CRITICAL SURVEY OF POETRY
Italian Poets

Editor

Rosemary M. Canfield Reisman
Charleston Southern University

SALEM PRESS
A Division of EBSCO Publishing, Ipswich, Massachusetts

Cover photo:
Dante (© STRINGER/ITALY/Reuters/Corbis)

Copyright © 2012, by Salem Press, A Division of EBSCO Publishing, Inc.
All rights in this book are reserved. No part of this work may be used or reproduced in any manner whatsoever or transmitted in any form or by any means, electronic or mechanical, including photocopy, recording, or any information storage and retrieval system, without written permission from the copyright owner except in the case of brief quotations embodied in critical articles and reviews or in the copying of images deemed to be freely licensed or in the public domain. For information address the publisher, Salem Press, at csr@salempress.com.

ISBN: 978-1-58765-913-3

CONTENTS

Contributors iv

Italian Poetry to 1800 1
Italian Poetry Since 1800 24

Ludovico Ariosto 51
Giovanni Boccaccio 61
Giosuè Carducci 67
Guido Cavalcanti 75
Christine de Pizan 81
Gabriele D'Annunzio 87
Dante 97
Ugo Foscolo 125
Girolamo Fracastoro 133
Giacomo Leopardi 145
Giambattista Marino 160
Michelangelo 166
Eugenio Montale 179
Cesare Pavese 188
Petrarch 194
Salvatore Quasimodo 205
Gaspara Stampa 214
Torquato Tasso 221
Giuseppe Ungaretti 231

Checklist for Explicating a Poem 243
Bibliography 246
Guide to Online Resources 249
Category Index 252
Subject Index 254

CONTRIBUTORS

Sidney Alexander
Virginia Commonwealth University

Jean-Pierre Barricelli
University of California, Riverside

Fiora A. Bassanese
University of Massachusetts, Boston

Joseph P. Byrne
Belmont University

Glauco Cambon
University of Connecticut

H. W. Carle
St. Joseph, Missouri

Joseph Carroll
Community College of Rhode Island

Luisetta Elia Chomel
University of Houston

Robert Colucci
Pittsburgh, Pennsylvania

J. Madison Davis
Pennsylvania State College-Behrend College

Desiree Dreeuws
Sunland, California

Ann R. Hill
Randolph-Macon Woman's College

Elizabeth A. Holtze
Metropolitan State College of Denver

Rebecca Kuzins
Pasadena, California

Adriano Moz
Spring Hill College

Patrizio Rossi
University of California, Santa Barbara

Robert W. Scott
American University

Roberto Severino
Georgetown University

Jack Shreve
Allegany Community College

Madison U. Sowell
Brigham Young University

Thomas A. Van
University of Louisville

ITALIAN POETRY TO 1800

Poetry and literature in the Italian vernacular, the common language that sprang from the ashes of Latin, arose in Italy around the beginning of the thirteenth century and soon displayed itself in literary works of major importance. This linguistic success is so extraordinary that one wonders how it was possible that such a literary phenomenon could take place in a language whose written tradition is so recent. The spoken language, however, had a long history, which is represented by the development of Latin into several vernaculars. The heritage and cultured structures of Italian have roots that are deep and extensive, developing from the culture and literature of the medieval period, the time from the fall of the Western Roman Empire to the beginning of the thirteenth century.

From Latin to Italian

During that long period of time, Italy developed a literature that, on one hand, was no longer in Latin but, on the other, was not yet in Italian. This language maintained the appearance of Latin but was quite different from classic Latin; it was the Latin used by the Roman Catholic Church and by educated people, a language that, after the fall of the Roman Empire, spread throughout Europe as the cultured language and remained as the official language of science until the modern age. Medieval literature, however, was not developed extensively, and its quality, from an artistic point of view, was rather limited.

During the Middle Ages, the Church had become the major source of knowledge and culture, and it had inherited from Rome its characteristic of universality. The major documents of medieval Christian thought profoundly shaped the values of the new vernacular literature; particularly influential were the works of the Scholastic philosophers, among whom towers Saint Thomas Aquinas and in which one can find the vital roots of Dante's writings.

Italian vernacular poetry began in the thirteenth century with the simultaneous flowering of written literature in several of Italy's competing dialects. In the twelfth century, it had appeared that the Sicilian dialect was going to acquire the status of a national language; Sicily, at the time of Emperor Frederick II (1194-1250), had become an important center of cultural life and art. This Sicilian superiority was ephemeral, however, vanishing after the death of the emperor. It was instead the Florentine tongue that, for several reasons, became the national language. The Florentine dialect prevailed primarily because, during the period of assertion of the vernacular, some of the greatest masterpieces of Italian literature were written in that dialect.

Early vernacular works

The earliest extant poetic compositions in the vernacular are religious works intended for doctrinal instruction; typical examples of this genre are Bonavesin della

Riva's *Libro delle tre scritture* (c. 1300; book of the three scriptures) and Fra Giacomino da Verona's *De Jerusalem celesti* (c. 1230) and *De Babilonia civitate infernali* (c. 1230). In the field of specifically religious poetry, which contains a clear and pure effusion of spiritual feelings, there is the *Laudes creaturarum* (c. 1225), by Saint Francis of Assisi, and the oeuvre of Jacopone da Todi, which includes 102 laudes. Though the majority of these religious poems narrate the deep mystical experience of the author, there are also several that are of a moral and satiric nature.

Of greater importance from an artistic and cultural point of view is the development in Italy of a lyric poetry of Provençal origin, which reflected a courtly concept of love that was conceived as an homage to "the lady" according to the principles dictated by the codes and rules of feudal society. The courtly content of this poetry and the very elaborate style rarely offered the possibility of expressing truly sincere and deep feelings. The poetry created by this style gave more importance to the artifice of the form than to the originality of the inspiration and was therefore characterized by a certain coldness.

The poetic genre had some success in northern Italy as a result of the troubadours, who traveled from court to court from Provence into northern Italy. The most consistent achievement of this lyric style, however, took place in Sicily at the court of Frederick II, where it assumed the status of a school. Among its most celebrated poets were Frederick himself and his sons, Enzo and Manfredi. In addition, there were resident courtiers such as Jacopo da Lentini and Giacomino Pugliese. The aesthetic value of the poetry of the Sicilian school is minimal; there, the worst traits of Provençal poetry were accentuated. Nevertheless, the historical significance of the Sicilian school is great: It constituted the first attempt to use the vernacular with a clear artistic intention. At this historical moment, as earlier mentioned, Sicilian could have become the national language. Historical events, however, prevented that. Frederick II died in 1250, and with his demise the power of his court soon disappeared and the cultural and literary effort which he so strongly supported collapsed.

Dolce stil nuovo

The poetry of the Sicilian school had, nevertheless, already found a fruitful development in Tuscany, where its poetic themes were enriched with political and religious elements—particularly in the works of Guittone d'Arezzo and in the amorous poetry of Chiaro Davanzati. Furthermore, the Sicilian experience was instrumental in suggesting a new development, a new conception of love poetry that was proposed by the advocates of the *dolce stil nuovo* ("sweet new style"). In this new style, feelings are based on a bourgeois experience—the culture of the communes—not on a feudal one as was the case with Provençal poetry. Supported by a mystical consciousness, the new poetry exemplified a greater sincerity of expression and was supported by deeper sensitivity and more ardent feelings. Guido Guinizzelli's lyric poem "A cor gentile ripara sempre amore" ("Love Seeks Its Dwelling Always in a Gentle Heart") established what could be considered the schematic structure of the new school. Originating in Bologna, this innovative way of creating verses reached Florence, where Guido Cavalcanti further developed it in his poem "Donna mi prega" ("A Lady Asks Me"). Cino da Pistoia brought to the *dolce stil nuovo* a new psychological concept of love, substantively humane, with a potential that Dante was to explore in *La vita nuova* (c. 1292; *Vita Nuova*, 1861; better known as *The New Life*), written shortly after 1292. *The New Life* narrates the spiritual unfolding of his pure love for Beatrice, a girl whom he met early in his life and who died young in 1290, leaving the poet grief-stricken. Under the influence of the *stilnovisti*, Dante cultivated his love for Beatrice as a pure—almost religious—feeling through which he might be led to spiritual perfection. This concept would be developed extensively in his masterpiece.

Dante

Dante (1265-1321) was born in Florence into a Guelph family that claimed ancient noble origins. He received his early education from the Franciscan friars of Santa Croce Church in his native town and, from the poetry of the Sicilian school that had spread into central Italy, he learned to write verses in the vernacular. Like many other citizens of Florence in his social condition, Dante participated in the tumultuous political life of the commune. As a consequence of these activities, he was exiled when the Black faction of the Guelph party, which was supported by Pope Boniface VIII, won political dominance over the White faction, to which Dante belonged. The Blacks banished the leaders of the Whites from Florence and its territory. Military attempts to regain power organized by the White faction failed. Dante resigned himself to the life of an exile and stayed at several courts in northern Italy, finally settling down in Ravenna at the court of Guido da Polenta. In Ravenna, he devoted his attention to completing his sacred epic, *La divina commedia* (c. 1320; *The Divine Comedy*, 1802). He died in Ravenna in 1321.

It is significant that Dante composed his masterpiece in exile. After a long period of tumultuous events, the moment for deliberation had come. On the one hand, the recent past appeared to him as a forest of mistakes; on the other hand, he could visualize the possibility of a transcending order, embracing Heaven and Earth. Dante believed that the misled and corrupt humanity of his time could organize itself into a new order which could reach the goal of temporal and eternal happiness. This empire would be universal and divinely ordained, and the emperor would be independent in his temporal power, his authority granted directly to him by God and not by the pope. Other motives that certainly influenced the composition of the poem were Dante's love for Beatrice and the desire to glorify her, his desire for justice, and his need to express his aesthetic insight and creative imagination.

In *The Divine Comedy*, Dante describes being lost in "una foresta oscura," a dark forest which represents the confusion of life. As a result of his experience, he acquires a consciousness of the sad condition of his spirit. He wants to free himself from this anguished state, but with human resources alone the soul cannot save itself. If a man with a soul in distress shows good intentions, however, he deserves the help of God; the Holy Virgin, representing "Divine Mercy," comes to his aid. She calls on Lucia (Saint Lucy), the "Enlightened Grace," who, in turn, goes to Beatrice, the symbol of knowledge in divine matters. Beatrice—who is also the human woman loved by Dante—descends into Limbo and begs Vergil, who represents "right reason," to bring help to Dante. Reason tells Dante that he cannot go suddenly from a sinful life to one of perfection; he must first face the dreadful consequence of sin by visiting Hell. He must then continue to Purgatory to make amends for his sins. Only then, after having reached the condition of natural perfection (the Terrestrial Paradise), will Dante be able to go to the Celestial Paradise and therefore reach the supreme reward, undergoing the beatific Vision of God. In this last part of Dante's mythical voyage, Vergil, "right reason," will not be a sufficient guide, and Dante will visit Paradise with the help of Beatrice.

The Divine Comedy is an epic poem of one hundred cantos. These cantos are collected into three parts, each of which is dedicated to one of the kingdoms of the life beyond: *Inferno, Purgatorio* (*Purgatory*), and *Paradiso* (*Paradise*). The *Inferno* is described in strong and vivid terms: the terrible heat and fires of the underworld, the agonies of the suffering, the terrors of the devils. In *Purgatory*, where the passions are appeased, there predominates a condition of melancholy generated by the recollection of the flawed past life and the interminable waiting for the state of eternal beatitude. In *Paradise*, Dante acknowledges the impossibility of conveying absolute happiness and holiness in earthly terms.

Although *The Divine Comedy* is Dante's masterpiece, he left other notable works as well. In addition to the poems that are included in *The New Life*, pervaded by mystical love, he composed a collection of *canzoniere* (lyric poetry) that documents the further artistic development that the poet had to undergo in order to reach the richness of motive that characterizes *The Divine Comedy*.

Dante's achievements mark a moment of great cultural change in the history of Italy. On the one hand, he summarizes the thought, life, and aspirations of the Middle Ages; on the other hand, he opens the door to a modern conception of life and culture. If Dante's gaze is fixed toward Heaven, he is not blind to temporal happenings, and he observes the Earth in all of its aspects and details. He does not ignore the mystery of the human soul. Rather, as exemplified in one of the cantos of *The Divine Comedy*, he embraces the courage of Ulysses, who ventured to discover new worlds. Thus, Dante anticipates the questing spirit of the Renaissance.

Petrarch

The political ideas of Petrarch (1304-1374), the other major poet of the thirteenth century and one of the major figures of Italian literature, present a historical ambience quite different from that of Dante. Politically, Petrarch is far removed from the conception of a universal empire. His interest is clearly concentrated on Italy seen as a country geographically and ethnically different from any other country beyond the mountain chain of the Alps. Culturally, Petrarch departs from the medieval worldview; for him, the classical world acquires a new interest. Thus, Petrarch could be considered a precursor of Humanism.

From a psychological point of view, Petrarch does not possess the self-assurance that is typical of Dante. He appears to be more introspective, with a tendency toward self-analysis, which may have accounted for his uncertainty and unhappiness—elements that constitute the essence of his poetry. The conflict between his religious desires and his worldly attitudes is never fully resolved. There is no serenity or dramatic resolution for him, only the constant melancholy that is characteristic of the modern spirit.

Petrarch was born Francesco Petrarca in Arezzo, the son of Pietro di Parenzo (commonly known as Ser Petracco), a Florentine notary who belonged to the White political faction and was exiled in 1302, the same year in which Dante was exiled. In 1312, the family moved to near Avignon, in France, where Petrarch's father had found employment with the papal court. Petrarch studied law at the universities of Montpellier and Bologna, but his interest was oriented more toward literature than law. In 1327, in the Church of Santa Chiara in Avignon, he first saw Laura, the woman who was the major source of inspiration for his poetry. Petrarch served several lords in Italy, especially those of Colonna, a powerful Roman family that contributed several popes to the Church. Petrarch traveled through the many regions of Italy as well as in France, Flanders, and Germany. Later, he returned to Provence and retired to Vaucluse, a small town not far from Avignon. He spent his time writing a long epic poem in Latin, *Africa* (1396; English translation, 1977), his most extended work in that language. The poem was inspired by Vergil's *Aeneid* (c. 29-19 B.C.E.; English translation, 1553) and was written in hexameter and subdivided into nine cantos. Petrarch felt this epic to be his major contribution to the literature of his time. It was successful during his lifetime, and in 1340, Petrarch was rewarded with the title of poet laureate by the Senate in Rome. During this period, he continued his activities as a diplomat at the service of various courts in Italy. He also continued with his literary endeavors, which included collecting ancient texts by Latin authors. Later, he went to live in the territories of the Republic of Venice and died in 1374 in Arquà, a small town near Padua, where he had gone into seclusion.

The true poetic glory of Petrarch, however, derives almost exclusively from the lyrics he wrote in the vulgar tongue, *Rerum vulgarium fragmenta* (1470, also known as *Canzoniere*; *Rhymes*, 1976). Though he dismissed these lyrics as *nugellae* ("little things"), he refined and edited them throughout most of his life. *Rhymes* consists of 366 poems, most of them sonnets recounting the melancholy story of his love for Laura, a love that did not cease even with Laura's death, which occurred in 1340 during the plague. Well acquainted with the love poetry of the Provençal troubadours, the Sicilian school, and the *stilnovisti*, Petrarch derived from these traditions elements that became vital and inseparable parts of his own poetic world. Nevertheless, the imprint, the essence of *Rhymes*, stems from his passion for Laura, the focus of an intense conflict between the seductions of the world and the enduring values of spiritual love.

The work is divided into two parts, usually designated "In vita di madonna Laura" (in the lifetime of Laura) and "In morte di madonna Laura" (after the death of Laura). In the first part, Petrarch's love has great impulses, prostrations, enthusiasms, and a gloomy bitterness. The poet blesses the moment of his falling in love and swears eternal fidelity to his feelings for Laura. Only rarely does sensuality appear in his verses, but at the same time the poet does not attempt to transform his feelings into a mystical thought that will raise him—through his love of the woman—to love of God. In the second part, those poems written after Laura's death, there is at first an expression of grief, the torture of separation, the tormenting thought that Laura's beautiful face, the "dolce sguardo," the endearing glance, are gone forever. Then, the image of Laura begins to live a new life in the soul of the faithful lover; she is no longer a temptress. Instead, Laura becomes a maternal figure and the consoler of Petrarch's sufferings. Also, with this new vision, Petrarch believes that his love, even if spiritualized, is still love for a human creature and therefore a distraction from the love for the Creator. Petrarch's *Rhymes* has been among the most influential poetic works not only of Italian literature but also of world literature. With a psychological acuity that anticipates the modern discovery of the self, Petrarch describes refined and sophisticated feelings, spellbinding in their perplexity but at the same time never completely detached from a lived human experience.

Giovanni Boccaccio

The third of the great Italian writers of this period is Giovanni Boccaccio (1313-1375), whose fame is founded on *Decameron: O, Prencipe Galetto* (1349-1351; *The Decameron*, 1620). A literary work in prose, it is a collection of one hundred short stories related to one another by a frame story.

Of limited artistic value, Boccaccio's poetry is nevertheless of historical interest. For the most part, it is allegorical, reflecting Dante's model and the general pattern of the medieval literary tradition. His most significant early works include *Il filostrato* (c. 1335; *The Filostrato*, 1873), a lyric composition somewhat biographical in style, which was followed by *Teseida delle nozze d'Emilia* (1339-1341; *The Book of Theseus*, 1974), an epic poem imitating the style of Vergil's *Aeneid* and Statius's *Thebais* (c. 92 C.E.; English translation, 1766). There is also *La caccia di Diana* (c. 1334; Diana's hunt), a mythological poem describing the life at the court of Naples where Boccaccio spent some time during his youth. Other works written before the *Decameron* are *Il ninfale d'Ameto* (1341-1342; also known as *Commedia delle ninfe*), an idyllic poem of popular love, and *L'amorosa visione* (1342-1343; English translation, 1986), an allegorical poem inspired by Dante's *The Divine Comedy*.

ITALIAN RENAISSANCE

Between the end of the fourteenth century and the beginning of the fifteenth century, there appeared in Italy the first signs of a profound change in Western culture. The typical representative of this period, which would be later called the Renaissance, sought above all the full and balanced development and enjoyment of his human potential. Transcendence was not explicitly denied but was simply neglected. The Renaissance person did not feel the need of divine grace to achieve these goals, and the ideal of the ascetic, who runs away from the world so that the spirit will thrive, was completely foreign—indeed, almost incomprehensible.

At the beginning of this period, there was a great interest in the studies of classical languages and literature. This interest in classical culture and the new critical sense with which these cultures were analyzed bred a large cultural movement called Humanism. In the infancy of the new movement, in the first part of the fourteenth century, there was little interest in the vernacular, since the aspirations of learned individuals were oriented toward classical languages. Among the Humanists who distinguished themselves as poets in this first part of the century, Giovanni Pontano entrusted all of his creative literary efforts to the Latin language; his works include an astrological poem, *Urania* (1505); an epic poem, *Lepidina* (1505); and three books of elegies, *De amore coniugalis* (1480-1484; conjugal love), which are dedicated to his wife.

LORENZO DE' MEDICI

At this historical moment, Tuscany no longer held predominance in the national literature but nevertheless was, along with Florence, a very active cultural center because of the patronage of Cosimo de' Medici and of his grandson Lorenzo the Magnificent (1449-1492). Lorenzo has a place in the history of Florence and Italy because of his great abilities as a politician and administrator and his munificent and intelligent patronage of the arts; in addition, he distinguished himself as a man of letters.

In Lorenzo's oeuvre one finds the influence of the most contrasting poetic currents of his time. His *L'altercazione* (after 1473) reveals the influence of the Platonist Center founded in Florence by the renowned Humanist Marsilio Ficino. In *Selve* (1515), Lorenzo narrates an allegorical love story which, as in Petrarch's *Trionfi* (1470; *Tryumphs*, 1565; also known as *Triumphs*, 1962), goes through several stages—jealousy, hope, despair—to conclude finally in the contemplation of the eternal beauty, God. In his *Rime* (1680), dedicated to Lucrezia Donati, he was inspired by the *stilnovisti*, whose philosophical ideas were close to Platonism. Also deserving of special consideration are *Nencia da Barberino* (c. 1474), a short lyric poem in which the peasant Vallera gives vent to his passionate love for the beautiful shepherdess Nencia, and *Canto trionfale di Bacco e Arianna* (c. 1490), a work in which Lorenzo becomes the interpreter of the soul and spirit of the Renaissance with the accomplished skill of a highly developed artist.

POLIZIANO

The most eminent poet of his century, Poliziano (1454-1494), was born in the Tuscan town of Montepulciano. Although born into a family of humble condition, Poliziano was able to educate himself at the school of noted Humanists in Florence. He also attracted the attention of Lorenzo the Magnificent, who took him into his house as the tutor of his children.

Poliziano was a brilliant Humanist and wrote verses both in Latin and in Greek. Some of his poems in classical languages have remarkable taste and artistic value, but his reputation as a poet is based on his vernacular poetry, especially on *Stanze cominciate per la giostra del magnifico Giuliano de' Medici* (1518; *The Stanze of Angelo Poliziano*, 1979; commonly known as *Stanze*), *Orfeo* (pr. 1480; English translation, 1879; also known as *Orpheus*), and *Rime* (wr. 1498, pb. 1814).

Stanze is an incomplete lyric poem, of which Poliziano wrote only the first book and part of the second. This work was supposed to celebrate the joust won in Florence in 1475 by Lorenzo's brother Giuliano, who was later killed during Pazzi's conspiracy in 1478. The poem describes how Giuliano, a handsome and vigorous young man, is living an intense and happy life in close contact with nature, spending most of his time riding and hunting and giving little attention to love and sentiment. Cupid is offended by this young man's attitude and plans to take revenge by making Giuliano fall in love with a beautiful nymph, Simonetta. In the second book of the poem, Venus and Cupid send Giuliano a dream that instills in him the desire for warlike glory, which is necessary in order that he be deserving of Simonetta's love. He prepares to organize a joust, and it is at this point that the poem is interrupted. The poem interprets with admirable grace that moment in which the sentimentally immature young man, who is completely involved with the exterior world, withdraws into himself and achieves for the first time a new awareness, noticing the rise of unsuspected love feelings.

Poliziano wrote *Orfeo*, his second major literary work, during his stay at the Gonzagas' court in Mantua. The tone of this composition is dramatic, but it lacks a true conflict of passions. The poem places instead a greater importance on the lyric and elegiac motives, but they seldom reach the expressive intensity of *Stanze*. Of more significant artistic value, from the lyric point of view, is *Rime*, a collection of love poems that also includes the famous "I' mi trovai fanciulle un bel mattino" ("I Went A-Roaming, Maidens, One Bright Day"). This poem ends with an invitation to capture the fleeting moment and to "gather ye therefore roses . . . ere their perfume pass away"—a topos which was to become one of the most pervasive in Renaissance poetry throughout Europe.

Jacopo Sannazzaro

The same accents are found in the poetry of the Neapolitan author Jacopo Sannazzaro (1458-1530), who, lacking the depth of inspiration, the vitality, and the human understanding of Poliziano, succeeds nevertheless in reaching a respectable artistic sophistication. Sannazzaro's reputation rests on *Arcadia* (*Arcadia and Piscutorial Eclogues*, 1966), a pastoral poem published in 1504. To his contemporaries, *Arcadia* appeared to be a unique combination of all the various motives of pastoral poetry, deriving its inspiration from classical poets such as Vergil, Ovid, and Theocritus.

Luigi Pulci

Another author of the fifteenth century, Luigi Pulci (1432-1484), profited from the enlightened patronage of Lorenzo the Magnificent. Pulci tried several forms of traditional poetry without great success, achieving fame only when he turned to an epic poem, *Morgante*, which he started almost as a joke. Instead, it introduced a genre that acquired a large popularity in Italy. The poem took up the subject matter of the *Chanson de Roland* (twelfth century; *The Song of Roland*, 1880) and the legend of Charlemagne—a theme that had found an unusual popularity among the simple people in Italy and had created a rich florescence of epic poems, none of which had arrived at any reputable artistic level. These epic poems had gradually taken a very definite structure, a structure that was monotonously repeated. The plot usually revealed the treacheries and evil deeds of the members of the House of Maganza, which had expelled from France the members of the House of Chiaromonte and called the Saracens to fight against Charlemagne, the leader of the Chiaromonte. These same adventures, usually narrated by storytellers in the streets, reappear in Pulci's *Morgante*. Pulci, however, succeeds in bringing the story to a level that is artistically moving and epic in scope.

Pulci ended his poem at the twenty-third canto, and his work was published as it was, incomplete, as *Morgante* (1481). Later, urged by a friend to complete it, the poet added another five cantos that tell of the defeat at Roncesvalles, where the rear guard of Charlemagne's army, returning from Spain and being led by the Paladin Roland, is destroyed by the Saracens. Thus completed, the epic poem was titled the *Morgante maggiore* (1483).

Matteo Maria Boiardo

This new literary genre was continued by Matteo Maria Boiardo (1440 or 1441-1494), who freed it from the popular tradition that still existed in Pulci's work and initiated with refined artistic awareness the poetic theme of the old chivalry, or Romantic epic. His major work, the *Orlando innamorato* (1483-1495; English translation, 1823), a grandiose enterprise originally planned to include 120 cantos divided into four parts (though interrupted after the second part), merges the two major themes of chivalric poetry: the events narrating the story of Charlemagne, from which Boiardo obtained his major characters and the plot of the Christian world fighting the Saracens, and the Arthurian legend, from which he deducted the individualistic spirit of love and adventure as well as the fair land aspect.

Love and adventure are evident in the *Morgante maggiore*, but both seem somewhat incidental to the story, lacking the well-organized and well-planned structure found in this new poem. In the *Orlando Innamorato*, love and adventure are closely connected, and it is indeed love that drives the restless knights to undertake the most unusual and risky endeavors. Boiardo is also credited with having created numerous characters with well-defined personalities; in turn, these characters were taken up by Ludovico Ariosto.

Several parts of Boiardo's *Orlando Innamorato* have a high poetic value, but the poem is not considered a true masterpiece: It lacks a unifying spirit that would give life to all parts of the story. There is, however, in Boiardo's poem an interesting taste for the primitive, from which stems a grandiosity that is not handicapped by exceptional or complicated psychological depth. One also perceives in his stories a fascinating and uncontrolled indulgence in the simple and powerful passions of love, vengeance, and a desire to conquer that is clearly an asset to his work and poetic conception. This raw energy, however, cannot be sustained throughout the poem. Little by little, the rich vein of inspiration exhausts itself, and the episodes of the story monotonously repeat themselves until the reader's interest in the adventure weakens and disappears. The spirit of the Renaissance, so deeply different from the one of the Middle Ages, demanded an entirely new vision of the world of the chanson de geste, and it was Ariosto who met this demand.

LUDOVICO ARIOSTO

Ludovico Ariosto (1474-1533) was born in Reggio Emilia. His father was in the service of the lords of that region, the Este family, and Ludovico inherited the position when his father died. He worked at first for the Cardinal Ippolito d'Este and then for the Cardinal's brother, the duke Alfonso d'Este, who had his court in the city of Ferrara. Often, however, the poet had to leave his favored city, sent by his patrons on missions to various parts of the duchy and Italy. Later in life, he was able to live in a house that he bought on the outskirts of Ferrara, where he could dedicate himself completely to writing, the greatest passion in his life.

In his youth, under the Humanistic influence, Ariosto wrote only in Latin, imitating Catullus and Tibullus. Ariosto first published a Latin ode, "Ad Philiroen" ("To Philiroe"), in 1494. After 1503, however, the poet rarely wrote in Latin; his lyric poetry was composed primarily in the vulgar tongue.

Ariosto began writing his masterpiece *Orlando furioso* (1516, 1521, 1532; English translation, 1591) around 1503 and published a first edition of sixteen cantos in 1516. After extensive revision, he published a second edition in 1521. Finally, yet another version, with several cantos added, was published in 1532. This careful revision produced a poem that for its excellent style could be compared to Petrarch's *Rhymes*. Moreover, the form in which the poem is written, the ottava rima, gave such musicality to Ariosto's verses that it was called the "golden octave."

Orlando Furioso is a continuation of the *Orlando Innamorato*; Ariosto's poem more or less begins where Boiardo concluded his story. Although the *Orlando Furioso* has an extraordinary number of episodes, its plot is based solidly and clearly on a few fundamental events. The multiplicity of the facts narrated does not create confusion or boredom but unfold in harmonious and orderly ways. All the characters, who may at times appear scattered, are intermittently collected at a specific point, be it the palace of the sorcerer Atlante or under the walls of Paris, walls from which they subsequently depart in search of new, wonderful adventures.

The spirit of the poem should be sought in the vision of life as a changing scene, a continuously changing spectacle, a vision that Ariosto had obtained from the Renaissance conception at its highest and most balanced stage of development. According to this conception, life should be observed with a certain detachment, without bitterness and without moralizing.

Late sixteenth century

In the second part of the sixteenth century, the great magnificence of the Renaissance faded, perhaps because of the natural exhaustion of the intense fervor of life, both elegant and merry, that had charmed the Italian courts. Politically, the change was particularly severe. The Spanish domination of Italy drastically changed life in the courts of several states. From a literary point of view, artistic production was tightly controlled and dominated by the rules and suggestions of several learned societies, especially the Accademia della Crusca ("academy of the chaff"), founded in 1583 with the intention of purifying the literary language.

There was, however, in the late sixteenth century an interesting ferment of new ideas. The theoretical elements implicit in the Renaissance conception of life became explicit only during this period. They were expressed in organized philosophical thought by thinkers such as Giordano Bruno (1548-1600), Bernardino Telesio (1509-1588), and Tommaso Campanella (1568-1639), a prolific author whose masterpiece is *La città del sole* (1623; *City of the Sun*, 1880). Inspired by Plato's philosophy, Campanella describes a utopian, egalitarian society ruled by a priest-philosopher in *City of the Sun*.

An important influence on Italian literary development after the Renaissance was exercised by the sweeping religious movement known as the Counter-Reformation. This Catholic movement tried to contain the spread of the Protestant revolution while renewing the life of the Catholic Church. In this period, literature followed the natural consequence of the exhaustion of the Renaissance, and the Counter-Reformation ideals succeeded from time to time in animating literary production with renewed religious spirit. Included among these works is the oeuvre of Torquato Tasso, who closed the Renaissance that Petrarch had opened.

Torquato Tasso

Torquato Tasso (1544-1595) was born in Sorrento, near Naples. His father, Bernardo, was an accomplished man of letters and had written a lyric poem, the *Amadigi* (1560), which had been somewhat successful. Bernardo Tasso was the secretary to the prince of Salerno, Ferrante di San Severino, and when the prince was forced to leave his state and go into exile for political reasons, Bernardo, accompanied by his son, followed his patron. This exile brought the Tassos to the courts of several Italian princes, and young Torquato pursued his studies in different universities, finally graduating from the University of Padua with a degree in literature. He was soon admitted to the retinue of Cardinal Luigi d'Este, to whom he had dedicated his pastoral drama *Aminta* (pr. 1573; English translation, 1591), a work that showed artistic maturity and that expressed in lovely forms the serenity of Tasso's spirit at that time in his life. Distinguished by this serenity and by its lighthearted sensuality, *Aminta* is the culmination of the Renaissance pastoral tradition.

Aminta was followed by *Gerusalemme liberata* (1581; *Jerusalem Delivered*, 1600), Tasso's major work. This period was not only the most prolific for the poet but also the happiest in his life. After 1575, the year in which *Jerusalem Delivered* was read publicly to the duke of Ferrara and his court, Tasso's mental health began to deteriorate. His sensitive mind was racked by doubts about the critical and religious soundness of his poem. He also became very suspicious of his friends and benefactors, and after some irrational episodes, the duke of Ferrara was compelled to confine Tasso to an asylum, where he remained for seven years. When he was released in 1586, the poet went to live at the court of the Gonzagas in Mantua, but only for a short time. He soon returned to his wanderings: Naples, Florence, back to Mantua, and Rome, where Pope Clement VIII planned to crown him with laurel. Tasso, however, could not manage to extend his life to the day of the coronation. Exhausted, he found shelter in the convent of Sant' Onofrio of the Giannicolo and there he died, on April 25, 1595.

Tasso had begun to work on his masterpiece, *Jerusalem Delivered*, with a greater concern than had characterized his earlier works. At the end of the sixteenth century, it was not conceivable that a poet would be starting to work on what was considered the most noble of the literary genre, the *poema epico* (the romantic poem), so much discussed by the supercilious academicians, yet without an adequate critical preparation. Tasso, therefore, expressed his ideas about the romantic poem in a short treatise, *Discorsi dell'arte poetica* (1587; discourses on the poetic art). The poet believed that the purpose of literature was more to entertain than to instruct and that in the romantic poem one should strive for credibility. For this reason, the poet should turn to history; tales of marvels and miracles should be religious in inspiration, it being undesirable for

Christian people to believe in the prodigies of pagan divinities. Finally, Tasso asserted that the poet should seek greatness and nobility in the characters and the events, excluding ridiculous, comical, and vulgar facts and creatures.

During his youth, Tasso had conceived a romantic poem on the Crusades and had written the first book of a work titled "Il Goffredo." Later he undertook the project again and, working intensively, completed it in twenty cantos of ottava rima in 1575, publishing it in the final form in 1581 as *Jerusalem Delivered*. In this literary composition, the poetic world of Tasso manifests itself in all of its richness and depth. At first it appears that, from an artistic point of view, one is confronted again by the world of the Renaissance with major elements including glory, expectation, anticipation, anxiety, heroic efforts, idyllic visions, pleasure, power, and melancholy. Moralistic and religious elements are present only in rhetorical and artificial forms, and there are only a few passages of sincerely felt spirituality and mysticism. If one observes the essence and the structure of the poem with greater care, however, one realizes that in those Renaissance motives there is hidden a new spirit, a new feeling that, without dissolving them, without transforming anything, gives to these realities a new expression, a new and deeper significance. Desire, expectation, enthusiasm, and heroic efforts are no longer an end in themselves, a pure expression of exuberant energies; they need now an ideal that will support and fulfill them. Force, power, has lost its barbaric beauty and opens itself to human feelings. Melancholy is not regret for the fleeting, transitory aspect of happiness, but rather an anxious desire for a more spiritual happiness and fulfillment, a fulfillment that Tasso's religiosity circumscribes. In this correct merging and balancing of the two opposing and contrasting forces—the love for the world and the attraction toward spirituality—Tasso supersedes his mentor, Petrarch.

After Tasso completed *Jerusalem Delivered*, his instability worsened. He began a new version of his epic, titled *Gerusalemme Conquistata* (1593; *Jerusalem Conquered*, 1907), an artistic failure on which he expended enormous labors. He also wrote a tragedy, *Il re Torrismondo* (pb. 1587; the King Torrismondo), inspired by Sophocles' *Oidipous Tyrannos* (c. 429 B.C.E.; *Oedipus Tyrannus*, 1715), as well as a poem of religious inspiration, *Le sette giornate del mondo creato*, published posthumously in 1607. None of these works could duplicate the intensity and the artistic fervor of his masterpiece.

BATTISTA GUARINI

Another work deserving of recognition and written in the same period is the pastoral tragicomedy *Il pastor fido* (pb. 1590; *The Faithful Shepherd*, 1602; translation by John Fletcher), by Battista Guarini (1538-1612), a poet from Ferrara who was for several years at the court in his own town and then in Florence and Urbino. More than for its dramatic qualities or artistic prominence of the protagonist, *The Faithful Shepherd* is famous for its musicality of expression, which brings Guarini's characters closer to those of the melodrama, a genre that had tremendous success in the seventeenth and eighteenth centuries.

The melodrama, as an artistic form, was created at the end of the sixteenth century by the Camerata dei Bardi, a group of literati and musicians who gathered at the Bardi's palace in Florence. Their intention was to effect a closer relationship between music and poetry, following the example of classical Greek authors. The first melodrama (or *favola per musica*) produced was *Dafne* (1600), written by Ottavio Rinuccini (1562-1621) with music by Jacopo Corsi and Jacopo Peri. In 1600, Rinuccini wrote *Euridice*, also with music by Peri, for the marriage of the king of France, Henry IV, and Marie de Médicis. A few years later, in 1608, he wrote the libretto for the opera *Arianna* (1608), by Monteverdi, which was performed at the court of the duke of Mantua.

Considerable success was enjoyed in the sixteenth century by lyric poetry that imitated Petrarch (*petrarchismo*), and among the numerous poets who wrote verses in this style, several are notable: Luigi Tansillo (1510-1568), Annibal Caro (1507-1566), Giovanni Della Casa (1503-1555), and Galeazzo di Tarsia (1520-1553), who is perhaps the best in this group. In addition, two women poets achieved artistic renown in this period: Vittoria Colonna (1492-1547), a member of the Roman aristocracy and a good friend of Michelangelo (1475-1564), the great sculptor and painter (who also wrote noteworthy poetry), and Gaspara Stampa (1523-1554), from Padua, whose powerful and passionate verses are regarded by many modern readers as among the finest in European literature of her time.

Seventeenth century mannerism

Poetry in seventeenth century Italy was characterized by a phenomenon that is usually identified as *secentismo* or *Marinismo*, from the name of the poet Giambattista Marino (1569-1625), who, more than anyone, was responsible for the vogue of this new poetic style throughout Europe. This new poetry gave an extraordinary importance to form, partly in consequence of slavish imitation of classical authors, a practice that gradually gave the impression that form was something detached from content. Artists used style as a means of attracting the attention of the reader. To generate a sense of wonder and amazement, poets tended to emphasize oddity, a characteristic that typified the literary production of the seventeenth century.

The most daring and applauded representative of this style was Marino himself, who was born in Naples. After a restless and adventurous youth, Marino, who had distinguished himself as a gifted and brilliant writer of verses, spent some time at the pontifical court in Rome and then was a guest in Turin at the court of Duke Carlo Emanuele I of Savoy, where he found glory and honor. Soon, however, he fell out of favor and was imprisoned. As soon as Marino was free, he left Italy for France, where he resided for many years in Paris, honored and admired at the court of Marie de Médicis. His reputation, especially after the publication of his major work the *L'Adone* (1623), was immense. When Marino returned to Italy, he was received with great celebration in Rome and Naples. He died in Naples shortly after his return in 1625.

Marino's lyric poems, which present various subjects, are collected in a book titled *La lira* (1615). Other compositions are *La galeria* (1619), a group of iconographic poems; *La sampogna* (1620), a pastoral idyll; and the sacred epic *La strage degli innocenti* (1632; *The Slaughter of the Innocents*, 1675), which enjoyed widespread and popular success.

L'Adone is by far Marino's most important work. It embodies both the strengths and the shortcomings of his art, and it stands as the most representative expression of the spirit of its epoch. *L'Adone* is a mythological poem, conceived at first as a short idyllic poem and then enlarged, with extraordinary richness of digressions and episodes, to reach the impressive size of five thousand verses. These five thousand verses were then subdivided into twenty long cantos which center on the love of Venus and Adonis.

Other poets

Although *secentismo* was predominant in this period, a number of other poets wrote according to the principles of more orthodox forms, those classical writers who opposed the group represented by Marino and his followers. They cannot, however, be separated from the previous group, because they, too, followed the same abstract conception that form and style are completely separate from content.

Among these poets, the best known is Gabriello Chiabrera (1552-1638), who lived at the courts of the Medici in Florence, the Gonzagas in Mantua, and the Savoias in Turin, and who was rewarded for his services and his art with honors and generous stipends. Chiabrera acquired his reputation through his *canzonette*, the pastoral poem "Alcippo," and his several odes imitating Horace, Anacreon, and particularly Pindar. His fame did not reach the heights of Marino's, but it was more constant, even if his artistic achievement was by far inferior.

Another poet who was also inspired by the classic tradition was Fulvio Testi (1593-1646), a courtier of the Estes in Ferrara. His artistic model was the lyric poetry of Horace, from which he drew erotic inspiration and moralistic reflections. Testi's poems have survived not because of their artistic achievement, but rather for their political significance: denouncing the political dominance of Spain over Italy during that historical period.

Among the minor poets of this century one could mention Francesco Redi (1626-1698), a poet who gained some reputation for a dithyrambic poem, *Bacco in Toscana* (1685; *Bacchus in Tuscany: A Dithyrambic Poem*, 1825), written in praise of the wines of his region.

To the creation of a new literary genre—the mock heroic or heroicomic—the poet Alessandro Tassoni (1565-1635) contributed *La secchia rapita* (1622, 1630; *The Rape of the Bucket*, 1825). A poem written in ottava rima, subdivided into twelve cantos, it narrates in epic style the struggle between the towns of Modena and Bologna over the possession of a bucket, which is a caricature of some of the trivial aspects of the life of his times. The poem is fragmentary and, with the exception of some shorter parts, is of rather limited importance.

Among the writers of dramatic poetry in this century was Federico Della Valle (1565-1628), author of several tragedies of substantial value. The *Reina di Scotia* (wr. 1590-1600, pb. 1628) projects the powerful figure of Mary Stuart, human in her grief and elevated in her dignity as queen. A second tragedy that had a good success is *Judit* (wr. 1590-1600, pb. 1627), in which the Jewish heroine hides in her heart the austere and dreadful duty that she must carry out against the savage figure of Holofernes, a primitive man dominated by his instincts. The pair tower over a background of Oriental splendor. Both of these works are of remarkable artistic quality; they are superb as dramatic works and could be considered comparable to some of the best tragedies of Vittorio Alfieri, who is, perhaps, the most outstanding Italian tragedian.

Eighteenth century neoclassicism

Toward the end of the seventeenth century, fourteen scholars and men of letters in the circle of Christina, queen of Sweden—who, after her abdication and conversion to Catholicism, resided in Rome—founded a literary academy, the Accademia dell'Arcadia, whose purpose was to exterminate the bad taste of *secentismo* and to return to Italian poetry the qualities of natural candor, simplicity, and classical purity. The members of the Accademia dell'Arcadia took names that were supposed to be of pastoral inspiration, and branches of the academy were soon established in every major Italian town.

The simplicity which the Accademia dell'Arcadia was planning to set against the despised mannerisms of *secentismo* was itself, however, a purely literary convention, and new affectations substituted for the old: Poetry remained imprisoned by the entanglements of rhetoric. Nevertheless, there were some positive aspects to this new literary movement. The Accademia dell'Arcadia represented a return to the pure classicism of the sixteenth century, and classical poets, both Greek and Latin, were once again the object of the attention that had been usurped by the dazzling Mannerist poets of the seventeenth century. Style and structure meant the reassumption of a composed and dignified form in poetry. The ideal of beauty was no longer confined to the expression of the unusual or the surprising, and poets were once again under the influence of the logic that had already guided men of letters during the sixteenth century, a logic that elaborated on the concepts of Aristotle's *De poetica* (334-323 B.C.E.; *Poetics*, 1705).

The only true poet produced by the Accademia dell'Arcadia was Pietro Metastasio, whose works constitute the fullest poetic expression of the Italian society of his time. Metastasio was born Pietro Trapassi in Rome in 1698. At a very young age, he showed an exceptional ability in improvising verses. This dexterity attracted the attention of

G. V. Gravina, who was one of the founders of the Accademia dell'Arcadia. Gravina was convinced that the renovation of poetry had to take place through the restoration of the concept of classical art. He thought that the young Trapassi, properly educated, could achieve what he, Gravina—who was a theoretician, not a poet—would never be able to do. Gravina then took the young poet to live with him, changed his last name to the Greek-sounding Metastasio, and saw that he was instructed in the philosophy of René Descartes and in Latin and Greek literature and language. Gravina never imagined that with that kind of education his pupil could have brought to the maximum height a dramatic genre that any true follower of Aristotle's poetic theories should have considered at least spurious.

At the death of his mentor, Metastasio almost abandoned his art, but a dramatic sketch, *Gli orti esperidi*, which he had written in 1721 for a festivity at the court of Naples, opened the gates to his fortune as a dramatist and a poet. Diva "La Romanina" (Marianna Bulgarelli) took a liking to the young Metastasio; she saw that he was educated in the art of music and introduced him to the melodramatic genre. In 1724, Metastasio completed his first melodrama, the *Didone abbandonata* (*Dido Forsaken*, 1952), which was received with great favor and was followed by *Catone in Utica* (pr. 1727-1728; *Cato in Utica*, 1767) and *Semiramide* (pr. 1729; *Semiramis Recognized*, 1767), all of them works of unusual mastery.

During the second part of the seventeenth century, the poetic aspect of the melodrama had been completely overwhelmed by musical and choreographic dramas. Early in the 1700's, Apostolo Zeno, a learned Venetian who was the official poet at the court of Vienna, attempted a reform of the melodrama and tried to make the plots less absurd in order to bring them closer to historical truth. Zeno was not a gifted poet, and he believed that what he himself had not been able to accomplish could be done by Metastasio, who was an extremely talented writer of verse. Zeno, therefore, recommended Metastasio as his successor at the Viennese court, where, free from financial concerns, the latter would be able to continue his artistic pursuits. After some hesitation, Metastasio went to Vienna in 1730. The decade that followed was the most prolific in the career of the poet. Besides *oratori* and other short dramatic compositions, Metastasio wrote eleven melodramas, among them some of his best: the *Olimpiade* (pr. 1733; *The Olympiad*, 1767), *Demofoonte* (pr. 1733; *Demofoone*, 1767), *La clemenza di Tito* (pr. 1734; *The Mercy of Titus*, 1767), *Temistocle* (pr. 1736; *Themostocles*, 1767), and *Attilio regolo* (pr. 1750; *Atilius Regulus*, 1767). Though his poetic inspiration weakened, his reputation remained unchanged for the rest of his life, and when he died in 1782, he was honored and remembered as the Italian Sophocles.

In spite of the dramatic and serious subjects with which Metastasio's melodramas dealt, it could be said that in reality they are lacking in the heroic and dramatic spirit that they presuppose; the protagonist on whom the action is centered never acquires the warm personality of a real character, because Metastasio has for these heroes an admiration that he has learned through books rather than an attraction that grows from an innermost conviction of feeling. The elegiac elements of his plays have instead a singular poetic consistency and find their most complete realization in the *ariette* (usually two stanzas that are supposed to be sung). In these brief compositions of crystalline clarity, the poet is free from any obstacle of heroic travesty, and he finds the way to convey the best expression of the Arcadian spirit.

The Enlightenment

In the second part of the eighteenth century, a crisis began in Europe that would eventually find its resolution in the French Revolution. In only a few years, this revolution would cause a deep transformation in people's ways of thinking, of living, and of expressing themselves, through the demolition of all the surviving forms of the Renaissance and of the period that followed. A new philosophy developed that had its precedents in the works of the Frenchman René Descartes, the German Gottfried Wilhelm Leibniz, and the Englishman John Locke—a philosophy that placed humans at the center of the universe. Humans were regarded as the supreme judge of reality, capable of subjecting any question to strictly rational analysis.

This movement was known as the Enlightenment; its spirit was epitomized by the Frenchman who created *L'Encyclopédie* (1751-1780), a rational and scientific dictionary of all the sciences and arts. This encyclopedia was published in France under the direction of Denis Diderot (1713-1784) and Jean le Rond d'Alembert (1717-1783), with the precise design of divulging new ideas and illustrating through the light of reason all the theoretical, moral, artistic, economic, and practical problems with which humans could be confronted. The representative members of this movement, even if they moved intellectually in different directions and carried different points of view, were other intellectuals and artists such as Charles de Montesquieu (1689-1755), Voltaire (1694-1778), and Jean-Jacques Rousseau (1712-1778). This movement, which affected all the ways of life and thought of European society, had a significant effect on literature as well.

Giuseppe Parini

In Italy, the highest poetic expression of the moral and spiritual renewal proposed by the Enlightenment was the work of Giuseppe Parini (1729-1799). Parini was born into a humble family in Bosisio, a small rural town near Milan. He appeared to be a very intelligent boy and was brought to Milan to study. In Parini's time, for a bright but poor youngster who wanted to acquire an education, the best course was to undertake a religious career. Parini entered a seminary and became a priest. He was very interested in literature and published, when still very young, a collection of poems. As was then fashionable for a poet, he became a member of the Accademia dell'Arcadia. From 1754 to 1762, he was a tutor in the house of Duke Serbelloni. He left his job and was for several months in severe financial difficulties. The publication of the first part of what is considered his major work, *Il giorno* (1763-1801; *The Day: Morning, Midday, Evening, Night*, 1927), a satiric poem in which he criticizes the sterile life of the aristocracy, brought him to the attention of the public and also of Count Firmian, who was the minister of Maria Theresa in Milan. Firmian was glad that Parini, with his writings, was calling on the aristocracy to assume more responsibility in their position in society. Firmian made Parini director of the *Gazzetta di Milano* for a year, and in 1769, Firmian appointed Parini as professor of literature at the Scuole Palatine.

When Napoleonic troops occupied Milan in 1796, Parini was called to be part of the new government; mistrusting any demagogic excess, he refused the offer and retired to private life. When the Austrians returned to Milan in 1799, he greeted them with joy. He died, on August 15, 1799.

Parini wrote several odes that reflect the credo of the Enlightenment and are of didactic and moralistic inspiration. Some of his poems expressing deep moral emotions include *La caduta* (1766), *A Silvia* (1795), and *Alla Musa* (1795). Others such as *Il pericolo* (1787), *Il dono* (1790), and *Il messaggio* (1793), are written in flattery of women; they are sparkling in their courtly, gallant fashion and full of aesthetic admiration for feminine beauty.

Parini's moral spirit and his conception of poetry are more fully expressed in *The Day*, the satiric and didactic poem in which he describes the futile day of a young lord of the Milanese aristocracy. The same Arcadian touches that are present in the *odi* are also part of the structure of *The Day*. A masterpiece that foretells the French Revolution, it nevertheless reflects Parini's excessive dependence on the conventions of his time. Proceeding with a slow documentary style, it is encumbered with too many details, and it has not aged well.

VITTORIO ALFIERI

The renewal of Italian moral consciousness in the eighteenth century had its first suggestive poetic expression in the works of Parini, but it was the work of Vittori Alfieri (1749-1803) that unambiguously announced the political renewal of the country. Vittorio Alfieri was born in Asti, into a family of the Piedmontese aristocracy. His father died when he was only a year old, and his mother soon remarried. As a child, Alfieri was withdrawn, dominated by a melancholy unusual in one so young. In 1758, he entered the Royal Military Academy of Turin, from which he was graduated after eight years of *ineducazione* (ineducation) with the rank of *portainsegna* (lieutenant) in the regiment of his own town. Military life did not attract him, since he was intolerant of any discipline. He was very fond of traveling, and between 1766 and 1772, he made three trips, the first within Italy, the other two through Europe, visiting all the major countries from Spain to Russia. When he returned to Turin, he allowed himself to luxuriate in a life of idleness and passion for horses. Even this rootless life, however, left him restless and dissatisfied, as reflected in the pages of his diary. Actually, his continuous discontent, his furious search without any apparent goal or purpose, was in reality caused by the clash of spiritual energies as he looked for a way of expressing his talents.

This expression he finally found in 1744 while assisting a sick friend. Alfieri scribbled down the sketch of a tragedy, *Antonio e Cleopatra* (pr. 1775; *Anthony and Cleopatra*, 1876), which after going through a process of painstaking revision, was staged with success at the Carignano Theater in Turin. This success did not make Alfieri vainly proud, but it made him conscious of his literary and moral mission and of the tremendous effort that he had to make in order to become worthy of his success. Until that moment, his education had been rather modest and fragmented, and he decided therefore to put aside horses, friends, and other pleasures and immerse himself in the study of letters. To improve his knowledge of the literary language, he went to live in Tuscany, and, to be more free in his pursuit, he renounced his aristocratic rights in favor of his sister and kept for himself a life annuity that would allow him to live comfortably. His tragedies were written one after the other, interspersed with other literary works, and all of them were pervaded by the burning ideal of freedom.

Alfieri was supported in his effort, which he thought was an artistic as well as a political mission, by a great love: his love for the countess Maria Luisa Stolberg of Albany, whom he met in Florence. In 1785, Alfieri went to live in France with Stolberg, whose husband, Charles Eduard Stuart, had died. There he had the opportunity to witness the outbreak of the French Revolution, which he greeted with a panegyric poem, *Parigi sbastigliata* (1789). He also had welcomed the American Revolution with a collection of five poems, *L'America libera* (1784; *Alfieri's Ode to America's Independence*, 1976). When the French Revolution degenerated into anarchy and terror, Alfieri left Paris and returned to Florence with Stolberg, living a quiet life while concentrating on his studies, until his death in 1803.

During the last years of his life, Alfieri wrote an autobiography in which he presented an interesting artistic version of his life and of the evolution of his personality. The same autobiographical spirit is present in his *Rime* (1789, 1804), which often is an analysis of his feelings and of his moods.

Alfieri's vocation as a tragedian was dictated by his desire to contribute to the Italian culture in a literary field that was not developed as it had been in France and other countries. The poet, in planning the structure of his tragedies, considered both the classical tragedy and the French tragedy as it had been developed by Corneille and Racine. He maintained in his work the three dramatic unities of time, place, and action, which had been imposed by the Renaissance interpreters of Aristotle's *Poetics*, as well as the division of each play into five acts. He did not continue the tradition of chorus and messengers, and he excluded the confidants that, in the French tragedy, through complicated introductory scenes, informed the public about the preceding action. Alfieri also minimized the love scenes and limited the number of characters so that he could concentrate the action on one or, at most, two of them. In Alfieri's tragedies, there is no description of the development of passion and spiritual tension. When the scene opens, these emotions have already reached the limits of human tolerance, and the tragic consequence cannot be avoided.

Because of these structures, the tragedies of Alfieri appear to be very close to the classical example and definitely classical in the precise clarity of his psychological implications as well as the precise separation between good and evil and the monolithic representation of the protagonist in his moral and spiritual composition. It is apparent, however, that all of these characters of unusual and solitary stature do not belong to the measured correctness of the neoclassical art at the end of the eighteenth century. Instead they predict the burgeoning Romantic movement, which established a drastically changed and renewed physiognomy of European art. This unusual aspect of Alfieri's tragedies is even more evident in those plays in which the protagonists have complex personalities full of contradictions and whose actions are projected on an anxious background which is threatened by obscure forces. Most representative of these dark plays are *Oreste* (pr. 1781; *Orestes*, 1815), *Rosmunda* (pr. 1784; English translation, 1815), *Agamennone* (pb. 1784; *Agamemnon*, 1815), *Saul* (pb. 1788; English translation, 1815), and *Mirra* (pr. 1789; *Myrrha*, 1815), which also represent some of his best works.

VINCENZO MONTI

Both Romantic and neoclassical elements are present in the poetry of Vincenzo Monti (1754-1828), a poet who in many respects concludes the literary activities of the eighteenth century and opens those of the nineteenth century and Romanticism. Monti was born in Fusignano, near Ferrara. As a young man, he received an education strongly based on classical culture, and since he had the unusual ability to write poetry, he captured the attention of Cardinal Scipione Borghese, who brought him to Rome to the papal court in 1778. There, Monti was soon involved with the dramatic political events of his times. At first he condemned the horrors and the excesses of the French Revolution in his poetic work *In morte di Ugo Bassville* (1793; *The Penance of Hugo: A Vision on the French Revolution*, 1805), commonly known as *Basvilliana*; subsequently, as a result of Napoleon's successful military campaign in Italy, he became a supporter of the new hero and wrote several panegyric poems in his honor. With the end of the Napoleonic Empire and the return of Austrian influence in Italy, Monti returned his support to the old master with new poems and other writings.

Among Monti's best-known work of his Roman period is "Presopopea di Pericle," which celebrates the finding of an ancient bust of the famous Athenian statesman. In *Al Signor di Montgolfier* (1784), he honors, according to the fashion of the Enlightenment, the greatness of the human mind. *The Penance of Hugo* is his best-known political work, and during the Napoleonic period, Monti's most noted works were *Il prometeo, Il bardo della Selva Nera* (1806), and *La spada di Federico II* (1806). This latter poem celebrates the victory of Napoleon over Prussia and has strong Romantic characteristics. After the fall of Napoleon, Monti celebrated the Austrian return with *Il ritorno di Astrea* (1816).

Unusually powerful and emotionally direct is his canzone "Per il giorno onomastico della sua donna" (for his lady's name day). Later in life, Monti resumed work on an earlier poem, "Feroniade," which was left unfinished; in it, he narrates the activities surrounding the draining and reclamation of the Pontine Marshes. This theme was dear to the hearts of the followers of the Enlightenment. Monti was not quite capable of creating the vital and complex structure of an extended or more engaging poem, although he had exceptional technical abilities in the composition of verses and therefore was greatly successful in his translations. Particularly masterful were his translations from classical languages, of which his translation of Homer's the *Iliad* (c. 750 B.C.E.; English translation, 1611) is considered his masterpiece.

Neoclassicism

Monti's oeuvre is characteristic of the period during which the ground was being prepared for Romanticism. At this time, art, literature, and public life in Italy were inspired by classical culture to a degree unprecedented even in the Renaissance. For the most part, this was a rather superficial and gaudy phenomenon fostered by the caesarism of the Napoleonic age and, perhaps, by an instinctive reaction of the Latin world against the surging German Romanticism. Thus, Italian neoclassicism, as this movement was called, bore the seeds of a Romantic sensibility. There was in Romanticism a torment and restlessness, an unsatisfied aspiration toward a perfected beauty— an unreachable region symbolized for the Romantics by classical Greece. This myth of Greece, present in all the best-known national literary compositions of the early nineteenth century, was the Romantic aspect of neoclassicism.

Monti is the most representative poet of this period, for his poetry is by nature oriented toward external forms. The new Romantic sensibility, preoccupied with the content of artistic reality, is not well assimilated in his art. This assimilation was to be the task of the poets who followed him, from Ugo Foscolo to Giacomo Leopardi, from Giosuè Carducci to Gabriele D'Annunzio. In D'Annunzio's poetry, the myth of the ancient world is no longer a serene and somehow superficial vision, but rather an island dreamed of and lost, a land of perfect beauty sought without hope.

Bibliography

Barnes, John C., and Jennifer Petrie, eds. *Dante and His Literary Precursors: Twelve Essays*. Dublin: Four Courts Press, 2007. A publication of the Foundation for Italian Studies, University College, Dublin. Scholarly essays on Dante's political and intellectual environment and on new ways of reading his works. Bibliography and indices.

Brand, Peter, and Lino Pertile, eds. *The Cambridge History of Italian Literature*. 2d ed. New York: Cambridge University Press, 1999. In this new, definitive volume, the first of its kind in four decades, leading scholars provide information about a wide range of writers, their works, and their significance. Translations are included. Maps, chronological charts, and bibliographical references.

Cavallo, Jo Ann. *The Romance Epics of Boiardo, Ariosto, and Tasso: From Public Duty to Private Pleasure*. Toronto: University of Toronto Press, 2004. The author combines analyses of the three poets, discussion of the literary tradition, comments on their social and intellectual environments, and summaries of previous criticism in order to provide the basis for a persuasive new theory about the relationship between them. An impressive achievement. Bibliography and index.

Everson, Jane E. *The Italian Romance Epic in the Age of Humanism: The Matter of Italy and the World of Rome*. New York: Oxford University Press, 2001. Demonstrates how the romance, or chivalric epic, owed its appeal to a fusion of traditional, medieval tales of Charlemagne and Arthur with the newer cultural themes developed by the revival in classical antiquity that constitutes the key to Renaissance culture.

Holmes, Olivia. *Assembling the Lyric Self: Authorship from Troubador Song to Italian Poetry Book*. Minneapolis: University of Minnesota Press, 2000. Examines the change in the concept of authorship that occurred in the thirteenth century when, because of the increase in literacy, poetic expression changed from oral to written form. Notes, bibliography, and index.

Jacoff, Rachel, ed. *The Cambridge Companion to Dante*. 2d ed. New York: Cambridge University Press, 2007. An updated edition of the standard introduction to Dante. Contains three new essays on *The Divine Comedy*, a current bibliography, and references to online resources.

Mallette, Karla. *The Kingdom of Sicily, 1100-1250: A Literary History*. Philadelphia: University of Pennsylvania Press, 2005. Applies postcolonial theory to the period when Sicily was a multilingual, multicultural country, producing literature in Arabic, Latin, Greek, and Romance dialects. Contains an extensive selection of poems in translation. Bibliography and index.

Stortoni, Laura A., and Mary P. Lillie, eds. *Women Poets of the Italian Renaissance: Courtly Ladies and Courtesans*. New York: Italica, 1997. This bilingual anthology contains eighty poems by nineteen poets, ranging from love lyrics to spiritual meditations. Includes introductory essay, biographies, first-line index, notes, and bibliographies.

Zatti, Sergio. *The Quest for Epic: From Ariosto to Tasso*. Translated by Sally Hill with Dennis Looney. Edited by Looney. Toronto: University of Toronto Press, 2006. Introduction by Albert Russell Ascoli. In this work, translated into English for the first time, one of Italy's most important critics traces the development of the narrative genre from chivalric romance to the epic and points out how that form, in turn, predates the modern novel. Notes, bibliography, and index.

Patrizio Rossi

ITALIAN POETRY SINCE 1800

At the time of Italy's unification in 1861, Alessandro Manzoni was the only living member of the great triad of early nineteenth century writers (composed of Manzoni, Ugo Foscolo, and Giacomo Leopardi), and he had written little poetry after the completion of his masterpiece, the novel *I promessi sposi* (1827, 1840-1842; *The Betrothed*, 1828, 1951). Also surviving were a trio of late Romantic poets, Aleardo Aleardi (1812-1878), Giovanni Prati (1814-1884), and Giacomo Zanella (1820-1888). The first was a patriotic poet; the second, although he was famous for his long Byronic poem of contemporary Venetian life, *Edmenegarda* (1841), had abandoned Romanticism and turned classicist; and Zanella, who has withstood the test of time somewhat better than the other two, was a priest interested in reconciling science and religion. His masterpiece, "Sopra una conchiglia fossile nel mio studio" ("On a Fossil Shell in My Study"), often compared to Henry Wadsworth Longfellow's "The Chambered Nautilus," is an imaginative history of Earth and a reflection on the higher destiny that awaits humanity.

The unification of Italy robbed its writers of one of their main inspirations; without a direct political mission, Italian literature lost some momentum during the last third of the century, fragmenting into various movements. Some writers wished to cling to a dying Romanticism, some returned to the classical past, and some looked ahead to realism. Those who championed realism, called *Verismo* in Italy, were chiefly novelists and dramatists.

THE SCAPIGLIATURA MOVEMENT

In the 1860's, there flourished a movement in Milan called the *scapigliatura*, from the disheveled or Bohemian appearance of its members, who reacted against the traditional forms of late Romanticism in their desire to achieve a spontaneous artistic expression. They looked toward such non-Italian poets as Gérard de Nerval, Charles Baudelaire, Henri Murger, Paul Verlaine, Arthur Rimbaud, and Heinrich Heine, and their work exhibited overtones of Decadence (art for art's sake), realism, and Satanism. At their worst, they substituted allegory and symbol for genuine thought and feeling.

Emilio Praga (1839-1875), a painter as well as a poet, wrote in the style of Baudelaire and died of alcoholism. The nostalgic motifs of his poetry are couched in pessimism and sensuality and can hardly be classified as examples of realistic writing. Arrigo Boito (1842-1918), offspring of an Italian father and a Polish mother, who ranks second after Giuseppe Verdi among Italian composers of the late nineteenth century, wrote poetry that sadly and sternly evokes the past, but his best lyric work, such as the legend of *Re orso* (king bear), has today been forgotten. Giovanni Camerana (1845-1905), also a painter, who committed suicide at the age of sixty, wrote landscape poetry with a painter's eye for color and form.

Peripheral to the *scapigliati* were Vittorio Betteloni (1840-1910), who was drawn to realism—a translator of Lord Byron and Johann Wolfgang von Goethe and a forerunner of the crepuscular movement—and his friend Olindo Guerrini (pseudonym of Lorenzo Stecchetti; 1845-1916), known for his peculiar brand of realism that approached pornography and for his satirical view of politicians.

While the *scapigliatura* movement failed to produce any great work of poetry, it created a commotion of new ideas from which other rebellious movements arose. Indeed, it could be argued that the decadent aspect of the poetry of Giovanni Pascoli and Gabriele D'Annunzio represents a continuation of the precepts of the *scapigliati*.

Giosuè Carducci

At that time, there arose a giant of a poet who would command and receive such respect from the Italian people as is rare in modern times, and who would receive the first Nobel Prize awarded to an Italian (1906). The Tuscan Giosuè Carducci (1835-1907)—rebellious, republican, and anticlerical—presented a drastic contrast to Abbe Zanella, who had fought for the Catholic ideal of a confederated Italy under the authority of a liberal pope. Carducci instead wrote "Inno a Satana" ("Hymn to Satan"); although Carducci's Satan is a progressive "avenging force of Reason" rather than a prince of darkness, Carducci continued for many years to harbor a grudge in response to what he deemed Pope Pius IX's betrayal of Italy in the secular interests of the Vatican.

Carducci was hostile toward Romanticism for its emotionalism and its deficiencies in formal expression. He equated Romanticism with the Middle Ages. Classicism for him was the glistening and gladdening Sun, while Romanticism was the infecund ghost of the moon (whose "stupid round face" Carducci said he hated), the haunter of ruins and cemeteries. Although his father admired Manzoni and had encouraged the young Carducci to read him, the poet was instead attracted to Homer and Vergil and the pre-Manzonian and pre-Romantic classicists (as well as these aspects in the poetry of Foscolo).

Carducci tried to subdue Romantic impulses by successfully adapting Greek and Latin quantitative meter to Italian verse, an achievement that his Italian predecessors (including Gabriello Chiabrera, 1552-1638; Leon Battista Alberti, 1404-1472; and Tommaso Campanella, 1568-1639) had attempted but had not attained. To the critics, his use of unrhymed Alcaics, Sapphics, hexameters, and Asclepiads seemed like nothing less than an insult to the Italian language. Carducci had foreseen this reaction and ironically called his three-volume collection *Odi barbare* (1877, 1882, 1889; *The Barbarian Odes of Giosuè Carducci*, 1939), not because the odes offended Italian readers but because Horace and Vergil would have been offended to hear their language corrupted in Italian. In his unbounded admiration for the sculptural lines of ancient Latin poetry, Carducci sometimes indulged a fascination with mere sound. His poetry is not often tender, but it is always cast in a mold of majestic form.

It is precisely Carducci's more tender poems, however, with their highly controlled emotionality, that are most alive for modern readers. His "Alla stazione in una mattinata d'autunno" ("To the Station on an Autumn Morning") is an impressive love poem reflecting the mood of his passion for Carolina Piva ("Lidia"); in the poem "Pianto antico" ("Ancient Lament"), while observing the greenness of a flowering pomegranate tree, he is reminded that his infant son, who once stretched out "his little hand" toward that very tree, is now dead.

Significantly, the poets whom Carducci chose to translate into Italian were Hellenistic Germans of the earlier part of the century, Friedrich Gottlieb Klopstock, August Platen, and Heine. Also revealing of his tastes are his eulogies for figures such as Giuseppe Garibaldi, the redeemer of Italy; Queen Margherita, the accomplished consort of King Umberto I; Homer; Vergil; Dante, whom he could appreciate but not love; Victor Hugo, to whom he writes: "Sing to the new progeny, O divine old man,/ time-honored song of the Latin people;/ sing to the expectant world: Justice and Liberty"; and even Jaufre Rudel and Martin Luther. A great orator, Carducci was often asked to make public addresses on literary figures of the past; at Pietole, he spoke on Vergil, at Arqua on Petrarch, at Certaldo on Giovanni Boccaccio, at Recanati on Leopardi. In Bologna on June 4, 1882, two days after the death of Garibaldi, Carducci delivered an extemporaneous tribute that has hardly been surpassed in any time or place. Carducci's heavy glorification of the past ("I stand on the mount of centuries"), however, became a suffocating burden from which his successors felt the need to free themselves.

As dogmatic as he was, Carducci was capable of changing his opinions and evolving with the times. The poet who wrote of ancient Rome, "No more she triumphs since a Galilean/ with russet hair, the Capitol ascending,/ thrust on her back a cross," gradually accepted a vigorous and loving morality touched with the divine, and even came to appreciate the historic mission of the Church. Indeed, the author of a savage poetic invective against Pope Pius IX mellowed to such an extent that he poetically invited "Citizen Mastai" (Count Giovanni Maria Mastai-Feretti, later Pope Pius IX) to drink a toast to liberty.

Though foremost a classicist, Carducci came to appreciate modern literature, both foreign and Italian. His "Colloqui con gli alberti" (conversations with the trees) even recalls one of Zanella's poems that Carducci admired, "Egoismo e carita" (selfishness and charity). In pre-Risorgimento days, Carducci was a staunch republican, but he slowly came to agree with Camillo Bensodi Cavour that Italy was not ready for democratic government, and he endorsed a kingdom under the House of Savoy. This decision led to a deep friendship with Queen Margherita, who in fact purchased his personal library a few years before his death to prevent it from being scattered.

Other neoclassicists

There were other Italian neoclassicists at that time, many of whom were devoted followers of Carducci and many, like Carducci himself, who were professors in the new lay university system. This group gave rise to the term "professorial poetry," characterized by its solemn tone and pedagogical intent. Carducci's lifelong friend Giuseppe Chiarini (1833-1908), with whom he had founded the literary society of the Amici Pedanti in 1856, is known for his *Lacrymae* (1879; tears), a collection of simple verses on the premature death of his son, Dante. Other *carducciani*, such as Enrico Panzacchi (1840-1904), Giovanni Marradi (pseudonym of G. Labronio, 1852-1922), Severino Ferrari (1856-1905), and Guido Mazzoni (1859-1943), were evokers of historical landscapes or poets of personal fantasies uninterested in realism. Another poet of rebellious spirit, but one antagonistic to Carducci, was the Sicilian Mario Rapisardi (1844-1912), professor and translator of Lucretius and Catallus and singer of the fatal unhappiness of humans and of the assault of science on long-accepted dogma. The same concern for the problem of human destiny is found in the poetry of Arturo Graf (1848-1913), the son of a Bavarian father and an Italian mother and, like Rapisardi, a professor.

GIOVANNI PASCOLI

Toward the end of the century, Carducci's position as unofficial poet laureate was assumed by his former student Giovanni Pascoli (1855-1912), who, like Carducci, was a professor and was interested only in the genre of poetry. As a humanist, he even surpassed Carducci, writing the finest Latin poetry since the age of Poliziano (1454-1494). By his emphasis on everday objects and activities, he shifted the focus of Italian poetry from the bourgeois to the petite bourgeoisie. As an outgrowth of his appreciation for the language of the common people, he incorporated many common and dialectal words into his Italian, and his example led to a more hospitable atmosphere for the ultimate acceptance of dialectal words into the standard language. His use and sometimes abuse of the onomatopoeic resources of language (for example, the *tellterelltellteretelltell* of sparrows, the *siccecce siccecce* of stonechats) was widely imitated. Because of his great love for little things, his poetry has been loosely termed "religious," yet, in his conception, religion was hardly more than a cause around which people could rally in order to become closer to one another.

In his youth, Pascoli was for a brief time partial to socialism, and in his maturity he lived always without material pretensions. However, the long years of prosperous peace that followed the unification of Italy were materialistic years during which social and religious concerns played a minor role, and Pascoli's message of simplicity and appreciation for small things had to be tempered somewhat. It was to Italy's classical past and to its more recent patriotic and historical themes that he turned in his last years. His treatment of the classical world, however, was peculiarly his own; his classical heroes are not remote ideals but rather real people with the problems of all people. Thus, Alexander the Great is portrayed not as a conqueror but as a man who laments that there are no more worlds to conquer. Pascoli also acted as spokesperson for the hopes and dreams of the Italian people for an empire in Africa. When the Italians were repulsed by the Ethiopians at Adua in 1896, Pascoli mourned the defeat in a poem, and when Italians wished to annex Libya in 1912, he wrote a treatise in agreement with their imperialistic ideals.

Pascoli presented his ideas about poetry in an essay called "Il fanciullino" (1897; the little boy), where he argues that the true poet sees things as a child sees them, spontaneously finding the analogies necessary to express his wonder. Pascoli, himself a child at heart, found fault with literary Italian, cramped by classical tradition and a limited poetic vocabulary, and he led a campaign for a "svecchiamento del lessico" ("updating of the poetic lexicon").

About the same time, Edmondo De Amicis (1846-1908), who also esteemed the childlike sense of wonder that is so often stifled in adulthood, was finding similar fault with literary Italian. In *L'idioma gentile* (1905; the noble language), he recommended that aspiring poets study the specialized vocabularies of the peasant trades; the aesthetician Benedetto Croce (1866-1952), who valued ideas above the words that dress them, asked in rebuttal if young Italians should become cooks in order to become poets. Croce, like other critics then as now, attacked Pascoli for his informality, sentimentality, and emotionalism, and was especially offended when Pascoli allowed his mother to address him in "La voce" ("The Voice") by his childhood (and dialectal) nickname, Zvanì. However uncontestable these charges seem, Italian (rather than British or American) critics today generally view Pascoli as the primary forerunner of most twentieth century Italian poetry.

Gabriele D'Annunzio

Pascoli's younger friend and admirer, Gabriele D'Annunzio (1863-1938), the third and last surviving member of the triad, was born "of pure Sabelian race" at Pescara, halfway down the Adriatic coast of Italy. A figure of European stature who occupies a significant place in the political and social, as well as literary, history of Italy, D'Annunzio was the most versatile of the triad, for when he realized that poetry no longer counted as the highest art, he applied himself to the novel and to drama. The crass sensuality of his novels and the exaggerated rhetoric of his plays, however, caused them to be forgotten in due time, while his poetry has proved to be of more lasting value. Because he attempted such a phenomenally wide range of stylistic and metrical possibilities in his poetry, D'Annunzio's legacy to subsequent generations has been great. To separate the enduring from the ephemeral in his vast output (a complete edition of his works, published by Mondadori from 1927 to 1936, makes up forty-nine volumes) has been an ongoing challenge to critics.

At the age of sixteen, D'Annunzio published an ode on the birthday of King Umberto I, written in the sapphic meter of Carducci. His first book of poems, *Primo vere* (1879, 1880; early spring), written while he was still at school, and his second, *Canto novo* (1882, 1896; new song), are imitative of Carducci and Olindo Guerrini and exhibit most of the characteristics for which he would become known—classical allusions *ad nauseam*, graphic description, linguistic and metrical dexterity, and an overwhelming joie de vivre. Another trait that became associated with him is his excessive use of the imperative mood, expressive of his sense of superiority and suggesting a master-novice relationship with his readers. The poems *Elegie romane* (1892) and *Poema paradisiaco—Odi navali* (1893) mark his attempt to free himself from the compulsion of the senses by means of human pity and sympathy—an attempt inspired by Leo Tolstoy and Fyodor Dostoevski.

D'Annunzio was also inspired by his mistress, Eleonora Duse; during the years of their affair (1894-1903), he produced his best works. His most ambitious undertaking bore the impressive title, *Laudi del cielo del mare della terra e degli eroi* (1899); he intended to expand this work into a series of seven books—each named for one of the seven Pleiades—but he never completed the project. The first book, *Maia* (1903), subtitled "Laus vitae" (praise of life), contrasts the myths of Hellas with the dogmas of Christianity in an ideal journey undertaken by the poet through Greece, celebrating joy in the perception of the natural beauty inherent in art, poetry, and legend. *Maia* takes up the theme of Carducci's *Barbarian Odes* and ends, in fact, with a tribute to Carducci. *Elettra* (1904), the second book of the proposed seven, offers an epic glorification of Garibaldi's efforts to liberate and unite Italy and sings the praises of other national heroes, of Hugo, and of Friedrich Nietzsche. *Alcyone* (1904; English translation, 1977), the third book, renews the Mediterranean tradition of the pastoral genre with its consummate simplicity and contains many of D'Annunzio's best-known poems; this volume is generally considered to represent the height of his poetic achievement.

Influenced by the French Parnassians and Symbolists, the English Pre-Raphaelites, and the German rhetoric of Richard Wagner and Nietzsche, D'Annunzio evolved a cult of Decadence centered on the relationship between beauty and decay. Not at all Christian, although always respectful to the clergy, D'Annunzio cultivated a fascination for Saint Francis of Assisi and went about his retreat, Il Vittoriale, in a dressing gown reminiscent of the Franciscan habit. The title of his poetic masterpiece, *Le laudi* (1949; expanded version of 1899 title, also includes *Maia, Elettra, Alcyone, Merope*, and *Asterope*), is from the *laudes* of the saint, and *Alcyone* includes pantheistic addresses that are paraphrased from the refrain of the "cantico delle creature." *Elettra* includes the poem "Assisi," in which D'Annunzio evokes Saint Francis from the very landscape, observing the "tortuous windings of desire" first in the "fresh breath of the evening prayer" and then in the "flesh of Francis/ inflamed by the demon of the flesh,/ bleeding on the roses' thorns." Daring to add outrageous detail to Christian myth, his boundless ego empowers him to transfer the turmoil of his own erotic fury to the landscape of Assisi and even to the saintly Francis himself, transforming his fantasy to the likes of a fertility rite. The same morbid mixture of carnality with Catholic myth and ritual is evident in D'Annunzio's mystery play, written in French, *Le Martyre de Saint Sébastien* (pr., pb. 1911), which was condemned as blasphemous by the bishop of Paris.

As a result of his fascist connections and his sympathy for Benito Mussolini (which, however, has been exaggerated by his detractors), D'Annunzio's fame faded rapidly after World War II. In the 1960's, glimmerings of a D'Annunzio revival began to appear: Some of his plays reopened; in 1976, Luchino Visconti made a film from the poet's novel *L'innocente* (1892; *The Intruder*, 1898); critics began to write about him again, and today tourists flock to his last home, Il Vittoriale, on Lago di Garda, to savor its historical implications. Two of D'Annunzio's more successful followers were women, Sibilla Aleramo (1876-1960) and Vittoria Aganoor Pompili (1857-1910). The suffocating influence of D'Annunzio's rhetoric, though less pervasive than Carducci's, did much to suppress genuine poetry and to push it to the sidelines of Italian literature, whence it had slowly to begin its way to recovery.

SIBILLA ALERAMO

The gifted and alluring Sibilla Aleramo (pseudonym of Rina Faccio) grew up in the Marches, where her Northern Italian father had been forced to take a position and where she made a bad marriage. Her free verse, often egocentric and cloyingly sensual, reaches lofty heights only when she describes the vanity of temporary carnal gratification. Her claim as Italy's foremost woman writer in the first century of the country's existence rests on the success of her novel, *Una donna* (1906; *A Woman at Bay*, 1908), in defense of women's rights. Among her lovers were the poets Vincenzo Cardarelli (1887-1959), Dino Campana (1885-1932), Clemente Rèbora (1885-1957), Giovanni Papini (1881-1956), and Giovanni Cena (1870-1917); she is sometimes compared to George Sand, whose correspondence with Alfred de Musset she translated into Italian. Although at earlier and later stages of her life she embraced socialism, in her poverty, she was obliged to use her literary talents on behalf of Mussolini. With hindsight, she expressed her envy of D'Annunzio, who died before the fascist debacle.

REGIONAL AND DIALECTIC POETRY

Traditional Italian poetry before the unification of Italy, as Ruth Phelps has noted, often lacks the "feeling of place" so evident in English poetry. Pascoli was the first of many modern Italian poets to convey this "English" love for a particular corner of the world. Salvatore Quasimodo (1901-1968), in *Il falso e vero verde* (1954), notes that Italian poets who are engaged most intensely by a world gathered up in a narrow landscape are often from the South, the tragic and much maligned South that has inspired even Northern poets to reflect on its destiny. Quasimodo himself wrote a "Lamento per il sud" ("Lament for the South") in which he noted that "the South is tired of hauling the dead/ on the banks of malarial marshes,/ is tired of solitudes, of chains,/ is tired of the curses/ in its mouth," and elsewhere in his poems he frequently alludes to his childhood in Sicily. The heat of the Sicilian midday sun is a major force in the amatory poetry of Giuseppe Villaroel (1889-1965), and Lucio Piccolo (1903-1969) sought to preserve the Baroque Sicily of agave plants, sirocco nights, and colored wagons in his poetry. The savage terrain of isolated Basilicata has inspired such native poets as Rocco Scotellaro (1923-1953), who wrote of "Backbones of mountains/ touched by the light winter sun," and Leonardo Sinisgalli (1908-1981), who celebrated this "Land of huge mamas, of fathers dark/ and radiant as skeletons, overrun by roosters/ and dogs."

Libero de Libero (1906-1981) conveys his deep attachment to the land of his native Ciociaria (between Rome and Naples) in his allusive and elliptical poetry written in the Hermetic tradition. Ada Negri (1870-1945), in *Canti dell'isola* (1924; songs of the island), paints the transcending beauty of the dream island of Capri. Diego Valeri (1887-1976) celebrated Venice, his city of adoption, in both poetry and prose. Umberto Saba loved Trieste and mentions his native city, "beautiful between the rocky mountains and the luminous sea," as one of the personal treasures denied him by the "vile Fascist and greedy German." Andrea Zanzotto (born 1921) writes of his bucolic Pieve de Soligo among the foothills of the Dolomites (especially in *Dietro il paesaggio*, 1951; beside the landscape) and assails real-estate developers poised for ecological rape. Pier Paolo Pasolini (1922-1975) tenderly sprinkles Friulian place-names throughout his poetry.

Eugenio Montale (1896-1981), who spent most of the first thirty years of his life in Genoa, painted the Ligurian landscape in terms of *petrosita*, *scabrezza*, and *aridita* (stoniness, roughness, aridity), and Camillo Sbarbaro (1888-1967), who also wrote lovingly of Liguria, is in fact mentioned in Montale's "Caffè a Rapallo" ("Cafe at Rapallo") as part of the beachside landscape. Other poets who used Ligurian themes in their poetry or drew upon the Ligurian Riviera for local color and veristic imagery include Ceccardo Roccatagliata Ceccardi (1872-1919), Mario Novaro (1868-1944), and Giovanni Boine (1887-1917), who turned his eyes yearningly back to his native town on the Ligurian coast from a sanatorium in the Swiss Alps.

Closely linked to poetry celebrating a particular region is that which employs a dialect in the face of pressure to employ the standard language. When Italy became a united nation in 1861, only slightly more than 2.5 percent of the population could speak Italian in addition to their native dialect. Although the Italian dialects all share the same Latin origin as the national language, and in fact share a vast quantity of lexical and grammatical features, there are also bewildering dissimiliarities that can make mastery of standard Italian a difficult task. As a result of the prescriptivist stance of linguistic arbiters since the time of Pietro Bembo (1470-1547), who argued for the purity of the Tuscan variety of Italian to the exclusion of borrowings from other dialects, the Italian language that the nation inherited in 1861 was a rigid medium of expression whose parameters would not be broadened until Pascoli undertook the task—a half century before television and radio would do the job more efficiently.

Coinciding with the rise of *Verismo* during the second half of the nineteenth century, an impressive number of talented poets chose to write occasionally or exclusively in their native dialects, and they have given to Italian literature a curious offshoot that is neglected in many surveys of Italian poetry. Although poets have been writing in their local dialects since the literary emergence of those dialects in medieval Italy, and although such preunification poets as the Sicilian Giovanni Meli (1740-1815), the Milanese Carlo Porta (1775-1821), and the Roman Giuseppe Gioachino Belli (1791-1863) enjoyed local followings, it was not until there was a united Italy that dialectal literature won a wider audience, and it was not until the emergence of Salvatore Di Giacomo (1860-1934) that Italian critics began to take dialectal literature seriously.

Salvatore Di Giacomo

The Neapolitan Salvatore Di Giacomo, who ranks as one of Italy's greatest lyric poets, employed a dialect that is musical, refined, and polished, not at all like street talk, though he frequently depicts street scenes in his poetry. Since Di Giacomo believed that his fame would rest on his scholarly studies (thirty-four volumes) treating the history and sociology of Naples, he wrote those works and some of his novelle in Italian, reserving his use of dialect for his poetry. He began writing during the vogue of *Verismo* and folklore studies, but his treatment of subject matter is sentimentalized and subjectivized to such an extent that the effect it achieves is quite different from that of *Verismo*. His poetry is dreamy and melancholy, sentimental but not mawkish, as in the sonnets of *O munasterio* (1887; the monastery), about a jilted sailor who becomes a monk and still longs for the freedom of the outside world, for green things growing, and for the water of the bay in the moonlight. Simple and innocent, Di Giacomo displays a childlike enchantment with the stars and moon. At times, too, he is fascinated by macabre elements. In his ghastly dream of a winter night, "Suonno 'e na notte 'e vierno," he sees before him all the women he has loved; when he fails to recognize one of them, who is veiled, she invites him to embrace her, and he realizes that she is Death.

Cesare Pascarella

Two poets of the same period, both writing in the dialect of modern Rome (*romanesco*), were also widely read and appreciated: Cesare Pascarella (1858-1940) and Carlo Alberto Salustri (1871-1950), called Trilussa. Pascarella wrote his *Sonetti* (1900; sonnets) in a medium close enough to standard Italian as to be understood easily (the glossary that accompanies the collection contains a mere forty words). The twenty-five sonnets of his *Villa Gloria* (1886) recount the ill-fated attempt by a group of patriots to wrest Rome from the Papacy (1867), and *Scoperta dell'America* (1894; the discovery of America), consisting of fifty sonnets, portrays Columbus, Ferdinand and Isabella, the Spanish sailors, and the American Indians all speaking the Roman dialect with humorous effects as they reenact the drama of discovering America.

Carlo Alberto Salustri

Carlo Alberto Salustri, or Trilussa, employed the *romanesco* dialect in its aspects of low-life (*gergo furfantino*) to construct fables in a variety of metrical forms. His art is witty, cynical, melancholy, epigrammatic, and not without a religious vein (as in "Sermone 1914," an antiwar poem). His cynicism is sometimes excessive, as in "L'omo inutile" (the superfluous man), about a six-month-old fetus under alcohol in a vat in a museum who claims that he is happier watching the people in the museum than dying as an adult in somebody's war; more often, his fables are simply delightful, as in "La carita" (charity), in which the president of an association for mistreated animals refuses to spare a dime to a beggar, claiming that only animals qualify for his sympathy, whereupon the beggar renews his appeal by displaying a headful of lice. Trilussa is probably best known for his political fables, which concern the freedom lost as a result of the fascist *ventennio*.

Other regional poets

Having produced Di Giacomo and a host of other poets during its centuries as the largest city in Italy (a distinction it retained for several decades even after the Risorgimento), Naples has been the most prolific source of dialectal literature. Next to Di Giacomo is his contemporary and competitor for recognition, the *verista* Ferdinando Russo (1866-1927), whose poetry portraying Neapolitan life is more dramatic and less tragic than that of Di Giacomo. His poems, like those of Di Giacomo, often deal with unrequited or impossible love. Other Neapolitan poets, less accomplished than Di Giacomo or Russo, clung to the melic tradition and contributed to the repertory of Neapolitan *canzonette*.

After Naples, the area around Venice has produced the richest vein of dialectal poetry. The Venetian Giacomo Noventa (1898-1960), who, with Alberto Carocci and Franco Fortini, in 1936 founded the Florentine review *Riforma letteraria* (which was closed down by the fascists three years later), was an aristocratic popular poet who embraced liberal, socialist, and Catholic views. The Veronese poet Berto Barbarani (1872-1945) wrote of the humble people and of his own loves and sorrows, depicting children with the warmth and sympathy of someone who has not had any of his own. Writing in the dialect of Trieste, Virgilio Giotti (1885-1957), abjuring historical and folkloric themes, elaborated a crepuscular inwardness, while Biagio Marin (1891-1985) is essentially a religious poet. In Friulian, Pietro Zorutti (1792-1867), author of humorous and sometimes sentimental sonnets and impressive epigrams, wrote his *Strolic furlan* (1847; Friulian almanac), a title echoed in the name of a poetry magazine, *Stroligut di cà da l'aga* (little almanac from this side of the water), published by a modern Friulian, Pasolini. Pasolini founded the Academiuta di Lenga Furlana at Casarsa, an institution that was active from 1946 to 1950, and compiled, in collaboration with the *romanesco* poet Mario Dell'Arco, an anthology of contemporary dialectal poetry from the entire Italian peninsula, *Poesia dialettale del Novecento* (1952; dialect poetry of the twentieth century). To the socialistic Pasolini, the dialect of his mother's native Friuli represented a sacred language spoken by the blessed poor, and he began his career as a poet describing the Alpine enclave, which for him represented an idyll of sexual (in his case, homosexual) freedoms opposed to the sexual corruption offered by the cities. Ironically, however, it was in Friuli that Pasolini's sexual activities with local male youths first led to blackmail and to lawsuits.

The Milanese dialect was represented by Delio Tessa (1886-1939), whose work embodies an invigorated crepuscularism, and the Ligurian dialect by Edoardo Firpo (1889-1957), whose poetry evokes the harsh Ligurian earth and the rigorous lives of those close to it. Nearer to the historical seat of the national language in Tuscany is the Pisan dialect, used by Renato Fucini (1843-1921) in his sonnets, which present vignettes of everyday life.

Writing in the harsh and little-known dialect of Basilicata is Albino Pierro (1916-1995), whose printed poems are characteristically accompanied by translations in Italian, as in *Nd'u piccicarelle di Tursi/Nel precipizio di Tursi* (1967; on the cliff of Tursi). Coming to poetry not from literary study but from inner need, he writes of the mystery of life and death, of the ancient landscape of the Italian South. From neighboring Calabria came the philosophizing poet Vincenzo Padula (1819-1893), who occasionally wrote in his Calabrian dialect.

Sebastiano Satta (1867-1914) is regarded as the national bard of Sardinia, even if his best poetry was written in Italian. His work is often shallow and his diction stilted, but at moments in *Canti barbaricini* (1910), he evokes a primitive epic grandeur.

Crepuscolari, Futuristi, and Vociani

In the twentieth century, Italian poetry escaped the provincialism that had dominated it for some time. Even the great figures Carducci and D'Annunzio came to represent a limiting classicism and an overblown rhetorical nationalism. To be sure, such figures exercised an influence on poets following them, but on the whole, the turn of the century saw a reaction against them. Of the triad, only Pascoli can be said to have anticipated contemporary poetry. The reaction took three forms: the style of the *crepuscolari* (crepuscular poets), that of the *futuristi* (Futurists), and the poetics of the writers associated with the magazine *La voce*, the *vociani*.

The crepuscular poets never constituted a school as such. Their name, which means "twilight," was derived from an article by Giuseppe Antonio Borgese (1881-1952) assessing the poetry of the turn of the century. In Borgese's view, the triad's achievements were so great that the younger generation of poets, men such as Sergio Corazzini (1886-1907), Guido Gozzano (1883-1916), Corrado Govoni (1884-1965), and Aldo Palazzeschi (pseudonym of Aldo Giurlani; 1885-1974), could hardly hope to express themselves in new ways; theirs could be only a waning poetry. Borgese found these poets to be filled with world-weariness and an unnaturally early awareness of death; the language of their works he thought Pascolian in its simplicity, its emulation of ordinary linguistic rhythms, and its concern for "small things." Though none of these poets was to become great, they established the Pascolian vocabulary and concern for ordinary cadences later employed by the great Italian modernists.

The poets identified by Borgese as *crepuscolari* wrote for only a short time. Either they died young, as did Corazzini, or they turned to other literary forms, as did Palazzeschi. Nevertheless, some of these writers should be given serious attention. In the poetry of Gozzano, for example, the danger of the crepuscular style, a self-indulgent melancholy, is balanced by a mordant irony, an irony especially incisive when directed against the foibles of the poet-self. In his fine poem "Totò Merumeni," Gozzano elaborates on a Prufrockian caricature. Totò, a fallen aristocratic type with "culture up to his ears," struggles, but without too much anguish, to comprehend his circumstances. He is a man with sensibilities but without will: "He's the *good man*, that fool of/ Nietzsche's. . . ." Totò incarnates an overripe culture and the malaise of a spirit without direction because its greatness is past. A chilly objectivity prevents any sentimentality. One line that could otherwise have been excessive states the theme of the poem: "One by one Life took all of its promises back."

The weakness of the crepuscular style, and the reason for its short vogue, is evident in Govoni's "La trombettina" ("The Little Trumpet"). This poem opens clearly and interestingly with a direct statement that all the magic that is left from a fair is in a trumpet carried across a field by a girl. The poet goes on to add: "But within its forced note/ are all the clowns, white ones and red ones,/ the band . . ." and so on. These added lines are not necessary and reduce the powerfully imagistic opening to pretty description that sinks to easy nostalgia. Even though the poet provides a surprising reversal of tone as an ending—finding "the wondrousness of spring" in the "flicker of a firefly"—he does not balance the sentimentality of the larger part of the poem. In fact, the ending substitutes another kind of sentimentality.

It was not the crepuscular poets who succeeded in reentering the European world. In 1909, publishing in the Parisian newspaper *Le Figaro*, Filippo Tommaso Marinetti (1876-1944) issued the *Manifeste du futurisme*. The Futurist movement, which embraced sculpture and painting as well as poetry, took one side of the Nietzschean philosophy of will and elevated it to a religion. Marinetti praised courage and boldness, unabashed egotism, and the purifying air of war. The machine age transcended all previous ages: Noise, speed, and mastery were its central values. Men such as Marinetti, Ardengo Soffici (1879-1964), Govoni, Papini, Palazzeschi, and even Giuseppe Ungaretti wrote under the Futurist banner.

Marinetti's call for the destruction of culture, though absurd in one way, was, in another way, prophetic, for World War I, which many of the Futurists foresaw and welcomed, threw European culture into a whirlwind of self-questioning. By the end of the war, it appeared as if Carducci had been forgotten. Ironically, the Futurist advocacy of war and its identification with fascism assured its fate: The reaction against the war meant that most writers turned their backs on Futurism as well.

Marinetti's "words in freedom," a poetic style in which syntax is interrupted or destroyed in order to achieve unusual juxtapositions of words, and in which words are stretched and given new, or absurd, meanings, became an element in a new poetic style emerging in Italy in the 1920's and focusing on the magazine *La voce*. Arturo Onofri (1885-1928) and Ungaretti were the major exponents of this style.

La voce saw its first number in December of 1908 under the editorship of Giuseppe Prezzolini (1882-1982). A center of social, political, and literary debate for eight years, the magazine became progressively more literary until, in December of 1914, under the editorship of Giuseppe De Robertis (1888-1963), it became completely literary. The writers published in *La voce* came from every side of the political spectrum. Even Mussolini and the dialectal poet Di Giacomo published in the magazine, but the writers who came to be known as *vociani* were men such as Sbarbaro, Papini (who had collaborated with Prezzolini on the magazine *Leonardo*), Rèbora, Piero Jahier (1884-1966), Palazzeschi, Cardarelli, Saba, and Campana.

Like Soffici, Palazzeschi, and Papini, Jahier had been a Futurist. For him, social issues were crucial in poetry, and in this belief he was typical of the *vociani*. His social concerns might have been colored, however, by his strict Protestant upbringing. Jahier's poetry was an antecedent of Ungaretti's, for it was fragmented, analogical, and aimed at an almost mystical apprehension of reality beyond any rational order.

Onofri had seen a crepuscular and Futurist phase, but his mature voice is identified with his *La voce* years. Following the French Symbolists, he insisted that the poem was a reality unto itself that had to be taken on its own terms. As Onofri's poetry developed, it became progressively more mystical, and his aesthetics reflected the influence of German Idealism, for he sought a union of the creative ego with the cosmos.

De Robertis, the editor of *La voce* from December, 1914 to December, 1915, saw the magazine through its most significant phase. With Ungaretti, De Robertis played an important part in the revaluation of Giacomo Leopardi, establishing the nineteenth century poet as perhaps the dominant native influence on Italian poetry in the first half of the twentieth century. The critic Silvio Ramat further asserts that this period in the history of *La voce* represented the beginnings of the Hermetic school, the most important movement in twentieth century Italian poetry.

DINO CAMPANA

Dino Campana, often called one of the *vociani*, must be treated separately, for he defies categorization. His association with the magazine was by default, for Soffici, to whom Campana had entrusted the manuscript of *Canti orfici* (1914; *Orphic Songs*, 1968), lost it; Campana thus had to publish his work himself. When Soffici read it, he praised it highly and was instrumental in arranging for a second edition.

Campana was influenced by the American poet Walt Whitman. A restless traveler, pathologically lonely and eventually mad, Campana wrote impassioned poetry. Imitating Whitman, he wrote in free verse, with erratic syntax and disquieting imagery. His sole work, *Orphic Songs*, lyrically depicts travels, women, loneliness. His writing is reminiscent of Vincent van Gogh's expressive power—as, for example, when he describes Genoa, making it any modern city: "And The City is aware/ And lights up/ And the flame titillates and swallows up/ The magnificent residues of the sun. . . ."

Campana's poetry is spontaneous, filled with brilliant insight, but sometimes without sustaining integument. True to their name, these poems seem, at their best, inspired in a demoniac fashion, and it is that quality that keeps them safe from pathos. Ironically, it might have been Campana's madness that preserved his work from melancholy. His life, however, was not thus preserved, for soon after the publication of his poems he was committed to a mental hospital at Castel Pulci near Florence, where he remained until his death in 1932.

GIUSEPPE UNGARETTI

Giuseppe Ungaretti (1888-1970) is the central figure of twentieth century Italian poetry. Next to him are Montale and Saba, and in the succeeding generation, Quasimodo. Only Ungaretti, Montale has said, could benefit from the air of freedom around the time of World War I. Though Saba was writing at that time also, his poetry remained derivative of Pascoli until he encountered Ungaretti.

Ungaretti was born in Alexandria, Egypt. His education was French, which probably accounts for the decidedly Symbolist influence on his poetry. His style brings together Symbolist, Futurist, and Leopardian techniques. The use of fragmented lines, analogy, nonmetrical but rhythmic cadences, and mysterium characterizes his early writing, the works of World War I: *Il porto sepolto* (1916; the buried port) and *Allegria di naufragi* (1919; the joy of shipwrecks).

In describing his verse, Ungaretti spoke of a poetics of the word, suggesting that words have a plethora of significations which it is the task of poetry to unearth. Ungaretti's spare style was a consequence of this belief. "I flood myself with light/ of the immense." So goes the poem "Mattina" ("Morning"); such a poem is evocative, incantatory. Even in those poems based on a narrative, Ungaretti removed all spare words—anything that served a merely decorative or metrical function—in order to get at the significant elements only. Such a narrative poem is "In memoria" ("In Memoriam"), about the suicide of his friend Mohammed Sheab. On its surface, the poem appears to be simply a whittled-down account of a tragic event, but when the reader takes into account the role of the poetic speaker, his condition as a soldier at the Italian front during World War I, and the fact that the poem stands as a successful song, such lines as "And he could not/ set free/ the song/ of his abandon" or "And only I perhaps/ still know/ he lived," it becomes clear that the apparent simplicity and directness of the poem conceal depths of meaning. This poem is not, in any simple sense, an effort to memorialize its subject through art; indeed, the poem suggests that the precariousness of things and of people is the very precondition of song.

After his first collections, Ungaretti turned to an intensive study of traditional Italian lyrics: Petrarch, Tasso, Leopardi. From the highly condensed line and music of his first works, he turned to traditional metrics as an inspiration, seeking, he said, "true Italian song." Without abandoning the lean quality of his early verse, Ungaretti managed in volumes such as *Sentimento del tempo* (1933; the feeling of time) and *La terra promessa* (1950; the promised land) to infuse his work with the music of the hendecasyllabic line. At the same time, his syntax became more complex, and he introduced subtle allusions to the classics. These features of his poems provoked resistance among some critics and inspired the label Hermetic—that is, requiring secret knowledge.

For Ungaretti, poetry and experience are in dialogue with each other (he called poetry "seemly biography"), so that a more complex poetry reflects a deepening experience. In fact, poetry is the vehicle by which experience is deepened, or, to put it in a more Ungarettian fashion, restored to its purity. Such an understanding of the role of poetry reveals how central language is to Ungaretti's worldview. For most human beings, caught up in a fragmented or clichéd language, experience is alienated from them at the very moment of its occurrence; though the poet might not come closer to the moment of experience, in recollection through poetry, he can uncover the truth of experience. Others, like Ungaretti, move from atheism to faith, suffer the loss of an only son, and confront old age, but they cannot capture the truth of these experiences as Ungaretti was able to do in his poetry.

Ungaretti's dialogue with tradition is an extension of his dialogue with experience. The essentials of experience do not change—love, death, memory—and the truth of these is held in the collective memory of tradition. The poet cannot work alone, but must return to the past creatively as a source. In one of his last poems, "Per sempre" ("For Ever") and written, perhaps, in memory of his wife, Ungaretti captured something of the sense of this twofold dialogue: "With no impatience I shall dream,/ Bend to the work/ That has no end. . . ."

Ungaretti gained an international reputation, lectured widely, and influenced almost every major modern poetic movement in Italy. He, along with Montale, Quasimodo, and others, was also active as a translator, helping to lead Italy out of cultural provincialism.

Eugenio Montale

While contemporary Italian poetry begins with Ungaretti, its greatest figure may be Eugenio Montale, though the bulk of Montale's work makes up only four modest collections: *Ossi di seppia* (1925; partial translation, *The Bones of the Cuttlefish*, 1983; full translation, *Cuttlefish Bones*, 1992), *Le occasioni* (1939; *The Occasions*, 1987), *La bufera, e altro* (1956; *The Storm, and Other Poems*, 1978), and *Satura, 1962-1970* (1971; English translation, 1998).

Montale's earliest poems are in the crepuscular mood, showing especially the influence of Gozzano as well as of Pascoli, but D'Annunzio is also present. Though Montale is not really a regional poet, his reflection of Sbarbaro, a fellow Ligurian, gives his poetry a regional feel. Unlike Sbarbaro's landscapes, however, Montale's settings verge on metaphysical realities, providing images emblematic of the human condition.

Not completely a pessimist, Montale nevertheless wraps whatever sense of extraordinary reality is attained in his poems in a language of desolation and spiritual fragmentation. In the poem "I limoni" ("The Lemon Trees"), for example—which many critics treat as thematically central to Montale's first collection, *Cuttlefish Bones*—there are several suggestions of a breakthrough into a heightened reality: "Here by a miracle is hushed/ the war of diverted passions,/ here even to us poor falls our share of riches,/ and it is the scent of the lemon trees. . . ." These openings, however, are quickly obscured: "But the illusion wanes and time returns us/ to our clamorous cities. . . ." In Ungaretti, the desolate landscape of modern existence is likewise seen as resulting from the reality of time, but for him there is also a way beyond depersonalized time; in Montale, the landscape is bleaker, the music more muted.

Montale's greatness lies in his ability to evoke cosmic order in the midst of ordinary things and events. A thunderstorm holds back ultimate reality, for example, in "Arsenio," a poem many critics take to be a self-portrait. Montale commented that at the time of the writing of this poem, he was under the influence of Henri Bergson, the French philosopher: "Miracle was as evident for me as necessity." For Montale, however, there was never a complete breakthrough to extraordinary reality; thus, Arsenio, after contemplating the possibility that the sound of castanets holds the key to a heightened reality, is suddenly swept along in a thunderstorm: "Everything about you is washing with overflow, the loose awnings/ flap in the wind, and immense rustling skirts/ along the earth, and down collapse with strident sounds/ the paper lanterns. . . ."

Montale's later poetry, beginning with *The Occasions*, became more difficult, more Hermetic: "I wanted a fruit that could contain its motives without revealing them, or better, without flaunting them." He was after an extreme concentration of meaning, an obscurity he considered good. The title of *The Occasions* suggests the difficulty of these poems; in them, one is immersed in occasions without introduction and must make one's way in the midst of objects suggestively arranged, but without any obvious relationships among them. Montale's is often a poetry of things imbued with meanings and memories.

For Montale, the central drama of existence is a striving for harmony with the self and the cosmos. Neither of these is finally achieved in life, but the poems themselves stand as a testament that Montale will not sink into cynicism or complete pessimism; although the poems do not offer ultimate consolation, they do limn a heightened experience. Thus, there is a kind of faith in beauty underlying these works, not aestheticism but an aesthetic stoicism: "The life that seemed/ so vast is briefer than your handkerchief."

Umberto Saba

Umberto Saba (1883-1957) lived and wrote during a period of tremendous poetic innovation in Italy, yet his own work remained close to the lyric tradition of Petrarch and Leopardi. To be sure, his poetry reveals the influence of his contemporaries (he himself acknowledges the influence of Ungaretti on his style), but the great body of his work cannot be categorized as belonging to any of the schools of twentieth century Italian poetry. Even though he is said to be a major force in the development of neorealism after World War II, he never shared any of the political themes of this school. Saba's poetry is fundamentally autobiographical. His recurring subjects are ordinary things, animals, and the people close to him—his mother, his father, and, above all, his wife.

Saba was born in Trieste, a city to which he remained passionately attached throughout his life. His mother was Jewish, and it was her religious identity that the poet chose for himself. His father deserted the family when Saba was a young boy. When he met his father years later, at the age of twenty, Saba says it was then that he discovered the origin of his poetic spirit. The images of Trieste found in his poetry were connected in his imagination with his wet nurse, a woman Saba loved; his emotional allegiance to her caused his mother some jealousy and pain. Saba suffered often during his adult life thinking of the pain he had given his mother, and it was probably only with his marriage that he found some sense of peace with himself.

Saba's major opus, *Il canzoniere* (1921, 1945, 1948, 1961, 1965), bears the title of Petrarch's great work—no doubt in homage to it. Written between 1900 and 1954, these poems are addressed to Saba's daughter Linuccia in an ironically offhand, self-deprecating way. The book is an autobiography in verse, and critics have often commented that the poet becomes self-indulent and technically lax in some of the poems, but, taken as a whole, the work has a greatness that is undeniable. Indeed, Saba's *Il canzoniere* is one of those rare masterpieces that combine unswerving artistic vision with great popular appeal.

A Pascolian, Saba balances potentially sentimental themes, such as the love he has for his wife, with a muted and ironic language. In "A mia moglie" ("To My Wife"), he develops a series of similes between his wife and barnyard animals. These images never become cute, and by the end of the poem, they ring with surprisingly passionate power: ". . . as in all the females/ of the peaceful animals,/ close to God;/ and in no other woman." Saba was a master of classical meters and forms. His career as a poet was traditional in the sense that he apprenticed himself to his craft, learning more and more difficult forms. This painstaking craftsmanship in the service of emotional authenticity made for great poetry. Though he valued simplicity, Saba was in no way simple.

Salvatore Quasimodo

Salvatore Quasimodo, born in Modica, Sicily, stands with Ungaretti, Montale, and Saba as one of the great poets of modern Italy. His winning of the Nobel Prize in Literature in 1959 aroused a great deal of critical debate, for many had expected the older Ungaretti or Montale to win. Quasimodo, furthermore, won the Nobel Prize based on his later work, such as *Giorno dopo giorno* (1947; day after day), which he wrote after his turn away from Hermeticism to a more socially and politically engaged poetry. For those critics who considered his early work superior, the Nobel Prize seemed a mistake. There is no doubt today, however, that Quasimodo is held in the highest critical esteem.

Educated as an engineer, though he discovered his love of poetry early in life, it was not until his late twenties that Quasimodo sought publication. His first poems were published in *Solaria*, a magazine whose internationalism, intellectualism, and political nonalignment were considered antifascist. In 1930, his collection *Acque e terre* (waters and lands) appeared, immediately establishing Quasimodo as a major new voice. These first poems were obscure, subdued, mysterious—Hermetic in the manner of Montale and Ungaretti. Though his early work revealed a strong sense of landscape, Quasimodo's main concerns—like Montale's—were spiritual. His was a voice of human loneliness and anguish. In "Ed è subito sera" ("And It Is Suddenly Evening"), this mood is beautifully, if epigrammatically, conveyed: "Each alone on the heart of the earth,/ impaled upon a ray of sun:/ and suddenly it's evening."

Quasimodo often evokes classical music, as in "Vento a Tindari" ("Wind at Tindari"): "Tindari, I know you mild/ among broad hills, above the waters/ of the god's soft islands. . . ." In the Italian, the cadences of classical Greek structure the line and add to the evocative power of the landscape. Like Ungaretti, Quasimodo sought a promised land which poetry somehow prefigured. In this case, it is Sicily sung in such a way that it becomes a mysticized realm. Just as Quasimodo practiced what Ungaretti called the "excavation of the word," so, too, he uncovered classical resonances in the scenes of his native island.

Quasimodo, along with many other Southern writers, lived in the North because of the deplorable condition into which the South had sunk, but in his writing, he remained a southerner, even ascribing to men of the South a capacity for creative invention because of their destitution. It was during his first stay in the North that Quasimodo encountered an important influence, Monsignor Rampolla del Tindaro, who encouraged him to study the classics. After teaching himself Greek and Latin, Quasimodo went on to the study of poetry and philosophy in the classical languages. In 1940, he published a powerful, controversial volume of translations, *Lirici greci* (1940; Greek lyrics), establishing himself as a major translator of the classics.

During World War II, Quasimodo went through a critical change. The involuted, obscure poetry of the 1930's came to seem to him a manifestation of self-indulgence, and he turned to a more socially engaged poetry. In this new poetry, he sought to communicate with a wider audience and to bear witness to the absurdity of the contemporary situation. In poems such as "Auschwitz," he called for a rejection of inhumanities: "Upon the plains, where love and lamentation/ rotted . . . , a no/ to death. . . ." His project, which he shared with many other artists of this century, was the remaking of humanity. The cry that closes "Uomo del mio tempo" ("Man of My Time") is as old as Greek tragedy, expressing, perhaps, humanity's only real hope: "Forget, O sons, the clouds of blood/ risen from the earth, forget the fathers:/ their tombs sink down in ashes,/ black birds, the wind, cover their heart."

Hermeticism

There are many ways of understanding the phenomenon called *Ermetismo*, or Hermeticism. Essentially an extension of Symbolism into Italy, the movement nevertheless developed distinctively Italian features. The term "hermetic" was first used in a 1936 article by the Crocean critic Francesco Flora (1891-1962), who deplored the lack of clarity in the poetry of Ungaretti and his fellow spirits. Flora criticized Ungaretti in particular for practicing an art that was French, an "analogical art"; like the French Symbolists, Ungaretti employed metaphor and ellipsis to bring out an inherent richness in words that went beyond any logical order. Flora's analysis, however, failed to acknowledge the native Italian influences that also shaped Ungaretti's art, particularly the "poetics of memory" elaborated in Leopardi's *Zibaldone* (1898-1900; notebook of thoughts).

Ungaretti, Montale, and later Quasimodo were the most important poets associated with Hermeticism; other poets identified with this school were Mario Luzi (1914-2005), Vittorio Sereni (1913-1983), Alfonso Gatto (1909-1976), and Sinisgalli. Sandro Penna (1906-1977) is also counted in this group, but the character of his poetry—like that of Saba's, to which it is sometimes compared—defies categorization.

Sinisgalli, a Lucanian poet, wrote of his region but also of urban life; his poetry is characterized by a remarkable precision that reflects his study of mathematics. As a poet, Sinisgalli moved from revelation to revelation. In his later poetry, leaving behind the mannerisms of Hermeticism, he became more epigrammatic, simpler and more direct. As he says of the poet in "Alla figura del poeta": "Like a rabbit in a hutch, every morning he finds—under his paws, before his eyes, near his nose—his portion of syllables and signs."

Of the other Hermetic poets, Luzi is perhaps the most significant, for he emerged, after the war, as a major spokesperson in defense of Hermetic poetry, which was coming under attack at that time by the emerging neorealists. The war had an effect on Luzi himself, however, and by the 1950's, his style had broadened considerably from that of his earlier poetry. Luzi's work is allusive, refined, and complex. He said of poetry: "The great adventure of modern poetry consists . . . in its attempt to reconstruct through language that unity lost by the ideal, practical, expressive world."

Gatto and Sereni both began in the analogical style of Hermeticism, and both changed direction as a result of the war. Gatto's earlier poetry—impressionistic, filled with landscapes—was highly melodic, perhaps reflecting his Neapolitan heritage

(Gatto was born in Salerno). Sereni explored the historical and ideological questions raised by the war.

Religious poetry

The patriotism that produced the Risorgimento and the prosperity that followed it were not conducive to the writing of lofty religious poetry. An exception is the poetry of the Calabrian Antonino Anile (1869-1943), a neoclassicist and follower of Carducci as well as a university professor of anatomy who saw no irreconcilable conflict between science and faith. Always deeply religious, his poems portray the beauty of nature as a manifestation of God.

Many of the *vociani* wrote what might be called religious poetry. Papini converted to Catholicism after the trauma of World War I and wrote his famous *La storia di Cristo* (1921; *The Life of Christ*, 1923), a work neither theological nor scientific but charged with love and hope. From 1921 until his death, he was constantly concerned with deepening his faith, as in "Domande al Signore" ("Requests of the Lord"), where he asks for simplicity, humility, a serene smile, the cleansing of his "turbid soul that reeks of the sewer," and the burning of his heart "so that, in pursuing pain, it would find/ Your irrefutable will."

The Milanese Rèbora, another of the *vociani*, started to write poetry as an atheist. The victim of shell shock in World War I, he was discharged in 1915, and the experience forced him to do more than ask the usual existential questions about war. In 1929, he retired to a monastery, was ordained a priest in 1936, and abjured the writing of poetry until 1955, when he wrote "Curriculum vitae," an autobiographical meditation on his spiritual pilgrimage.

The response of *vociani* such as Rèbora, Onofri, and Jahier to the rhetoric of the nineteenth century was a moral indignation. Rèbora became traditionally religious, Onofri became a mystic, and Jahier expressed himself in philosophical terms. Jahier, unlike Rèbora, saw war as the symptom of a corrupt capitalistic society and as such saw it as God's way of destroying that corruption. Onofri, on the other hand, embarked upon a mystical quest that produced poems less successful than his earlier attempts.

The spiritual crisis that Ungaretti underwent after 1928 led to his return to Catholicism and ultimately is reflected in the most important part of his collection *Sentimento del tempo*. In the central poem of the section, titled "La pietà" ("Pity"), the poet expresses serious doubts about the power of his poetry and seems to waver between two poles: the solipsism of a poetry pursued in a world without God, and the certitude of a renewal of faith. Though Ungaretti expresses a tone of greater harmony in his later works, the struggle persists. Ungaretti remained the paradoxical agnostic believer; every introduction of a Christian value or image in his verse is balanced by a pagan or a humanistic counterweight.

Always insistent that he belonged to no school, Carlo Betocchi (1899-1986) cultivated his own style and his own sympathetic outlook toward objects of ordinary life. Although his post-World War II poetry is more somber, all experiences are interpreted as proof of his love for God and humanity. A land surveyor and construction engineer, Betocchi was instrumental in the organization of *Il frontespizio*, a Florentine review for Catholic poets (1929), of which he and Papini were coeditors.

Quasimodo was probably the most conventionally religious of the first-rank poets of this era. His work translating the New Testament and his knowledge of the Old Testament are echoed allusively in all of his poetry, and religious references are not always treated Hermetically. His poem "Man of My Time" takes on the directness of a sermon: Man, with his "exact science bent on extermination," is "without love, without Christ," and the poet then includes a scriptural quotation: "The blood smells as on the day/ when one brother said to the other brother: 'Let us go out to the fields.'" His great antiwar poem "Alle fronde dei salici" ("On the Branches of the Willows"), in which the poet asks, "And how could we have sung/ with the alien foot upon our heart?" and in which lyres hung on willow branches swaying in the sad wind form a counterpart to the "black howl" of a mother who meets her son crucified on a telegraph pole, was inspired by the Psalm 137, in which the children of Israel, who have hung their harps "upon the willows in the midst thereof," ask "How shall we sing the Lord's song in a strange land?" The most important lesson that Quasimodo learned from his faith was the acceptance of suffering, an acceptance that gives his mature poetry great moral authority.

The poet-priest David Maria Turoldo (1916-1992), of Friulian origin, published his first book of poetry, *Io non ho mani* (1948; I have no hands), in the painful years after World War II, establishing himself as a lover of all living things, even of the earth itself. His imagery is sensuous and uninhibited ("And while the kisses of others/ stopped at the mouth,/ I ate You at every dawn"). Although he inveighs against the destructiveness of the Western world, he can praise even the cities and the machines of the world, for they are human handiwork and are not in themselves profane.

La Ronda and the Rondisti

The review *La ronda*, founded by Cardarelli and published in Rome between 1919 and 1923, represented an attempt to encourage a renewal of Italian letters after World War I. The *rondisti* wished to restore good writing in poetry and prose by a return to classical tradition, well-constructed syntax, clear style, and a literary vocabulary. The creation of literature was once again to be viewed as a craft with as few infractions of the rules as possible. In their task of reeducating Italians in the art of writing, they chose as their model Leopardi, ultimately emphasizing his prose over his poetry. They failed for the most part to achieve these goals, for the world was changing, and although they rejected fascism, the academicism that gradually developed from their aims came dangerously close to suiting the needs of fascism.

Only in the work of Cardarelli did the *rondisti* produce a significant contribution to poetry. Cardarelli, whose critical work revealed a particular distaste for Pascoli and a virtually idolatrous regard for sixteenth century literature, wrote of the seasons as emblems for the cycle of human life, of landscapes in the harsh light of a sun that often obliterates hopes and dreams. Some of the other writers associated with *La ronda*, such as Emilio Cecchi (1884-1966) and Riccardo Bacchelli (1891-1985), were influential in propounding the vision of art as an autonomous sphere, a notion that became an important aspect of Hermeticism. Initially Ungaretti, from 1919 to 1920, was involved with the *rondisti*, but he split with them because he felt they wanted prose poems instead of creations approaching song.

Like the *rondisti*, Ada Negri (1870-1945), who was the first woman member of the Italian Academy, held traditional views about poetry. In her poems, she exalts the virtue of the working classes and, in those written after her marriage to a wealthy Piedmontese industrialist, the joys of motherhood. After a period of disillusionment, she wrote *Il libro di Mara* (1919), a powerful love poem that has been likened to the lyrics of Sappho and the Song of Solomon.

Poetry of the Resistance

It is an understatement to say that for the Italian people, the experience of World War II was traumatic and that they emerged from it with changed values. The fact that virtually all postwar literary movements are introduced with the prefix "neo-" (for example, neorealism, neoexperimentalism) is but a single example of the rupture caused by the war. A great polemic arose after the war over charges that Italian poets had done little or nothing to stop the rise of Fascism. One result of the charges was that previously Hermetic poets such as Quasimodo, Sereni, and Luzi underwent profound changes of attitude; another was that poetry reflecting on the mission of the Resistance movement came to be highly esteemed. In an attempt to unify poets, some critics have amplified the meaning of "Resistance" poetry to include any antiwar poetry of the period. Thus, the very fine *Antologia poetica della resistenza italiana*, edited by Elio Accrocca and Valerio Volponi and published in 1955, includes poets such as Ungaretti, who initially admired Mussolini and only later became disillusioned, and Sereni, who was imprisoned by the Americans in North Africa.

Italian poets sympathetic to the Resistance poured forth torrents of verse to commemorate the heroism of the fallen, and torrents of deeply felt invective, such as Saba's refrain, "All this the vile Fascist/ and the greedy German took from me," or Palazzeschi's cry, "Death to the Germans." Italians of Jewish descent were especially vocal: Saba, Natalia Ginzburg, and Franco Fortini, who wrote, speaking of Italy, "Now it is not enough just to die/ for that empty ancient name." The death of Corrado Govoni's son at the Fosse Adreatine (the massacre in Rome by the Germans of 335 partisans on March 24, 1944, about which De Libero also wrote movingly) inspired an elegy, *Aladino: Lamento su mio figlio morto* (1946; Aladino: lament for my dead son), reminiscent in breadth and length of Alfred, Lord Tennyson's *In Memoriam* (1850).

Especially significant among the Resistance poets are Cesare Pavese (1908-1950), Pasolini, and Gatto. Pavese, one of those who attacked the Hermeticists for their failure to speak out against Fascism, was arrested for antifascist activities in 1935 and then imprisoned. He was profoundly affected by the deaths of his friends Giaime Pintor and Leone Ginzburg, killed in their partisan undertakings, but his feelings about the period were given fuller development in his novels than in his poetry.

Pasolini was just as deeply affected by the death of his younger brother Guido at the beginning of 1945, and it is Guido's tale that Pasolini tells in "Il testamento Coran" (the Qur'ān testament), later incorporated into *La meglio gioventì* (1954; the finest youth). For Pasolini, who was drafted into the Italian army in September, 1943, but who deserted after a mere week, the Resistance was "a style all light, memorable/ awareness of sun."

Like Pavese and Pasolini, Gatto was a Communist. Seeds of his moral dilemma were evident in his *Amore della vita* (1944), and in 1944 and 1945, his verses circulated secretly; in 1949, they were assembled in *Il Capo sulla neve* (the head on the snow).

Because he failed to join the Fascist Party, Montale was investigated by the Questura of Florence in 1937 and in the following year was discharged from his employment at the Gabinetto Vieusseux, at that time the largest lending library in Europe. Adolf Hitler's visit to Florence in the spring of 1938 is recalled in Montale's "Primavera hitleriana" ("Hitlerian Spring"), in which the poet observes the cries of "alala" and the swastikas (the Italian term for which means "hooked crosses") with consternation and irony. Some readers, however, felt that in his later poetry, Montale did not make that consternation explicit enough.

Quasimodo, who was active in the Resistance and was imprisoned by Mussolini for a time at Bergamo, felt impelled after the war to reconsider his role as a poet. His conversation was no longer with a vague and generalized humanity but with humans specifically. He emerged from his poetic seclusion and became committed to helping humans remake themselves. His Resistance poems are contained in *Giorno dopo giorno*, in which there abound references to this change in self-perception, to the difference between his previous and his present poetic mission ("I can no more return to my elysium"), and denunciations in savage terms of human inhumanity toward other people ("You are still the one with the stone and the sling,/ man of my time"). In "Auschwitz," he tells the soldier that he will find the smoke-immolated victims within him, but adds as an afterthought, "or are you, too, but ash/ of Auschwitz, medal of silence?"

Hermetics versus neorealism

The passions released by the ordeal of World War II and the bitter civil strife of the Resistance could not help but spill over into literary debate, and this was especially the case in Italy, where poetry aligned itself with schools in which political ideology was explicitly or implicitly supported. Because of their passive resistance, the Hermetic poets came under attack from the Left; the attack was initiated in an article published in *La rinascita* in 1944 and went on for several years, finally wasting itself in mere verbal exercise. In the meantime, the political realities of Italy had changed considerably, for the Italians, along with other Europeans, entered a period of economic well-being.

Several of Italy's most significant writers participated in the debate. More significant, however, these were the years in which neorealism emerged as the most vital form of Italian artistic expression, and though neorealism is associated to a large extent with the novel and the cinema, this movement also had its poetic exponents.

Pavese anticipated the neorealist art of the postwar period in *Lavorare stanca* (1936; *Hard Labor*, 1976). These poems are generally expressions of unromanticized landscapes filled with people from daily life. Though they have lyrical moments, they are informed by a pervasive bitterness. In "Instinct," Pavese speaks of dogs copulating and then refracts the attitudes of various emblematic persons through this act in such a way as to humble human pretenses: "Anything can happen out in the/ open. Even a woman, shy when face to face with a man,/ stands there...."

Of all the exponents of neorealism, it is Pasolini who stands out as the central figure. Born in Bologna but at heart a Friulian, Pasolini was the quintessential *homme engagé*. A filmmaker, novelist, and political essayist as well as a poet, he showed not only a love for the great classics and for the Hermetic style of Ungaretti, but also a devotion to leftist apologetics and Roman Catholicism. Pasolini was lionized and rejected by almost every group with which he came in contact. His poetry cannot be said to follow any specific style, but it is clear that his interests are in an art of social relevance. His volume *Le ceneri de Gramsci* (1957; *The Ashes of Gramsci*, 1982) was in part an act of homage to Antonio Gramsci, the head of the Italian Communist Party who was imprisoned under Mussolini but who managed to send out letters and journal entries expressing his vision of society and art.

In the title poem, "The Ashes of Gramsci," Pasolini combines historical reflections on the years before World War II with personal confession: "I live in the non-will/ of the dead postwar years: loving/ the world I hate...." It may be that there is no resolution for the conflict between the artist's absorption in art and the artist's moral duty to communicate with his fellow humans; in Pasolini, one finds a man living this contradiction.

A simpler case of neorealism is evident in Scotellaro, whose poetry is of a regional character. Scotellaro was born in Basilicata in 1923; a Socialist, he became mayor of his town but died at an early age in 1953. His poetry expresses his understanding of the peasantry, from which he himself came; his lyrics depict the life of his region and its ancient, even atavistic, character.

Fortini (pseudonymn of Franco Lattes; 1917-1994) began as a Hermetic poet but turned to a poetry of social engagement. A prominent Marxist critic, Fortini, a Jew, went through a period of disillusionment during the war. Despite his Marxist orientation, his poetry maintains classical references and style; he writes, as Ramat puts it, in the Petrarchan-Leopardian tradition.

Although neorealism was dominant in the years after World War II, several prewar poets, among them Luzi and Sereni, continued in the postwar era to write in the Hermetic style. In the 1950's, a number of younger poets associated with Luzi came to be regarded as neo-Hermetic; two principal figures of this group are Zanzotto and Luciano Erba (born 1922). What distinguished them from the Hermetics of the 1930's was a greater concern for language per se—an attempt to regain a poetically significant language in a world in which language itself has been technologized.

Zanzotto's poetry, beginning with *Dietro il paesaggio*, poems written between 1940 and 1948, shares with Hermeticism a surface difficulty, a highly condensed but personal symbolism suggesting the need to penetrate appearances in order to apprehend the real. In his later poetry, access to the real is permitted only by linguistic experimentation, for the language of everyday usage has been enslaved for superficial, purely utilitarian ends. Shattering syntax, struggling to unearth what he calls a "nether language," Zanzotto has much in common with that of the avant-garde experimentalists. At its most radical, Zanzotto's poetry virtually eschews content, suggesting the fragmentation, asymmetry, and nonnaturalism of much modern music.

Erba's development was the reverse of that of many later poets, for he began as a socially committed poet and then moved to neo-Hermeticism, one of a group of Lombard poets who sought to move beyond the heroics of neorealism to the expression of disillusionment. In many ways, there is a Pascolian streak in the poetry of Erba, for he develops a poetry of "small things" in order to focus on the insignificant lives of modern humanity. Erba's poetry has a clarity of line that gives the people portrayed in his work a vividness belying their ordinariness. This quality is exemplified in "Tabula rasa?": "Do you see me going along as usual/ in the districts without memory?/ I have a cream tie, an old burden/ of desires. . . ."

Another important postwar poet is the Sicilian Bartolo Cattafi (1922-1979). A recurring motif in Cattafi's poetry is the figure of a traveler or nomad set in a precisely and vividly described landscape. Cattafi strives to build blocks of words, to create poems that are thinglike assemblages of images: "Ex nihilo God/ from tatters scraps/ carrion trash me."

Avant-garde and later poets

Other changes in poetry in the 1950's all centered on the role of language. The avant-garde focused on the absurdity of any rational philosophy—even worldviews as diverse as those of Croce and Gramsci—in the modern world. The poets of this avant-garde, such as Antonio Porta (1935-1989), Alfredo Giuliani (1924-2007), Nanni Balestrini (born 1935), Edoardo Sanguineti (1930-2010), and Elio Pagliarani (born 1927), are reminiscent of Surrealism in their insistence that art must reflect the schizophrenia of modern society. They also employ the open form of American poets such as Charles Olson and William Carlos Williams. Influenced by literary theory, often to a crippling degree, the avant-garde poets reflect the ideas of the New Novel in France (in their insistence on an art of things) and of semiotics (in fact, Umberto Eco, a noted semiotician, is usually considered a poet of this group).

As the twenty-first century began, Italian poetry was characterized by a bewildering diversity, in marked contrast to the time-honored Italian tendency to form schools. In part, this fragmentation seemed to be the result of the failure of the protests that swept Europe in 1968 to effect genuine social change. Italian poetry after the Cold War embraces computer poets and experimentalists who tear language apart and attempt to rebuild it in new forms, but also more traditional poets who continue to ply their trade.

BIBLIOGRAPHY

Blum, Cinzia Sartini, and Lara Trubowitz, eds. and trans. *Contemporary Italian Women Poets: A Bilingual Anthology*. New York: Italica Press, 2001. Selections from the works of twenty-five women poets published in the last half of the twentieth century. Though they represent various literary traditions and different regions of Italy, they are alike in having produced memorable poetry. Introduction, notes, and bibliography.

Bohn, Willard, ed. and trans. *Italian Futurist Poetry*. Toronto: University of Toronto Press, 2005. A bilingual collection of more than one hundred poems, arranged in chronological order, reflecting the diversity and the very real creativity of a movement that the editor believes has previously been mislabeled. Bibliographical references and index.

Brand, Peter, and Lino Pertile, eds. *The Cambridge History of Italian Literature*. 2d ed. New York: Cambridge University Press, 1999. In this definitive volume, the first of its kind in four decades, leading scholars provide information about a wide range of writers, their works, and their significance. Translations are included. Maps, chronological charts, and bibliographical references.

Cary, Joseph. *Three Modern Italian Poets: Saba, Ungaretti, Mondale*. 2d ed. Chicago: University of Chicago Press, 1993. Focuses on the work of Umberto Saba, Giuseppe Ungaretti, and Eugenio Montale. Biographical and critical studies of three poets who flourished in the first half of the twentieth century, along with a thoughtful discussion of the historical period in which they lived. Bibliography and index.

Condini, Ned, ed. and trans. *An Anthology of Modern Italian Poetry in English Translation, with Italian Text*. New York: Modern Language Association of America, 2009. The thirty-eight poets in this collection represent all the dominant poetic genres and movements of post-Unification Italy, from symbolism and feminism to neo-avant-gardists and neorealists. Excellent introduction by Dana Renga, who also provided notes. Bibliographical references.

Frabotta, Biancamaria, ed. *Italian Women Poets*. Translated by Corrado Federici. Toronto: Guernica Editions, 2002. A volume whose purpose is to address the issue of gender differences among poets. Included are poems by twentieth century Italian women poets and interviews in which specific poems are discussed, as well as such topics as a definition of poetry.

Payne, Roberta L., ed. *Selection of Modern Italian Poetry in Translation*. Montreal: McGill-Queen's University Press, 2004. A bilingual collection that surveys Italian poetry between the 1860's and the 1960's, with special attention to groups that the editor feels have been neglected by critics, such as the Futurists and women poets. Includes ninety-two poems by thirty-five poets. An excellent introduction to modern Italian poetry.

Picchione, John. *The New Avant-garde in Italy: Theoretical Debate and Poetic Practices*. Toronto: University of Toronto Press, 2004. Describes the theoretical tenets of the experimental movement that flourished between the late 1950's and the late 1960's and explains how those ideas were applied in the creation of poetry. Of particular interest is the author's account of the growing friction between members of the movement and the split that eventually occurred. Bibliographical references and index.

Ridinger, Gayle, and Gian Paolo Renello, eds. *Italian Poetry, 1955-1990*. Boston: Dante University of America Press, 1996. This anthology of the work of three generations of Italian poets presents the poems in Italian followed by their English translations. Provides examples of recent experimental works, such as prose poetry. Biocritical essay and list of publications for each poet are included.

Jack Shreve and Robert Colucci

LUDOVICO ARIOSTO

Born: Reggio Emilia, duchy of Modena (now in Italy); September 8, 1474
Died: Ferrara (now in Italy); July 6, 1533

PRINCIPAL POETRY
Orlando Furioso, 1516, 1521, 1532 (English translation, 1591)
Satire, pb. 1534 (wr. 1517-1525; *Ariosto's Satyres*, 1608)
Cinque canti, 1545

OTHER LITERARY FORMS

Ludovico Ariosto (or-ee-AW-stoh) was an influential verse dramatist of his time, following the form of the Latin comedies of Plautus and Terence and rigorously adhering to the unities of time and place, though setting the plays in Ferrara and using the society of that city for his plots. His plays include *La cassaria* (pr., pb. 1508; *The Coffer*, 1975), *I suppositi* (pr. 1509; *The Pretenders*, 1566), *Il negromante* (wr. 1520; *The Necromancer*, 1975), and *La Lena* (pr. 1528; *Lena*, 1975). His final play, "I studenti," written in 1533, was completed posthumously by his brother Gabriele and retitled *La scolastica* (pb. 1547; *The Students*, 1975).

ACHIEVEMENTS

Ludovico Ariosto was one of the greatest Italian poets, his supreme achievement being the long poem *Orlando Furioso*. Many writers and thinkers of the Renaissance regarded *Orlando Furioso* as one of the greatest works ever composed, and its influence lasted well into the Romantic period, though it is little read today. Although Ariosto's patrons, the Este family, did not fully recognize the importance of the poet who was under their care, Ariosto's epic poem established a proud, if fictitious, line of descent for the Estensi, pleased the court at Ferrara, and spread Ariosto's name across Europe; even bandits were said to hold him in awe. *Orlando Furioso* captured the essence of Renaissance thought in its dynamic combination of classical form, fantasy, chivalry, medieval romance, irony, morality, and style. Fiercely independent as an artist, Ariosto obsessively wrote and rewrote his epic until it became, along with the works of Michelangelo, Leonardo da Vinci, and Raphael, one of the supreme artistic expressions of the Italian Renaissance.

BIOGRAPHY

Ludovico Ariosto was the son of Niccolo Ariosto, captain of the guard of Reggio Emilia, and vassal of the duke of Ferrara. Niccolo was a stern father and a harsh ruler who was hated by the people of Reggio Emilia. In 1484, he moved to Ferrara with his ten

Ludovico Ariosto
(Library of Congress)

children and set Ariosto to the study of law, despite the boy's inclination toward poetry. Ariosto resisted and was eventually permitted to study literature with Gregorio de Spoleto, until 1499, when Gregorio left for France as the tutor of Francesco Sforza. Ariosto was fluent in Latin (Horace became his favorite poet, exerting a significant influence on his later poetic forms and style), but as a result of Gregorio's departure and subsequent events, he never learned Greek, a failure that he regretted for the rest of his life. His first poetry was in Latin and earned the praise of Pietro Bembo, who urged him to continue writing in Latin. Ariosto, however, with his taste for simple things, preferred the vernacular and soon wrote only in Italian.

In 1500, Ariosto's father died and the young man was forced to take up the management of his mother's dowry and put aside his studies to care for his four brothers and five sisters. His dream of a simple life filled with humanistic studies was shattered; he found himself preoccupied with the banal tasks of finding positions for his younger brothers and administering the estate, an experience on which he would comment bitterly in *Ariosto's Satyres*. In 1502, he wrote a long Latin poem in honor of the marriage of Alfonso d'Este to Lucrezia Borgia and was rewarded with a captaincy in Reggio. He worked his way up to gentleman-in-waiting to Cardinal Ippolito d'Este, the brother of Duke Alfonso, and was sent on various diplomatic missions for the Este family. In 1509, for example, he went to Rome to seek the aid of Pope Julius II against Venice. On two other occasions, he visited the pope, trying to tighten the relationship between Julius and the Estensi, who were allied by marriage to Louis XII of France. Julius, however, became instrumental in driving the French from Italy with the League of Cambrai. Indeed, Ariosto irritated Julius so much that the pope threatened to have him tossed into the Tiber; he was forced to flee over the Apennines with Duke Alfonso in order to escape the consequences of Julius's fury.

In 1513, Ariosto visited the new pope, Leo X, who had been his friend as a cardinal, expecting the pope to become his patron. Leo, however, was a Medici (son of Lorenzo de' Medici), and that family hated the Estensi, so Ariosto went home empty-handed. In the same year, on his way home from a diplomatic mission in Florence, he began a long romantic attachment to Alessandra Benucci. He had carried on a number of previous romances, several leading to the birth of illegitimate children. One son, Virginio, born in 1509 to Orsolina Catinelli, became Ariosto's favorite and resided with Ariosto until the old man's death, even after Ariosto married Alessandra.

In 1516, Ariosto completed his first version of *Orlando Furioso* and dedicated it to his unappreciative patron, Ippolito. (The cardinal coarsely asked Ariosto where he had come up with all that foolishness.) Ariosto was thoroughly disillusioned with his patron, who, he suspected, gave him his pension to compensate the poet only for his life-threatening duties as a diplomatic messenger and not at all for his poetry. Furthermore, Ariosto was irregularly paid. A year later, when Ippolito was appointed bishop of Budapest, Ariosto pleaded his ill health, the poor health of his mother, and a desire to continue with his studies and refused to accompany Ippolito to Hungary. The poet was not disappointed when the angry cardinal released him from his service and even denied him an interview. Ariosto proudly said that if the cardinal had imagined he was buying a slave for a miserable seventy-five crowns a year, he was mistaken and could withdraw the pension.

Ariosto entered the service of Duke Alfonso and became governor of Garfagnana, a wild area between the provinces of Modena and Lucca, claimed by the Luchesi, Pisans, and Florentines. It had surrendered to the Estensi, however, and though given only half-hearted support by the duke, Ariosto proved himself a capable, honest, and diligent administrator. His letters to the duke from his headquarters in Castelnuovo show that, despite his feeling of being in exile, he was a wise ruler in meting out justice, exacting tribute, and controlling the bandits. He was constantly called on to settle squabbles, feuds, and complaints and to coax one faction to make peace with another. There is a story of his having been captured by bandits and taken to their chieftain. When the bandit leader discovered that he was addressing the author of *Orlando Furioso*, he humbly apologized for his men's failure to show Ariosto the respect he deserved, a respect not shown even by his patrons. Ariosto did his best in extraordinarily difficult circumstances and was delighted when, after three years, he was allowed to return to Ferrara. One critic has observed that sending the gentle Ariosto to Garfagnana could be compared to Queen Victoria sending Tennyson to subdue a rebellion in Afghanistan; such were the absurdities of the patronage system.

Seeking a tranquil existence, Ariosto bought a vineyard in the Mirasole district with money he had set aside. He had always been frugal, and he built a small, simple house with a Latin motto on the facade: "Parva sed apta mihi, sed nulli obnoxia, sed non/ Sordida, parta meo sed tamen aere domus" (A little house, but enough for me; to none unfriendly, not unclean, and bought with my own money). Living with his son Virginio and his lame brother Gabriele, he was married to Alessandra Benucci (secretly, so that he could still collect his ecclesiastical income) and spent his time gardening, reading the Latin classics, writing comedies, and superintending their performance and the construction of a theater. He also made his third revision of *Orlando Furioso*, increasing the number of cantos from forty to forty-six. When this task was completed, he traveled to Mantua to present a copy to Emperor Charles V, to whom the Estensi had become allied after abandoning the French. Charles appreciated the arts; allegedly, he once stooped to pick up Titian's brush, and there was a rumor that he intended to crown Ariosto in a special ceremony. This never came about, however, and the poet died of tuberculosis a year after his trip to Mantua. He was buried in the church of San Benedetto, though his remains were later transferred to the Biblioteca Comunale of Ferrara.

The posthumous success of Ariosto's great epic was extraordinary. It went through 180 editions in the sixteenth century, often in expensive illustrated formats. It was translated into all the languages of Europe and imitated in all of them.

Analysis

About 1494, Ludovico Ariosto began writing poetry, and, for about ten years, he wrote almost exclusively in Latin, primarily using the poetic forms of Catullus and Horace but influenced by many classical poets as well, including Albius Tibullus and Sextus Propertius. Although his verse in Latin is not equal in technical skill to that of Giovanni Pontano or Pietro Bembo, it has distinctive qualities, particularly its sincerity, which caused Bembo to urge Ariosto to continue writing in Latin. Ariosto's first published Latin ode, of 1494, is an Alcaic (the form most frequently employed by Horace), "Ad Philiroen" ("To Philiroe"). Written just as Charles VIII of France was about to invade Italy, it extols the blessings of peace and love. Catastrophe threatens, but it is good to lie under the trees gazing at Philiroe and listening to the murmur of a waterfall. Critic Francesco De Sanctis observes that Ariosto, in his Latin verse, thinks, feels, and writes like Horace. Political upheavals are not worth worrying about as long as one can wander in the fields in pursuit of Lydia, Lycoris, Phyllis, Glaura, or any other woman given a Latin pseudonym.

In these lyrics, such as "De puella," "De Lydia," "De Iulia," "De Glycere et Lycori," "De Megilla," and "De catella puellae," one immediately perceives the personality of Ariosto and the general aspiration of artists in the Renaissance to transcend ordinary events for the higher realms of art. Despite his diplomatic career, Ariosto always preferred a simple existence in unpretentious surroundings, but not until late in his life was he able to settle in his little house near Ferrara, where he could spend his time on poetry and gardening. His preference for this type of life is apparent even in his earliest works. He found no satisfaction in the complexities of court and politics and attempted to achieve classical serenity in the pleasures of nature, love, and poetic form. It hardly mattered to him whether Italy was tyrannized by a French king or an Italian one: Slavery is slavery.

Despite Bembo's advice, Ariosto preferred to write in the vernacular, though his lyrics in Italian are a great deal less sensuous than are their Latin counterparts. Heavily influenced by Petrarch, the passions become Platonic, and the physicality of kisses and embraces is replaced by worshipful comparisons of the love object with divinity and the sun. Most of these poems are respectable but workmanlike imitations of Petrarch and are far from Ariosto's greatest work. The poet himself showed a great deal of indifference to the scattering of lyric poems he wrote throughout his life, never collecting and publishing them. He wrote in a number of forms: elegies, sonnets, canzones, madrigals, *capitoli*, and one eclogue. In the case of many poems ascribed to Ariosto, there are serious questions of authenticity. His most famous lyric poem is the sonnet "Non so s'io potro ben chiudere in rima" (I know not if I can ever close in rhyme), which touches on his falling in love with Alessandra in Florence on Saint John's Day as the accession of Leo X was being celebrated.

ORLANDO FURIOSO

Were it not for his great epic poem, *Orlando Furioso*, Ariosto would be regarded as no more than a minor poet whose lyrics influenced the French Pléiade and whose Roman-style comedies made a mark on Renaissance English drama through George Gascoigne, who adapted *The Pretenders* for the British stage in 1566, and William Shakespeare, who used part of it for the subplot of *The Taming of the Shrew* (pr. c. 1593-1594). *Orlando Furioso*, however, is one of the great works of the Renaissance, dwarfing the numerous romances of other writers of that period. It served as a model for Miguel de Cervantes' *El ingenioso hidalgo don Quixote de la Mancha* (1605, 1615; *The History of the Valorous and Wittie Knight-Errant, Don Quixote of the Mancha*, 1612-1620; better known as *Don Quixote de la Mancha*) and Edmund Spenser's *The Faerie Queene* (1590, 1596). It influenced Bernardo Tasso's *Amadigi* (1560) and Torquato Tasso's *Gerusalemme liberata* (1581; *Jerusalem Delivered*, 1600). Robert Greene wrote a play entitled *The History of Orlando Furioso* (pr. 1594), and Shakespeare's *Much Ado About Nothing* (pr. c. 1598-1599; pb. 1600) derives from an episode in Ariosto's epic. John Milton made some use of the poem, and *Orlando Furioso* left its mark on the Romantic period as well, particularly on the poetry of Lord Byron. Sir Walter Scott faithfully read through *Orlando Furioso* every year and relished the epithet bestowed on him by Byron, who called him "the Ariosto of the north." Though not widely read today, *Orlando Furioso* is nevertheless considered one of the masterpieces of the Italian Renaissance.

Ariosto's great poem began with his desire to complete the *Orlando innamorato* (1483, 1495; English translation, 1823) of the Homer of Ferrara, Matteo Maria Boiardo. The Orlando of Boiardo's poem is descended from the hero of the Carolingian epic *Chanson de Roland* (twelfth century; *The Song of Roland*, 1880). Boiardo merged the traditions of the Arthurian romance with those of the Carolingian, and in his hands Orlando becomes much more than a warrior battling Saracens. The love theme of Arthurian romance assumes a dominant role, as the title reveals. The epic is complex, with supernatural events, subplots, battles with infidels and dragons, strange people and islands, fairies, giants, and the rescues of fair maidens. In the latter part of the poem, Boiardo intended to have the Saracen knight Ruggiero convert and marry Bradamante and to make them the ancestors of the Este family. Boiardo, however, died in the same year the French invaded Italy, and his Ruggiero remains Muslim and unmarried.

In 1506, Ariosto began *Orlando Furioso* to complete Boiardo's epic, and over a lifetime of writing and revising, he proved himself the best Italian poet of the genre. As his predecessor had integrated the Carolingian and Arthurian traditions, so Ariosto added to them the classical tradition. Many critics have commented that the title of Ariosto's epic echoes Seneca's *Hercules furens* (first century C.E.). Ariosto's opening words, "I sing of knights and ladies, of love and arms, of courtly chivalry, of courageous deeds . . . ," are very close to the opening words of Vergil's *Aeneid* (c. 29-19 B.C.E.; English translation, 1553): "Of the arms and the man I sing." In fulfilling Boiardo's intention to establish an illustrious lineage for the Estensi, Ariosto was also paralleling Vergil's attempt to establish a great ancestry for Augustus Caesar. The following line, "I shall tell of the anger, the fiery rage of young Agramante their king . . . ," is reminiscent of the opening of Homer's *Iliad* (c. 750 B.C.E.; English translation, 1611) and the "wrath of Achilles." Critics have also noted the influence of Ovid, Lucan, and Statius on Ariosto's epic.

To summarize the story line of *Orlando Furioso* would take many pages. The poem is longer than Homer's *Iliad* (c. 750 B.C.E.; English translation, 1611) and *Odyssey* (c. 725 B.C.E.; English translation, 1614) combined, and simply cataloging its characters is a major task. Some critics have therefore asserted that the poem is episodic and lacks unity. Most, however, point to the story of Ruggiero and Bradamante as the central plot around which the themes revolve, although many episodes seem to have no explicit connection with the conflicts between duty and love which constantly interfere with their relationship. Bradamante refuses to marry Ruggiero unless he converts to Christianity, and Ruggiero hesitates to do so while his lord Agramante is in danger. Later, Ruggiero becomes the friend of Leo, the man Bradamante's father had chosen to be her husband, and, out of loyalty, agrees to fight Bradamante in disguise, as Charlemagne has proclaimed that only he who defeats Bradamante in combat may marry her. Leo, however, asks Charlemagne to give his rights over her to Ruggiero (yet another act of selfless friendship and chivalry). As Ruggiero and Bradamante are being married, however, Rodomonte, a Muslim African king, calls Ruggiero an apostate, and they fight a duel. The poem ends with Rodomonte's condemned soul, in typical Renaissance style, blaspheming on its way to Hell.

Besides recounting the difficulties that Ruggiero and Bradamante must overcome in order to establish the Este line, *Orlando Furioso* tells the story of Orlando, driven to madness by his love for Angelica, daughter of the emperor of Cathay, who has been sent to destroy the court of Charlemagne. Despite the title of the poem, his story seems secondary to that of Ruggiero. After Angelica flees Paris, Orlando searches the world for her, like a knight of the Round Table in quest of the Holy Grail, encountering various adventures along the way but always one step behind her. He rescues a woman from being sacrificed to a monster, for example, just after Ruggiero has lifted Angelica off the same island by means of the hippogriff, a flying horse.

Midway through the epic, Orlando goes mad—God's punishment for abandoning the Christian armies—and rampages naked across France. He stumbles across Angelica as she is about to set sail, but because of his state, they do not recognize each other, and Angelica sails out of the poem. Orlando swims across the Strait of Gibraltar to Africa and does not recover his senses until another madman, Astolfo, travels with Saint John in Elijah's chariot of fire to the Moon, where all the things humankind has lost are collected. Astolfo recovers his own senses and puts Orlando's in a jar, so that he can transport them to Orlando. Restored, the knight devotes himself to the Christian cause and kills Agramante and several others in battles at Bizerta and Lipadusa.

This brief outline of the action of *Orlando Furioso* can give only a partial idea of the epic's complexity. The range of Ariosto's imagination is enormous, and that the poem manages to maintain any coherence at all, considering its myriad characters and supernatural intrusions, is testimony to Ariosto's genius. Besides being unified by its major plots, the poem is unified by its warning to Christendom that its internecine troubles can only increase the Islamic threat. The Turkish advance into Europe was stopped only in 1529, four years before Ariosto's death, when the siege of Vienna was abandoned. The poet did not live to see the Battle of Lepanto in 1571, which ended the Ottoman threat to Europe, and throughout his life, the Turks seemed to be growing in power, while Christians squabbled among themselves.

Many critics argue that *Orlando Furioso* is unified primarily by its style and tone rather than by its plot. With fantastic episodes occurring in every canto, Ariosto sustains the suspension of disbelief by deft use of details, imbuing scenes with the texture of familiar reality. He avoids the bombast and overt rhetorical flourishes that damage the style of so many epic poems of the period.

As De Sanctis points out, there are many tales concerning Ariosto's absentmindedness while composing the epic. It is said, for example, that he once walked halfway to Modena before remembering that he was still in his slippers. Few works of art in any age have been created with the intensity that Ariosto brought to *Orlando Furioso*. As his satires prove, Ariosto took the role of the artist very seriously. Art was his faith; religion, morality, and patriotism were secondary. Ariosto's incessant reworking of the poem shows his artistic obsession with finding the ideal form for his creation. Just as Dante had captured the essence of the end of the Middle Ages, so Ariosto synthesized the essence of the Renaissance, merging classical form with medieval romance and balancing the ironic detachment of a poetic craftsman with an earthy sense of reality.

SATIRE

Between 1517 and 1525, Ariosto wrote seven verse epistles in tercets, modeled after Horace's *Sermones* (35 B.C.E.). Published posthumously, as *Satire* (translated into English as *Ariosto's Satyres*), because of the real people and situations mentioned in them, these poems reveal much of what is known of Ariosto's personality. Written to friends and relatives such as Bembo and Ariosto's brothers Alessandro and Galazio, the satires are autobiographical and use his personal experiences and observations to make larger moral generalizations. The writer's need for independence is expressed, corruption in the Church and court is exposed, and the dangers of ambition are shown in an Aesop-like fable of a pumpkin that climbs a pear tree. Other poems express Ariosto's regrets at not having completed his education, his views on marriage, his love for the simple life, and his unhappiness at being separated from his family by his patrons' business.

Frequently witty, the satires lack the aristocratic sophistication of Horace and often seem rambling and coarse. Instead of offering incisive observations on human weakness and foolishness, Ariosto often seems to be using the satires as a device to release his pent-up frustrations with a world that will not leave him alone. Nevertheless, the satires do tell a reader much about the atmosphere of the Italian Renaissance, especially the obsessive scrambling for power among noble families.

OTHER MAJOR WORKS

PLAYS: *La cassaria*, pr., pb. 1508, 1530 (*The Coffer*, 1975); *I suppositi*, pr. 1509 (*The Pretenders*, 1566); *I studenti*, wr. 1519 (completed by Gabriele Ariosto as *La scolastica*, pb. 1547, and completed by Virginio Ariosto as *L'imperfetta*, pr. c. 1556; *The Students*, 1975); *La Lena*, pr. 1528 (*Lena*, 1975); *Il negromante*, pr., pb. 1529 (wr. 1520; *The Necromancer*, 1975); *The Comedies of Ariosto*, 1975.

BIBLIOGRAPHY

Ascoli, Albert R. *Ariosto's Bitter Harmony: Crisis and Evasion in the Italian Renaissance*. Princeton, N.J.: Princeton University Press, 1987. Ascoli's close reading of *Orlando Furioso* uncovers Ariosto's "poetics of concord and discord," the evasion of historical crises, and the relationship of this "text of crisis" to others of the genre.

Brand, C. P. *Ludovico Ariosto: A Preface to the "Orlando Furioso."* Edinburgh: Edinburgh University Press, 1974. An excellent overview of Ariosto's life and works. Contains full chapters on life, lyrics, satires, and dramas while concentrating on a thematic study of *Orlando Furioso*. Emphasizes the opposition of love and war. Contains brief bibliographies for each chapter and two indexes.

Carroll, Clare. *The "Orlando Furioso": A Stoic Comedy.* Tempe, Ariz.: MRTS, 1997. Analyzes the poem's stoic view of harmony through a dialectic of contradictory meanings (wisdom through madness, juxtaposition of excess and restraint) and the balance of the poem's structure. The poem is envisioned as "a miniature animated cosmos," an organism ordered yet changing, accomplished through the imagery of circle, wheel, ring, and *tondo*.

Finucci, Valeria, ed. *Renaissance Transactions: Ariosto and Tasso.* Durham, N.C.: Duke University Press, 1999. Collection of six articles on *Orlando Furioso* by Ronald Martinez (Rinaldo's journey as epic and romance), Daniel Javitch (Ariosto's use of arms and love), Katherine Hoffmann (his juxtaposition of honor and avarice in the criticism of courtly society), Finucci (the problematic masculinity of Jocondo and Astolfo), Eric Nicholson (early theatrical adaptations), and Constance Jordan (the woman warrior Bradamante).

Griffin, Robert. *Ludovico Ariosto.* Boston: Twayne, 1974. Good introductory work on Ariosto, beginning with a chapter on his life and ending with a survey of criticism. Also contains chapters on lyrics, satires, dramas, and a thematic analysis of *Orlando Furioso*. Argues that the unity of the poem rests on man's inability to accept the will of fortune in a world beyond his limited comprehension. Contains chronology, notes, selected bibliography with brief annotations, and two indexes.

Javitch, Daniel. *Proclaiming a Classic: The Canonization of "Orlando Furioso."* Princeton, N.J.: Princeton University Press, 1991. Studies sixteenth century reception of the poem and how readers determined its literary value.

MacPhail, Eric. "Ariosto and the Prophetic Moment." *MLN* 116, no. 1 (January, 2001): 30-53. This essay, which looks at the historical context of Ariosto's epic poem, helps readers understand the times in which he wrote.

Wiggins, Peter De Sa. *Figures in Ariosto's Tapestry: Character and Design in the "Orlando Furioso."* Baltimore: The Johns Hopkins University Press, 1986. Agreeing with Galileo's early comments on the psychological consistency of Ariosto's characters and his exact knowledge of human nature, Wiggins suggests that their complex inner lives are universal human types. This invisible interior world, at odds with an exterior world of folly and depravity, is a major theme of the work. Excellent index and notes for each chapter.

_____. *The Satires of Ludovico Ariosto: A Renaissance Autobiography.* Athens: Ohio University Press, 1976. A bilingual text, using the Italian original edited by

Cesare Segre with Wiggins' clear prose translations on the facing page. Each satire is placed in biographical and historical context with its own separate preface and notes. Argues that the narrator of the satires is an idealized poet courtier in typical situations rather than a factual mirror of Ariosto himself. Suggests that the satires share similarities with *Orlando Furioso*: the theme of illusion and reality, the ironic humor, and the use of a dramatic persona as narrator.

J. Madison Davis
Updated by Joseph P. Byrne

GIOVANNI BOCCACCIO

Born: Florence or Certaldo (now in Italy); June or July, 1313
Died: Certaldo (now in Italy); December 21, 1375

PRINCIPAL POETRY
Rime, c. 1330-1340
La caccia di Diana, c. 1334
Il filostrato, c. 1335 (*The Filostrato*, 1873)
Il filocolo, c. 1336 (*Labor of Love*, 1566)
Teseida delle nozze d'Emilia, 1339-1341 (*The Book of Theseus*, 1974)
Comedia delle ninfe fiorentine, 1341-1342
Il ninfale d'Ameto, 1341-1342 (also known as *Commedia delle ninfe*)
L'amorosa visione, 1342-1343 (English translation, 1986)
Elegia di Madonna Fiammetta, 1343-1344 (*Amorous Fiammetta*, 1587, better known as *The Elegy of Lady Fiammetta*)
Il ninfale fiesolano, 1344-1346 (*The Nymph of Fiesole*, 1597)
Buccolicum carmen, c. 1351-1366 (*Boccaccio's Olympia*, 1913)

OTHER LITERARY FORMS

Although Giovanni Boccaccio (boh-KOCH-ee-oh) was an excellent poet, his long-lived literary reputation is founded on his prose works. As a scholar and humanist, he wrote long encyclopedic works, including genealogies of the pagan Greek and Roman gods, geographies, and biographies of famous men and women from history, myth, and legend. *De casibus virorum illustrium* (1355-1374; *The Fall of Princes*, 1431-1438) as well as *De mulieribus claris* (c. 1361-1375; *Concerning Famous Women*, 1943) were influential in Geoffrey Chaucer's composition of "The Monk's Tale" in *The Canterbury Tales* (1387-1400). One of his most curious prose works, *Corbaccio* (c. 1355; *The Corbaccio*, 1975), is a long vernacular work, misogynistic in its theme, that parodies the conventions of the medieval dream-vision genre.

It is Boccaccio's *Decameron: O, Prencipe Galeotto* (1349-1351; *The Decameron*, 1620) that reveals his literary genius and narrative gift. Set during the Black Death, this large prose work consists of an outer narrative frame describing the effects of the plague on the city of Florence and the subsequent flight of three young men and seven women to the countryside, where they tell a hundred tales to amuse one another and pass the time. Often labeled the "mercantile epic," *The Decameron*, with its focus on the vices and virtues of everyday life, is decidedly Renaissance in its outlook and tone.

Achievements

Giovanni Boccaccio, along with his friend and fellow humanist Petrarch, can be classified as one of the architects of the Italian Renaissance. Boccaccio, Petrarch, and Dante are the crown jewels of fourteenth century Italian poetry. Boccaccio was both a scholar and a poet, and his writings in Latin and Italian took inspiration and delight in the classical past and his contemporary world. While he was instrumental in encouraging the reading and translating of ancient Greek literature, he also continued the tradition started by Dante of promoting vernacular Italian as a worthy vehicle for great poetry and prose. Read in the original or translated into a variety of languages, his works were instrumental in spreading Renaissance values and ideas throughout Europe. His prose and poetry were foundational and inspirational for later poets and writers, including Chaucer, Christine de Pizan, Ludovico Ariosto, William Shakespeare, and Miguel de Cervantes. Boccaccio is also credited with popularizing the ottava rima; this verse form, used in his long poetic narratives, would become the mainstay for epic poetry written in Italian for centuries.

Biography

Giovanni Boccaccio was born in 1313, in Florence or Certaldo, as the illegitimate son of Boccaccino di Chellino and an unknown mother. His father, a fairly well-to-do merchant banker for the Bardi banking family, made his home in the village of Certaldo some twenty miles southwest of Florence. Despite the circumstance of Boccaccio's birth, his father recognized his son's legitimacy by 1320 and sought an education for him. By the age of seven, Boccaccio had had his first taste of Latin verse, in particular that of Ovid and Vergil. His father, however, hoped for his son to follow him in his career as a merchant-banker, and by the time Boccaccio was fourteen, he was brought or sent to Naples to be apprenticed as a merchant in one of the banking houses operated by the Bardi family.

At the time, Naples was a cultural, artistic, and intellectual center, and it fed the young Boccaccio's passion for literature more than it incited any pecuniary interests. His position within the banking industry allowed him access to a broad social and cultural spectrum. Boccaccio frequented the royal libraries in Naples and became acquainted with some of the age's greatest Humanist scholars, jurists, artists, and theologians. They introduced him to the great poetic traditions of the ancient world and his own time, including the poetry of his future friend and fellow poet, Petrarch. Eventually, Boccaccio abandoned his father's profession for a literary career and began composing his own poetry. It is during this time that he is supposed to have met and fallen in love with Fiammetta, a woman whose beauty and charm would inspire his poetry throughout his life. Although there has been speculation over her true identity, most scholars maintain she was a fictitious but convenient muse for the poet.

In 1341, Boccaccio returned to Florence and immersed himself further in his study

Giovanni Boccaccio
(Library of Congress)

of the classics and poetic composition. For much of his adult life, his literary pursuits were supported by his public role as ambassador for Florence. This position would take him to the courts of Rome, and Lombardy and even to the papal court of Urban V in Avignon.

In 1348, Boccaccio, along with the entire city of Florence, experienced the Black Death. It would claim the lives of his father and stepmother and, by some reports, more than a third of his community. Shortly thereafter, he began his most ambitious work, *The Decameron*, which uses the devastation of Florence by the plague as the starting point and narrative frame for the telling of his hundred prose tales. In 1350, he met Petrarch, and their lifelong friendship began. Although he never married, Boccaccio fathered at least five children, none of whom survived beyond adolescence.

Boccaccio's later life was fruitful both artistically and in terms of scholarship. He wrote the satire *The Corbaccio* and spent much of his time studying ancient texts and writing his encyclopedic works. For all of his work, he was held in high esteem by contemporary poets, Humanists, and scholars, and he would meet with many of them when he could. At this stage in his life, his mind turned to more spiritual matters, and he possibly took minor religious orders. Sometime after the death of his friend Petrarch in 1374, Boccaccio's health began to deteriorate. He suffered from gout and scabies, both made worse by obesity. He remained in Certaldo, and on December 21, 1375, at the age of sixty-two, he died.

Analysis

Although Giovanni Boccaccio is a foundational figure in Renaissance Humanism and literature, his life and work are, nevertheless, an outgrowth of the literary and cultural sensibilities of the late medieval period. Like Dante, whose works he admired tremendously, he chose to write in the vernacular and employ the *dolce stil nuovo*, "the sweet new style," which emphasized personal introspection on matters of love and relied on a vocabulary of accepted metaphors and symbols to express the fruit of that introspection. In addition, his devotion to his muse, Fiammetta, and the poetry and prose she inspired reflect the tendency of contemporary poets to spiritualize the older courtly love traditions that originated in the writings of the twelfth century writer Andreas Cappellanus and the poetry of the troubadours and medieval romance poets. To this late medieval tradition, however, Boccaccio brought a burgeoning Renaissance way of thinking, as seen in his passion for the ideals, literary models, and narrative texts of the classical world. Specifically, his long narrative poems reflect a conscious imitation of epic and have for their subject matter classical myth and heroic tradition; he also wrote eclogues, *Boccaccio's Olympia*, in Latin in imitation of Vergil.

In his narrative poetry, Boccaccio frequently explores the conflict between love and fortune and how each tests the lovers involved. Two of the most important in this genre are *The Filostrato* and *The Book of Theseus*.

The Filostrato

Boccaccio based *The Filostrato* on the twelfth century *Le Roman de Troie* (the romance of Troy) by Benoît de Sainte-Maure. In this work, Boccaccio creates a complex poem of love, passion, and intrigue divided into eight cantos. The poem is set against the famed Trojan War, and the main character Troilo, a prince in the house of King Priam of Troy and a great warrior in the ongoing battle with the Greeks, is smitten with love for Criseida, a young widow whose father, Calchas, has defected to the Greek side. Her cousin Pandaro, a friend of Troilo, discovers his friend's love and orchestrates a meeting and later romantic trysts. The vicissitudes of war interrupt their love, however, as Calchas arranges to have his daughter returned to him. Though Troilo and Criseida swear fidelity and plan for a swift reunion, Criseida is soon courted by the Greek Diomede and abandons Troilo, whose pain and sorrow at the loss of his love can find no solace. His subsequent death on the battlefield is the only thing that relieves him of his emotional pain. Throughout the poem, Troilo's quick and complete surrender to an overwhelming and seemingly boundless love for Criseida is contrasted with her slow and deliberate yielding to the advances made on his behalf by Pandaro.

For Troilo, love is an overwhelming emotion that afflicts the will; it possesses him and renders him completely helpless in either working to fulfill his desires or extricating himself from them. Not so for Criseida, as she rules the relationship and to a great degree her own heart. She chooses to love Troilo and does so fully, but she is quite capable of leaving him behind when the circumstances of her life change. Ultimately, the poem presents how those who love deeply are subject to the whims of a fickle universe that brings lovers together and ultimately separates them. The proem to the text suggests that the theme and events reflect Boccaccio's own love affairs, although literary historians have long debated how much of the poem is infused with autobiographical details. *The Filostrato* would eventually serve as the source for Chaucer's *Troilus and Criseyde* (1382), which in turn would be the source for Shakespeare's *Troilus and Cressida* (pr. c. 1601-1602).

THE BOOK OF THESEUS

Set in ancient Greece, *The Book of Theseus*, a twelve-canto poem, is Boccaccio's attempt to write a poem in Italian that is consciously modeled on the classical epics of Vergil and Statius. Like his *The Filostrato*, it fuses the subjects of classical heroic poetry with a courtly love tradition. The plot of the narrative relates how Teseo (Theseus) conquers the Amazons, marries their queen, Ippolita (Hippolyta), and then returns to his homeland. After defeating Thebes in battle, Teseo takes two Thebans prisoner, the cousins Arcita and Palemone. While imprisoned, the two catch sight of Emilia, Ippolita's sister, and are immediately smitten with love for her. Eventually their freedom is gained, and with Teseo's approval, they compete in a tournament for Emilia's hand in marriage. All three pray to the gods for intervention to resolve the conflict and receive answers. Mars intercedes on behalf of Palemone, who wins the battle and Emilia for his bride. Shortly thereafter, Venus, on behalf of Arcita, strikes down Palemone. After Palemone's funeral, Emilia and Arcita are married.

Interestingly, the poem presents the matters of love and war as situations that paradoxically allow human beings to achieve the highest expressions of their virtues, such as loyalty, bravery, piety, and compassion, while at the same time engaging in acts of war and in brutal conflict. In the end, Boccaccio balances the turmoil and strife that both war and love can bring to the world with the balance and order of the world as ordained and maintained by the gods. Teseo is the human counterpart of the gods, as he too is a source of order, wisdom, virtue, and power.

Over the years, critics have debated Boccaccio's success in reviving the classical epic in *The Book of Theseus*. For some, his ambition and hopes for the work as epic were not matched by his poetic abilities. They claim that the poem, rather than achieving the lofty seriousness of epic narrative, instead tends toward the melodramatic and that the plot is stretched to meet the required twelve cantos necessary for an epic. Nevertheless, Chaucer found the work to be intriguing enough to use its plot, characters, and passages as the basis for "The Knight's Tale" in *The Canterbury Tales*.

OTHER MAJOR WORKS

SHORT FICTION: *Decameron: O, Prencipe Galeotto*, 1349-1351 (*The Decameron*, 1620).

NONFICTION: *Il filocolo*, 1338; *Genealogia deorum gentilium*, c. 1350-1375; *Trattatello in laude di Dante*, 1351, 1360, 1373 (*Life of Dante*, 1898); *Corbaccio*, c. 1355 (*The Corbaccio*, 1975); *De casibus virorum illustrium*, 1355-1374 (*The Fall of Princes*, 1431-1438); *De montibus, silvis, fontibus lacubus, fluminubus, stagnis seu paludibus, et de nominbus maris*, c. 1355-1374; *De mulieribus claris*, c. 1361-1375 (*Concerning Famous Women*, 1943); *Esposizioni sopra la Commedia di Dante*, 1373-1374.

BIBLIOGRAPHY

Bergin, Thomas Goddard. *Boccaccio*. New York: Viking Press, 1981. This is a good introduction to the life of the poet and is a thorough critical study of all of his works.

Boitani, Piero. *Chaucer and Boccaccio*. Oxford, England: Society for the Study of Mediaeval Languages and Literature, 1977. Most students of English literature will come to Boccaccio's works through Geoffrey Chaucer. This is an excellent critical study of the literary connection between the poets.

Branca, Vittore. *Boccaccio: The Man and His Works*. Translated by Richard Monges and Dennis McAuliffe. New York: New York University Press, 1976. This English-language biography is a respected source and is frequently referenced by critics.

Stillinger, Thomas, and F. Regina Psaki, eds. *Boccaccio and Feminist Criticism*. Chapel Hill, N.C.: Annali d'Italianistica, 2006. The most recent trend in Boccaccio scholarship has been to examine his depiction of women. The essays contained in this work examine both his poetry and his prose in regard to feminism.

Joseph Carroll

GIOSUÈ CARDUCCI

Born: Val di Castello, Duchy of Lucca (now in Italy); July 27, 1835
Died: Bologna, Italy; February 16, 1907
Also known as: Enotrio Romano

PRINCIPAL POETRY
Rime, 1857
Juvenilia, 1863
Giambi, 1867 (also known as *Giambi ed epodi*, 1882)
Levia gravia, 1868
Decennalia, 1871
Poesie, 1871
Nuove poesie, 1872
Odi barbare, 1877 (*Barbarian Odes*, 1939)
Nuove odi barbare, 1882 (*New Barbarian Odes*, 1939)
Ca ira, 1883
Rime nouve, 1887 (*Rime nouve of Carducci*, 1916; *The New Lyrics*, 1942)
Rime e ritmi, 1899 (*The Lyrics and Rhythms*, 1942)
Terze odi barbare, 1889 (*Third Barbarian Odes*, 1939)
A Selection of His Poems, 1913
A Selection from the Poems, 1921
The Barbarian Odes of Giosuè Carducci, 1939, 1950 (includes *Barbarian Odes*, *New Barbarian Odes*, and *Third Barbarian Odes*)
Selected Verse, 1994

OTHER LITERARY FORMS

Giosuè Carducci (kor-DEWT-chee) had a long career as a scholarly critic as well as a poet and also combined the two activities. He wrote many volumes of literary history and criticism and edited several editions of Italian authors, including Petrarch and Politian. His two volumes on Giuseppe Parini have been called "the most impressive monument of his indefatigable industry." The major fault in his prose, as in his poetry, is a tendency toward bombast, though at his best he was the finest essayist of his time. Often asked to speak on public occasions, he displayed disciplined classical eloquence, speaking on Vergil, Dante, Petrarch, Giovanni Boccaccio, Alessandro Manzoni, and Giacomo Leopardi. His greatest speech, delivered in Bologna on June 4, 1882, was his extemporaneous eulogy for Giuseppe Garibaldi, who had died two days previously: "Per la morte di Giuseppe Garibaldi" (on the death of Giuseppe Garibaldi). All his nonfiction, as well as his poetry, is collected in his complete works, *Opere complete* (1940).

Achievements

The first Italian to win the Nobel Prize in Literature, which he received in 1906, Giosuè Carducci synthesized two great literary traditions to create a distinctive, original body of work. Although he came to maturity in the Romantic era, Carducci adhered to and helped maintain the values of the classical tradition; indeed, he became the outstanding exponent of the classicism which lay beneath the surface of Romanticism throughout the seventeenth century. Unlike his contemporaries, who looked nostalgically back to the Middle Ages, Carducci turned his attention toward ancient Rome and Greece. His fusion of a classical aesthetic with essentially Romantic sentiments exerted a powerful influence, particularly in the last decades of the century. Poets such as Enrico Panzacchi, Lorenzo Stecchetti, Giovanni Marradi, and Severino Ferrari were all part of Carducci's circle. Both for his influence and for his work, Carducci is recognized as the major Italian poet of the late 1800's.

Biography

Giosuè Carducci was born to Michele Carducci and Ildegonda Celli in Val di Castello, a small town near Viareggio, in Tuscany. Carducci's father, a physician, was greatly affected by the patriotism which would lead to the Risorgimento. An active Carbonaro (a member of a secret society seeking the unification of Italy), he was confined for a year in Volterra because of his participation in the Revolution of 1831. When Carducci was three, his family moved to Bolgheri, in the wild and desolate Maremma region south of Pisa. Maremma, with its Etruscan tombs, became the emotional landscape of Carducci's later poetry, appearing in such poems as "Idillio maremmano" ("Maremma Idyll") and "Traversando la Maremma Toscano" ("Crossing the Tuscan Maremma"). Carducci's mother reared him on the tragedies of Vittorio Alfieri, a writer in the French neoclassical style who had sought to revive the national spirit of Italy. For his part, Carducci's father attempted to impart to his son his own fervent enthusiasm for the writings of Manzoni, but Carducci, always an independent thinker, never acquired a taste for Manzoni. The boy was also taught Latin by his father and delighted in the works of Vergil and other ancient authors. He avidly read Roman history and anything dealing with the French Revolution. His first verse, satirical in nature, was written in 1846.

In 1848, the Carduccis were obliged to move when the attempt at independence failed. The threat of violence became too great for Carducci's father, and the family relocated first to Laiatico, then to Florence. Carducci went to religious schools until 1852, and was influenced by his rhetoric teacher, Father Geremia Barsottini, who had translated into prose all the odes of Horace. The boy became further impassioned in the cause of Italian reunification and discovered the works of Ugo Foscolo and Giuseppe Mazzini. After completing his education, Carducci followed his wandering father to Celle on Mount Amiata but soon after won a scholarship to the Normal School of Pisa.

Giosuè Carducci
(Library of Congress)

In 1855, he published his first book, *L'arpa del populo*, an anthology, and a year later he received his doctoral degree and a certification for teaching. He took a position as a rhetoric teacher in a secondary school at the *ginnasio* in San Miniato al Tedesco.

With several friends, among them Giuseppe Chiarini, Carducci founded a literary society, Amici Pedanti, a group that was essentially anti-Romantic and anti-Catholic. They believed that Italy's only hope for the future was in the revival of the classical, pagan spirit of the ancient world, which was emphasized as still existing in the Italian land and blood. Such opinions naturally provoked violent objections, both from Romantics and from those who favored the status quo. Carducci freely and ferociously responded in prose to the attacks many times. His first collection of poetry, *Rime*, appeared in July, 1857.

Although Carducci won a competition for the chair of Greek in a secondary school in Arezzo, the granducal government did not approve his appointment, so in 1857, he returned to Florence and eked out a living by giving private lessons. In November, his depression became worse when his brother Dante killed himself for unknown reasons. A year later, Carducci's father died, and Carducci became the head of his impoverished family. In 1858, he moved his mother and brother Walfredo into a very poor house in Florence, continuing his private lessons and editing the texts of the Bibliotechina Diamante of publisher Gaspare Barbèra. Together with Barbèra, he founded a short-lived periodical, *Il poliziano*. Despite his financial situation, Carducci married Elvira Menicucci in March, 1859.

With the union of Tuscany and Italy, Carducci's fortunes turned for the better. First, he was offered the chair of Greek in the secondary school of Pistoia, where he remained for nearly a year; then, the minister of education, Terenzio Mamiani, appointed him to the chair of Italian Eloquence at the University of Bologna. Carducci was somewhat ambivalent toward his professorial role and its traditional philological orientation and fretted about its effect on his poetry, but the position allowed him to deepen his acquaintance with the classics and with the literature of other nations. His political views also changed. Under Victor Emmanuel II, Carducci had been an idealistic monarchist in support of the union of Italy, but after Garibaldi was wounded and captured by government troops at Aspromonte in 1862, Carducci allied himself with the democratic republicans and became more pronouncedly Jacobin and anti-Catholic, venting his intense feelings in aggressive poetry.

Carducci published his *Giambi* (iambics; later *Giambi ed epodi*), a collection of polemical poems, under the pseudonym Enotrio Romano; the poems reveal Carducci's affinities with Victor Hugo and Heinrich Heine. "Inno a Satana" ("Hymn to Satan") was in a similar vein and became one of his most famous poems, though his work suffered in quality as he became more vituperative. By 1872, however, he had begun to control his polemical instincts, and some of his finest poems, later collected in *The New Lyrics*, were written in the 1870's. *Barbarian Odes*, begun in 1873, became his most influential work.

Indeed, following the publication of the collection *Barbarian Odes*, Carducci became an object of adulation for younger poets throughout Italy. Periodicals such as *Fanfulla della Domenica*, *Cronaca bizantina*, and *Domenica letteraria* helped spread his fame. *New Barbarian Odes* solidified his reputation, and he assumed the role of national poet.

In part, Carducci's position as a leader of young Italian poets was the result of the efforts of Angelo Sommaruga, who had founded *Cronaca bizantina* to encourage native Italian writing and gathered newcomers such as Marradi, Matilde Serao, Edoardo Scarfoglio, Guido Magnoni, and Gabriele D'Annunzio for its pages. Sommaruga sought out Carducci to give credibility to the group, and Sommaruga's encouragement spurred Carducci to intense activity in verse and prose. During this period, Carducci's political and philosophical views shifted; he resigned himself to the monarchy and acquired a more religious attitude, with some appreciation of the Roman Catholic Church's mission, though he remained fundamentally anticlerical.

The last two decades of Carducci's life were filled with misery. In 1885, he became ill. Five years later, he was made a senator, but in 1899, a stroke paralyzed his hand and nearly deprived him of speech. He continued working, despite the setbacks, publishing his last volume of poetry in 1899 and collecting his works from 1850 to 1900. In 1904, he resigned from teaching. He received the Nobel Prize in Literature the year before he died.

Analysis

When granting Giosuè Carducci the 1906 Nobel Prize in Literature, the Swedish Academy stated that the award was given "not only in consideration of his deep learning and critical research, but above all as a tribute to the creative energy, freshness of style, and lyrical force which characterize his poetic masterpieces." Carducci's works are exceptional in their synthesis of literary qualities often seen as opposites. Though his life coincided with the height of Romanticism in Italy, he took the classical mode as his paradigm of artistic creation. This might have made him a curious anachronism, but his passion and his agility with classical form kept his works free of the servility that mars much neoclassical poetry. Carducci had too great a heart to let formal considerations neuter him and too much poetic skill not to exploit the opportunities of form.

Indeed, Carducci's great learning gave him the ability to scrutinize his own work, to evaluate and revise it with a living sense of literary history. Full of the passions of the Risorgimento and the nationalism of the new Italian state, he nevertheless viewed his work as part of a long historical tradition; whatever the Romans had been in essence was still in the Italian landscape, soil, and blood. Though Italy had drifted from the unity and glory of its past, it was always possible to restore those qualities, which were not dead but merely submerged. Classicism thus became a way of restoring to the Italian nation and people their rightful identity and heritage. Carducci himself wrote:

> Great poetry aspires ceaselessly to the past and proceeds from the past. The dead are infinitely more numerous than the living, and the spaces of time under the Triumph of Death are incomparably more immense and more tranquil than the brief moment agitated by the phenomenon of life.

Juvenilia

Carducci collected his earliest poetry (that written between 1850 and 1860, including that published in *Rime*) in *Juvenilia*. In these early poems, the young Carducci was searching for his voice, but he had already adopted many of the values which inform his mature work. *Juvenilia* reveals a familiarity with Greek and Latin models as well as with Italian poetry; the values that antedate Romanticism are stressed, along with a natural humanism free of the sentimentality and egotistic aberrations of Romanticism. *Juvenilia* is highly patriotic in tone and often violently anti-Catholic because of the Church's opposition to the reunification of Italy. Carducci revives the memory of ancient poetry and pagan strength by saluting the ancient gods; he praises ancient Greece, "Mother Rome," and "free human genius." He reminds Italy of the greatness of Rome and the heroic example of the French Revolution. He salutes the heroes of Italian unity, such as Garibaldi, Mazzini, and Victor Emmanuel II, the latter in a joyous celebration of the imminent war with Austria in 1859. Many of the poems are violently emotional: Carducci attacks those whom he perceives as the enemies of Italy and plunges into depression over the contemporary state of the country and its people.

One of Carducci's most famous and controversial poems was "Hymn to Satan." Later in his life, the poet would disavow the poem and call it "vulgar sing-song," but he stood defiantly behind it when it was published, astounding the public and causing great outrage at the University of Bologna and elsewhere. The critic Querico Filopanti, for example, asserted that it was not a poem at all but an intellectual orgy. In it, Carducci gives full vent to his anticlerical feelings, seeking to shock Italians out of their spiritual apathy. Satan becomes the symbol of nature and reason: He is Lucifer, carrier of light, enemy of asceticism and of a Church which denies the natural rights of human beings. Free thought, progress, and physical vitality are Satan's promises. Curiously, the poem praises Girolamo Savonarola for his defiance, ignoring the religious reformer's own asceticism. Carducci's Satan has been likened to Charles Baudelaire's in *Les Fleurs du mal* (1857, 1861, 1868; *Flowers of Evil*, 1909), but a more fruitful comparison can be drawn with the English Romantics' interpretation of John Milton's Satan in *Paradise Lost* (1667, 1674) as a Romantic hero. Carducci's Satan is clearly more Promethean than Satanic.

Levia gravia and Giambi ed epodi

Levia gravia (light and heavy) has a tone of somberness and bitter disappointment, reflecting the events of the 1860's. During this time, the conquest of Rome was delayed, the disaster at Aspromonte occurred, and Carducci himself was drifting from his belief in the monarchy. The largely political inspiration and the tendentiousness which characterize *Levia gravia* also mar *Giambi ed epodi*, in which Carducci's combative nature overcomes his sense of poetry. "Canto dell'amore" ("Song of Love"), the last poem in *Giambi ed epodi*, provides a departure from this combativeness and reveals a depth greater than that of many of his earlier works. Most of this collection simply attacks and satirizes Pope Pius IX and the problems of the newly formed Italian government. "Song of Love," however, expresses a simple, robust view of life. Looking from Perugia, where the fortress of Paolina (a symbol of tyranny razed by the people in 1860) once stood, the poet is filled with the beauty of spring and lifted above the level of ordinary human struggle. The song of love fills him. The ancient Etruscans and Romans and foreign invaders of the Umbrian plain are evoked as symbolic of the ongoing cycles of nature. The poet even invites his enemy the pope to drink a glass of wine to liberty with him. He hears a chant rising from the hills, the voice of people of the past saying, "Too much we hated, suffering. So love!/Holy and fair the world shall be always."

NUOVE POESIE

Some critics, such as Eugenio Donadoni, remark on the gracefulness of images and rhythms in *Levia gravia* and date Carducci's beginnings as a major poet from this volume. Others, however, would delay his "arrival" as a major poet to the more mature *Nuove poesie*, four years later. One notable poem from the latter is "I poeti di parte bianca" ("Poets of the White Faction"), which makes reference to the factions in Dante's Florence and evokes that moment in history as well as the poetry of the fourteenth century. "Francesco Petrarca" celebrates the great sonneteer and speaks of raising an altar to him in the deep, green woods, combining Carducci's sense of landscape with his love for the tradition of Italian poetry.

BARBARIAN ODES, NEW BARBARIAN ODES, AND THIRD BARBARIAN ODES

At the center of Carducci's oeuvre is the highly influential and original sequence comprising *Barbarian Odes*, *New Barbarian Odes*, and *Third Barbarian Odes*. "I hate the outworn meters," Carducci proclaimed, and he began to adapt such classical forms as the Alcaic, the Asclepiadean, and the Sapphic, all commonly used by Horace. His adaptations of classical meters are extraordinarily successful; the demanding requirements of the ancient forms are satisfied gracefully and unobtrusively. When, late in life, he returned to modern forms, the musicality and facility of his verse were markedly enhanced.

Among the most successful poems of the *Barbarian Odes* is the pensive love poem "Alla stazione in una mattinata d'autunno" ("To the Station on an Autumn Morning"), in which Carducci evokes the melancholy feeling of the autumn season. "Miramar," the title of which is derived from the name of the castle near Trieste from which Maximilian began his voyage to Mexico, also conveys a tragic, pensive mood, using vivid natural imagery of the Adriatic Sea in the context of the story of the ill-fated Emperor Maximilian of Mexico. "Alla fonti del Clitunno" ("At the Sources of the Clitumnus"), a protest against Christianity, lacks the sharp edge of Carducci's earlier poems on the same topic. The poet celebrates the peasants who live along the quiet river, condemns the fanatic humility of medieval life, and hails the fecund vitality of Italy, mother of crops, laws, arts, and industry. "Presso l'urna di P. B. Shelley" ("Near the Urn of P. B. Shelley") is one of Carducci's many poems making reference to great persons, living or dead. Written in elegiac distichs (a dactylic hexameter followed by a pentameter), the poem portrays a faraway island where mythical and literary figures meet. Siegfried and Achilles walk along the sea; Roland and Hector sit together under a tree; Lear tells his story to Oedipus. Ophelia and Iphigenia, Cordelia and Antigone, Durendala and Andromache, Helen and Iseult, Lady Macbeth and Clytemnestra are paired. Shelley, the only modern poet present, has been brought to the island by Sophocles. The narrator speaks: "The present hour is in vain; it but strikes and flees;/ only in the past is beauty, only in death is truth." Like many classicists, Carducci believed that it is possible to cheat death only by the immortality of art.

The Lyrics and Rhythms

In *The Lyrics and Rhythms*, his final book of poetry, Carducci abandoned the classical meters of *Barbarian Odes* and returned to modern forms. Many of the poems in this volume were composed in the Alps and have a clear, wide-ranging vision, as if written in imitation of the clear, broad expanses visible from the mountains. Standing on the "mount of centuries," the poet looks deeply into the past in order to see the future. The landscape is rich with associations from his memory, from history, from ancient myth and legend. The tone of the collection is generally solemn, as if Carducci, who had been obsessed with death since his brother's suicide and the death of his infant son, were contemplating his own end. In the gravity of its tone and the sweep of its vision, this last book of poems offers a fitting valediction.

Other Major Works

EDITED TEXT: *L'arpa del populo*, 1855.

MISCELLANEOUS: *Opere*, 1889-1909 (includes prose and poetry); *Opere complete*, 1940 (30 volumes; includes all his prose and poetry).

Bibliography

Bailey, John Cann. *Carducci*. Oxford, England: Clarendon Press, 1926. A brief biographical and critical study of Carducci.

Brand, Peter, and Lino Pertile, eds. *The Cambridge History of Italian Literature*. Rev. ed. New York: Cambridge University Press, 1999. Contains a short discussion of Carducci and classicism. Includes bibliographical references and index.

Carducci, Giosuè. *Selected Verse*. Translated and edited by David H. Higgins. Warminster, England: Aris & Phillips, 1994. The introduction and commentary to this collection of Carducci's verse provide information on his life and poetic works.

Scalia, S. Eugene. *Carducci: His Critics and Translators in England and America, 1881-1932*. New York: S. F. Vanni, 1937. A history of the critical reception of Carducci's work in England and America. Includes bibliographic references.

Sherby, Louise S., ed. *The Who's Who of Nobel Prize Winners, 1901-2000*. 4th ed. Westport, Conn.: Oryx Press, 2002. Contains a short entry on Carducci, a prize recipient.

Williams, Orlo. *Giosuè Carducci*. 1914. Reprint. Whitefish, Mont.: Kessinger, 2008. A short biography of Carducci. Includes bibliographic references.

J. Madison Davis

GUIDO CAVALCANTI

Born: Florence (now in Italy); c. 1259
Died: Florence; August 27 or 28, 1300

PRINCIPAL POETRY
Le rime, 1527
The Sonnets and Ballate of Guido Cavalcanti, 1912 (Ezra Pound, translator)
The Complete Poems, 1992

OTHER LITERARY FORMS

Guido Cavalcanti (ko-vol-KON-tee) is remembered only for his poetry.

ACHIEVEMENTS

The extant poems of Guido Cavalcanti number fewer than threescore; when taken together, however, they are compelling evidence that he was one of the finest Italian poets of his age. Ezra Pound, Cavalcanti's translator into English, even exalted him above Dante, noting in 1929 that "Dante is less in advance of his time than Guido Cavalcanti." While Pound's enthusiasm for Cavalcanti was perhaps excessive, there is little doubt that, except for Dante, Cavalcanti was the most outstanding member of the famous school of *dolce stil nuovo* ("sweet new style"). Although some critics question the existence of such a school in late thirteenth century Italy, it is generally conceded that a number of poets of the period constituted an informal group defined by common linguistic and thematic concerns. In addition to Dante and Cavalcanti, this group included Guido Guinizzelli, the founder of the school, and several writers of love lyrics: Lapo Gianni, Gianni degli Alfani, Dino Frescobaldi, and Cino da Pistoia.

The major themes of the *dolce stil nuovo* are outlined in Guinizzelli's seminal canzone "Al cor gentil ripara sempre amore" ("To the Noble Heart Love Always Returns"). Foremost is a new concept of nobility, which is no longer tied to birth or social rank but rather to spiritual perfection or moral worth. Second is the identification of love with the noble heart, meaning that love is reserved for the heart of a truly noble soul (as defined above) and that the noble heart is likewise reserved for love. Last is the theme of the spiritualization of woman. Since women inspire love, and love in turn is the cause and product of a noble heart, women may prove to be instruments of moral perfection. Every lady is a potential *angelicata crïatura* (angelic creature), to use Cavalcanti's phrase and to employ terminology characteristic of the *stilnovisti*.

The phrase "the sweet new style" derives from *Purgatorio* (*Purgatory*) in Dante's *La divina commedia* (c. 1320; *The Divine Comedy*, 1802). It is Bonagiunta Orbicciani da Lucca's term for the poetics espoused by Dante, Cavalcanti, and several of their contemporaries. The "sweetness" of the new style refers primarily to the gentleness of the subject matter (love), the purity of the language (vernacular Italian), and the graciousness of the chosen poetic rhythms (implying an avoidance, for example, of harsh rhymes). The "newness" derives from the originality of the poets' inspiration—that is, an inner, emotional need to write verse as opposed to a purely intellectual decision to compose—and from the abundance of new expressions, rather than stereotypical phrases, designed to communicate the psychological state of the poet. Cavalcanti's careful depiction of the various states of his emotions, such as self-pity and bewilderment, is noteworthy for its innovative departure from timeworn clichés. An even more important achievement, however, was the remarkable influence Cavalcanti exerted on his onetime friend Dante, who early in his career referred to Cavalcanti as his *primo amico*, or "first friend," and to whom he dedicated *La vita nuova* (c. 1292; *Vita Nuova*, 1861; better known as *The New Life*). It was Cavalcanti who encouraged Dante to write his poetry in the vernacular instead of in Latin; Dante's decision to follow his friend's advice changed forever the course of Italian poetry.

Biography

Guido Cavalcanti was born in Florence, a few years prior to Dante's birth. The exact year of Cavalcanti's birth has never been established. While some have placed it as early as 1240, Natalino Sapegno and many others believe that the poet was born just before 1260. His father was Cavalcante de' Cavalcanti, a descendant of Guelph merchants and the same figure who appears next to the Ghibelline Farinata degli Uberti in one of the burning tombs of the heretics in the *Inferno*. Dante's treatment of Cavalcanti's father and father-in-law in this famous episode has led to much speculation about Cavalcanti's own philosophical and religious beliefs and was in part responsible for the depiction of Cavalcanti as a heretic in various stories by Giovanni Boccaccio and others. What is known of Cavalcanti's life comes in large part from the contemporary chronicles of Filippo Villani and Dino Compagni. At an early age, Cavalcanti was betrothed by his father to Beatrice (Bice) degli Uberti, daughter of Farinata. This was essentially a political marriage, one designed, like so many of the time, to put an end to the internecine wars between the Guelphs and the Ghibellines, who supported the papacy and the emperor, respectively. Cavalcanti was among the Guelph representatives at the peace negotiations held by Cardinal Latino in 1280; he took part in the general council of the commune in 1284, together with Compagni and Brunetto Latini, and his friendship with Dante dates from this period. He was a fierce adversary of Corso Donati, leader of the Black Guelphs. Because of his hatred for Donati, he joined the opposing White Guelph faction. His allegiance to that faction led to his exile in Sarzana, Italy, on June 24, 1300. It was on that date that the priors of Florence, of which Dante was one, attempted to resolve the city's political strife by banishing the leaders of both factions. While banished, Cavalcanti contracted malaria. Although he was recalled to Florence soon thereafter, he never recovered, and he died in his native city on August 27 or 28 of the same year. His death was recorded on August 29, 1300, in the register of the dead in the Cathedral of Santa Reparata.

These meager facts about Cavalcanti's life and death shed little light on the poet's personality, which is largely shrouded in legend. Perhaps because Dante attributes *disdegno* (disdain) to him in a verse of the previously cited episode in the *Inferno*, other authors have also characterized Cavalcanti as haughty, aristocratic, and solitary. Dante's portrayal of his supposedly best friend as disdainful has led many to conclude that their friendship sharply diminished at some point during their later years. Some speculate that this happened because of conflicts over literary values, with Dante preeminently interested in ethical understanding and Cavalcanti in aristocratic expression. Others argue that the differences in their perception of love formed the basis for the breakdown of their friendship. A disagreement over political matters is yet another possible explanation, although both Dante and Cavalcanti were White Guelphs, and Dante's permanent exile followed Cavalcanti's temporary exile by only a year or so. Whatever the case, Compagni describes Cavalcanti as a "noble knight" and as "courteous and bold" but also as "disdainful and solitary and devoted to study." Villani writes that the poet was a "philosopher of antiquity, not a little esteemed and honored for his dignity." It is Villani also who outlines the rancor and bitterness that Cavalcanti felt toward Donati, who evidently attempted to assassinate Cavalcanti as he made a pilgrimage to Santiago de Compostela. Boccaccio, in his commentary on the *Inferno*, speaks of Cavalcanti as a "most well-bred man and wealthy and of a lofty intellect." Regardless of who paints the portrait, Cavalcanti always appears as intelligent but a man apart, a solitary person destined to exile by his temperament if not by his politics.

ANALYSIS

Guido Cavalcanti's poetry, like that of other *stilnovisti*, may be viewed, in part, as a reaction to the poetry of Guittone d'Arezzo and his followers. Guittone's mid-thirteenth century poetry was largely imitative of the Provençal tradition: Hermetic in nature, it also emphasized rhetorical, metrical, and verbal complexities. Poets of "the sweet new style," on the other hand, deemphasized technical elements so that aspects such as meter and rhyme were generally subservient to meaning. Also, whereas Guittonian poetry covered a wide range of subjects, Guinizzelli and his disciples focused almost entirely on love and its effects. Cavalcanti, however, should not be seen as a mere conformist to Guinizzelli's dicta, for Cavalcanti in turn distinguished himself from many of his own school. In his concentration on love's psychology, he was philosophically more sophisticated than all other *stilnovisti* except Dante. He introduced, for example, the concept of *spiriti* (spirits) into his poetry to dramatize the conflicting emotions and behaviors that love elicits. The term "spirit" is a technical term of Scholasticism; it refers, according to Albertus Magnus, to the "instrument of the soul" or the "vehicle of life." Spirits represent the essence of life. They shine in the eyes of the beloved and console the heart of the lover. They are forced to flee, however, when love invades. Their flight results in humankind's metaphorical death. It is not surprising, then, that closely related to the theme of spirits in Cavalcanti's poems is the theme of death.

Lyrical works

If one facet of Cavalcanti's poetry may be characterized as highly philosophical, the other can be described only as profoundly lyrical. The preoccupation with love and death, for example, results in a melancholy portrayal of the poet's mercurial emotions: Happiness is poignantly juxtaposed to sadness. Tears and sighs become appropriate symbols of the persona's ever-changing state of being because they can stand either for joy or sorrow, pleasure or pain. Love is always the culprit that renders the lover defenseless, a helpless observer. Love causes both agony and ecstasy; eventually, it generates a deep-seated desire for release via death. The poet's sense of helplessness before such an all-powerful conqueror is reflected in the presentation of the lover as spectator. This distancing technique leads to a highly dramatic tension and a beautiful lyric expression. It allows the poet to observe and record the effects of love but does not permit him to intervene.

Sonnets

Cavalcanti's known works include thirty-six sonnets, eleven ballads, two canzones, two isolated stanzas, and one motet. In addition, two ballads of questionable authenticity are occasionally attributed to him. The sonnets, because of their large number, seem to represent the poet's preferred form. The major theme of most of the sonnets relates, not unexpectedly, to the pain and weakness that love inflicts on the lover. Love, however, is not the only argument in the compositions. The sonnets of correspondence, for example, are the most important in the collection from a historical perspective, and they show the range of topics covered. These sonnets were dedicated or written to other men, including the poets Dante, Alfani, Guittone d'Arezzo, Guido Orlandi, and a certain Bernardo da Bologna (about whom very little is known).

The five sonnets addressed to Dante are either responses to rhymes on love by Dante or words of friendly encouragement. "Vedeste, al mio parere, onne valore" ("You Saw, in My Opinion, Every Valor") is a reply to Dante's famous call to love's faithful, "A ciascun' alma presa e gentil core" ("To Every Captured Soul and Noble Heart"). On the other hand, one sonnet to Orlandi, "Di vil matera mi conven parlare" ("Of a Vile Matter I Must Speak"), constitutes a rather caustic personal attack. Another sonnet, addressed to Guittone and entitled "Da più a uno face un sollegismo" ("From Many to One Makes a Syllogism"), falls in the tradition of the harsh literary criticism of Guittone also found in Dante's writings. A sonnet to Nerone Cavalcanti, "Novelle ti so dire, odi, Nerone" ("News I Know to Tell You, So Hear, Nerone"), testifies to the fierce fight between the Cavalcanti and Buondelmonti families.

Ballads

In the ballads, one finds themes such as that of exile in "Perch'io non spero di tornar giammai" ("Because I Hope Not Ever to Return") and of country delights in "In un boschetto trova' pasturella" ("In a Woods I Found a Shepherdess"). As noted earlier, the theme of death often accompanies or weaves through the prevailing theme of love. This is seen in the ballad "Quando di morte mi conven trar vita" ("When I Must Take Life from Death"). On the poet's pilgrimage to Santiago de Compostela, he stops in Toulouse. There, in the Church of the Daurade, he imagines an encounter with Mandetta, a beautiful woman recalled in the ballad "Era in penser d'amor quand'io trovai" ("I Was Thinking of Love When I Found"). The beauty of Mandetta is also described in the sonnet "Una giovane donna di Tolosa" ("A Young Woman of Toulouse"). The young woman reminds him of his faraway lady, whom Cavalcanti never mentions by name in his poetry. Dante, however, refers to her as Vanna, short for Giovanna, and states in *La vita nuova* that she was also known, because of her beauty, as Primavera, or Springtime.

"My Lady Asks Me"

The poet's most famous poem, which is also his most difficult, is neither a sonnet nor a ballad. Perhaps the most-discussed canzone in all Italian literature, "Donna me prega" ("My Lady Asks Me"), a poem of seventy-five lines, has been described by John Colaneri as "an intellectual, philosophical, and somewhat obscure exposition of the essence of love." Most scholars would agree with this description, especially the reference to the poem's obscurity. Interpretations of the work differ widely, drawing variously on Arab mysticism, Averroist thought, Arab-Christian Platonism, Thomist philosophy, and neo-Aristotelianism.

From a technical viewpoint, "My Lady Asks Me" is a virtuoso performance, offering unequivocal proof of the poet's exceptional rhyming ability. The poem is meant to be a treatise on the philosophy of love as well as a highly lyrical composition, however, and in the canzone's opening stanza, Cavalcanti raises the following questions: Where does love exist? Who creates it? What is its virtue, its power, and its essence? The answers to these queries are contained in the remainder of the poem but in a rather complicated philosophical knot.

In most of his poetry, Cavalcanti has a great desire to render visible that within humans that is invisible, such as the movements of the human soul. The poet transforms these actions into images of real beings. Thus, "spirits" (as the term was used in Scholastic philosophy, to designate the vital faculties of humans) were introduced into love poetry. All the *stilnovisti* made use of them for the purpose of artistic representation, but it was principally with Cavalcanti that the systematization of the spirits took place. Indeed, it was primarily because of Cavalcanti that spirits became an integral part of the literary expression of the amorous theme and that they remained there for centuries.

BIBLIOGRAPHY

Ardizzone, Maria Luisa. *Guido Cavalcanti: The Other Middle Ages*. Buffalo, N.Y.: University of Toronto Press, 2002. Ardizzone provides criticism and interpretation of the works of Cavalcanti, along with biographical information.

Cavalcanti, Guido. *The Complete Poems*. Translated and with an introduction by Marc A. Cirigliano. New York: Italica Press, 1992. Features parallel texts in English and Italian of Cavalcanti's poems. Introduction and notes contain discussions of his poetic works and life. Bibliography and index.

_____. *Thirty-three Sonnets of Guido Cavalcanti*. Translated by Ezra Pound. San Francisco: Arion Press, 1991. The introductory essays by Hugh Kenner and Lowry Nelson, Jr., provide useful information on Cavalcanti's works and life.

Dronke, Peter. *Medieval Latin and the Rise of European Love Lyric*. 2d ed. New York: Oxford University Press, 1968. In the chapter on Cavalcanti, Dronke depicts the poet as a master of *stilnovisti* poets. He briefly examines the canzone in the light of contemporary lyric poetry and Scholastic philosophy.

Lind, L. R., ed. *Lyric Poetry of the Italian Renaissance*. New Haven, Conn.: Yale University Press, 1954. An anthology containing several of Cavalcanti's poems, including the famous translation by Ezra Pound of the canzone "Donna me prega." Presents a synthesis of Cavalcanti's theory of love.

Nelson, Lowry. "Cavalcanti's Centrality in Early Vernacular Poetry." In *Poetic Configurations*. University Park: Pennsylvania State University Press, 1992. This short overview places Cavalcanti's work in his own cultural and intellectual contexts and discusses his influence on poets from Dante to Ezra Pound.

Pound, Ezra. *Literary Essays of Ezra Pound*. London: Faber and Faber, 1954. Pound's classic essay "Cavalcanti" offers his view of the poet who influenced him deeply early in his career. He has a scholar's eye as well, for his analysis of "Donna mi prega" is thorough in both senses.

Rebay, Luciano, ed. *Italian Poetry: A Selection from St. Francis of Assisi to Salvatore Quasimodo*. New York: Dover Books, 1969. Besides containing several fresh translations of the poems, the book is a good brief source of background material, particularly on the *dolce stil nuovo*.

Wilhelm, James J. *Dante and Pound: The Epic of Judgment*. Orono: University of Maine Press, 1974. Chapter 4 details Cavalcanti's influence on Dante and Dante's reaction to Cavalcanti, especially as registered in the *Inferno*. Chapter 5 explores Pound's critical attitude toward Cavalcanti and how this differed from his poetic use of him.

Wilkins, Ernest H. *A History of Italian Literature*. Cambridge, Mass.: Harvard University Press, 1954. Eminently readable, easily accessible, this work is a standard assessment of Cavalcanti's achievement, discussing his poetic voice and his emphasis on the psychology of love.

Madison U. Sowell

CHRISTINE DE PIZAN

Born: Venice (now in Italy); c. 1365
Died: Probably at the Convent of Poissy, near Versailles, France; c. 1430
Also known as: Christine de Pisan

PRINCIPAL POETRY

L'Epistre au dieu d'Amours, 1399 (*The Letter of Cupid*, 1721)
Le Livre du dit de Poissy, 1400
Le Livre de la mutacion de fourtune, 1400-1403
Le Dit de la Rose, 1402
Le Livre du chemin de long estude, 1402-1403
Le Livre du duc des vrais amans, 1405 (*The Book of the Duke of True Lovers*, 1908)
Cent Ballades d'amant et de dame, c. 1410
Le Ditié de Jeanne d'Arc, 1429 (*The Tale of Joan of Arc*, 1977)

OTHER LITERARY FORMS

The oeuvre of Christine de Pizan (krees-TEEN duh pee-ZON) was not limited to poetry but included an impressive number of prose works as well. Composed primarily between 1400 and 1418, these works cover a broad thematic range and bear witness to a powerful and erudite ability; they include letters, short narratives, memoirs, manuals, autobiography, treatises, allegorical psalms, and meditations. Many represent an expansion and development of ideas expressed initially in her poetry; her early poetic commitment to scholarship, political ethics, religious devotion, and women's rights was amplified in the prose works of her maturity.

ACHIEVEMENTS

Christine de Pizan is rightly recognized as France's first woman of letters, professional writer, and feminist. Although scholars of the past acknowledged and respected her ability, modern scholarship has elevated Christine (as she is known by scholars) to a deserved place in world literature. If this recognition has been somewhat tardy, the delay has been the result of the general inaccessibility of her work, spread among dispersed manuscripts. A number of modernized versions from the original Middle French, translations, editions, and critical studies have dramatically heightened interest in her work. Especially remarkable are her learned vocabulary, her knowledgeable use of mythological allusions, and her feminism.

Christine excelled thematically and structurally in both traditional and innovative forms. As an accomplished lyrical poet, she received acclaim from her contemporaries for her conventional courtly poetry. In this category, for example, she demonstrated mastery of the ballade, rondeau, lay, pastoral, and lover's lament. These poems were designed to please the aristocracy at court through an idealized concept of love. Her skill in writing traditional poetry earned the admiration and support of many important members of the nobility, such as the dukes of Orléans, Burgundy, and Berry as well as King Charles V. Although she was composing in the conventional style, Christine often interjected her own personality by describing events in her life, by referring to a noble benefactor, or by expressing her opinions on the important issues of her day. In this regard, the works possess a documentary value.

Although Christine's poetry exhibits a high degree of technical mastery, she was never content with virtuosity for its own sake. Central themes of the necessity for justice and responsibility in government, concern for all women, and religious devotion imbue her writings. As a whole, Christine's works bear witness both to a vast knowledge of history and to a profound moral commitment to the age in which she lived.

Biography

Although Christine de Pizan ranks as France's first woman of letters, she was not of French but of Italian birth. Born about 1365 in Venice, she spent only her first years in Italy, leaving her birthplace when her father received the position of astrologer at the court of Charles V of France. Tommaso di Benvenuto da Pizzano, known as Thomas de Pizan after his arrival in France, brought his family to Paris around 1368, and it was there that Christine had an experience that was to shape the course of her lifework. With her father's encouragement, she received the kind of education usually reserved for boys in the Middle Ages. A precocious child, Christine was eager to learn, and this unique educational opportunity proved to be the single most important factor in her life, for it provided the young artist with the scholarly tools and knowledge on which she was to draw during her entire career. On these early foundations in classical languages, literature, mythology, history, and biblical studies, Christine would build a rich and varied literary edifice. In addition, her educational background influenced her perspective by prompting her to view her subjects in a historical, comprehensive, and ethical light.

Because of her creative talent and her ability to please the court with her poetry, Christine became a favorite and never lacked noble patronage. However, at age fifteen, in 1380, she married not a nobleman but a court notary from Picardy, Étienne de Castel. According to *L'Avision-Christine* (1405; *Christine's Vision*, 1993), an autobiographical work, it was a happy marriage, and the couple had three children.

Two extremely unhappy events sharply influenced Christine's life and career before she was twenty-five years old. The first of these was the death of Charles V in 1380 and the subsequent government during the minority of Charles VI. During the regency period of the dukes of Bourbon and Burgundy, Christine's father lost his court position. This demotion meant a loss of prestige as well as severe financial losses from which the scholar and former court astrologer never recovered. A few years later, in 1385, Thomas de Pizan died. Then, in 1389 or 1390, a second, even more devastating, event occurred when Christine's husband died in an epidemic. Thus, her ten-year marriage came to an abrupt end, leaving her with the heavy responsibility of rearing three children alone.

Instead of lamenting the loss of those who had supported and encouraged her literary talents, Christine turned to her art as a source of income as well as a refuge from grief. She was successful in her literary pursuits and regained noble patronage, moving gradually yet not exclusively into prose and producing a wide range of works. Although it is difficult to reconstruct her biography for these years, it is thought that she entered the Dominican convent at Poissy around 1418, the time of the Burgundian massacres. Scholars base this hypothesis on the description of a visit to her daughter at Poissy in "Le Dit de Poissy" (the proverb of Poissy). She did not break the silence of her retreat until 1429, when she composed *The Tale of Joan of Arc*. Thus, Christine concluded her literary career appropriately, honoring a woman who, like herself, had risen above adversity to pursue her goals. The exact date of her death is not known, but she is believed to have died around 1430.

Analysis

The most striking characteristics of Christine de Pizan's work are her breadth of knowledge and her active engagement of the social and political issues of her day. Although these attributes would be considered typical rather than extraordinary in a modern writer, they are indeed intriguing in a woman living at the turn of the fifteenth century. Clearly, credit for the wealth of knowledge seen in her works must be given to the exceptional education that she received. Nevertheless, an analysis of the artist must include recognition of the artistic sensitivity and the reverence for life that she brought to her career. Because of the broadness of her vision, she transcended the traditional courtly style of poetry in which she was trained and began to include significant personal, political, and moral issues in her poems. Her works weave innovation into traditional background by passing from idealized medieval expression to realistic humanist concerns that are closer in spirit to the Renaissance.

Cent Ballades d'amant et de dame

Christine's first published works in verse reveal her conformity to the literary standards of the era. The aesthetic canon governing late medieval poetry did not accept expressions of individual joy or sorrow but instead required these emotions to be placed in a universal framework. Christine's early works demonstrate not only her respect for the existing literary system but also her mastery of it. In her ballades, lays, and rondeaux, there is a harmonious relationship between form and meaning. An example of the traditional mold can be seen in *Cent Ballades d'amant et de dame* (one hundred ballades of a lover and his lady). In ballade 59, following the social code of the era, the poet advises young lovers to be noble, peaceful, and gracious. Written in decasyllabic lines, the ballade follows the prescribed form in stanzaic composition, regular rhyme, and refrain. The tone is appropriately elevated by the use of virtuous, abstract vocabulary, and verbs in the imperative and subjunctive moods. This ballade is typical of Christine's courtly love poems, which in their grace and elegance meet and even surpass the criteria of the times.

At the beginning of her career, Christine depended on the approval of her patrons, and it was important to please them by adhering to acceptable forms and also to amuse them with clever versatility and occasional flattery. She accomplished this by writing a group of rondeaux, very brief poems in lines of two to four syllables in equally short stanzas. These poems on the chagrin of love are typical of the clever, though sometimes exaggerated, metric exercises with which late medieval poets experimented. Christine also excelled at occasional verse; several of her poems in this category go beyond flattery by conveying a secondary message which in the course of the poem emerges as the main theme. For example, in a series of poems honoring Charles d'Albret, a patriotic high constable, Christine salutes his royal lineage, then hastens to one of her favorite and most important themes, the defense of the honor of women, particularly those in need. Although Christine continues to observe the fixed form of the ballade, she transmits her intense interest in her subject through a passionate tone, a concrete vocabulary, and a rhythmic pattern that dramatically emphasizes key words. The contemporary theme is anchored to ancient history as the poet compares the champion of her sex to the virtuous Roman Brutus.

Many of Christine's poems are centrally concerned with women's rights. It would appear that the genesis of this theme in her work was twofold. First, as a woman who herself had to work for a living, Christine could identify with women who had suffered misfortune, most of whom did not have her advantages. Many times in her works, she pleads for widows and orphan girls. Although Christine's feminism thus had its roots in her own experience, it was also given force by her rejection of widely accepted literary stereotypes of women. She abhorred, for example, the image of her sex in Guillaume de Lorris and Jean de Meung's *Le Roman de la rose* (thirteenth century; *The Romance of the Rose*, partial translation c. 1370, complete translation 1900), in which women are portrayed as greedy, inconstant, and egocentric.

THE TALE OF JOAN OF ARC

Christine's final literary work provides an appropriate conclusion to a survey of her poetic career. In terms of both theme and structure, *The Tale of Joan of Arc* represents a culminating point because in it, the poet restates and unites both forcefully and creatively the concerns that inspired her whole literary career. Of the inspirations, the most prominent is religious devotion. The poem, which extols Joan of Arc's mission to save France, is a pious work, praising God's grace and power. Joan is uniquely qualified to champion France because she is God's handmaiden: "Blessed is He who created you!/ Maiden sent from God," exclaims the poet in the twenty-second stanza. Two secondary themes, patriotism and political concern, are welded to the religious motif; they also give the poem documentary value.

The poem reflects the attitude of a nation already weary from what was to be known as the Hundred Years' War (1337-1453) yet exhilarated by the victory of Orléans and the coronation of Charles VII at Rheims in 1403. Christine's sense of reality does not allow her to be swept away by optimism. Instead, realizing that there are further civil dangers to be faced, she encourages mutual cooperation between citizens and their king.

The final theme of the poem, yet certainly not the least in importance, is explicitly feminist: The heroine, supported and uplifted by the author's belief that women are able to do all things, confers unity and balance to this hymn of praise. In her enthusiastic expression of admiration for Joan as a woman, Christine employs a range of technical devices that convincingly reinforce her message. Written in sixty-one stanzas of eight octosyllabic lines each, the poem adheres to a traditional stanzaic structure, yet within the stanzas, all formality disappears; marked by exclamations, direct address, rhetorical questions, concrete and picturesque vocabulary, and conversational movement, the style is highly innovative. In this final work, Christine left an eloquent testimony to her accomplishments as a woman and as a poet.

OTHER MAJOR WORKS
NONFICTION: *L'Epistre d'Othéa à Hector*, 1400 (*The Epistle of Othea to Hector: Or, The Boke of Knyghthode*, c. 1440); *Les Epistres sur "Le Roman de la Rose*," 1402; *Le Livre des fais et bonnes meurs du sage roi Charles V*, 1404; *L'Avision-Christine*, 1405 (*Christine's Vision*, 1993); *Le Livre de la cité des dames*, 1405 (*The Book of the City of Ladies*, 1521); *Le Livre des trois vertus*, 1405 (*The Book of the Three Virtues*, 1985); *Le Livre du corps de policie*, 1406-1407 (*The Body of Polycye*, 1521); *Les Sept Psaumes allégorisés*, 1409-1410; *La Lamentation sur les maux de la guerre civile*, 1410 (*Lament on the Evils of Civil War*, 1984); *Le Livre des fais d'armes et de chevalerie*, 1410 (*The Book of Fayttes of Arms and of Chivalry*, 1489); *Le Livre de la Paix*, 1412-1413; *L'Epistre de la prison de la vie humaine*, 1416-1418.

BIBLIOGRAPHY
Altmann, Barbara K., and Deborah L. McGrady, eds. *Christine de Pizan: A Casebook.* New York: Routledge, 2003. A collection of essays on various aspects of Christine de Pizan, including her role as defender of women, and analyses of various works.

Birk, Bonnie A. *Christine de Pizan and Biblical Wisdom: A Feminist-Theological Point of View.* Milwaukee, Wis.: Marquette University Press, 2005. While this work deals more with Christine de Pizan's prose, it includes biographical information and discussion of her religious views.

Blumenfeld-Kosinski, Renate. *The Compensations of Aging: Sexuality and Writing in Christine de Pizan, with an Epilogue on Colette*. Paris: Peeters, 2004. Studies sexuality in the works of Christine de Pizan.

Campbell, John, and Nadia Margolis, eds. *Christine de Pizan 2000: Studies on Christine de Pizan in Honour of Angus J. Kennedy*. Atlanta: Rodopi, 2000. A collection of papers on Christine de Pizan, focusing on her poetry and her poetic techniques.

Forhan, Kate Langdon. *The Political Theory of Christine de Pizan*. Burlington, Vt.: Ashgate, 2002. An analysis of the political and social views of Christine de Pizan. Bibliography and index.

Green, Karen, and C. J. Mews, eds. *Healing the Body Politic: The Political Thought of Christine de Pizan*. Turnhout, Belgium: Brepols, 2005. A collection of essays on politics in the writing of Christine de Pizan. Although it focuses on her prose, it sheds light on her poetry.

Kelly, Douglas. *Christine de Pizan's Changing Opinion: A Quest for Certainty in the Midst of Chaos*. Cambridge, England: D. S. Brewer, 2007. This examination of opinion in Christine de Pizan's writings notes that this focus was found in other late medieval French literature.

Kennedy, Angus J., et al., eds. *Contexts and Continuities: Proceedings of the Fourth International Colloquium on Christine de Pizan, Published in Honour of Liliane Dulac*. Glasgow, Scotland: University of Glasgow Press, 2002. A collection of papers from a conference held in Glasgow in July, 2000, on Christine de Pizan. Bibliography.

Richards, Earl Jeffrey, ed. *Christine de Pizan and Medieval French Lyric*. Gainesville: University Press of Florida, 1998. Nine critical essays on the lyrical works, all but one written expressly for this volume and first published here.

Smith, Sydney. *The Opposing Voice: Christine de Pisan's Criticism of Courtly Love*. Stanford, Calif.: Humanities Honors Program, Stanford University, 1990. Smith examines the political and social views of Christine de Pizan, in particular her opposition to the idea of courtly love. Bibliography.

Ann R. Hill

GABRIELE D'ANNUNZIO

Born: Pescara, Italy; March 12, 1863
Died: Gardone, Italy; March 1, 1938

PRINCIPAL POETRY
Primo vere, 1879, 1880
Canto novo, 1882, 1896
Intermezzo di rime, 1884, 1896
Isaotta Gùttadauro ed altre poesie, 1886, 1890
San Pantaleone, 1886
Elegie romane, 1892
Poema paradisiaco—Odi navali, 1893
Laudi del cielo del mare della terra e degli eroi, 1899
Maia, 1903
Alcyone, 1904 (English translation, 1977)
Elettra, 1904
Merope, 1912
Canti della guerra latina, 1914-1918
Asterope, 1949
Le laudi, 1949 (expanded version of 1899 title, also includes *Maia*, *Elettra*, *Alcyone*, *Merope*, and *Asterope*)

OTHER LITERARY FORMS

In addition to poetry, the literary production of Gabriele D'Annunzio (don-NOONT-syoh) encompasses many other genres: short stories, novels, autobiographical essays, political writings, and several plays, in Italian and in French.

The whole of D'Annunzio's production is available in three major editions: *Opera omnia* (1927-1936), *Tutte le opere* (1931-1937), and *Tutte le opere* (1930-1965), which also includes D'Annunzio's notes under the title *Taccuini*. Forty-one volumes of D'Annunzio's collected work were issued under the title *Opera complete* (1941-1943).

ACHIEVEMENTS

Gabriele D'Annunzio dominated the Italian literary scene from 1880 until the end of World War I. His literary work and his personal conduct challenged existing models with such an exuberant vitality that even the less positive aspects of his art and life have been influential, if only for the reaction they have provoked.

Extremely receptive to foreign influences, D'Annunzio, through a series of experiments with new forms and styles of composition, evolved an original poetic language.

Gabriele D'Annunzio
(Library of Congress)

Replacing traditional grammatical links with paratactic constructions, he forged a style in which assonance, onomatopoeia, and alliteration prevail, achieving enthralling effects of pictorial and musical synesthesia.

Historically, D'Annunzio's most original achievement was to help break the highly academic literary tradition that had been dominant in Italy for centuries and to reintegrate Italian culture into the mainstream of European intellectual life. He was the first modern Italian writer. His literary work in its amplitude and variety served as an invaluable source of motifs, themes, and suggestions for the brilliant generation of poets who came to maturity in the 1920's. As Eugenio Montale has observed, an Italian poet who has learned nothing from D'Annunzio is truly impoverished.

Biography

Gabriele D'Annunzio was born in Pescara, a small port city in the Abruzzi region, on March 12, 1863, to a well-to-do family. He received a solid classical education at the Liceo Cicognini, in Prato, and when he was only sixteen years old, he published his first collection of verses, *Primo vere* (early spring).

In 1881, D'Annunzio moved to Rome, where he registered at the university in the department of Italian literature, but he never completed his university studies. He chose instead to pursue a writer's career, consolidating his fame as a young poetic genius in the literary and aristocratic circles of the capital. During that time, he contributed verses, short stories, and articles to several publications, while enjoying an intense social life punctuated by love affairs, intrigues, and scandals. His second collection of verses, *Canto novo* (new song), was both more accomplished and more personal than its predecessor.

D'Annunzio's Roman period, interrupted by adventurous cruises and occasional sojourns in the Abruzzi region, lasted until 1891. By that time, he had already gained national recognition, sealing his social and literary success with his marriage to Maria Hardouin, duchess of Gallese, and with the publication of a novel. These were fruitful years for D'Annunzio, as witnessed by the production of numerous novels and collections of short stories. D'Annunzio led an extravagant and magnificent life, a life of debts and scandals, of new loves and adventures. At the same time, he maintained an unrelenting rhythm of work. Indeed, all his activities were encompassed and absorbed by a total engagement in literature.

D'Annunzio also nourished political ambitions. In 1896, he published *Le vergini della rocce* (*The Maidens of the Rocks*, 1898), a novel whose antidemocratic message is emblematic of the writer's political choices. One year later, he entered the political arena and was elected as a representative to the Italian parliament. His activity there was unremarkable until 1900, when, during the controversy over the exceptional laws proposed by Luigi Pelloux's government, he theatrically shifted to the left wing, declaring: "I am going toward life." In the same year, he presented himself as a candidate in the Socialist list but was not elected; with this defeat, D'Annunzio closed his parliamentary experience.

In 1894, D'Annunzio had met Eleonora Duse, the great actress, who played a considerable part in his sentimental life and had a substantial influence on his literary activities. This union of love and art gave rise to a period of great literary achievements. At La Capponcina, a villa in the hilly countryside of Florence, surrounded by horses, dogs, and works of art, D'Annunzio wrote another novel, a number of plays, and the first three volumes of *Le laudi*, which represent the highest expression of his poetic art. His relationship with Duse was interrupted in 1903 by new temptations. After a few years of extravagant expenses, D'Annunzio, driven by his taste for luxury and his passion for cars and planes, was insolvent. In 1909, La Capponcina was seized by the creditors, and one year later D'Annunzio left Italy for France, choosing what he pompously called a "a voluntary exile." There, he split his time between his residence in Arcachon and Paris, where he was soon introduced into the literary and social circles. To this period belong several works in Old French, the most prominent of which is *Le Martyre de Saint Sébastien*, a theatrical text with music by Claude Debussy, which was presented in Paris in 1911.

The French period came to a close at the outbreak of World War I. Faithful to the idea of traditional alliance between France and Italy, D'Annunzio returned to Italy to campaign in favor of Italy's intervention in the war against Germany. D'Annunzio's political speeches were a clamorous success, significantly contributing to the victory of the interventionist party.

As soon as Italy entered the war, D'Annunzio enlisted as a volunteer; he fought first on the front line and then participated in several actions on the sea and in the air. In January, 1916, as a result of a plane accident, he lost his right eye and had to spend three months immobilized and in darkness. During this period of forced inactivity, he painfully scribbled notes that were to become *Il notturno* (1921), a work in prose without a precise narrative line, in which he registered impressions and notations in a stream of consciousness in which past and present are intertwined.

The end of the war and the peace negotiations, quite unsatisfactory for Italy, found D'Annunzio in the role of the poet-prophet, the voice of the people demanding their rights. The polemics over the peace negotiations reached their height when it appeared that the city of Fiume would not be annexed to Italy. With his famous "Marci dei Ronchi," D'Annunzio, at the head of a group of volunteers, entered Fiume and established a temporary government. His action interrupted the diplomatic negotiations between Italy and Yugoslavia; the Italian government first ordered D'Annunzio to leave the city and then sent the fleet to force him out.

Fiume was officially annexed to Italy in 1924. D'Annunzio's action may have had some weight in this decision, but its immediate result was a failure. Meanwhile, in Italy, D'Annunzio's prophetic role had been assumed by Benito Mussolini. D'Annunzio, disillusioned, retired to a large estate on Lake Garda which he renamed Il Vittoriale. There, he spent the rest of his life, surrounded by a rich library and by the mass of disparate objects that he had collected with obsessive passion.

The relations between D'Annunzio and the Fascist government were respectfully cold. The poet, while subscribing to certain principles of fascism, considered Benito Mussolini a poor imitator of his own style; Mussolini, for his part, chose to keep D'Annunzio at a proper distance while bestowing on him honors and subsidies.

When he was not traveling, D'Annunzio led a quiet life at Il Vittoriale, devoting his time to editing his *Opera omnia*. In 1924, under the title *Le faville del maglio*, he gathered and published some of his previous writings; a second volume appeared in 1928. D'Annunzio's *Le cento e cento e cento pagine del libro segreto di Gabriele D'Annunzio tentato di morire* (1935) clearly referred to a strange accident in 1922 (he had fallen from a window) that could have been a suicide attempt. He died in 1938.

ANALYSIS

The "D'Annunzio phenomenon" has stirred a century-long argument between Gabriele D'Annunzio's admirers and detractors, and his reputation has endured alternating periods of favor and disfavor, often related to historical circumstances. Later, under the impetus of a revival both in Italy and abroad, his works were reevaluated in the light of new critical methods.

Considering the number of D'Annunzio's poetry collections, novels, plays, and memoirs, it would be unrealistic to expect a consistent artistic level throughout his oeuvre, but it should be recognized that, in its vastness and diversity, his work is an invaluable documentation of half a century of European intellectual life. In this perspective, it is difficult to isolate certain verse collections from the context of his entire production. The pattern of receptivity and experimentation that characterizes D'Annunzio's poetry can be appreciated only by following the arc of his poetic achievement from *Primo vere* to *Le laudi*, where the voice of the poet reaches the plenitude of his expressive means.

PRIMO VERE

In *Primo vere*, the choice of language, images, and versification is clearly inspired by Giosuè Carducci's model. A second edition of the work in 1880, enriched with fifty-nine new poems, offers greater insight. The delicate musicality of certain verses, and the attention devoted to the description of landscapes as the privileged scenery for love encounters, anticipate the distinctive tone that D'Annunzio was to achieve in *Canto novo*. The driving inspiration of this collection is the poet's yearning for identification with nature. A pervasive pagan sensuality saturates the atmosphere as nature and man vibrate with the same impulses: A woman's breath has the perfume of the forest, and her haunches are like those of an antelope; lovers are entwined like "virgin trees interlacing their branches." The metaphors unify Earth, sea, and man in a vitalistic élan in which all forms merge.

CANTO NOVO

Canto novo establishes the alternation between two themes that constitutes a favorite pattern of D'Annunzio's dialectic: an unresolved conflict between the vitalistic impetus and a fin de siècle introspection and sadness. The tendency to magnify the elegiac and melancholic component in the poet's writings is evident in the prevalent interpretation of the collection's most celebrated poem, "O falce di luna calante" (oh, sickle of waning moon), which has often been read as an expression of weariness and consuming despair; as Barberi Squarotti has noted in *Invito alla lettura di D'Annunzio* (1982), this interpretation takes the poem out of its context in the collection, for the next poem is an invitation to another day of joyous life and love.

INTERMEZZO DI RIME

D'Annunzio's negative note decidedly does prevail, however, in *Intermezzo di rime*, which was later revised and published under the shorter title *Intermezzo*. This new collection presented a sharp change in versification, tone, and inspiration. Influenced by the

French Parnassianism, D'Annunzio abandoned Carducci's versification for the traditional meters of sonnets and ballads. The volume also reveals a renewed taste for mythological reminiscence, while the polished elegance of the compositions suggests a new concern with aestheticism. Here, closed gardens substitute for natural landscapes, bucolic pagan eroticism gives way to a refined experimentation with morbid sensuality, and vitalism turns into sadistic cruelty. The entire collection is informed by a spirit of willful transgression. The protagonist, "l'Adolescente," dissipates his vital energies in enervating lust. His attempt to achieve full control of life through the exaltation of the senses results in failure, as the satisfaction of pure sensuality rapidly wears out in disgust.

Several other important themes make their first appearance in this collection: the promenade, a privileged moment for erotic emotions; woman, the luxurious female whose castrating power destroys man's energies; art, the fruit and carrier of corruption; the poet, the supreme artificer, the jeweler chiseling the hard, resistant metal of language. Other, less significant sections of *Intermezzo* reveal a taste for the macabre and the sadistic, quite in fashion at that time.

POEMA PARADISIACO

Following several collections of poems that refined the manner of *Intermezzo*, *Poema paradisiaco—Odi navali* introduced a new style. Here, following the French Symbolists and influenced as well by Giovanni Pascoli's *Myricae* (1891; tamarisks), D'Annunzio proposes a new musicality studiously built on a rhythm of verses broken by enjambments and interrupted by exclamations, questions, and invocations, where rhymes are hidden and assonance prevails. Memory, contemplation, and melancholy govern this poem of gardens (from the Greek *paradeisos*, "of the garden"), where "gardens" signify the closed space of interiority and meditation away from intellectual and sensual turmoil.

Poema paradisiaco evokes the languid melancholy of things that are no more, of sentiments that could have been. The memory of a brief encounter rouses a longing for an opportunity forever lost. The poet recalls flowers that have not been gathered, loves that have not been lived, privileged moments that have not been enjoyed. In "La passeggiata," the poet prefers a sweet and melancholy relation with a woman to the ardor of love, concluding with a subtly ironic comment: "o voi dal dolce nome che io non chiamo!/ perchè voi non mi amate ed io non vi amo" ("You, with the sweet name I do not call!/ because you do not love me and I do not love you"). *Poema paradisiaco* remains one of the fundamental works of nineteenth century Italian poetry for its innovative language and rhythm and for its influence on the following generation of poets.

LE LAUDI

Although all the preceding poetic works of D'Annunzio have provoked contrasting critical opinions, *Le laudi* has by general agreement been recognized as the poet's masterpiece. This vast work was to include seven books dedicated to the seven stars of the Pleiades, but only four books of the projected seven were published during D'Annunzio's lifetime: *Maia, Elettra, Alcyone*, and *Merope*. A fifth book, *Asterope*, published posthumously in 1949, includes the poems that D'Annunzio wrote during World War I.

Maia is mainly devoted to "Laus vitae," a long poem based on D'Annunzio's voyages in Greece in 1898 and 1899. In this poem, he celebrates the creative power of the classical world, comparing the vital drive of Greek civilization with the sterility of contemporary society. Hymns to Hermes, the creator, alternate with descriptions of modern cities where corruption and vice dominate, culminating with a vision of the "Great Demagogue," a mass leader who preaches the destruction of everything that is beautiful and noble. The populace is portrayed as an instinctively violent and somehow innocent animal, exploited by demagogues and sacrificed without pity. Destruction and suffering, the poet-prophet predicts, will be followed by the birth of a new society in which work and beauty will be equally respected and loved.

In these fiery images, D'Annunzio expresses his antidemocratic and aristocratic sentiments, inspired by Friedrich Nietzsche, but the complex system of the philosopher is narrowed down to serve a limited political program. The poem concludes with an invocation to Nature, the immortal Mother, who is the source of creation and renewal.

Elettra, named for the second star in the constellation, is divided roughly into two parts. In the first part, the celebratory and commemorative inspiration of many of the poems and their oratorical manner reveal D'Annunzio's ambition to create a new mythology, to become the epic bard of the new Italian nation. This effort is not always sustained by authentic inspiration, and in many poems rhetoric and artificiality prevail. The second part, "Le città del silenzio," is a celebration of the old Italian cities, silent and forgotten in the enclosure of their glorious past. Evocations of ancient events and descriptions of splendid monuments and palaces dissolve into a subdued musicality tinted with melancholy.

In the third volume of the series, *Alcyone* (which has been translated into English), D'Annunzio reached his highest lyric expression. After the heroic tension of *Maia* and *Elettra* and their fervid affirmations and denunciations, *Alcyone* stands as a pause, a moment of total participation in the joyous blossoming of nature in its fullest season. The book opens with "La tregua" ("The Respite"), an invocation to "il magnanimo despota" (the generous despot), Nietzsche, the master of willpower. After a period of intense commitment to the fight against brutal ignorance, corruption, and vulgarity, the poet asks for a respite. He wants to be reinvigorated, forsaking public squabbles for the pure sources of life. The poem concludes with a celebration of pagan nature, the realm of fauns, nymphs, and satyrs.

In the following poems, a series of mythological passages translates the introductory hymn to nature into the apotheosis of poetry. In the poem "Il fanciullo," the divine flute player who modulates the most delicate murmurs of nature is the image of the youthful god of poetry: Here, poetry is the privileged activity where art and nature meet and merge. In "Lungo l'Affrico nella sera di giugno dopo la pioggia," a description of the fresh calm of nature in the twilight after a summer rain evolves into a meditation on the power of poetry. Nature offers itself like ductile clay to the poet, who shapes it into a durable work of art. In the following poem, "La sera fiesolana," this concept evolves into a conception of poetics which is central to an understanding of the collection. The landscape vibrates with a secret urge to express itself; hills and rivers, leaves and drops of rain, all nature utters silent words that only the poet can hear. The voice of nature is the language of poetry itself. "La spica" and "Le opere e i giorni" carry the message even further, affirming that all forms of nature live only as a function of the poetic word, which, by naming them, calls them into existence.

After *Alcyone*, D'Annunzio was chiefly concerned with other literary genres. He seldom returned to poetry and then only for occasional lyric fragments. *Merope*, the fourth book of *Le laudi*, includes ten canzones composed on the occasion of the Italo-Turkish war. These poems do not add anything to D'Annunzio's reputation; the flamboyant rhetoric of the volume betrays its essentially political function.

With *Alcyone*, D'Annunzio's poetic inspiration achieved its fullest expression. The feeling of joyful participation in nature that informed his early verse reappeared in *Alcyone*, decanted, refined, and enriched by the variety of D'Annunzio's painstaking experiments with new forms and techniques and by his unrelenting meditation on poetry. Themes, motifs, and discoveries of the preceding collections merge in *Alcyone*. Mythology, no longer an artificial ornament, is integrated with nature, which speaks through myths and transfers to the poet its creative force. In this world created by poetic language, everything harmonizes in a unique song celebrating the eternal beauty of life and nature in their multiform aspects.

D'Annunzio's art, based on classical culture yet renewed by the European avant-garde, represents the link between traditional and modern forms of poetry. Like all great writers, D'Annunzio created a personal poetic language to give life to his imaginative world; at the same time, his verse transcended personal concerns to serve as a testing ground for modern Italian poetry.

OTHER MAJOR WORKS

LONG FICTION: *Il piacere*, 1889 (*The Child of Pleasure*, 1898); *Giovanni Episcopo*, 1892 (*Episcopo and Company*, 1896); *L'innocente*, 1892 (*The Intruder*, 1898); *Il trionfo della morte*, 1894 (*The Triumph of Death*, 1896); *Le vergini della rocce*, 1896 (*The Maidens of the Rocks*, 1898); *Il fuoco*, 1900 (*The Flame of Life*, 1900); *Forse che si forse che no*, 1910; *La Leda senza cigno*, 1916 (*Leda Without Swan*, 1988).

SHORT FICTION: *Terra vergine*, 1882, 1884; *Il libro della vergini*, 1884; *San Pantaleone*, 1886; *Le novelle della Pescara*, 1902 (*Tales from My Native Town*, 1920); *Le faville del maglio*, 1924, 1928 (2 volumes).

PLAYS: *Sogno di un mattino di primavera*, pr., pb. 1897 (*The Dream of a Spring Morning*, 1902); *La città morta*, pb. 1898 (in French), pr. 1901 (in Italian; *The Dead City*, 1900); *Sogno di un tramonto d'autunno*, pb. 1898 (*The Dream of an Autumn Sunset*, 1904); *La Gioconda*, pr., pb. 1899 (*Gioconda*, 1902); *La gloria*, pr., pb. 1899; *Francesca da Rimini*, pr. 1901 (verse play; English translation, 1902); *La figlia di Jorio*, pr., pb. 1904 (*The Daughter of Jorio*, 1907); *La fiaccola sotto il moggio*, pr., pb. 1905 (verse play); *Più che l'amore*, pr. 1906; *La nave*, pr., pb. 1908 (verse play); *Fedra*, pr., pb. 1909 (verse play); *Le Martyre de Saint Sébastien*, pr., pb. 1911 (music by Claude Debussy, choreography by Ida Rubinstein); *Parisina*, pr., pb. 1913 (music by Pietro Mascagni); *La Pisanelle: Ou, La Mort parfumée*, pr., pb. 1913 (music by Ildebrando Rizzetti and Mascagni); *La Chèvrefeuille*, pr. 1913 (*The Honeysuckle*, 1915).

SCREENPLAY: *Cabiria*, 1914.

NONFICTION: *L'armata d'Italia*, 1888; *L'allegoria dell'autunno*, 1895; *Contemplazione della morte*, 1912; *Vite di uomini illustri e di uomini oscuri*, 1913; *La musica di Wagner e la genesi del "Parsifal,"* 1914; *Per la più grande Italia*, 1915; *La penultima ventura*, 1919, 1931 (2 volumes); *Il notturno*, 1921; *Il libro ascetico della giovane Itali*, 1926; *Le cento e cento e cento pagine del libro segreto di Gabriele D'Annunzio tentato di morire*, 1935; *Teneo te, Africa*, 1936; *Solus ad solam*, 1939.

MISCELLANEOUS: *Opera omnia*, 1927-1936; *Tutte le opere*, 1930-1965; *Tutte le opere*, 1931-1937; *Opera complete*, 1941-1943 (41 volumes); *Nocturne, and Five Tales of Love and Death*, 1988.

BIBLIOGRAPHY

Becker, Jared. *Nationalism and Culture: Gabriele D'Annunzio and Italy After the Reisorgimento*. New York: Peter Lang, 1994. A look at D'Annunzio and his links to Italian fascism that places his works within the history of his time. Bibliography and index.

Bonadeo, Alfredo. *D'Annunzio and the Great War*. Cranbury, N.J.: Associated University Presses, 1995. A scholarly examination of D'Annunzio's role and stance in World War I. Bibliography and index.

D'Annunzio, Gabriele. *Alcyone*. Edited by John Robert Woodhouse. New York: Manchester University Press, 1978. A collection of D'Annunzio's poetry in English with an informative introduction and annotations by the editor. Includes bibliography and index.

Gullace, Giovanni. *Gabriele D'Annunzio in France: A Study in Cultural Relations*. Syracuse, N.Y.: Syracuse University Press, 1966. Biographical and historical account of D'Annunzio's life.

Jullian, P. *D'Annunzio*. New York: Viking Press, 1973. An in-depth biography of D'Annunzio's career.

Ledeen, Michael Arthur. *D'Annunzio: The First Duce*. Rev. ed. New Brunswick, N.J.:

Transaction, 2002. An examination of the political beliefs and activity of D'Annunzio. Bibliography and index.

Pieri, Giuliana. *The Influence of Pre-Raphaelitism on Fin de Siècle Italy: Art, Beauty, and Culture*. London: Maney Publishing for the Modern Humanities Reseach Association, 2007. Pieri's discussion of pre-Raphaelitism's influence contains a chapter on D'Annunzio.

Rhodes, A. *The Poet as Superman: G. D'Annunzio*. New York: McDowell, Obolensky, 1960. Narrative biography of D'Annunzio's life in politics and literature.

Valesio, Paolo. *Gabriele D'Annunzio: The Dark Flame*. New Haven, Conn.: Yale University Press, 1992. A critical examination of the works of D'Annunzio. Bibliography and index.

Woodhouse, John Robert. *Gabriele D'Annunzio: Defiant Archangel*. New York: Clarendon Press, 1998. An authoritative biography, presenting D'Annunzio's relationships with the worlds of Italian culture, theater, and politics. Includes extensive bibliographic references.

Luisetta Elia Chomel

DANTE

Born: Florence; May or June, 1265
Died: Ravenna (now in Italy); September 13 or 14, 1321
Also known as: Dante Alighieri Durante Alagherius

PRINCIPAL POETRY

La vita nuova, c. 1292 (*Vita Nuova*, 1861; better known as *The New Life*)
La divina commedia, c. 1320, 3 volumes (*The Divine Comedy*, 1802)

OTHER LITERARY FORMS

The prose works of Dante (DON-tay) are not usually taken as major literary achievements in themselves, although they provide many useful sidelights and clarifications to a reader of *The Divine Comedy*. Dante titled the work *Commedia*. It was Giovanni Boccaccio, forty years after Dante's death, who called the work *La divina commedia*, the name by which it is commonly known. *Il convivio* (c. 1307; *The Banquet*, 1887) was probably written between 1304 and 1307. An unfinished work of some seventy thousand words in Italian prose, it is a commentary on three canzones or odes in which the poet proposes a theory of allegory for moral readings of his poetic compositions, so that it will be clear that virtue, not passion, is the topic. A digressive apologia, *The Banquet* is a mine of information about medieval literary culture. *De vulgari eloquentia* (c. 1306; English translation, 1890), a Latin prose work of nearly twelve thousand words, was probably composed in the period from 1304 to 1306. It is believed to be the first study ever written about vernacular language and poetic style and contains fascinating conjectures about the origin of language, Romance linguistics, verse forms, metrics, and poetic sounds. *De monarchia* (c. 1313; English translation, 1890; better known as *On World Government*) is a Latin prose work of nearly eighteen thousand words, probably written in 1312 and 1313; it is a series of arguments for world rule unified under the Holy Roman Empire. Dante's explanations of his ideas about the separate but complementary functions of church and state are particularly valuable. Only a few of Dante's letters survive, but several of them contain seminal passages of Dantean thought.

Many of Dante's lyrics are probably lost forever, but if the eighty or so miscellaneous ones attributed to him are a fair sampling of his efforts, he put his finest in *The New Life*. Many of these smaller poems show only average craftsmanship and are interesting because they reveal a poet who actively participated in his society. Some of the sonnets are exchanges of opinions with friends; six are part of an invective, a contest both socially and intellectually (which was common then), between Dante and Forese Donati. There are love poems to various ladies, some of them real individuals, others clearly allegorical. The lyrics show a very human poet, playful and experimental, heated by anger and love, embittered by exile.

Dante
(Library of Congress)

Achievements

Dante is among the greatest and most influential figures in the long history of Western literature, and no brief summary can do justice to the scope of his achievements. Perhaps his most enduring legacy has been the astonishing supply of signs and symbols for describing and evaluating inner experience that succeeding generations of readers have found in *The Divine Comedy*. Dante was ultimately a mystic in his approach to God, but he wrote with systematic clarity about every spiritual event, stopping only at the point where language and reason had to be abandoned. Probably the most learned, articulate voice in the Christian West since Saint Augustine, Dante created a powerful mindscape able to reflect every movement of the soul. He did this without subjectivism and narcissism. Dante's vision is both a mirror of the self and a window onto the outside world, the cosmos, and the divine. His inward journey is recounted with great intensity and variety, but with no surprises, for that inner world is no more ambiguous or mysterious than the outer world, and Dante did not confront either world in a metaphysical void. His vision is not a hallucinatory refuge, but a site where the interconnectedness of all things can be rationally presented and the consequent need for spiritual discipline and social duty can be argued.

Dante responded to two primary imaginative impulses. One drove him to put all his experiences into an ordered relationship: eros, history, politics, and faith. Behind these ideal forms and schematizations lies a genuine love of the created world in all its density. Dante insists that experience be known as actual and metaphorical, and that virtue be attained through historical processes. The other impulse moved him continually beyond each part of his creation, always ascending, so that each epiphany becomes a curtain to be drawn back to reveal a higher one. One reads Dante with an awareness of the elaborations of each part and the upward movement of the whole.

Dante was the most important voice in the vernacular love lyric before William Shakespeare. Dante's mastery of lyric form and meter was unparalleled, and he used the intellectually demanding conventions of *dolce stil nuovo* ("sweet new style") with simplicity and ease. Had he taken Holy Orders, he could have given the world a pastoral voice worthy of John Donne or George Herbert. Dante's vocational decision was singular and uncompromising. He decided to be a citizen and a philosophical poet. The pains of citizenship fired the creator in him, so that he ultimately became the grandsire of Italian literature and indeed of much of Western literature written since his time. Dante excelled in the poetry of direct statement, in making thought melodic. He found ways to energize moral knowledge, so that it could both persuade and delight. He never wrote to be obscure or ambiguous, but it is important to remember that he was addressing keen, well-educated medieval minds. His mastery of narrative technique and symbolic detail encourages some readers to evaluate his art for its own sake, but Dante always wrote to make the reader look beyond his words to the vision that they served.

Biography

Dante Alighieri was a citizen, and his city was Florence. Medieval Italian cities were for the most part independent states, free of feudal allegiances, with power based not on land, but on harbors, commerce, and industry. The nobility within these cities had gradually yielded power to the new bourgeois interests, but the traditional lines of that struggle were still evident, the nobles seeking support from the emperor and the bourgeois and popular elements tending to oppose the empire and join with the pope.

Those in the imperial faction were called Ghibelines, and those in the papal, or at least the anti-imperial faction, were known as Guelphs. The faction one chose to support often had more to do with current and particular needs and where one's friends and enemies were than with hereditary considerations. Dante's Florence was Guelph, which was enough to make rival cities support the Ghibelline cause—not that the Florentine Guelphs were able to live peaceably for long among themselves. A feud between two branches of a family in Pistoia, who called themselves "Whites" and "Blacks," spread to the Florentine upper classes. The Whites attracted the older families and papal supporters, while the Blacks tended to attract the newly rich commercial classes.

Little is known of Dante's youth in Florence. It is clear that he read widely among Provençal and contemporary Italian poets as well as classical Latin writers; his writing also reveals a practical knowledge of music and painting. He may have attended the University of Bologna. He fought in the Florentine army and seems to have enjoyed many friendships throughout his city. The most important event in his life occurred at a May Day festival when he was nine years old. There he first saw Beatrice Portinari, who was eight at the time. They did not see each other again until nine years later, but Dante's devout fascination with her image and its significance lasted throughout his life. When she died in 1290, Dante diverted his grief by plunging into the difficult politics of the city and the study of philosophy. Between 1296 and 1301, the government of Florence entrusted him with high responsibilities in politics, finances, and diplomacy. His election as one of the city's six priors in the summer of 1300 exemplifies the public trust he enjoyed, a trust he justified when he validated the banishment of his close friend, the poet Guido Cavalcanti.

The year 1300 brought a convergence of several crises, political, spiritual, and economic, in the poet's life. So far as Dante's personal misfortunes are concerned, there are few details in the historical records. The larger event involved Charles de Valois, whom Pope Boniface had invited into Italy to help with the reconquest of Sicily. Charles was permitted to enter Florence with all his troops, after assurances that he would not take part in the struggle between the Whites and the Blacks. Almost immediately, Charles allowed the Blacks to have the upper hand, at which point they began severe reprisals against the Whites. Dante was in Rome at the time as part of a delegation sent to secure guarantees from the pope that the French forces would not interfere in Florentine politics. Dante was accused in absentia of barratry, extortion, impiety, and disloyalty, accusations that ultimately carried with them the death sentence. Dante never returned to Florence. As an exile, he drew closer to the exiled Whites and Ghibellines, but neither negotiations nor armed conspiracy succeeded in restoring them to power in Florence. Dante became disenchanted and impatient with his fellow exiles, who resented him, and may even have blamed him for the military reversals they were suffering.

A restless Dante may have spent time in at least a half dozen Italian cities and perhaps Paris at one point. He was unable to right things between himself and Florence, so that he might return. When Henry VII was elected emperor, Dante envisioned an Italy unified under the empire, with an end to the destructive rivalry between church and state, but several key cities, aided by Florentine money, resisted Henry. When Dante angrily urged the emperor to conquer Florence, he probably eliminated his last chance of entering the city alive. Florence excluded him from the general amnesty offered to the Whites, and then withstood the emperor's assault; Henry died shortly thereafter. In 1315, probably because it needed talented citizens to help against a rival army, Florence declared itself willing to have Dante return, but he proudly rejected the terms. He was in

Verona shortly after that, at work on *The Divine Comedy* under the patronage of Can Grande della Scala and his family. He spent his last days in Ravenna at the court of Guido da Polenta. In 1321, da Polenta sent him on a diplomatic mission to Venice. On his return, Dante fell desperately ill and did not recover. He was buried in Verona wearing Franciscan dress.

Analysis

Dante wrote *The New Life* to give an essential history of his own spirit, which was first aroused, then illuminated by his love for a woman. Here together are the narcissism and ecstasy of youth with the intricate design and perceptions of an older, uncompromising intelligence. The work consists of forty-two passages of prose commentary in which thirty-one poems are set at varying intervals. There are twenty-five sonnets, five canzones, and one ballad. The reader is not meant to abide the prose patiently until he reaches the next poem. Medieval poets believed that it should be possible to state in prose the core idea of any poem they created. Furthermore, no poem existed for its own sake—that is, solely for an aesthetic purpose. The prose keeps the reader in touch with the invisible realities and spiritual implications that were far more important to Dante than personal expression or artistic technique. The poems of *The New Life* describe and deal with romantic and sexual passion. Within the close boundaries and strict internal laws of poetic form, they either exemplify the point Dante is making in prose, or give way to a prose examination of the meanings beneath their surfaces. The poetic voice contains the original turmoil; the prose voice carries the more complete understanding of later personal reflection. The reader is thus able to share in the warmth of the original feelings and the sequence of epiphanies about them.

The topic of *The New Life* is love-suffering, which the poet will complain about but never abandon, for love-suffering is a way of life—indeed, part of the credentials of a noble person. The nobles whom Dante addressed constituted an elite, intelligent group who shared a sensitivity about love and who communicated easily with one another about its subtle doctrines. Traditionally, the medieval love poet did not concentrate on the real presence of the lady so much as on his own feelings about her. The poet would cry out against the upheavals his passions were causing and voice his fear and resentment of her coldness and elevated distance. Despite it all, he would vow to continue his martyrdom. These conventions of refined love were distorted and exaggerated, but they proved fit equipment for capturing the values of romantic experience. They take the reader past appearances into mental and spiritual realities that a camera eye can never see. The new ideas about love, which began emerging less than a century before Dante was born, caused a revolution in the sensibilities of Western European culture. Dante mastered them, then added a revolution of his own. He transcended the devouring egotism of his predecessors by identifying his own erotic drive and the mental processes it stimulated with the Divine Love that beckons to every soul. The lady thus becomes not merely the outer boundary of the lover's consciousness but a mediating presence between self and Deity. No longer a mirror of the poet's feelings, she stands as a window onto the infinite beauty of the Divine Presence and the way of salvation. *The New Life* records Dante's discovery of what he owed to several "God-bearing" ladies whom he encountered on his journey, Beatrice foremost among them.

The work begins with the intelligent and chastened voice of experience: Dante has learned to read the book of Nature, and he knows that the mystical significance of numbers can validate his spiritual discoveries. He has found a *vita nuova*, a new and miraculous life epitomized by the number nine, which the word *nuova* also signifies. Nine is the square of three, a number that, to the medieval imagination, represented perfection and the spiritual life. Dante explains how he first saw Beatrice when she was in her ninth year of life, and not again until nine years later, at the ninth hour of the day. Numbers are the clues to what Heaven has planned for him, so that when Dante writes this book of personal memory, made according to the laws of sequence and cause and effect, the reader is also aware of the perennial present of an unchanging ideal realm. For example, in section 3 of *The New Life*, Dante has a dream that is not only an erotic fantasy but also a prophecy. After he has seen Beatrice for the second time, the God of Love appears in a fiery cloud carrying Beatrice, who is asleep and flimsily clothed. Love wakens her and skillfully makes her eat of Dante's burning heart. Then the God begins to weep and folds his arms around her, and the two ascend heavenward. Dante notes that he had this dream at the first of the last nine hours of the night. Thus, the historical event of the lady's death, through the significance of numbers, reflects eternity.

The structure of Dante's book of memory suggests infinite harmony and reconciliation, particularly through the numbers three and nine. The thirty-one poems of *The New Life* fall into three groups, each group attached to one of the three canzones, or longer poems. At the center of the second or middle group is a canzone with four poems on either side of it. The first and third groups each have ten poems and one canzone; in the first group, the poems precede the canzone, and in the second, they follow it. Besides the obvious symmetry of the entire structure, there are nine poems in the middle group. If Dante had intended the first poem to be an introduction and the thirty-first to be an epilogue, the numbers nine and one would dominate the plan, although this is only a reasonable conjecture. Of more significance is the merger of numerical sign and literary idea in the middle group: The canzone that is at the exact center of the work refers to Beatrice's possible death with imagery traditionally associated with the Crucifixion of Christ. Thus, the center of the poet's book of memory and the center of Christian history are connected, through the analogy drawn between Beatrice and Christ.

The cast of *The New Life* is small, and the narrative is almost without setting and background. There are really only two actors: the poet and the feminine presence who provides all the imaginative milestones in his life. Some women are useful distractions to prying eyes, so that he can conceal his true love's identity. The death of one of them tunes his grief for the eventual death of Beatrice, as does the death of Folco Portinari, Beatrice's father. If one takes this little history of a pilgrim's soul as an analogy for God's created time, where events can be understood either to anticipate or to look back toward Christ's Passion, death, and Resurrection, one immediately appreciates the suggestiveness of the format. When Dante contemplates the possibility of Beatrice's death, it seems to him that the sun grows dark and violent earthquakes occur. The next dream presents Beatrice following her beautiful friend, Giovanna, just as Christ followed John the Baptist. Her death will be comparably momentous and fruitful for his own life and later ages. Not that these insights enabled the poet to bear the actual death of Beatrice; the sonnets and canzones that follow that event are almost all to which a lyric poet can aspire, fusing intellect and pathos so perfectly that readers are reminded how imperfectly united their own souls are; at the same time, they are uplifted by the unity Dante has found. For long moments, the reader can believe that the alleged incompatibility between poetry and philosophy is but a jealous rumor.

As Dante decorates his own love story with signs of what he would come to understand about it in retrospect, he also means to show the progress of his own mind as events teach and shape him. He remembers himself as a self-preoccupied courtly lover, more educated and intellectually demanding than the troubadour poets from whom he learned, but, like them, emaciated by love-suffering, anxious, easily embarrassed, inclined to enjoy nursing his wounds in private, and completely under the rule of his master, Love. When, out of concern for her good name, Beatrice refuses to recognize him, he takes to his bed like a punished child. Then he begins to realize the limitations of this infantile mode. That night in a dream, the god appears and tells Dante that not he, but Love, is at the center of things, equidistant from all points on the circumference. Until he can accept the possibilities of this subtler and more comprehensive definition, the paradoxically painful and pleasurable qualities of his subjective experience will continue to vex him. Then, some town women, gently ridiculing his emaciated condition, suggest logically what Love had put more mysteriously: Happiness can come from the words he uses to praise Beatrice, not the words that concentrate on his own condition. With this nobler theme, his new life begins.

The famous canzone from section 19 that begins "Donne ch'avete intelletto d'amore," or "Ladies who can reason out Love's ways," describes the source of the lady's nobleness and perfection, which make all in Heaven want her with them, so that Heaven itself can be more perfect. On Earth, her glance can banish an evil intention or transform it to a noble one, and the worthy will feel salvation from having looked at her, for God has granted that whoever has talked with her will not come to a bad end. Having shifted his attention to a site outside himself, and having identified Beatrice as an emissary of Divine Love (able like it to create something where nothing has existed), Dante now has a talismanic axiom that will help him meet all future experience—even Beatrice's death, for everything coming to him from her will lead heavenward.

After Beatrice's death, a disconsolate Dante is temporarily distracted by the earthly beauty and compassion of a lady who looks at him sympathetically, but a vision of Beatrice resolves his inner struggle between reason and sensuality, and from then on the image of Beatrice is all he contemplates. The last sonnet of *The New Life* tells how his sigh passed the world's outermost sphere, moved by a new intelligence to the radiance of Beatrice in Heaven. When the sigh tries to report what it saw, its words are too subtle for Dante's comprehension; he is certain only that he hears Beatrice's name again and again. The highest and most serene image of the poet's renewed life is, paradoxically, beyond words. In the final section, Dante tells of a miraculous vision that included sights so profound that he made the resolution to say no more about Beatrice until he could find a suitably elevated vehicle. He closes with the wish that the Lord will grant him a few more years, so that he can compose a work about her that will contain things never said about any woman.

A diary unlike any written before it, *The New Life* was the work of a poet ready for sublime tasks who chose to review the development of his spiritual vision and poetic powers as the first step in the direction of carrying out those tasks. A finished masterpiece in its own right, it also served as a prelude to the greatest sustained poetic achievement in the West since Homer.

The Divine Comedy

There probably never has been a piece of literary imagination as great in scope, as intricate in relationships among its parts, as fastidiously shaped to the smallest detail as Dante's *The Divine Comedy*. Besides the exacting challenge of maintaining poetic intensity for some fourteen thousand lines, there were the perils of dealing with interpretations of religious doctrine and Holy Writ in a fictional context. Even more perilous was the interpretation of Divine Justice, as it applied to specific historical incidents and individuals. Dante's genius and pious imagination flourished among these boundaries and obstacles. He used the appearances of the created world to describe the human heart in a theocentric universe. The three-part narrative pictures the soul deprived of God, in hope of God, and with God. Dante needed a design to mirror the unchanging realities beyond time and space, and he needed an action that would be an imitation of the soul's movements toward these realities. The symmetrical design of the entire work reflects divine perfection, as does its threefold narrative division and three-line stanzas. Each part, *Inferno Purgatorio* (*Purgatory*), and *Paradiso* (*Paradise*), is divided into thirty-three cantos. With the introductory canto, these total one hundred, a number that also traditionally suggested divine unity and perfection.

The world of Dante's *The Divine Comedy* is vertical. The reader always moves downward or upward with the poet: the spiral descent into Hell, the climb up the purgatorial mountain, then up through the various planetary spheres, until the notions of movement up and down are no longer pertinent. The medieval model of the universe was similarly vertical, with Heaven above, Earth at the middle, and Hell below. Everything in God's creation was located at some point or other on a chain or ladder of being, which descended from his divine presence to the lowest form of inert matter. Each being was put at a particular step or degree on this scale, so that it could realize whatever purpose the Creator intended for it, but each thing or being was also understood in terms of what was above it and what was below it. The three realms of Dante's *The Divine Comedy* are vertically related, and each realm has its own vertical plan. The reader is continually urged to compare each spectacle with the one viewed previously and to ponder in retrospect its connection to the spectacle that follows it.

Writing a comedy was also imitating the world, at least as Dante used the term "comedy." In the medieval conception, comedy presented the happy resolution of a difficult situation. Thus, time and history could be seen as parts of a comic action, because Providence, working behind the superficial chaos of Fortune's wheel, would ultimately turn every earthly change to good. Human time and all its pains began with the Fall of Adam, but that Fall looked forward to Christ's redemptive sacrifice. The sacrifice of Christ, who is often referred to as the "Second Adam," made it possible for the pattern of each life to be comic—that is, for humankind to conquer sin and win salvation. Dante's *The Divine Comedy* takes place at the end of Holy Week, during the most spiritually intense hours of the Christian year. For a time, darkness appears to triumph, as the God-Man is slain and buried, but out of seeming defeat comes a victorious descent into Hell and a resurrection that is the archetype of every spiritual rebirth that will come after it. When Dante descends into Hell on Good Friday and reaches Purgatory on Easter morning of the year 1300, the reader contemplates that holier comedy thirteen hundred years before.

The Divine Comedy offers more than structural symmetry and Christian values. It is also an imitation of the swarming variousness of the world of time and space: dreams, boasts, accusations, haunting beauties and catastrophes, wisdom, and reconciliation. The opening words hurry the reader into the narrator's dilemma and impasse, until, ninety-nine cantos later, the vision moves beyond human language and sensation. In his treatment of things invisible, Dante makes the reader touch with understanding almost every texture of earthly existence. To the medieval mind, the world was a book to be read, but a book could imitate the world by being an exhaustive compendium of information about geography, history, the nature of flight, even the spots on the moon. Dante's imagination is alert and curious, not satisfied with building a warehouse of facts. Dante further wishes the reader to visualize and experience the logistics of every step of the journey, feeling the heat, smelling the foulness, seeing different kinds of light and darkness, confronting the monstrosities, and struggling along the broken causeways.

The Divine Comedy is Dante's report of a journey he took into the anagogical realm of existence—that is, the afterlife—to witness the rewards and punishments that God's justice apportions to humankind on the basis of choices freely made in life. Dante himself said this much about his masterpiece. The reader learns while watching him learn, and because of that, even in the *Inferno*, moving toward the center of Earth, the place farthest from God, there is a sense of the intelligence and soul expanding. The journey around which the narrative is constructed is also about the movement of every individual life. It intended to provide equipment for living in a City of God on Earth until the grander city of Jerusalem can be attained.

Although the meticulous physical detail encourages the reader to imagine himself or herself on a journey in time and space, the reader is moving in a mindscape, a spectacle of the sinful human heart. Nowhere in Hell is he or she shown an attitude or act of which every living soul is not capable. Dante's descent involves a lowering of self through the admission of fault and capacity for fault, and the realization that the difference between human sin and Satan's sin is one of degree rather than kind. Self-accusation and contrition make cleansing and regeneration possible, so that the climb to salvation can begin. Dante makes himself fall so that he may rise a stronger man, but his is a controlled fall. The vision of Hell could lead to despair and insane fascination, but with a guide who has been there before, Dante can have this terrible knowledge and survive. Having a second individual on the journey is also a useful narrative strategy, because the guide can interact dramatically with Dante the pilgrim and provide a normative presence, so that Dante the poet need not stultify the narrative with endless digressions about what the pilgrim cannot see.

That Dante should choose Vergil, the greatest of all Latin poets, to accompany him is not surprising. In one way or another, Vergil's writings had nourished every medieval poet. In his epic, the *Aeneid* (c. 29-19 B.C.E.; English translation, 1553), Vergil had described a hero's visit to the underworld, and in that sense had been there once himself. His medieval admirers believed him to be a saint, a moralist, a prophet, even a magician. He was also a pagan and, as Dante strictly reasoned, had not been saved, but he was thought to embody natural wisdom unaided by revelation, which would make him a fit companion for a trip into the region of the damned. Vergil was also a poet of the Empire. He used the story of the fall of Troy to celebrate the founding of Rome and all the achievements of the divinely favored nation that followed it. Vergil predicted an era of world order and prosperity under Roman imperial rule. Many Christians believed that he foresaw in one of his pastorals the coming of the Redeemer and the Christian era. In his essay *On World Government*, Dante had argued that the Empire and the Church were two discrete but complementary modes by which divine purposes could be realized in human history, one emphasizing reason, the other revelation. Vergil epitomizes both the grandeur and the limitations of that gift of natural reason. He travels with Dante as far as he—that is, reason—can, and then is replaced by Beatrice, who personifies the light of divine revelation denied to pagans.

Part 1, Inferno

The world of *The Divine Comedy* is so wide and various that a comprehensive introduction to it is not possible in a brief essay, but canto 1 of the *Inferno* is a useful place to begin observing how Dante's composition works. It is Maundy Thursday night, the day before Good Friday in the year 1300. The poet's first words are about personal time, the midpoint of life at which he awakened to discover himself in a dark wood, with no idea where the right road was. Because the very first line refers to a stage of life, the reader is not likely to imagine a search through a literal wood for an actual road. A few lines later, as Dante painfully recalls the harshness and recalcitrance of the forest, it becomes clear that he is talking about his own former willfulness. As horrid as this time of error was, says Dante, good came of it. This mixture of fear and optimism sets the tone perfectly for the *Inferno* and for the rest of *The Divine Comedy*. The opening lines involve the reader in the experiences of another being as though they were his or her own (which, in a sense they are). Eschewing biographical or historical detail, Dante presents only the essential, the elementary: At a crossroads in life, another human realized that he or she had lost touch with an important part of himself or herself.

The poet does not know exactly how he lost his way in that wood, but the torpor from which he suffered at the time was obviously spiritual. Struggling out of the wood, he is aware of a steep mountain, and as he looks up at the sun that lights the ways of men, he feels some comfort. Somehow, his awareness of his own poor spiritual state and the grace of a loving God have helped him through a dangerous maze, a place, he notes, from which no one has escaped, once entrapped there. Clearly, the forest is a form of spiritual death, or sin, but all the pilgrim has done so far is avoid the worst. To climb the mountain and achieve the spiritual perfection it implies, he will need to gain control of the complicated forces within himself.

A quick-stepping leopard first impedes his progress, but a look at the morning sun, as beautiful as it was during the first moments of Creation, restores Dante's hopes, which are again shattered when a lion, head held high, approaches menacingly. Most intimidating is a gaunt, ravenous wolf, which Dante says has conquered many men. The wolf begins to edge Dante back down the path into the dark forest. Dante does not say what each of these beasts symbolizes, but probably they represent types of sinful living. This notion exists because, to the medieval mind, beasts usually stood for the lower or unreasonable parts of the personal hierarchy. The leopard seems to have the flair and energy of youth, the lion the more powerful intellectual pride that can dominate later years, and the wolf the avarice for possessions that comfort advanced years. Any one of these sins could weigh down a traveler throughout life. Dante makes the point that inability to deal with the three brings despair and spiritual disaster. The light of the sun offers encouragement; grace is available, but it has to be used. As he stumbles downward, Dante sees a shadow. Although it seems unaccustomed to speaking, the shadow answers when Dante calls to it for help, just as the way out of the woods appeared when Dante admitted to himself that he was lost. The shadow is Vergil, who stands for the natural good sense that Dante had allowed to lie dormant.

Vergil does not want Dante to take on the she-wolf directly, for she has been the ruin of many. There is another way out of the wood, Vergil says. The person who confronts his or her own demons without a guide or a strategy is inviting failure. Dante first needs to use his reason to understand the nature of unforgiven sin and its punishment. Then he can visit the purgatorial realm, where the vestiges of forgiven sins are removed, and finally a worthier guide will show him the vision of ultimate reward. Vergil also cautions Dante against becoming preoccupied with the sins of his fellow countrymen. In time, says Vergil, a greyhound will come to chase the avaricious wolf from Italy. Whether this greyhound represents a great earthly prince or some divine apocalypse is not clear. The central point of this first canto is that, beginning with his own conscience, then using the legible signs in the book of the natural world and the revival of his own rational faculty, Dante is ready to journey toward whatever perfection he can hope to attain.

The above remarks are not an ambitious reading of obscure material. Dante saw clearly and wrote to be understood. He did, however, believe that it was natural and beneficial to require an audience to be alert to more than the literal in what he said. An extremely sophisticated tradition of biblical interpretation had prepared his audience to do that and to take pleasure in understanding more than surface meanings in a piece of writing. If the created world was a fair field of symbols, and if the revealed word could be read on several metaphorical levels, why not a story of the mind's journey to God? Thus, Dante wrote allegorical fiction, in which what is said is frequently intended to mean something else. The "literal" aspect of allegorical narrative is usually the least important, for it is the sense of the figurative and the symbolic that the author wants to exercise. The reader needs a fine set of interchangeable lenses to see the multiple levels.

Dante's Hell is in the center of Earth, which was thought to be the center of the created world, but in a theocentric universe, Earth was really on the outside looking in. The lowest point in Dante's Hell is therefore the farthest possible point from God; it is frozen, signifying the total absence of human or divine love. This Hell is fashioned from religious tradition and popular belief. Spectacular as some of the punishments are, the chief source of pain is indescribable: the eternal loss of the sight of God.

Although many modern readers reject the idea of eternal punishment, medieval Christian thinkers had concluded that an all-perfect Being had to embody justice as well as mercy. When an individual died, the reign of mercy ended and that of justice began. In this view, the damned have willfully rejected the power of grace, the teachings of the Church, and the Sacraments. If after this, God relented, he would be unjust. Justice also determines the nature of the punishments and the consequent degree of suffering. The punishment Dante imagines for each sin is a symbolic definition of the sin itself, which the sinner has to repeat for eternity. Only the living can learn from this infernal repetition. For all the uproar and movement in Hell, nothing changes. A medieval definition of change would be the movement of things toward the ideal form that God intended for them; not a single gesture in Hell does that.

Dante's Hell is an inverted hierarchy, with each level revealing a more serious sin below. Hell has nine circles, in addition to an outer vestibule. The upper five circles contain punishments for sins committed through misdirected or uncontrolled emotions; they reflect the perils of natural vitality and appetites, as the image of the leopard suggested. Next, behind the walls of the city of Dis, are crimes that require a stronger determination of the will to disrupt the plan of existence. The violence that appears here (circles six and seven) may be connected with the lion that threatened Dante earlier. The eighth circle is a long sheer drop below this and contains the violators of the various kinds of promise-keeping that make social life possible. The more complicated frauds of treason and betrayal in the ninth and lowest circle may be related to the ravenous wolf. Far more ingenious than the schematic layout of Hell is Dante's ability to keep a sense of spontaneity and discovery in what could have been merely a dutiful walk through a catalog of sin. Dante's skill at variation, which every medieval poet would have coveted, is perhaps the chief source of the poem's excellence. Even in *Purgatory*, where the treatment of each sin runs to a pattern, Dante somehow handles every section uniquely.

One of the sources of variety and sense of forward movement in the *Inferno* is the interaction between Dante and Vergil. Vergil chides, encourages, and revives his pupil as they travel through Hell. The pilgrim Dante becomes stronger and more sure of himself, less frightened by the nightmarish circus about him and more able to despise intelligently the evil he sees. At first, Dante does not believe himself to be fit for such a journey, but when Vergil tells him that Beatrice wills it, he immediately agrees to follow. Two cantos later, in Limbo, the greatest pagan poets are welcoming him to their company. Whenever he has need of Reason, Vergil is always there—even literally at one point—to lift and carry him out of danger. The danger and inhospitableness increase as the two proceed deeper. Everything they see is an inversion or distortion of Charity, the love of God and neighbor in which every Christian act is rooted. At the start, Charon, the underworld boatman, refuses to ferry Dante and Vergil across the river Acheron; in the ninth and lowest circle, Count Ugolino devours the head of the bishop whose betrayal caused the Count and his sons to be starved to death. The reader becomes increasingly aware of Dante's obsession with the two Florences: the City of God on Earth that he wanted it to become and the ungrateful zone of corruption it had been to him. In his darkest hour, Dante was nearer to Beatrice and all that she stood for than Florence would ever be to Jerusalem. Almost until the final instants of *Paradise*, Dante rails against the city that nourished and exiled him.

Somewhat like a gothic cathedral, *The Divine Comedy* is a huge structural support covered with crafted sections of varying size and content, each section somehow finding a place in the totality. A very limited sampling of sections might begin with Upper Hell, where the sins of the incontinent are punished. It may be surprising to find that lust is the first sin viewed here, which makes it the least serious offense in Hell. Medieval moralists tended to treat sexual love as a natural behavior in need of a supernatural perspective. This is quite different from treating sexuality as a taboo, as later ages would. Even so, the reader should consider the mixture of feelings within Dante—who began as a lyric poet in the tradition of erotic courtship—as he watches the souls of the lustful tossed on a roaring black wind, an image of the uncontrollable passion to which they surrendered their reasoning power. They are like flocks of starlings and cranes borne up and down forever, shrieking as they go. The scene conveys the restlessness of human passion and the crowded commonness of the sin itself. The world's most famous lovers are in those flocks: Dido, Helen, Paris, and Tristram. Seeing them, Dante grows dizzy with sympathy.

Two of the lovers are still together, dovelike as they waft along hand in hand. They are Paolo and Francesca, who suffered and died for love at the hands of Francesca's husband. Francesca delivers a courtly lyric celebrating the power of love that brought her and Paolo together, a lyric that ends with the assurance that damnation awaits the one who murdered them. Deeply moved by the lovers' tragedy, Dante asks to know more. What he hears is not the spell of romance but a rather ordinary process of young lechery: leisure time, suggestive reading, and the knowing glances that precede coupling. Dante has to be true to the old conventions of love here, the ones he transformed in *The New Life*; he also has to maintain the clear-eyed antiromanticism of Christian morality. It is all too much for the pilgrim, who falls into a dead swoon, until he awakes to find himself in the third circle, with the Gluttonous.

Like the Lustful, the Gluttonous have allowed themselves to be controlled and distorted by a natural urge. The image Dante uses to describe the punishment here is startling in the manner of a metaphysical conceit. First, he describes a cold, heavy rain soaking a putrid earth. Cerberus, the three-headed watchdog of the Underworld, is there, each head gorging on the souls of the Gluttonous as they wallow in the mud. To distract the monstrous beast, Vergil throws filthy mud down its throats. Cold rain seems to have no connection with excessive eating, until one considers the motivation that is often behind that excess: self-centered loneliness with indiscriminate sieges of oral gratification. One Ciacco ("Fats"), a fellow Florentine, addresses Dante from the slime. He vents his own alienation and misery, then gives an acid survey of the rottenness that will continue to seep from their native city.

The metaphoric effect is equally powerful in canto 12, when Dante and Vergil enter the pathless wood of the suicides, where the souls have been turned to dead trees that bleed at the touch and are fed on by Harpies, who represent the guilt of self-destruction. Through this same wood run the souls of persons who in life madly spent all they owned. They are being chased and torn to pieces by hunting dogs. Dante's decision to put suicides here among souls who have been violent against themselves seems reasonable. That he should sense a comparable wish for death among those who are impatient to destroy their wealth shows a marvelous awareness of the darker corners of the human situation. Like the cold rain on the Gluttonous, it is a superb reach of intelligence and intuition.

The last four cantos describe the ninth and lowest circle of Hell, which contains the perpetrators of the subtlest, most complicated frauds imaginable. First described are the giants of classical legend who tried to scale Heaven and challenge Jove, and the biblical Nimrod, who directed the attempt to build the Tower of Babel. At the bottom of Hell's pit is the frozen lake Cocytus. There, the traitors, who through intellect and will achieved the most drastic perversion of love, are frozen in unrepentant attitudes of hatred. These are the souls of those who betrayed kin, fatherland, guests, and, lowest of all, those who betrayed their lords. Fed ultimately by all the rivers of Hell, the ice itself may be blood-colored. Tears, a symbol of compassion, freeze instantly there. The famous agony of Count Ugolino of Pisa, who, with his children, starved to death in prison, mirrors perfectly these pitiless surroundings. Ugolino and the others are at Hell's bottom because they violated the promise-keeping that is the root of every social and spiritual relationship, for humans become ethical on the basis of their fidelity to promises of loyalty, hospitality, and the like. The cannibalism that the traitor Ugolino enacts as he devours the skull of the person who betrayed him suggests the ultimate negation of social behavior, where humanity and bestiality are no longer distinguishable.

Satan, the angel once nearest to God, now occupies the lowest extremity of Hell, held in ice up to his chest. This is the summary image of the first third of *The Divine Comedy*. At the center of the heart of darkness is this living death, presided over by the first of God's creatures to defy him. Satan has three faces here, red, yellow, and black, which probably refer to the races of humanity through which his first evil is continued. A parody of the Triune God, his face is the inversion of the spiritual number three. Two bat-like wings flap under each face, making a freezing wind that keeps the lake frozen. There is no other movement observable here, unless one includes the tears from those three pairs of eyes, which drip in a bloody mixture from Satan's chins. The draft from his wings evidently freezes all tears but his own. If these tears and blood, which are appalling reminders of the sacramental water and blood that flowed from the side of the Redeemer on the first Good Friday, represent the misery that sin causes, they reveal no contrition whatsoever, for the wings are operated by a will that is still rebellious and an icy egotism that will never cease to oppose God. Even the blindly passionate wind that heaved Paolo and Francesca about would be a welcome alternative to those hopeless gusts.

Each of Satan's mouths chews on a famous traitor. Situated highest, the mouth of the red face tortures the most notorious traitor of all: Judas Iscariot. In the lower mouths are the two others who make up this Satanic Eucharist, Brutus and Cassius, who subverted

God's plan for world empire under Rome by assassinating Julius Caesar. In Dante's conception, sacred and imperial history, although they are separate, are both founded on God's will, and therefore must stand responsible before his justice. In this sense, the things of God and the things of Caesar must ultimately converge. In the midst of these ironies is the supreme irony of Satan's powerlessness, which makes him, for all his gigantic size, ridiculous. He and the giants are mastodons in a museum. Dante and Vergil climb down this hulk out of Hell and see the stars for the first time since early Friday morning.

When Vergil and Dante have climbed down past Satan's navel, they have reached the point farthest from God. What was below is now above them, and Satan appears upside down, a fitting final aspect of the Arch-Rebel. The pair are now in Earth's southern hemisphere, facing an island with a mountain called Purgatory, formed of the land that retreated to avoid Satan when he fell. The Earthly Paradise is on the top of that mountain. It was closed at the expulsion of Adam and Eve, but since Christ's death it has been open to souls purified in Purgatory. Actually, Scripture gives few specific details about Hell, and none at all about Purgatory.

In Purgatory, medieval Christians believed, the residual effects of sins admitted, confessed, and forgiven were removed before the soul entered Paradise. The soul permitted to enter Purgatory was saved and would surely see God someday. Furthermore, these souls could be helped by the prayers of people still on Earth and could enjoy communication with the suffering souls around them. This is quite different from the isolation and hopeless sense of loss in Hell.

PART 2, PURGATORY

If the topic of the *Inferno* is the just punishment of sin, the topic of *Purgatory* is the discipline of perfection. It is a more serenely organized piece of writing, with a pace that is generally more constant. After the terraces of the ante-Purgatory, the mountain has seven cornices, each devoted to purging the stain of one of the deadly sins. Every cornice contains a penance, a meditation, a prayer, a guardian angel, and a benediction. The ascent from one area to another is often accompanied by a brief essay on some topic in natural or moral philosophy. The idea of an ante-Purgatory was probably Dante's own. In its two terraces are the souls of those who delayed repenting until the moment of their death. Having waited too long in life to do what was necessary to be saved, they must wait for some time before they can begin the ascent. In the first terrace are the souls who, although excommunicated by the Church, delayed repentance until the last moments of life. In terrace two are those who delayed similarly, although they always lived within the Church; included here are the souls of the indolent, the unshriven, and the preoccupied.

Saint Peter's Gate is the entrance to Purgatory proper. Three steps of Penance lead up to it: confession, contrition, and satisfaction. At the gate, an angelic custodian inscribes seven *P*'s signifying the Seven Deadly Sins (*peccatum* is the Latin for "sin"), on the forehead of each soul. The letters will be erased one at a time as the soul passes from cornice to cornice. The Seven Deadly Sins were the most widely used description of human evil in the Middle Ages. Somehow or other, every transgression was thought to have come from one of those seven: Lust, Gluttony, Avarice, Sloth, Wrath, Envy, and Pride. Each cornice has a penance appropriate to the stain left by one of those sins. The soul may be made to perform a penitential exercise that symbolically describes the effects of the sin committed, or as counterbalance it may have to perform actions that suggest the virtue directly opposed to the sin. Sometimes souls are assigned to do both.

The meditation in each cornice consists of a whip, or example of the opposing virtue, and a bridle, which is made up of horrid instances of the sin in question. These are followed by a prayer taken from the Psalms or hymns of the Church, then by a benediction (one of the Beatitudes), which is spoken by the angel of the cornice, who then erases a *P* from the soul's forehead. The soul then moves up the Pass of Pardon to the next cornice.

The boundary line for a Hell or Purgatory can be difficult for even a severely legalistic planner to draw. Those souls closest to the entrance of Hell had lost all hope of salvation, though by a narrow margin. In *Purgatory*, those closest to the boundary have avoided that loss by a similarly narrow margin. Dante's Hell begins with the neutrals, those who chose not to choose. They are a faceless mob condemned to chase a whirling standard forever. Next is the Limbo of the unbaptized and virtuous pagans. Dante could not imagine salvation for them, even though their poetry and ideas had nurtured him, but neither could he condemn them for light denied. Thus, the virtuous pagans appear in a dim but pastoral setting, and the poets among them admit Dante to their number. The first terrace of Purgatory also involves fine distinctions, but ones in which the poet is less personally involved. To be excommunicated was not a sin in itself, but a person who was separated from the Church by a sin that called for excommunication, and who put off repentance until the last minutes of life, was grasping salvation by its coattails. Appropriately, these excommunicates and the other late repentants in the second terrace are the only souls in Purgatory who have to undergo a punishment—that is, a wait. All the others are cheerfully engaged in a healing process that will continue until they are ready for Paradise.

Ascending through the cornices of Purgatory is in one way like backing up the spiral road out of Hell. The lowest part of Hell, where the proudest act ever committed is being punished, corresponds to the first cornice, where the stains of pride are being removed. The cornice of Lust, the least of the Seven Deadly Sins, is nearest the top of the mountain, as Lust was farthest from the frozen lake at the bottom of Hell. The descent became increasingly difficult for Dante and Vergil as each circle delivered something more bleak or dangerous. The trek upward in Purgatory is a happy jettisoning of old heaviness, done in the midst of general enthusiasm and encouragement. Instead of Charon, who grudgingly ferried the two across Acheron, an angel of the Lord lightly takes a hundred singing souls across to the island where Mount Purgatory stands. Indeed, the change of mood exhilarates Dante so thoroughly that he all but loses his sense of mission as he listens to the singing of Casella, an old friend and musician.

There are subtle changes in Vergil's presence at this point. He is temporarily eclipsed in the early cantos by the appearance of the astringent Cato, who represents the discipline that will be needed for the lively chores ahead. Moreover, Vergil has not been here before, so although he is still a fount of good sense, he is seeing everything for the first time. He can only partly answer certain questions Dante asks, such as the one about the efficacy of human prayer. Dante will have to wait for Beatrice to explain such matters fully, and interpreters will come forth intermittently to talk about what Vergil cannot be expected to recognize.

Dante and Vergil emerge from Hell on Easter morning at dawn and reach the island shortly after that. They are in the second terrace of ante-Purgatory when the sun begins to set. Night climbing is not permitted, so the two are led to a beautiful valley, where the souls of preoccupied rulers dwell. The cycle of day and night and the natural beauty of the valley indicate their presence still on Earth, in the middle state. The significance of not attempting a penitential climb in the dark is fairly clear, but as night falls, two angels descend to keep watch over the valley. They immediately chase off a serpent who has marauded there. Dante is brilliantly suggestive here. The sentry angels are dressed in green, which is a sign of both hope and penance, but that they should be there at all is puzzling. The point seems to be that, at least in ante-Purgatory, temptation is still a possibility. The fiery swords that the angels bear and the presence of the enemy serpent recall the Fall in Eden, and indeed the theme at the core of this journey is the return to that garden and man's state before he sinned.

The morning dream that Dante has in that valley is also charged with details that add significance to all that will happen. Having his own share of Old Adam's nature, he says, he nods off, and in the first light, the time of holy and prophetic dreams, he sees a golden eagle in midair, about to swoop toward its prey. He thinks of Zeus snatching the boy Ganymede up to Heaven, but then he conjectures that this eagle must always hunt here, so it need not have anything to do with him. Then the eagle comes for him like lightning and takes him up to the circle of fire that surrounds Earth, where they burn together with a heat that wakens him and ends the dream. He finds that Saint Lucy has carried him to Saint Peter's Gate—the beginning of Purgatory proper.

This dream illuminates the rest of the story until the final line, although it is possible to interpret its simpler elements at once. Lucy is one of the three ladies (the other two are Beatrice and the Blessed Virgin) who decided to help Dante out of the dark wood earlier. Lucy personifies the beckoning power of Divine Light by literally transporting Dante to the start of this second phase of his journey. The golden eagle, a bird sacred to Jove and also an emblem of the empire, is doing a comparable thing. Here are two faces of the Godhead, one maternally encouraging, the other ravenously assertive, together making up a richly complicated insight that comes not from a Vergilian lecture or the remark of a dead soul, but from a dream, where the discourse is intuitive and mystical. The progress up the mountain will for the most part involve intellectual and ethical knowledge, but as it is happening the totality of Dante's being will be moving toward a Divine Love that is beyond language and rational understanding, and for which a burning heaven is the most appropriate metaphor. The movement up the cornices will be clear and steady, so uniform as to be tedious at times. It will require the light of day, but the total movement of the self with the Deity is perhaps best reflected in dream light, because Dante is giving his readers not only an encyclopedia of morality but also an imitation of a psychological process.

The removal of the vestiges of sin will render the soul fitter and more able to see the Beatific Vision in its full glory. In Purgatory, all souls are headed homeward, and each step is easier and more satisfying. Innocence, humans' state before sin, is the first destination, and from there a more glorious vision will begin, one that the most artful words can only partially describe.

Signs that Eden is near begin in the sixth cornice, with the Gluttonous. By this time, Publius Papinius Statius, a pagan Latin poet who became a Christian, has joined the party; Dante believes that Vergil's reason and literary art need the supplement of revelation so that everything that is about to happen can be fully appreciated. Vergil had pagan glimmerings of Eden and the prelapsarian state when he wrote of a virtuous Golden Age once enjoyed by humankind, but glimmerings are not enough. Before them in the path, they see a tall tree, watered from above by a cascade. The tree bears ambrosial fruit, but a voice forbids anyone to eat it. Examples of Temperance are then described, which are the goad or whip to counter the vice. The souls of the Gluttonous, all emaciated, suffer from being denied the sweet-smelling fruit, but as one of them tells Dante, they come to the tree with the same desire that Christ brought to the Cross, for both sufferings bring redemption. They see another tree that also keeps its fruit from a gathering of gluttonous souls. A voice tells them to ignore the tree, which is the sort that fed Eve's greed. The connection between the sin of Gluttony and the eating of the forbidden fruit was a point commonly made from medieval pulpits. Particularly noteworthy here is the easy flow of allusions to the Fall of Man and to the suffering on the Cross that compensated for it. The classical story of Tantalus's punishment in the Underworld may have inspired Dante's description of the Gluttonous, but the tree of Eden and the tree of the Cross are clearly the central points of reference here.

PART 3, PARADISE

When the three travelers finally reach the Earthly Paradise, they see not a garden but a forest, a sacred wood wherein dwells the primal innocence that seemed so far away in the dark wood of the *Inferno*, in canto 1. The sacred wood has a single inhabitant, Matilda, who is there to explain these environs and make straight the way of Beatrice, who appears in a spectacular allegorical event called the Procession of the Sacrament. Only eyes that have regained the first innocence are ready for such a vision. Looking eastward, which is by tradition the holiest direction, Dante sees a brilliant light spread through the forest, and a procession led by seven candlesticks to a chanting of "Hosanna." Next come twenty-four elders, heads crowned with lilies, and after them four beasts surrounding the triumphal cart drawn by a griffin, whose birdlike features are gold, and elsewhere red and white. Three ladies, colored respectively red, green, and white, dance in a circle by the right wheel; four in purple dance by the left wheel, led by one who has a third eye. Two old men come next, one dressed as a physician, the other carrying a sword. They are followed by four humbly dressed individuals, and then by a very old man, going in a visionary trance. These last seven all wear red flowers.

Medieval religious processions were usually staged to affirm a crucial matter of doctrine or devotion. The key notion in this masquelike procession is the unity of sacred revelation since the Fall of Man. The twenty-four elders refer to the books of the Old Testament, their lily crowns suggesting pure righteousness. The Benedictus they sing is a reminder that the Old Testament symbolically anticipates events in the New Testament. The four beasts are the beasts of the Apocalypse and the signs of the four Evangelists. The griffin, which is part eagle and part lion, traditionally refers to the two natures of Christ, its gold suggesting divinity, its red and white, humanity. White and red are also the colors, respectively, of the Old and New Testaments, and of the bread and wine in the Eucharist. The ladies by the right wheel are Faith (white), Hope (green), and Charity (red); by the left wheel are the four cardinal virtues: Prudence (with the third eye), Temperance, Fortitude, and Justice. Behind the cart are Luke, Paul, and the Epistles of Peter, James, John, and Jude. The old man is the Revelation of Saint John. The red flowers they all wear signify the New Testament.

Then Beatrice appears on the cart in a red dress and green cloak, her head crowned with olive leaves. At this moment, Dante realizes that Vergil, the man of natural wisdom, is no longer with him. Beatrice, who might as well be called Revelation here, tells Dante to look at the entire procession. All of it is she, Beatrice says. Beatrice's words are the fullest manifestation so far of the significance of one passionate event that occurred when the poet was nine years old. What the God-Man brought into history, she is. The Incarnation that the Old Testament faintly surmised and the New Testament celebrates, she is, with every holy virtue in attendance. The same can be said of the transsubstantiated Host on the altar.

After a rebuke from Beatrice for the wandering ways of his own life, which is perhaps his own rightful dose of the purgatorial suffering he has been content to watch, Dante faints with shame. When he revives, Matilda is drawing him across the stream of forgetfulness. With the memory of evil now gone, he can watch with original innocence as the procession heads toward the Tree of Knowledge, where human sin began. Many medieval writings connected the Tree of Knowledge with the tree on which Christ was crucified. Lore had it that the seeds of the fruit from the first tree were buried on the tongue of Adam and then grew to become the tree of the Cross. Christ was often referred to as the Second Adam, come to reverse the catastrophe caused by the first. Here, the Griffin (Christ) moves the cart with Beatrice (the Word and its Incarnation) past the site on which the temptation and Fall occurred and joins the shaft of the cart to a barren tree, which immediately blossoms. The Griffin then ascends, leaving Beatrice at the roots of the tree. She now represents the Church that Christ at his ascension left behind to care for the humans he had redeemed.

The role of the Empire in God's plan is stressed here, too. An eagle slashes at the tree, just as Roman persecution maimed the Church. Then a gaunt fox appears, probably to represent the heresies of the Church's early history. After the fox has prowled about the cart, the eagle descends again, this time to feather the cart from its own breast. This no doubt represents the symbiotic relationship between church and state in the Holy Roman Empire. That liaison is followed by a dragon that damages the cart, causing it to change into the many-headed beast of the Apocalypse, on top of which is enthroned a whore consorting with giants. The imagery suggests the later corruption of the Church caused by its consorting with earthly powers. Thus, Dante sketches a symbolic history of the decay of the Church that Christ and Peter founded. The point is one he makes directly in many places: that in Christian history, Church and Empire need to maintain separate identities as they pursue God's plan. The atmosphere of these last cantos has been gradually shifting toward Apocalypse, which Beatrice continues by prophesying revenge for what has been allowed to happen to Christendom, but the final canto returns to the theme of a purgatorial journey. Dante now drinks from Eunoe, the water of Good Remembrance, which renders him finally free from the tarnish of an earthly life and ready for a direct vision of the Godhead.

Readers who think of Dante as the poet of Hell often have read only the first third of his masterpiece. The joy that quickens every step of the *Purgatory* makes it an exhilarating sequel to the *Inferno*, but that joy is only a hint of what awaits Dante in the vision of Paradise. The *Inferno* and *Purgatory* are preparatory visions, the first stressing the reality of evil and its effects, the second showing that it is possible to remove every one of those effects. *Purgatory* and *Paradise* form the main part of the comedic structure, which leaves the unhappiness of the *Inferno* far behind.

Dante's *Paradise* is a description of Godhead, as much of it as his eyes could register, and as much as his memory could retain. Medieval literary audiences loved well-executed descriptions, and the *Inferno* and *Purgatory* contain some extraordinarily effective ones. Once the poet has left the substantive world, images on which to base descriptions are no longer obvious. Hell and Purgatory are constructed and described according to sinful human actions, which had been traditionally identified and discussed in concrete images. Social history abounds with vivid examples of depravity, but there has never been a great store of fictions or metaphors to describe the state of the soul enjoying Heavenly rewards. Moreover, the step-by-step journey into Hell and up the purgatorial mountain involves a sense of time and space that is inappropriate to the simultaneity of eternity. Thus, the metaphor of the journey does not quite fit a vision of Heaven, although to accommodate human communication and understanding, the vision had to be subdivided and presented in some sequence. Dante reminds his audience, however, that this is only a strategy to help them see.

Until one reaches the presence of God, the Being than Whom none is higher, one has to understand every phenomenon, even heavenly bliss, hierarchically. Every soul in Heaven is completely happy, but even heavenly bliss has its degrees. To describe Paradise, Dante looks outward from Earth to the concentric spheres of the planets and beyond them to the Empyrean, where the Divine Presence begins. Because, moving outward, each successive planet is closer to God, each one can be a gathering point for increasingly elevated forms of blessedness. With the rather technical exception of the souls on the Moon, the imagery Dante uses to describe the souls he meets is nonrepresentational, even approaching abstraction with voices, lights, and patterns. Dante was familiar with the tradition of the cosmic voyage, a literary form that went back to the Stoic philosophers, in which a guide takes a troubled individual to the outer spheres, to provide consolation by demonstrating the littleness of troubled Earth when compared to the grand harmony of all Creation. A powerful counterpoint develops in *Paradise* between accounts of the sordidness of contemporary Italian society and the charity and communion above. Part of the image of Paradise is thus accomplished through negative description, using earthly examples to emphasize what Heaven is not.

The *Inferno* does not start with a poetic invocation. Dante rushes directly into the troubled middle of things. *Purgatory* has an invocation to Calliope, the Muse of epic poetry. It is crucial but perfunctory, and it suits the hopeful premises of that work. The invocation to *Paradise* is a fitting start to a sublime task. It tells what a poet requires to describe his Creator. He starts with the notion that what he has seen is not possible to relate, because when the mind nears that which it has always wanted, memory weakens. Even so, he will sing about that part of it that has remained with him. He calls on Apollo, a god traditionally associated with light, wisdom, and prophecy, to breathe into him and use him like a bellows to utter song worthy of what memory of Paradise he still has left. Dante's audience would have been comfortable with an invocation to a pagan deity, because they believed that many pagan myths were glimpses of Christian light that could be used to make poetry more articulate. As an inspiration to soul and art, Apollo resembles the Holy Spirit, but he also carries all the rich associations of the classical literary tradition.

If Apollo will be generous, Dante continues, he will approach the laurel tree to take those famous leaves, now so neglected by an unheroic and unpoetic age, to create poetry that will ignite better imaginations than his own. From that tree, then, may come light for all future ages. The highly prophetic *Paradise* deserves to be under the keeping of

Apollo. The poet approaches the laurel tree sacred to Apollo as he gathers strength to take his pilgrim self from Eden and the last visible traces of earthly things. The tree of tantalizing punishment for the Gluttonous and the tree of the first sin are replaced here by a tree reflecting the highest moral calling of art. As the images of Eden and sin recede, the laurel tree and the tree of Redemption converge. Dante looks at Beatrice looking at the sun, which is both Apollo's planet and a traditional symbol for God. It is the same sun he saw that morning in the dark wood, but then he was looking through sinful eyes. The eagle, Dante's symbol for the Empire, was thought to be able to look directly into the sun; the suggestion here is that Beatrice, who stands for all revelation, and the eagle are one. It might seem curious that an image of imperial order should be presented at a moment of intimacy between self and Godhead, but Dante will make a similar point throughout *Paradise*: that religious mysticism and social history are different but not antithetical routes to God. The eagle that seized Dante in a dream and took him on high to burn was as much the call of empire as it was a private religious impulse.

Dante is not able to look directly at the sun for long. As he looks at Beatrice looking at eternity, he begins to hear the music coming from the harmonious motion of the heavenly spheres, a sound no mortal has heard since Adam sinned. Instantly, Dante realizes that he has left Earth with Beatrice. The vision that follows, the organization of which is only a metaphor for the ineffable, involves ten Heavens, each of the first seven associated with a planet—Moon, Mercury, Venus, Sun, Mars, Jupiter, Saturn—the eighth Heaven with the zodiac and fixed stars, the ninth the Crystalline Heaven of the *Primum Mobile*, or First Mover, through which motion was imparted to all the other spheres, and beyond that the Empyrean, or realm of God. In the first seven Heavens, the souls are located in the planet with which their earthly activities could be associated, although in actuality each of them is in the Empyrean with God. According to Dante, the first three Heavens are touched by the shadow of Earth. On the Moon, the planet nearest Earth, are those souls who through no fault of their own proved inconstant in vows they had made to God. They were not sinners, only less perfect in salvation. Next is the Heaven of Mercury, filled with souls who lived virtuous lives serving the social order, but who were motivated at least in part by worldly ambition. The sphere of Venus is for those who followed Eros in life but now are delighted to wheel with celestial movement.

In the Heaven of the Sun are spirits whose wisdom furthered the understanding of God on Earth. Mars houses those who gave their lives for the Christian faith, while Jupiter houses the souls of the Just. The second three Heavens (Sun, Mars, and Jupiter) celebrate the virtuous achievements of the active life, but the contemplatives abide above them, in the circle of Saturn. The theme of the eighth Heaven is the Church triumphant, with Christ and the saints in full radiance. The ninth and tenth Heavens, respectively the *Primum Mobile* and the Empyrean, are given to the various direct manifestations of God. They take up the last six cantos, which trail off as even Dante's imagination begins to fade before its task.

The mood of *Paradise* is perfect joy that has no end and leaves not even a trace of unfulfilled desire. The spirits describe that joy by what they do and say. There is a hierarchy of blessedness here, but it exists without anyone feeling envy or deprivation. Just as the courtesy and charity of Purgatory take one above the hatred and cupidity of Hell, so the perfect happiness here lifts one even higher, particularly through the praises for its perfect Source. The points of Christian doctrine and philosophy that are explained to Dante as he moves from Heaven to Heaven with Beatrice are rarefied, some barely fixable in mind or language. To follow these thoughts, the reader must move with Dante past the recognizable specifics of time and place. This commentary can only sample that exquisite brightness. One might begin with the notion that the rewards of Heaven justify everything that humans can know about God's plan. *Paradise* is a celebration and vindication of the Church and all its traditions, and of the plan for justice on Earth through Empire. It is also an opportunity for a citizen poet and visionary to justify himself to the audience of the world.

The Heaven of the Sun provides a satisfying example of Dante's love for the true Faith and the ideal Church. When he and Beatrice ascend to this Heaven, twelve lights carol around them, and one, Saint Thomas Aquinas, speaks. Aquinas belongs with the wisdom and illumination of the Sun. Mastering Aristotelian thought, he put its processes at the service of Christian theology. Among medieval Scholastic philosophers, he was supreme, and as a member of the Dominican Order (whose standard is a blazing sun), he studied and wrote to combat the heresies of unbelievers. Aquinas speaks not to praise a great university scholastic, however, but to praise Saint Francis of Assisi. Saint Francis was a street preacher, a disciple of the poor, whose spontaneous, instinctive love of God did not move through learned syllogisms. Aquinas tells a lively allegory about Saint Francis and the woman in his life, Lady Poverty. Poverty had been a neglected widow since her first spouse died on the Cross twelve centuries before. Indeed, Poverty and Christ were so inseparable that during the Crucifixion she leapt on the Cross, like a wanton lover. Aquinas compares Francis's taking the vow of poverty to a wedding, an orgiastic celebration at which the guests (Saint Francis's followers) all hasten to follow this couple; as an Order, they will spread preaching and conversion throughout the world. This earthy description of Saint Francis's love for an ideal is no blasphemy: It is a charming reminder of how far the saint actually was from sensuality.

Then a Franciscan, Saint Bonaventure, praises the life work of Saint Dominic, founder of the order to which Aquinas belonged. Dominic, says Bonaventure, was the skillful gardener, sent to cull, trim, and order the plot of Faith and bring it new vitality. It is, like Aquinas's remarks about Francis, a graceful compliment, from lights that glow more brightly as they praise others. The ecstatic preacher and the systematizer of doctrine both work God's will and complement each other. At the same time, the reader cannot forget the diatribes of Aquinas and Bonaventure against the state of those orders.

Dante continually arranges his descriptions of Heaven to portray the idea of perfect happiness, although he relentlessly turns to bitter reminders of what human choice has rendered impossible on Earth. He never puts down the lash of satire for long. If *Paradise* is the happy conclusion of a comedy, it is also filled with astringent reminders that human history is a process of social and moral decay, much like the image of the Old Man of Crete in *Inferno* 14, which starts with a golden head and ends with rotting feet. At points Dante is apocalyptic about this decay, and he foretells destruction for his sinful age. He also implies that one day a strong figure will punish those selfish wrongdoers and usher in an age of justice.

Despite his outcries as an embittered satirist and doomsayer, Dante knows that both sacred and secular history are processes of God's justice, even when they seem to be operating at cross-purposes. In the Heaven of Mercury, Dante interviews Justinian, the Roman emperor and codifier of law, who outlines the historic progress of the Empire. For Justinian, history is the flight of God's sacred eagle. He describes the earliest tribes in Italy, the Punic Wars, and the emperors. Justinian's most startling point is that the highest privilege of Roman justice was the punishment of Christ. The Crucifixion was a legal act, conducted by duly constituted Roman authority, with Pontius Pilate as the agent. It made the Redemption possible. At the same time, as Beatrice will later explain, the legality of the act under Roman law did not remove the need to avenge what had been done to Christ's person, so, somewhat paradoxically, the destruction of Jerusalem was also justified. The path of Divine Justice moved from ancient Rome to the Holy Roman Empire, thanks to Charlemagne, but that magnificent progress has fallen to puny, contemptible heirs, as the Guelphs and Ghibellines of Dante's time continually ruin that justice with their feuding.

Dante's view of the workings of Divine Justice comes with surprises, as when he puts in the Heaven of Jove one Rhipeus, whom Vergil in the *Aeneid* called the most just among the Trojans. Presumably, Rhipeus was a pagan. That he should be in Heaven and the author who wrote about him in Hell is an irony, but Dante means to emphasize the presence of an appetite for justice in the Trojan line even before it settled in Italy.

If the ways of Justice can seem mysterious, Dante had no doubt that they would someday set in balance all the wrongs he had suffered. In Hell, Dante's anger at old enemies sometimes made him spiteful and almost pruriently interested in their pain. He paid particular attention to the part of Hell where barratry, the crime of making personal profit out of public trust, is punished by immersion in a pit of boiling tar. The episode is personal, for Dante was convicted and sentenced to exile on charges of barratry. For all the thrashing about among devils and damned souls in the pit of barrators, not so much as a drop of tar touches the poet. That is his answer to the capricious charges against him.

By placing his fictional journey in 1300, several years before the beginning of the political turmoil in Florence that resulted in his exile, Dante was able to present himself as a pilgrim ignorant of what is to come. This allows the heavenly hosts to refer to his coming suffering as an unjust but transient ordeal. It is a powerful response to his oppressors, because it allows him to assert the righteousness of his own cause and the maliciousness of his enemies through voices that are not to be contradicted, because their foreknowledge comes from the Divine Presence. The highest and most justified reaction to his future sufferings will come when Dante sees how little they amount to in the eye of eternity.

Dante's self-justification in *Paradise* shows a legitimate holy pride in ancestry and a certainty about his own destiny, despite the disgrace that is brewing for him. In the Heaven of Mars, the souls of those who died for the Faith form a cross. One of them, Dante's great-great-grandfather Cacciaguida, reminds him of the simple and virtuous old stock from which he is descended, in a line extending back to ancient Roman times. Cacciaguida hails Dante as a solitary continuation of this earlier nobility, then names clearly what had been hinted about in Hell and Purgatory: exile, poverty, a life at tables and under roofs not his own. Cacciaguida instructs Dante not to temper so much as a word, but to be a gadfly to degenerate Florence as Justice works its way.

Paradise is always ascending toward the vision of God, at which paradoxically it will evaporate, because it is only a human artifact. Actually, Dante is given three manifestations of God's presence. In the *Primum Mobile*, he sees God symbolically as a point of light surrounded by nine rings, each ring representing an order of angels. These nine rings of angels are in pointed contrast to the geocentric world, where the most slowly moving sphere, that of the Moon, is closest to the corruptible center. Here, as Beatrice explains, the fastest and brightest angelic circle, that of the Seraphim, is closest to the point of light. The definition of God as an indivisible point of light may seem unusual, given the traditions of a transcendent, all-encompassing Divinity. Dante was familiar with a definition of God as a sphere whose center is everywhere and whose circumference is nowhere, a concept that neatly implies the traditional idea of God's absolute and indivisible simplicity and his absolute interminability and simultaneity. The image of the point of light and the concentric circles of angels is perhaps as close as the human intelligence can come through symbols to understanding God's essence.

The image of God that Dante is given when he enters the Empyrean is a product of faith and revelation; it is the closest Dante can come directly to God, and this is the image with which *The Divine Comedy* must end. The Empyrean contains the souls of the Blessed on ascending tiers of thrones arranged to form petals of a white rose, as they will appear on Judgment Day. With the rose, a symbol of Divine Love, Dante moves finally beyond time and space in a blinding brightness as a river of Divine Grace pours from an incalculable height. In the center of the rose is a circle of light, the glory of God. It is time now for the final vision, but Dante discovers that Beatrice has left him to take her place among the Blessed. She has sent the great mystic and contemplative Saint Bernard to be his final guide. Doctrine and revelation, which Beatrice represented, have advanced as far as they can. Only ecstasy can go beyond that.

Under Bernard's direction, Dante's journey ends where it was first conceived, for there are the Virgin, and Lucia, whom the Virgin had sent to Beatrice, who in turn summoned Vergil to aid Dante in the descent to Hell. Now Saint Bernard prays for Mary's intercession, so that they can look at God without the instruments of metaphor or symbol. It is, as Dante says, the end of all yearning, satisfying and rendering obsolete the last vestiges of desire in the soul. In one mystical moment, Dante sees all creation held together by love. Then he sees three circles, each one a different color, occupying one space. It is the Trinity. The first two circles (the Father and the Son) reflect on each other, and the third (the Holy Ghost) seems a flame coming equally from the first two. It is a vision beyond logic and intellect. In trying to encompass it, Dante falls, like Icarus, back to his everyday human self. Dante ends with the remark that, whatever the limitations of his own understanding, Love was at the heart of what he saw, that same Love which moves the sun and the stars.

OTHER MAJOR WORKS

NONFICTION: *Epistolae*, c. 1300-1321 (English translation, 1902); *De vulgari eloquentia*, c. 1306 (English translation, 1890); *Il convivio*, c. 1307 (*The Banquet*, 1887); *De monarchia*, c. 1313 (English translation, 1890; also known as *Monarchy*, 1954; better known as *On World Government*, 1957); "Epistola X," c. 1316 (English translation, 1902); *Eclogae*, 1319 (*Eclogues*, 1902); *Quaestio de aqua et terra*, 1320 (English translation, 1902); *Translation of the Latin Works of Dante Alighieri*, 1904; *Literary Criticism of Dante Alighieri*, 1973.

BIBLIOGRAPHY

Bloom, Harold. *Dante Alighieri*. Philadelphia: Chelsea House, 2003. A biography of Dante that also examines his works. Bibliography and index.

Gallagher, Joseph. *A Modern Reader's Guide to Dante's "The Divine Comedy."* Liguori, Mo.: Liguori-Triumph, 2000. A canto-by-canto guide to *The Divine Comedy* that is especially helpful for beginning readers of the work. Provides insightful character analysis from a specifically Roman Catholic perspective, along with accessible explanations of Dante's many obscure references. Includes a helpful outline.

Havely, Nick. *Dante*. Malden, Mass.: Blackwell, 2007. Havely looks at the life and work of Dante, focusing on literary and cultural traditions; key themes, episodes, and passages, and on how his work has been received.

Hollander, Robert. *Dante: A Life in Works*. New Haven, Conn.: Yale University Press, 2001. An intellectual biography, drawing on the works of its subject rather than on what little is known (and has already been well covered) of Dante's life.

Jacoff, Rachel, ed. *The Cambridge Companion to Dante*. New York: Cambridge University Press, 1995. An excellent guide to Dante's life, work, and thought. Especially useful for those readers of *The Divine Comedy* who want more information on specific allusions than most footnoted editions supply. Includes fifteen specially commissioned essays that provide both background information and critical commentary and a chronological outline of Dante's life.

Lansing, Richard. *Dante: The Critical Complex.* 8 vols. New York: Routledge, 2003. A collection of criticism and analysis, with volumes looking at Dante's relation to Beatrice, philosophy, theology, history, critical theory, and interpretation.

_____, ed. *The Dante Encyclopedia.* New York: Garland, 2000. An encyclopedia devoted to Dante. Covers his life and works and contains numerous appendixes. Index.

Raffa, Guy P. *Divine Dialectic: Dante's Incarnational Poetry.* Toronto, Ont.: University of Toronto Press, 2000. A study of Dante's worldview as revealed in incarnational images in his poetry.

Reynolds, Barbara. *Dante: The Poet, the Political Thinker, the Man.* 2d ed. Emeryville, Calif.: Shoemaker & Hoard, 2007. A biography of Dante that looks at his political life as well as his poetical life.

Thomas A. Van

UGO FOSCOLO

Born: Zante, Ionian Isles, Greece; February 6, 1778
Died: Turnham Green, near London, England; September 10, 1827

PRINCIPAL POETRY
Bonaparte liberatore, 1797
Poesie, 1803
Dei sepolcri, 1807 (*On Sepulchers*, 1835, 1971)
Le grazie, 1848

OTHER LITERARY FORMS

Ugo Foscolo (FAWS-koh-loh) is best known for his *Ultime lettere di Jacopo Ortis* (1802; *Last Letters of Jacopo Ortis*, 1970), an epistolary novel written after the Treaty of Campoformio (October 17, 1797), in which Napoleon Bonaparte ceded Venice to the Austrians. Napoleon's action shocked Foscolo, who had previously written an ode entitled "A Bonaparte liberatore" ("To the Liberator Bonaparte"). In this autobiographical novel written in the form of letters from the student Jacopo Ortis to his friend Lorenzo Alderani, eroticism and politics (of a strong anti-Gallic strain) are merged. In the same year, Foscolo wrote a tragedy, *Tieste* (pr. 1797), in the style of Vittorio Alfieri, the success of which owed much to its revolutionary democratic spirit.

Between 1804 and 1805, while in France, Foscolo began work on an Italian translation of Laurence Sterne's *A Sentimental Journey* (1768). This translation was finished in 1813 in Pisa and was published as *Viaggio sentimentale di Yorick lungo la Francia e l'Italia* concurrently with an autobiographical work, *Notizie intorno a Didimo Chierico* (1813; news about Didimo Chierico). On January 22, 1809, in support of his nomination for a professorship at Pavia University, Foscolo published an important work titled *Dell'origine e dell'ufficio della letteratura* (about the origin and function of literature), in which he promotes a sociohistorical approach to literature.

Among Foscolo's most important nonlyric works are the tragedies *Aiace* (pr. 1811) and *Ricciarda* (pr. 1813). *Aiace* was not successful at its premiere but has come to be considered one of Foscolo's best works. Foscolo's *Epistolario* (1949-1970; letters) is outstanding, from both a literary and a political standpoint, and is characterized by sincerity even in the most intimate matters. In Switzerland, Foscolo published his speeches under the title *Della servitu d'Italia* (1823; on the servitude of Italy), a work that shows Foscolo's pessimism concerning the then-fermenting Risorgimento, the movement for the unification of Italy.

From 1816 until his death in 1827, Foscolo lived in England and dedicated himself to producing scholarly, critical works such as *Saggi sul Petrarca* (1821; *Essays on*

Petrarch, 1823). Through these works, Foscolo helped to initiate in Italy a modern critical awareness of the psychological and sociohistorical background of literature.

ACHIEVEMENTS

Ugo Foscolo was a man of strong commitment and even stronger will, never afraid to follow the path of truth in the pursuit of the ideals he held worthy. Like many Italian writers from Petrarch and Dante on, Foscolo brought a strong thread of classical culture to the Romanticism that dominated the entire European scene during the early 1800's. His personal experiences and his cultural background became the raw material from which he worked all his life. Foscolo's writings, in some sense, summed up much of the achievement and many of the trends of Italian literature of his day (the critical studies of Dante, Petrarch, and Giovanni Boccaccio are notable in this respect), and he stood as a significant milestone for writers of succeeding generations. His burial at the Church of Santa Croce in Florence, where he is entombed among the greatest figures of Italian literary and political history, suggests his place in Italian culture and letters.

BIOGRAPHY

Niccolò Ugo Foscolo was born to parents of mixed heritage; his mother, Diamantina Spaty, was Greek, while his father, Andrea Foscolo, was Venetian. When Foscolo was ten years old, his father died. He and his mother then moved to Venice, where he stayed until 1797, during which time he began to attend political and literary gatherings such as those of the Countess Isabella Teotochi. In this period, he developed an admiration for the revolutionary doctrines of Jean-Jacques Rousseau, Alfieri, and Robespierre while attending classes taught by Melchiorre Cesarotti at Padua University.

In 1797, because of his political ideas, Foscolo was forced to flee to Bologna, where he received the nomination of honorary lieutenant for the French army in Italy. He performed this role as a strict republican until the infamous Treaty of Campoformio, which caused Foscolo to hate Bonaparte so much that he moved to Milan, where he lived from 1797 to 1815. In Milan, Foscolo made the acquaintance of Vincenzo Monti and Giuseppe Parini, and he also pursued love affairs with Teresa Pickler, Isabella Roncioni, and the Countess Antonietta Fagnani Arese.

When, in 1798, the second coalition of the Austrians and Russians reconquered northern Italy from Napoleon (who was at that time in Egypt), Foscolo fought against this action under General Jean-Étienne Championnet, but his open aspiration for Italian independence provoked great hostility from the French. Nevertheless, he went to France for two years (1804-1806) and made the acquaintance of the famous Italian writer Alessandro Manzoni, as well as an English girl, Fanny Emerytt, by whom he had a daughter, Floriana. Returning to Milan in 1806, Foscolo pursued more love affairs and dedicated himself to various writing activities. In 1812, after the presentation of his second tragedy, *Aiace*, in which certain characters were seen as anti-French, the poet was forced to flee to Florence. There, Foscolo involved himself in the circle of the countess of Albany until the Austrians took Milan in 1813. Unable to pledge allegiance to the Austrian government, Foscolo went into voluntary exile in Switzerland in 1815. One year later, he moved to England, where he collaborated in the publication of magazines and journals, gave classes in literature, and was reunited with his daughter, Floriana. He quickly exhausted Floriana's savings, some three thousand pounds, and remained deeply in debt until his death in 1827. Only in 1871 was his body brought to Florence and buried, as requested in his will, in the Church of Santa Croce, next to the tombs of Michelangelo, Machiavelli, Alfieri, and Galileo.

Foscolo's achievements were acknowledged during his lifetime, but it was only after his death that his writings were fully recognized as a milestone in Italian literature. He succeeded in detaching himself from the regionalism of his predecessors. From political realism, he went on to pessimism, though he never espoused the fatalism expressed by his younger contemporary Giacomo Leopardi; Foscolo's was a dynamic pessimism that organized his heroic and lyric behavior. If the function of poetry, as Natalino Sapegno states in his *Disegno storico della letteratura italiana* (1973), is to discover amid the contradictions of this earthly life that universal harmony by which humans restore their own existence, Foscolo, amid a troubled life, found support in his art and created a personal vision of the sublime.

Analysis

The Romantic movement dominated Italian literature during the first half of the nineteenth century, and Ugo Foscolo, along with other writers, such as Vincenzo Monti and Alessandro Manzoni, was part of it, though at a rather different level. Foscolo's personal life and his involvement in the political, social, and literary history of Italy are closely meshed in his poetry.

"Sonetti"

Foscolo's twelve sonnets (known collectively as the "Sonetti"), which combine the strength of Dante and the melancholy of Petrarch, have much in common with his novel *Last Letters of Jacopo Ortis*: the oppressive influence of Fate on politics and personal life, hints of suicide, the pleasures and despair of love, and a sense of hostility against the invaders of Italy. There is in these sonnets, however, a new sense of nature, a more ironic and melancholic approach to the political problems of Italy, and a more lyric treatment of autobiographical themes such as love, exile, death of loved ones, and exhortations to achieve glory through poetry.

In the sonnet "Te nudrice alle muse" ("You Nurturer of the Muses"), addressed to Italy, Foscolo complains about the proposed abolition of the Latin language, a proposal made by the legislature of the Cisalpina Republic. This sonnet at first appears to be academic and traditional in structure, theme, and style, reflecting the influence of Alfieri and the neoclassical literary forms of the late eighteenth century. There is, nevertheless, an innovative element in this sonnet: the first use by Foscolo of a technique, later perfected in *On Sepulchers*, by which the various sections of a poem are related by larger, "historical" logic rather than by conventional syntactic logic. The two quatrains of this sonnet refer to the past, while, without any apparent connective tissue, the tercets ironically address Italy on the inconveniences that would be caused by the abolition of the Latin language. The logic that related quatrains and tercets reflects the overlying concept that there can be no contemporary Italian language and culture without reference to the language and culture of the past.

The sonnet "E tu?" ("And You?") also contrasts quatrains and tercets: The quatrains have an *abba-abba* rhyme scheme and are historical in content, while the tercets rhyme *aba-cbc* and are erotic in theme and mood. The poet starts by using heroic, quasi-Ossianic terminology to recall the medieval fights in Florence; then, in a more lyric fashion, he praises Florence as the dwelling place of his beloved.

"Ne più" ("Never Again"), another sonnet from this collection, speaks of the tragedy of the exiled Foscolo. The poet, though Italian by birth and education, will never be able to forget that he was born of a Greek mother in the luminous and wooded Zacinto, and that his poetry echoes Homer and Theocritus. Foscolo recalls his island and the myths of Venus and Ulysses with a surge of melody in full rhymes. The first statement nostalgically affirms that he will never again set foot on the sacred shore of his native island and, unlike Ulysses, will not be granted burial in his native land. The last tercet, however, brings the consolation that, if not his body, at least his song will return to Zacinto: Poetry will be his means of immortality.

The Foscolo of the "Sonetti" reaches a climax of poetic inspiration when he turns from history and mythology to treat his personal life or naturalistically perceived objects. A vein of melancholy emerges in sonnets such as "Perché taccia il rumor di mia catena" ("To Hush the Clangor of My Chain"), "Forse perché della fatal quiete" ("Perhaps Because of the Fateful Quiet"), and "Un dì, s'io non andrò sempre fuggendo" ("One Day, Should I Not Always Flee"). In these sonnets, for example, there are autobiographical references to his unfortunate love for the Florentine Isabella Roncioni and to the death of his brother John, which reminds him of his exile.

The sonnet "Perhaps Because of the Fateful Quiet" is a dialogue with the evening; it moves in a thickly harmonious structure from the proposal of the theme through a central part to the conclusion. Its merit, as Foscolo himself said, lies in producing, through a broken structure, the same effects that musicians achieve through dissonance and painters achieve through shading. The poem starts with monosyllables and bisyllables, pauses at the fourth line in perfect lyric hendecasyllables until the eighth line, and then begins again the tormented rhythmic pattern. In a fashion reminiscent of Edward Young and Giuseppe Parini, Foscolo writes of the evening that is dear to him because it is the image of death; it keeps the secret paths of his heart, promising rest for his ever-warring spirit.

"To Louise Pallavicini Fallen from a Horse"

During the same years in which these sonnets were composed (1800-1802), Foscolo also wrote two *odi*: "A Luigia Pallavicini caduta da cavallo" ("To Louise Pallavicini Fallen from a Horse") and "All'amica risanata" ("To the Healed Friend"), for Antonietta Fagnani Arese. These two odes praise the beauty of and virtually deify the two women to whom they are dedicated. The autobiographical elements and controlled poetic expertise of the sonnets continue in these odes, which are additionally characterized by literary eclecticism and imagery drawn from pagan mythology.

The first ode describes a fall that the beautiful Louise took from a horse and expresses the wish that she will recover and become more beautiful than before. The whole poem is supported by mythic prototypes: Venus stung on the foot while leaning over the dead body of Ado, the "bath of Pallas," the intervention of Neptune against the enraged horse, and finally the fall of Diana into the volcano Etna, followed by her recovery. Though the poem's structure (eighteen stanzas of six lines each) is taken from Carlo Frugoni, and its imagery is inherited from poets such as Ludovico Ariosto, Poliziano, and Alfieri, Foscolo proves his mastery of form, style, and imagination by achieving a certain degree of seriousness in a lyric genre which in eighteenth century Italy had a rather light, occasional status. In Foscolo's work, goddesses care for human suffering and exchange feelings of love with mortal creatures. The highly artificial tone characteristic of occasional verse does not diminish the sense of beauty and serenity which this ode evokes, foreshadowing Foscolo's more mature work in *Le grazie*.

"To the Healed Friend"

The second ode, "To the Healed Friend," usually viewed in relation to the passionate letters that Foscolo wrote to Antonietta Fagnani Arese, is, by contrast, carefully controlled in emotion. The process of deification is more stylized here than in the ode to Louise Pallavicini. The poet begins with a description of the healing of his beloved, again using mythological allusions. The deification reaches its climax when the poet declares that his verses will be the woman's salvation from death and from the jealousy of others. The conclusion reiterates the mood of the earlier sonnet to his native island, "Ne più mai toccherò le sacre sponde" ("I Will Never Touch Again the Sacred Shore") and anticipates the poem *Le grazie* with a recollection of the spirit of Sappho and the sound of Greek poetry. As in the first ode, Foscolo contemplates evil and death only to distance himself from them, to aspire to a higher sense of beauty and eternity.

On Sepulchers

In considering *On Sepulchers*, Giovanni Getto, in *La composizione dei "Sepolcri" di Ugo Foscolo* (1977), observes that the three images—suggesting nature, civilization, and death—presented at the beginning of the poem, represent the complex symbol of *On Sepulchers*'s entire figurative world. The poem draws together all the poetic motifs of Foscolo's earlier work into a new and powerful synthesis. The dialectic of this poem is, ultimately, between death and immortality. If the evils of this life cannot be avoided, immortality may be attained through memory, as evidenced by burial monuments, for after death, the hero will obtain at least this measure of glory. In the various shadings of *On Sepulchers*, Foscolo continuously fuses images and contrasting tones and creates the highly individual syntax that distinguishes his verse.

On Sepulchers is infused with a sense of melancholy, mystery, and historicism. After evoking life, nature, poetry, and hopes broken by death, Foscolo blames the new Napoleonic law for having placed the bones of great men and those of thieves in the same tomb. He remembers then the sensible pagan rituals in honor of the virtuous dead, contrasting them with the superstitious rites of Christianity, which are characterized by a fear of the next world. He then passes to a historical vision in praise of Florence, where Dante and the parents of Petrarch were born, and where Machiavelli, Michelangelo, and Galileo are buried in Santa Croce. The sense of heroism and of the regeneration of the Italian nation comes from a tie between the living and the dead. This is why the heroic spirits of the past inspired Homer, especially the spirit of Hector, the greatest and most unfortunate of all heroes.

For Foscolo, poetry was one of the most pure and significant achievements of humankind. His translations from Homer in the period preceding the composition of *On Sepulchers* inspired him to celebrate the heros of the past in order to unite former times with the present in an ineffable harmony. The occasional, the meditative, the narrative, and the fantastic impulses all converge in this poem. Unlike *Last Letters of Jacopo Ortis*, which echoes the Titanism of Alfieri, and unlike the "Sonetti," which expresses the solitude and the horror of Foscolo's life, *On Sepulchers* testifies to the poet's liberation from his past passions. From the beginning, the reader of *On Sepulchers* has in front of his eyes not a bare tomb but a sepulcher comforted by the tears of the living, because "Hope, the last Goddess, flees the sepulchers." From reason to fantasy, from the past to the present, from the dead to the living, from autobiographical references to the recollection of the great poets and heroes of the past, Foscolo develops his themes like a symphony. The initial rhetorical question in *On Sepulchers*, in which the desolation of death is clearly stated, is finally transformed into the attitude that all people worthy of glory, such as Hector, will have the "honor of tears as long as the sun will shine over human afflictions."

LE GRAZIE

The interrelationship between poetry and the other arts, while present in Foscolo's earlier poetry, becomes central in *Le grazie*. The vision of poetry that eternalizes heroism through emulation of living people, as found in *On Sepulchers*, is here replaced with poetry that focuses on beauty, which educates the human spirit to reveal the secret consonance of the universe.

Aldo Vallone, in *Le Grazie nella storia della poesia foscoliana* (1977), has remarked that the neoclassicism of *On Sepulchers* becomes for Foscolo in *Le grazie* the natural way of composing poetry. The expressive elements contained in this ambitious allegorical and didactic poem, which remained unfinished at Foscolo's death, reveal his absolute mastery of his material. By technical devices such as the usage of certain prepositions, of narrative sections, and of repetition of key words, Foscolo suggests at one moment the shading of the verse, while at another moment he reestablishes equilibrium among the various segments of the poem, producing an effect of musical lyricism.

Composing *Le grazie* while at the villa Bellosguardo, near Florence, Foscolo was inspired by the Venus of Canova and the statuary group of the Graces. The poem also reveals the influence of the neoclassical aesthetics of Johann Joachim Winckelmann, and marks Foscolo's passage from pure to critical lyric. This is not to say that there is any lack of images or lyric pleasure; on the contrary, critical and poetic thoughts are here combined. The philosophical intuition of reality as harmony goes side by side with passion and melancholy.

In the tradition of Homer and Callimachus, three hymns compose *Le grazie*. The first hymn is dedicated to Venus, goddess of beauty, the second to Vesta, goddess of the hearth, and the third to Pallas, goddess of the arts. According to *Le grazie*, aesthetics were born in Greece, and with them civilization began. Italy became the major theater of civilization, and there music, dance, lyric language, greatness of mind, and physical beauty gave rebirth to the Graces—that is, to Harmony. This concept is presented in the second hymn and poetically developed by the image of a sacrifice made by three of the women Foscolo loved: Nencini, with a harp; Martinetti, with a honeycomb; and Bignami, with a swan. The last hymn takes the reader to the middle of an ocean on an ethereal Earth. Pallas, in fact, weaves a veil that exalts youth, love, hospitality, maternal affection, and filial piety. With this veil, she covers the Graces so that they can protect themselves from passion.

The form of the three hymns seems to be less impetuous than that of *On Sepulchers*: Dissonances are softened, and the verse has a smoother and less luminous modulation.

OTHER MAJOR WORKS

LONG FICTION: *Ultime Lettere di Jacopo Ortis*, 1802 (*Last Letters of Jacopo Ortis*, 1970).

PLAYS: *Tieste*, pr. 1797; *Aiace*, pr. 1811; *Ricciarda*, pr. 1813.

NONFICTION: *Orazione a Bonaparte pel Congresso di Lione*, 1802; *Dell'origine e dell'ufficio della letteratura*, 1809; *Notizie intorno a Didimo Chierico*, 1813; *Essay on the Present Literature of Italy*, 1818; *Saggi sul Petrarca*, 1821 (*Essays on Petrarch*, 1823); *Della servitu d'Italia*, 1823; *Discorso storico sul testo del "Decamerone,"* 1825; *Discorso sul testo e su le opinioni diverse prevalenti intorno alla storia e alla emendazione critica della "Commedia" di Dante*, 1825; *On the New Dramatic School in Italy*, 1826; *Epistolario*, 1949-1970 (7 volumes).

TRANSLATIONS: *La chioma di Berenice*, 1803 (of Callimachus's poetry); *Esperimenti di traduzione della "Iliade" di Omero*, 1807 (of Homer's *Iliad*); *Viaggio sentimentale di Yorick lungo la Francia e l'Italia*, 1813 (of Laurence Sterne's *A Sentimental Journey*).

BIBLIOGRAPHY

Cambon, Glauco. *Ugo Foscolo: Poet of Exile*. Princeton, N.J.: Princeton University Press, 1980. A critical study of the works of Foscolo. Includes index.

Franzero, Charles Marie. *A Life in Exile: Ugo Foscolo in London, 1816-1827*. London: Allen, 1977. A biography focusing on Foscolo's life in London.

Magill, Frank N., Dayton Kohler, and Laurence W. Mazzeno, eds. *Masterplots: 1,801 Plot Stories and Critical Evaluations of the World's Finest Literature*. 2d ed. Pasadena, Calif.: Salem Press, 1996. Contains an in-depth analysis of *On Sepulchers*.

Matteo, Sante. *Textual Exile: The Reader in Sterne and Foscolo*. New York: Peter Lang, 1985. A study of Foscolo and Laurence Sterne. Substantial bibliography.

O'Neill, Tom. *Of Virgin Muses and of Love: A Study of Foscolo's "Dei sepolcri."* Dublin: Irish Academic Press, 1981. In-depth study of *On Sepulchers*. Includes bibliographical references and index.

Parmegiani, Susan. *Ugo Foscolo and English Culture*. London: Maney, 2010. Focuses on Foscolo's experiences in England and the effect on his writings.

Radcliff-Umstead, Douglas. *Ugo Foscolo*. New York: Twayne, 1970. An introductory biography and critical analysis of selected works by Foscolo. Includes bibliographic references.

Adriano Moz

GIROLAMO FRACASTORO

Born: Verona, Republic of Venice (now in Italy); c. 1478
Died: Incaffi, near Verona, Republic of Venice (now in Italy); August 6, 1553
Also known as: Hieronymus Fracastorius

PRINCIPAL POETRY

Syphilis sive morbus Gallicus, 1530 (*Syphilis: Or, A Poetical History of the French Disease*, 1686)
Ioseph, pb. 1555 (wr. c. 1540-1545; *The Maiden's Blush: Or, Joseph*, 1620)

OTHER LITERARY FORMS

Foremost among the prose work of Girolamo Fracastoro (fro-ko-STAW-roh) is the treatise *Syphilis* (wr. 1553, pb. 1939). Other scientific pieces include *Homocentricorum sive de stellis* (1538; homocentricity on the stars), *De causis criticorum dierum libellus* (1538; on the causes of critical days), *De sympathia et antipathia rerum* (1546; on the attraction and repulsion of things), *De contagionibus et contagiosis morbis et eorum curatione* (1546; *De contagione et contagiosis morbis et eorum curatione*, 1930), and *De vini temperatura* (1534). Also of interest are three Humanistic dialogues: *Naugerius sive de poetica dialogus* (1549; English translation, 1924), and the unfinished "Turrius sive de intellectione dialogus" and "Fracastorius sive de anima dialogus," which were published posthumously in the *Opera omnia* of 1555.

A play, *La Venexiana* (the Venetian, or Venetian comedy), was discovered in 1928 by Emilio Lovarini, deciphered from manuscript miscellany collected in 1780 by Iacopo Morelli. No other text is known, and no mention was made of the play in its time, although it seems to have been written after 1509. The play was published twice by Lovarini, in 1928 and in 1947. A pseudonym, Hieronymous Zarello, was applied to the work, but the Fracastoro expert Girlando Lentini attested its authenticity in his August, 1948, article, "Non piu anonima la Venexiana," in the *Giornale di Sicilia*. The play was published in 1950 in a bilingual edition with introduction and English translation by Matilde Valenti Pfeiffer. The work has been described by Pfeiffer as "one of the earliest character plays in world literature." Its alternation of long and short episodes during the course of four days and its shift of place and mood anticipate the dramaturgy of William Shakespeare. In five acts, its six characters convey the vulnerability of romantic love. The play moves quickly; the characters are quaint and boldly drawn; the language is unusually pithy and droll. It is a rare document of Venetian life, as its epigraph avers: "Non fabula non comedia ma vera historia" ("Neither fable, nor comedy, but real history").

Another work, "Apocalisse" (apocalypse), extant among Fracastoro's manuscripts as late as 1700, is now lost. W. Parr Greswell notes as well that Fracastoro's "Citriorum epigrammata" and many of his smaller pieces are lost. In referring to Fracastoro's accumulated writings, it is important to note Murray Bundy's observation that "little attempt has ever been made to establish a critical text or to determine chronology."

Achievements

Girolamo Fracastoro was a Renaissance man in the finest sense of the term. As poet, scholar, scientist, and physician, he embodied the essence of sixteenth century curiosity and Humanistic commitment. Greswell states that "perhaps the productions of no other modern poet have been more commended by the learned, than those of Fracastoro."

Fracastoro's research and writing on infectious diseases drew attention in 1530 when he determined the origin of an epidemic of syphilis in Naples at the time of Charles VIII. It is generally believed that Fracastoro named the disease after the amorous shepherd of Greek mythology, who was punished by the sun god for his infidelity. (Other sources assert that the word derives from *sifilide*, a term in common usage in the local dialect.) A later work, *De contagione et contagiosis morbis et eorum curatione*, dealing with typhus, tuberculosis, and syphilis, developed the concept of infection by transfer of minute organisms from diseased individuals to healthy ones.

In *De sympathia et antipathia rerum*, Fracastoro discussed a concept of *simpatia* different from that of his Humanist contemporaries. For him, it was a *species spiritualis* that unified the world, a cosmological principle that was to be studied naturalistically, one that applied to both anthropological and aesthetic concepts. This concentration of research is also present in *De causis criticorum dierum libellus*. Fracastoro's emphasis in this treatise was so advanced (he located the causes of disease in microorganisms rather than in astral or numerological relationships) as to cause his biographer, Bruno Zanobio, to comment that "the traditional position of philosophy is turned upside down: philosophy is such to the extent that it investigates not abstract but concrete nature."

Fracastoro was renowned as a physician, but his knowledge of astronomy, literature, and philosophy reflected the comprehensive talents of the learned men of his time. Familiar with the new theories made possible by the use of the telescope, he criticized the employment of epicycles and deferents in astronomy and was the first to use the geographical term "pole" when referring to the magnetic extremes of the Earth. In his work *Homocentricorum sive de stellis*, Fracastoro declared that experience was the only valid scientific method, and he furnished illustrations of the movements of celestial bodies, their orbits, the seasons, and the various types of days (civil, solar, and sidereal). The work was apparently known to Giordano Bruno, who included Fracastoro as one of the interlocutors in Bruno's dialogue *De l'infinito universo et mondi* (1583; *Of the Infinite Universe and Worlds*, 1950). The biographer Roberto Massalongo went so far as to assert that the work "paved the way" for the great theories of Nicholas Copernicus. Indeed, Fracastoro was read carefully in the nineteenth century by Alexander von Humboldt, who considered Fracastoro's geological investigations significant enough to classify him with Leonardo da Vinci as a scientist far in advance of his time.

Biography

Girolamo Fracastoro was born around 1478 into a very ancient and honorable patrician family, the son of Paolo Philippo and Camilla dei Mascarelli, of a wellborn family of Vicenza. An esteemed ancestor, Aventino Fracastoro, was a celebrated physician of Scala and a gentleman of Verona; he died in 1368, and his tomb in the Church of San Fermo must have been a constant reminder to the young Girolamo of his noble lineage.

Two oddities regarding Fracastoro's birth and early years have been noted by numerous biographers. At birth, his lips were so tightly sealed that a surgeon's knife was required to separate them. Julius Caesarus Scaliger referred to the event in one of the twenty-seven epigrams in his *Altars in Honor of Fracastoro* (1554), relating that the god of medicine and poetry, Apollo himself, intervened at Fracastoro's birth to create a mouth for the poet. The other extraordinary event was the death of his mother (some say his nurse), who was struck and killed by lightning while holding the young Fracastoro in her arms. There is no further record of the effects of these events on the young poet. Reports agree, however, that his intellect was early noted and that no expense was spared regarding his education.

Fracastoro entered the University of Padua as an adolescent and exhibited a desire to master every science that occupied his attention, demonstrating a singularly advanced proficiency in mathematics. In addition, he studied literature, astronomy (astrology at that time), medicine, and philosophy, the last with Nicolo Leonico Tomeo and Pietro Pomponazzi. Pomponazzi was a tutor in Aristotle, Averroës, and Alexander of Aphrodisias, and received considerable attention for a paper he wrote that was incorrectly interpreted as calling into question the immortality of the soul.

Upon receiving his degree in 1502, Fracastoro became an instructor in logic and also served as *conciliarius anatomicus*, giving lectures on medicine and anatomy. It was at this time that he met a young medical student named Nicolaus Copernicus. Other colleagues and acquaintances who were to play roles in his literary activities were Alessandro Farnese (later Pope Paul III), Gaspar Contarenus and Ercole Gonzaga (later made cardinals), Giovanni Matteo Giberti (subsequently bishop of Verona), Pietro Bembo (dedicatee of his most significant work of poetry and personal secretary to Pope Leo X), Andreas Navagero (dedicatee of Fracastoro's work on poetics and a national historian and ambassador), and the brothers Marcus Antonius, Joannes Baptista, and Raymundo della Torre (all utilized as characters in Fracastoro's literary "dialogues").

Fracastoro married young, possibly in 1500; his wife, Elena, who was apparently five years older than her husband, died in 1540. They had five children, four sons and one daughter, only two of whom survived their father. During the period of national strife after the League of Cambria, Fracastoro took refuge in the Republic of Venice, where he enjoyed the patronage of General Alviano, serving as personal physician and as an instructor in the informal academy that Alviano had established in Pordenone. Niccolò Machiavelli commented on the precarious situation of the Venetian and

Veronese states at this time. German, Spanish, French, and Swiss troops were all garrisoned in the area at one time or another, and plague was rampant. Soon after the defeat of the Venetian forces, Fracastoro retired to the villa in Incaffi and alternated residence between there and Verona, some fifteen miles distant. The villa was a peaceful retreat, frequented regularly by writers, scientists, philosophers, and artists. Fracastoro himself has described it in the eulogy for Marcus Antonius della Torre:

> Here acts, absolv'd from modish fashion's school
> Nor moves in measur'd steps, nor stands by rule
> But drinks at pleasure, and reclines at ease
> No laws to trammel, no fops to tease.

Between 1509 and 1530, Fracastoro actively practiced medicine and continued his research in botany, cosmography, and infectious diseases. Fracastoro was an eminent physician, serving Catherine de Médicis, and was once called to serve as court physician to Marguerite of Navarre. The early version of *Syphilis: Or, A Poetical History of the French Disease* (not to be confused with Fracastoro's treatise on the same subject) was completed by 1525, and Fracastoro's retirement to study and to write coincides with its publication in 1530 (his first work to issue from a printing press). By that time, he was no longer happy to be recognized primarily as a physician, though it was in this capacity that he was subsequently called on by Pope Paul III (Alessandro Farnese) to serve as medical adviser (*medicus conductus et stipendiatus*) to the Council of Trent in 1545.

At the time, the pope was very concerned about both security and the political ramifications of holding the Council in Trent; his preference was Bologna. Fracastoro's assessment of the danger of epidemic convinced the authorities of the wisdom of the change. Fracastoro's influence on the decision to move the council from Trent to Bologna suggests the stature of his professional opinion. In 1546, Fracastoro was made a canon of Verona. Though always interested in politics, he never held public office.

Fracastoro died of cerebral apoplexy on August 6, 1553. He had predicted such a death, which occurred without the attendance of either physician or priest. Earlier, he had saved the life of a nun who was suffering from the same affliction by application of a remedy of his own devising. Ironically, his servants failed to understand his motions calling for medical aid in his own case, and he is said to have died quite resigned to his fate. Though there is some controversy concerning his place of burial, his body reputedly rests in the ruins of the parish church of Saint Eufemia, near the villa in Incaffi; the church itself has been destroyed. Soon after his death, an effigy in bronze was placed in the Benedictine cloister near Verona. In Verona itself, south of the Porta Vittoria, is a *cimitero* with monuments to the city's greatest citizens. Fracastoro's name can be found most prominently over the alcove designated number one. In 1559, a statue of Fracastoro by Danese Cataneo was erected in the Piazza dei Signiori, near those of Catullus, Napos, Macer, Vitruvius, and Dante.

Analysis

Girolamo Fracastoro flourished in the atmosphere of the Italian Renaissance, when the diminished influence of theological study gave way to an increased interest in science and nature. The contemplative attitude was gradually replaced by a more aggressive operative one. Nature was viewed as an autonomous reality with its own laws before which supernatural intervention was of minimal use. Humans were forced to rely on their capacity for progressive understanding of the principles that regulated the natural world.

Syphilis

Such were the ideas that made up the narrative poem *Syphilis*, on which rests Fracastoro's literary fame. Written in 1521 and dedicated to Bembo, the poem consists of thirteen hundred verses in Latin hexameter (not verses in the contemporary sense of stanzas, but blocks of copy in his handwritten manuscript); in the words of Bruno Zanobio, it "represents a magnificent paradigm of formal sixteenth century virtuosity in refined Latin of a didactic quality reminiscent of Vergil's *Georgics* (37-30 B.C.E.). The work reveals the author's early concept of *seminaria* (microorganisms), a concept that he derived from the pre-Socratic philosopher Democritus by way of the *semina morbi* of Lucretius's *De rerum natura* (c. 60 B.C.E.; *On the Nature of Things*, 1682), available to Fracastoro in a 1515 translation by his friend Andreas Navagero.

It is significant to note the exercise of poetic license in the application of some scientific terms. Meter altered the use of terminology in these cases: *contages* was used for *contagio* (contact or touch); *seminaria* for *semina* (seeds); *achores* for *pustula* (sores, infections). This was the case earlier, when Lucretius used *pestilitas* for *pestilentia* (pestilence or plague). Fracastoro's *seminaria* differ from traditional *semina*, however, and it is difficult to know if the author foresaw the actual existence of microbes. The inability at the time to distinguish between organic and inorganic and the belief in spontaneous generation would probably have prevented Fracastoro from assigning to his *seminaria* the characteristics of microorganisms as they are known today.

Fracastoro developed the concept further in a prose treatise, also entitled *Syphilis*, which was completed in 1553 but not published until 1939. Zanobio interprets Fracastoro's work on syphilis to be his new premise for the construction of a philosophy of nature: "Nature creates and destroys and gives misery and happiness, and it is useless to appease the gods. Science, whose power alone can give joy, dictates man's actions." Fracastoro's most significant contribution to the scientific side of syphilography was *De contagione et contagiosis morbis et eorum curatione*, published sixteen years after the poem *Syphilis*. Leona Baumgartner and John F. Fulton observe that in his concept of animate contagion, Fracastoro was "a precursor of [Louis] Pasteur and [Robert] Koch."

The poem *Syphilis* was an immediate success and earned extravagant praise from many sides. Bembo announced that the work equaled that of Lucretius and Vergil.

Jacopo Sannazzaro, a contemporary and a cruel critic of anyone who threatened to challenge his own supremacy, commented that it surpassed his *De partu virginium* (1527; of Virgin birth), a work twenty years in process. It was neither the first nor the last poem on the subject, but it was the longest, the most serious, the most eloquent, and by far the best publicized.

An early version of the poem was completed by 1521; the date has been established through Fracastoro's mention of Pope Leo as being still alive (the pope died in 1522). The author first presented the work to Bembo in a two-book version. Bembo suggested changes, among which was the deletion of a myth on the origin of mercury as a remedy. He thought it too obvious an imitation of Aristaeus in Vergil's *Georgics*. Fracastoro rejected most of the suggested changes but did expand the work to three books.

The earliest extant version, published in 1530, is referred to as the "Verona text." In this text, two verses are omitted, while the lines beginning "Quo tandem . . ." and "Aetheris inuisas . . ." have been entered, apparently in Fracastoro's own hand, on the "authorized" or "Rome text" of the following year. This change is not found in other contemporary editions, and there were no other changes in seven subsequent editions published in the author's lifetime. The omitted lines are not included in the *Opera omnia* of 1555 but are in the one of 1574. The poem is found in more than one hundred editions; it has appeared many times in Latin editions, eleven Latin versions of which are in the *Opera omnia*. Many bilingual editions exist, with several editions in English. It has appeared in six languages.

SYPHILIS, BOOK 1

Book 1 of *Syphilis* begins with a consideration of the "varied chances of things" that appear responsible for the dread disease. The author observes "how number governs moved things and things moving," a possible reference to the theories of Pythagoras and Heraclitus. Fracastoro, as a protobacteriologist, determines that the "origin of the affliction" is to be found in the air; the *semina morbi* (diseased seeds) are *semina coeli* (germs of the heavens). References to seeds, germs, atoms, and corpuscles can be traced to the writings of Lucretius and Epicurus, but Fracastoro makes the observation that this affliction strikes only the *humanum genus* (human race), Vergil's *ingens genus*, the race having mind and reason.

"Into Italy, it broke with the Frenchmen's war and after them it was named [*morbus Gallicus*]." Although the disease did not at that time carry the onus of immorality it subsequently assumed, it was referred to by the Italians as "the French disease," by the French as "the Neapolitan evil," by the Germans and English as "the French pox and Bordeaux evil," in Holland and North Africa as "the Spanish pox," in Portugal as "the Castilian disease," in Persia and Turkey as "the Christian disease," in Russia as "the Polish disease," and in Poland as "the German disease."

Italy at the time of the poem's composition was torn by conflicts with Louis XII of

France and Maximilian of Germany. The country was suffering from plague, famine, and war. It is not surprising, then, that the author should designate Mars as influential in the country's misfortunes: "Venus and Mars the dire/ Against all humans, planets would conspire/ . . . when they converge at some spot in the skies." Giovanni Boccaccio in his *Decameron: O, Prencipe Galeotto* (1349-1351; *The Decameron*, 1620) had referred to the influence of celestial bodies that resulted in the Black Death. Guy de Chauliac, a famous fourteenth century French surgeon, had attributed the plague to the conjunction of Saturn and Mars on March 22, 1345, in the fourteenth degree of Aquarius: "Two centuries before this, in the skies/ Saturn and Mars would lock their silent cars." Fracastoro himself drew an astrological parallel to the syzygy of the same planets in the sign of Cancer: "Jupiter calls a congress of the stars/ Evoking Saturn and the war god Mars . . . he calls the Crab . . . to open the double doors of heaven's halls." By the "god's decree . . . to the air is this new poison given, the effluvium of homicide." With the introduction of Sirius, the air carries "the seeds of poison everywhere." Here, the author invents a new god who has no basis in classical mythology and is indeed a fictitious character offering prophecy. Such an expediency was often resorted to by fifteenth and sixteenth century writers.

Fracastoro, however, writes as a physician, a man of science, and he proceeds to reveal the difficulties of his investigation. The halting speech of the poet results from the delay with which the heavens confront the scientist as he seeks to link the disease to the things that cause it. "Making no advance," he fears that much "hangs on the play of chance." As he proceeds to "comb the symptoms," he finds that the disease is at home both in hovel and in court. Its symptoms are never quite the same. "Its form and seed vary everywhere/ Knowing no bounds and limits, peoples, states . . . it flashes through the air." He does, however, ascertain that it survives four months of incubation, "shutting the moon's disc four times." To more dramatically delineate this "hideous leprosy," Fracastoro describes the personal plight of a handsome youth of Brescia: "Gone is the brilliance of his youth and spring/ Dying by inches his soul sinks. . . ." This graphic depiction is extended to include the suffering of Fracastoro's native land as well as the personal grief he feels with the premature death of his friend Marcus Antonius della Torre. Wright refers to this final section of book 1 as "some of the finest verse ever done by Fracastoro, indeed by any Latin poet of the period." The following invocation to Italy has been deemed by Mario Truffi as the equal of Petrarch and Giacomo Leopardi:

> Dear land, my land, that only yesterday
> Hoped for the happiness of peace profound.
> O soil of heroes! God's land! Holy ground,
> Where is your ancient treasure? Torn away.
> Your breasts, prodigious for Adige's flood,
> Gave you fecundities so passing good.
> Today, O Italy, what colors drear

Depict your suffering, your ills, your fear?
Trembling are all the strings of my poor lute
To tell of your misfortunes, but are mute.
Garda, go hide your shame amidst your reeds.
Laurels no longer seek your water's needs.

Fracastoro demonstrates dramatic concern on many levels. One analogy connects the desolate River Adige and Lake Garda, into which it flows near his home, with the desecrated blood of his nation: "The Adige bathes in new sterility, having lost its ancient force." Another parallel is drawn between the decline of the country and the death of della Torre: "Noble Anthony passes and naught can save him from the tomb, still in the bloom of spring, O Italy!" Fracastoro finally resorts again to the poetic muse to save his country: "The mellow lyre of old Catullus hand/ Might stir your woods again, O Fatherland." This allusion to classical poetry would not have been lost on the author's contemporaries. Bembo related that the work "makes me think the soul of Vergil has passed into [Fracastoro]."

SYPHILIS, BOOK 2

Book 2 of *Syphilis* includes, as did book 1, the customary encomiums to Bembo ("armed in his humility, whose sheer ability is equal to the grandest name") and to Pope Leo X ("Prince, whose fame is more than great"), that they might turn a willing ear to the poet's voice. It also pays tribute to Sannazzaro, the "Christian Vergil," as "Fornello's god, a new poet's voice/ That made old Vergil's epic heart rejoice."

Soon, "in fear and trembling," Fracastoro "takes up his pen" to prescribe medication and treatment. His prescriptions are many and varied—some, clearly, dated folk remedies and others still in use today. One of the first is "Spain's ornament, the pride of Italy," the lemon tree. "Beloved of Venus," it acquired its power through the tears Venus shed for Adonis, which were "shut within the golden rind a gift/ Of heav'nly virtues, energetic, swift." There follow in rapid succession both exotic and common reliefs: myrrh of Arabia, frankincense from Libya, and apopanax from the Nile, as well as cinnamon, bittercress, cassia, cucumber, turpeth, saffron, mint, thyme, ladysmantle, briony, chicory, hartstongue, and hops, these last as common "pharmacopia of the day." In addition, one finds salves and ointments made from oil, wool fat, honey, goose fat, linseed paste, starwort, and narcissus. Other applications include copper and potassium nitrates and oxides of lead, antimony, and storax. Considering that bloodletting was also part of the cure, the activities prescribed are strange: hunting, a form of tennis, and wood chopping—"Be active if you wish to keep alive."

The use of mercury is traced at this point to a mythological origin. The Syrian shepherd Ilceo has incurred the wrath of Diana and Phoebus for killing a favorite deer. He has been stricken with a disease for which no remedy exists under the sun. The goddess

Calliroe appears to him, however, and directs him to a nymph, Lipare, who leads him to a cave below Mount Etna wherein is found a stream in which flows a liquid metal (quicksilver). It is interesting to note that this substance, mercury, was known for its medicinal properties to Aristotle as *arguron chuton*, and to Pliny the Younger as *argentum vivum*. Such treatment was also applied in the intervening centuries by Rhazes and Avicenna.

The Ilceo myth probably represented a nonclassical reference for Fracastoro. The name is not found elsewhere, and Bembo thought it a poor choice of material. It is of interest to note, however, that it is this section of the work that Greswell chose to excerpt in the *Memoirs of Angelus Politianus, Joannes Picus of Mirandula, Actius Sincerus Sannazzarius, Pietrus Bembus, Hieronymous Fracastorius, and the Amalthei* (1801). Wright observes that the author's language becomes less poetic in the closing section of the book, after the telling of the myth, as Fracastoro relates the therapeutic marvels of the common herbs as skin treatment.

Syphilis, Book 3

Truffi finds the third book of *Syphilis* to be the "best from the poetic side." In this section, Fracastoro praises Christopher Columbus for his explorations in the New World ("yoking the mountains in a mighty quest"); Fracastoro was the first to use Columbus's achievement as poetic material. Fracastoro's Columbus desperately invokes the moon to reveal land to him and his fatigued mariners. There then appears a sea nymph, who directs him to the island of Ofiri (Haiti, scene of the first European landing in the Americas on December 6, 1492). The sailors anger the gods by shooting forest birds sacred to Apollo, whereupon they are cursed. This episode parallels scenes in the *Odyssey* (c. 725 B.C.E.; English translation, 1614) and in Vergil's *Aeneid* (c. 29-19 B.C.E.; English translation, 1553). The remedy for their affliction is to be found in "seeking aid from the same forest they profaned."

The "aborigines" whom they encounter on the island are descendants of the Atlanteans, the cursed remnants of an ancient race, who are afflicted with a disease that demonstrates "a living path/ Of what the gods invented in their wrath." Fracastoro relates their plight through the legend of Sifilo (Syphilis). During a particularly long and devastating drought, Syphilis, a shepherd for King Ilceo, inveighed against the sun god and instead venerated King Ilceo. Syphilis advocated similar conduct on the part of others until they, "braving gods, denying gods, devastating temples fair," convinced Ilceo of his own glory, and the King, in "mad joy and blinded thus, commanded that each state receive him as a god." It was at this point that the "island paradise received the evil of a subtle seed.... He who wrought this outrage was the first, and after him this malady is called Syphilis, and even the King escaped not its attack."

Upon consultation, the nymph America advised a sacrifice. Initially, Syphilis was designated, but through the intercession of Juno (recalling the legend of Iphigenia and the biblical story of Isaac), a substitution was made—in this case, a black cow's blood to appease Terra (Tellus, Latin deity of the earth) and a white heifer to change Juno's mood. The blood of the beast created "fecund seeds in Tellus's vast breast," which became the *lignum-sanctum* (Guaiacum tree) from which was extracted the syphilis cure: "the lignumsanctum you must/ Cull, lest disaster fall on every one/ For a bird-murder and an outraged sun." Thus, it was determined that "Every year a shepherd symbolizes/ The victim; ancient are the sacrifices." The author ends his work by appealing to Apollo (and to Bembo) that his poem be remembered, "as descendants may one day wish to read of signs and appearance of the disease."

Again, it should be noted that there was in Fracastoro's time no hint of immorality involved with the disease. To the contrary, Fracastoro asserts in his poem that the disease "hatched from a poison that no vice has wrought," though he does refer to it as venereal (from Latin *venereus*, love) in the prose adaptation written later.

NAUGERIUS SIVE DE POETICA DIALOGUS

In *Naugerius sive de poetica dialogus*, the focus of Fracastoro's aesthetics is revealed. According to Zanobio, Fracastoro determined that neither content nor form rendered the essence of the poetic but rather "intuition, the universal present in all things and expressing itself in the judgment that regulates them." Bundy sees this as "the view of a pagan of the Renaissance quite in sympathy with the frank aestheticism of the majority of contemporary [1924] artists." John Addington Symonds praised Fracastoro's writing from a literary standpoint, suggesting that it "recalls the purity of phrase of Catullus." Bundy further notes that Fracastoro's use of the dialogue is Ciceronian in both form and substance, in that Fracastoro employed the later Latin variation on Plato of using less dramatic, more real characters, as did Fracastoro's contemporaries Giovanni Pontano, Sperone Speroni, Antonio Minturno, and Gimabattisto Gyraldus. Ciceronian as well is the "absence of philosophical first principles directing the course of the dialogue; [Fracastoro] is frankly eclectic rather than a great original thinker."

Fracastoro's *Naugerius sive de poetic dialogus* not only presents a theory of the poetic but also presents it as "consummate art" itself. According to Bundy, "The symmetry, the beauty of external form, illustrates the ideal which he sets forth." Bundy further asserts that in this work Fracastoro was one of the first writers of the Renaissance to formulate in elegant manner a concept close to Aristotle's intentions in his *De poetica* (c. 334-323 B.C.E.; *Poetics*, 1705) and that *Naugerius sive de poetica dialogus* "is one of a few Renaissance treatises which insists upon an aesthetic standard." Wilmer Cave Wright has commented that to be immortal, one needs only to write a treatise telling poets what the aim of poetry is. The poets, of course, will not read the work, but it will be mandatory reading for all subsequent historians of criticism.

THE MINOR POEMS

Of Fracastoro's works of poetry other than *Syphilis*, Truffi notes "the poem on the death of della Torre, that to G. B. della Torre, to Rainerio, to Bishop Giberti, to Marguerite de Valois (Queen of Navarre), to Francesco della Torre, to Alessandro Farnese, to Pope Giulio III and minor poems all praiseworthy for their purity of style and classicity of verse." The eulogies for Marcus Antonius della Torre are included in various versions of the collected works; the "minor poems" are less commonly available. Henry Wadsworth Longfellow included two of them in his anthology *The Poets and Poetry of Europe* (1896), commenting that Fracastoro wrote "A few poems in the mother tongue which show liveliness and facility of poetical composition." One, "To a Lady," retains the familiar hexameter and identifies the woman's "all perfect symmetry" as the eternal model of beauty wherein love finds its future home. In "Homer," the Horatian motto *ut pictura poesis* is employed by the author to indicate how, through the depiction of "sunny banks and grottoes cold," Homer became "the first great painter of scenes of old." Fracastoro is said to have written a madrigal, "Madrigal al sonno" (to slumber), on the occasion of his wife's death. The "Madrigal al sonno" is a hymn on the power of narcotics to alleviate suffering, written in the vernacular and lacking the weight of Fracastoro's Latin verse. "Alcon seu de cura canum venaticorum" (Alcon, or: how to take care of dogs for the hunt) is a short poem about the training of dogs for the hunt, known to have been among Fracastoro's favorite pastimes. The poem is included only in works appearing later than the sixteenth century, and Emilio Barbarani rejects it as spurious, mainly because it was not included in the volume of the author's poetry that was organized in 1555.

As a major writer of the Italian Renaissance, Fracastoro exhibits the comprehensive thinking of the period. He was equally at ease in the speculative and in the applied fields of science and art. Though securely based in the classical form of his predecessor, Vergil, Fracastoro's poetry embraced common topics and rendered them with grace and sensitivity. His versatility lends a particular vitality to his writing that will assure his work a permanent place in the respect and esteem of future generations.

OTHER MAJOR WORKS

PLAY: *La Venexiana*, pb. 1928 (wr. after 1509; English translation, 1950).

NONFICTION: *De vini temperatura*, 1534; *De causis criticorum dierum libellus*, 1538; *Homocentricorum sive de stellis*, 1538; *De contagionibus et contagiosis morbis et eorum curatione*, 1546 (*De contagione et contagiosis morbis et eorum curatione*, 1930); *De sympathia et antipathia rerum*, 1546; *Naugerius sive de poetica dialogus*, 1549 (English translation, 1924); *Syphilis*, wr. 1553, pb. 1939.

MISCELLANEOUS: *Opera omnia*, 1555 (includes "Turrius sive de intellectione dialogus" and "Fracastorius sive de anima dialogus").

BIBLIOGRAPHY

Fracastoro, Girolamo. *Fracastoro's "Syphilis."* Translated with introduction, text, and notes by Geoffrey Eatough. Liverpool, England: Francis Cairns, 1984. Written mainly from the point of view of a literary scholar who stresses Fracastoro's poetic achievements. Contains a detailed analysis of the poem *Syphilis*. Includes a computer-generated word index.

Gould, Stephen Jay. "Syphilis and the Shepherd of Atlantis." *Natural History* 109, no. 8 (October, 2000): 38-42. Gould discusses the "Syphilis sive morbus Gallicus" by Fracastoro and the genome of syphilis.

Greswell, W. Parr, trans. *Memoirs of Angelus Politianus, Joannes Picus of Mirandula, Actius Sincerus Sannazarius, Petrus Bembus, Hieronymus Fracastorius, Marcus Antonius Flaminius, and the Amalthei*. Manchester, England: Cadell and Davies, 1805. An early biography of Fracastoro, based primarily on an even earlier life by F. O. Mencken. It is concerned primarily with Fracastoro as a literary figure. Especially good on reporting on his contemporaries' opinions about him. Contains notes and observations by Greswell.

Hudson, Margaret M., and Robert S. Morton. "Fracastoro and Syphilis: Five Hundred Years On." *Lancet* 348, no. 9040 (November 30, 1996): 1495-1496. The authors pay tribute to the physician who spread knowledge of the origin, clinical details, and available treatments of syphilis throughout a troubled Europe.

Pearce, Spencer. "Nature and Supernature in the Dialogues of Girolamo Fracastoro." *Sixteenth Century Journal* 27, no. 1 (Spring, 1996): 111-132. Fracastoro was one of the first philosophers of nature during the Italian Renaissance. In his dialogues, Fracastoro attempts to construct a philosophical anthropology in which humanity's supernatural vocation may be accommodated within the rational framework of a philosophy of nature.

Pfeiffer, Matilde Valenti. Introduction to *La Venexiana*. New York: S. F. Vanni, 1950. Pfeiffer's introduction offers some historical information on the discovery of the play and Emilio Lovarini's conjecture that the play was written by Fracastoro.

Rosebury, Theodor. *Microbes and Morals: The Strange Story of Venereal Disease*. New York: Ballantine, 1973. Two chapters are devoted to Fracastoro, dealing specifically with syphilis as a medical problem. This book presents the best semipopular treatment of the origins of syphilis and whether it was brought from the Americas by the sailors of Columbus.

Simmons, John G., ed. *Doctors and Discoveries: Lives That Created Today's Medicines*. New York: Houghton Mifflin, 2002. Contains a biography of Fracastoro and a discussion of his poem.

H. W. Carle

GIACOMO LEOPARDI

Born: Recanati, Papal States (now in Italy); June 29, 1798
Died: Naples (now in Italy); June 14, 1837

PRINCIPAL POETRY
Versi, 1826
Canti, 1831, 1835 (includes expanded version of *Versi*; English translation, 1962)
I paralipomeni della batracomiomachia, 1842 (*The War of the Mice and the Crabs*, 1976)
The Poems of Leopardi, 1923, 1973
Poems, 1963
Selected Poems of Giacomo Leopardi, 1995

OTHER LITERARY FORMS

Giacomo Leopardi (lay-oh-POR-dee) was a child prodigy who began exercising both his talents and his erudition at the age of eleven. While as a poet he is best known for the *Canti* (literally, "songs") and to some extent for the political satire *The War of the Mice and the Crabs* and other lyrical poems not included in the *Canti*, he did leave a great number of shorter poetic pieces or fragments, including translations, together with a similar number of brief prose pieces that in the aggregate round out an active literary personality. His philosophical "Imitazione," on Antoine Vincent Arnaut's "La Feuille," is possibly of 1818, or of 1828, the year of his polemical poem on style, "Scherzo." Four or five years before, he had freely translated a fragment of Simonides and followed it with another translation of the same author. As early as 1809, inspired by Homer's *Iliad* (c. 750 B.C.E.; English translation, 1611), Leopardi produced his first poem, "La morte di Ettore," and in 1812, he wrote *Pompeo in Egitto*, a tragedy denouncing tyranny. A number of extant poetic fragments cannot be dated accurately. In 1819, Leopardi wrote the pastoral tragedy *Telesilla*. In addition, he created many prose works, such as the remarkably erudite *Storia dell'astronomia* (1813; *History of Astronomy*, 1882), ranging from the beginning of the science to the comet of 1811, and the long *Saggio sopra gli errori popolari degli antichi* (1815; *Essay on the Popular Superstitions of the Ancients*, 1882), which revealed, among other things, the budding philologist. This philological dedication was to produce a number of projects in translation, vulgarization, and editing throughout his life, albeit more frequently in his earlier than in his later years because of his failing eyesight and health. As examples, one might mention his translations from the poetry of Moschus in 1815; the *Discorso sopra la vita e le opere de M. Cornelio Frontone*, the essay *Il salterio Ebraico*, and various vulgarizations of Homer and Vergil, all of 1816; and the *Crestomazia* (1827-1828) of Italian literature in two volumes, as well as editions of Cicero and Petrarch, and an *Enciclopedia delle cognizioni utili e delle cose che non si sanno* during the 1820's, many volumes of which he never completed. A fundamental work is his 4,526-page notebook titled *Zibaldone*, which he began in 1817 and which represents an encyclopedic medley of thoughts and analyses, observations and recollections—philosophical, philological, critical, and personal—that occupied his mind until the end of 1832. It was published from 1898 to 1900. From this notebook, in large part, he compiled a collection of thoughts titled *Cento undici pensieri* that was also published posthumously, in 1845 (*Pensieri*, 1981). To be noted, too, is his essay *Discorso di un Italiano intorno alla poesia romantica* (*Discourse of an Italian Concerning Romantic Poetry*) of 1818. Next to the *Canti*, Leopardi's most important work remains the collection of twenty-four short masterpieces of satirical prose known as the *Operette morali* (*Essays and Dialogues*, 1882), published and augmented three times during his lifetime: 1827, 1834, and 1836. Finally, an indispensable companion to Leopardi studies is his published correspondence, *Epistolario* (its nucleus was published in 1849), not only for its wealth of biographical indications but also, often in the manner of the *Zibaldone*, for its innumerable intellectual premises.

Achievements

Giacomo Leopardi left an indelible mark on Italian poetry, in which he is considered second only to Dante, and while Leopardi's influence on European letters does not match that of a number of transalpine contemporaries (Lord Byron, Victor Hugo, and Ludwig Tieck, for example), he is surely a greater poet than most of them and closer to the modern psyche—indeed, one of the truly significant poets of the nineteenth century. Leopardi was not only a consummate philologist in the classical sense, with all the linguistic and historical erudition that that term implies, but also one of those rare poets who, like Dante and Johann Wolfgang von Goethe, have been deemed worthy of consideration as a philosopher. Lyrical expression and philosophical reflection maintain a harmonious balance in his poetry at all times. Some critics see Leopardi chiefly as a scholar of broad humanistic and historical dimensions; others, as one of the sacred voices inspiring the movement for Italian unification; still others, as a pessimistic philosopher, a precursor of twentieth century Existentialism. Even in *Essays and Dialogues*, however, Leopardi was above all a poet—which is perhaps the most appropriately encompassing term available for him.

Biography

Count Giacomo Talegardo Francesco di Sales Saverio Pietro Leopardi was born in Recanati, in the province of the Marches, of a wealthy and noble family with a long tradition of service to the Church. His father, Count Monaldo, prided himself on his intellectual accomplishments, among which he included reactionary and scholarly writings and the building of an extensive and erudite family library in which the young Leopardi spent most of his formative years. Monaldo's sense of infallibility did not help him manage his inherited fortune, a responsibility undertaken by his wife, Marquise Adelaide Antici, an austere, bigoted, and despotic woman, whose harshness toward the sensitive Giacomo contrasted with her husband's affectionate paternal disposition. The priest who tutored Giacomo until he was thirteen declared at that time that there was nothing more he could teach the boy, who read and studied daily until very late. Leopardi's interests—theology, mathematics, history, rhetoric, Greek, Latin, Spanish, French, Hebrew, English, German, the philosophers, the Enlightenment, the Italian classics, the commentators, and astronomy—encompassed an encyclopedic range of intellectual activities, as described in *Zibaldone*, a "mad and most desperate [regime of] study," which inevitably and irreparably damaged his naturally frail constitution. His eyesight, his bones (rachitis), his back (he became a humpback), and other ailments (such as a cerebrospinal disease) were to plague him painfully for more than half of his brief life.

At first, Leopardi's consuming ambition was the acquisition of fame, "a very great and perhaps immoderate desire," but as the years passed, he realized that he had sacrificed his youth in pursuit of his ambition. Youth, "dearer than fame and laurels, than the pure light of day," lost "without a pleasure, uselessly," became a recurrent theme in his poetry. Frequently, he sat depressed in the library, or, during an afternoon stroll around the countryside, waves of melancholy overcame him, "an obstinate, black, horrible, barbarous melancholy," which convinced him that life could produce only misery.

Pietro Giordani, an Italian writer and patriot, befriended Leopardi, and for a while his spirits lifted. The subdued tones of earlier poems such as "Le rimembranze," "Appressamento della morte," "Primo amore" ("First Love"), and "Memorie del primo amore" were replaced by the more energetic tones of patriotic songs such as "All'Italia" ("To Italy") and "Sopra il monumento di Dante che si preparava a Firenze" ("On the Monument to Dante"). He tried to leave his "native savage town" of Recanati, but his parents discovered and frustrated the attempt, in the wake of which they imposed a close surveillance of his actions, complete with censorship of his correspondence. This situation produced meditations of deep melancholia, out of which grew a philosophy of sorrow, which for him constituted the necessary condition of the universe, in which beauty, love, glory, and virtue emerge as illusions that deceive wickedly and promote universal unhappiness. However, illusion provided the only refuge from devastation occasioned by reason and reality, and the need for it made repeated claims on his soul and his worldview. During this period, from around 1819 to around 1822, many fine idylls came to light, such as "Il sogno," "L'infinito" ("The Infinite"), "La vita solitaria" ("The Solitary Life"), "La sera del dì di festa" ("Sunday Evening"), "Alla luna" ("To the Moon"), as well as the philosophical canzones "Ad Angelo Mai" ("To Angelo Mai"), "Nelle nozze della sorella Paolina," "A un vincitore nel pallone," "Bruto Minore" ("The Younger Brutus"), "Alla primavera, o delle favole antiche" ("To Spring: Or, Concerning the Ancient Myths"), "Inno ai patriarchi" ("Hymn to the Patriarchs"), and "Ultimo canto di Saffo" ("Sappho's Last Song").

Finally, in 1822, Leopardi received permission to journey to Rome—an experience that he anticipated with great enthusiasm, only to find in a short time disappointment and disillusionment. The capital, once the classical city of Caesar and Brutus, now the pontifical abode of Pius VII, academically still unemancipated from the corruption and veneered pomp of the eighteenth century Arcadia, appeared like everything else: It partook of the vanity of all things.

In 1823, the Milanese editor Antonio Stella offered Leopardi, by then returned to Recanati, the job of publishing the complete works of Cicero, a venture that saw the poet leave "the sepulcher of the living" for the Lombard capital in 1825. Completed by this time were the philosophical poem "Alla sua donna" ("To His Lady") and his famous prose work, *Essays and Dialogues*, his acid reflections on an undependable world. In Milan, he also worked on a commentary on Petrarch's poetry and on a double anthology of Italian verse and prose. Another poem, also in the philosophical vein, "Al Conte Carlo Pepoli" ("To Count Carlo Pepoli"), appeared. His reputation spread beyond Italy, so that offers of chairs reached him from the universities of Bonn and Berlin, but fear of the intemperate northern winters prompted him to refuse.

After a lapse of several years, Leopardi returned to his creative writing: "A Silvia" ("To Sylvia"), "Il risorgimento" ("The Revival"), "Il passero solitario" ("The Solitary Thrush"), "Le ricordanze" ("Memories"), "La quiete dopo la tempesta" ("The Calm After the Storm"), and "Il sabato del villaggio" ("Saturday Evening in the Village") are poems of sorrow and illusion, of simple joys and lost youth, of evil and the pain of living. One of his greatest poems, "Canto notturno di un pastore errante dell'Asia" ("Night Song of a Nomadic Shepherd in Asia"), is dated 1829. Financial difficulties, aggravated by his parents' characteristic insensitivity, dented his pride when, in 1830, he accepted a sum of money raised by charitable friends headed by the historian Pietro Colletta. "I have lost all; I am a trunk which feels and suffers." In 1832, Leopardi was forced to ask his family for a modest allowance, an improbably small sum that, together with the previous year's Florentine printing of the augmented *Canti* (the idylls had appeared in Bologna in 1826 as *Versi*, and the broader and final collection appeared again in Naples in 1835), provided some economic respite.

Life continued to disillusion Leopardi, especially in his experience of unrequited and disappointing love. First, there had been a distant cousin, Gertrude Cassi, a lovely young lady of twenty-six who had come to Recanati for a brief visit that had filled the somber family mansion with some cheer, but had left the shy youth disenchanted ("First Love," written in 1817); then came Countess Carniani-Malvezzi of Bologna, a poet herself, with whom he established a comfortable intellectual relationship until his own emotions, growing warmer, forced a reluctant break in 1826; finally, between 1830 and 1833, having fallen in love with the wife of a Florentine professor, Fanny Targioni-Tozzetti, Leopardi discovered that she had merely been flattered by the attentions of a great man and had given him insincere encouragement. She became his "ultimate deception," the wounding return to reality from his illusions, echoes of which are heard in "Il pensiero dominante" ("The Ascendant Thought"), "Aspasia," "Amore e morte" ("Love and Death"), and "Consalvo," as well as in his most bitter poem, "A stesso" ("To Himself").

Leopardi knew many of the important figures of his day, and many others yearned to know him. Still, his circle of friends remained limited. Toward the end of his life, he became close companions with a young Neapolitan exile, Antonio Ranieri, first in Florence and then, after Ranieri was pardoned by King Ferdinand II, in Naples. Leopardi's health, already strained, declined rapidly, despite the more salubrious climate of Torre del Greco in the neighborhood of Mount Vesuvius; the loving attention of Ranieri and his sister Paolina, as well as the doctors, could do nothing for Leopardi. By this time, he had written "Sopra un basso rilievo antico sepolcrale" ("On the Ancient Sepulchral Bas-Relief"), "Sopra il ritratto di una bella donna" ("On the Portrait of a Beautiful Lady"), and "Palinodia al marchese Gino Capponi," as well as his monumental poem "La ginestra, o il fiori del deserto" ("The Broom: Or, The Flower of the Desert"). On his deathbed, just before he died, he dictated to Ranieri the end of his last poem, "Il tramonto della luna" ("The Setting of the Moon"). Death, which he had so often invoked as a liberation from the anguish of having been born, overtook him on June 14, 1837. He was buried in the small church of San Vitale in Fuorigrotta. Giordani provided the epitaph, in the course of which one reads: "philologist admired outside of Italy, consummate writer of philosophy and poetry, to be compared with the Greeks...."

ANALYSIS

Giacomo Leopardi's prominence as a poet stems from the lyrical greatness of the *Canti*, but as *Essays and Dialogues* demonstrates, there was in him a talent for biting sarcasm and sardonic humor that *The War of the Mice and the Crabs* brings forth in no uncertain terms. He thought about this work from 1830, when he conceived it in Florence, to the end of his life, in Naples, where he completed it. An ironic fantasy, ringing with sociopolitical overtones, it was published abroad (by Baudry, in Paris), posthumously, in 1842, thanks to the faithful guardianship of Ranieri. The work, whose full original title means "things left out of the [pseudo-Homeric] War of the Frogs [also Crabs] and the Mice," is in eight cantos of eight-line stanzas (Leopardi had translated the original *Batrachomyomachia*, a work originally attributed to Homer, three times), and takes to task any optimism based on the notion of social progress, liberals who claim to have the solution for national problems, the antimaterialistic postures of early nineteenth century philosophers, and political absolutism. Mixing together many elements, including the grotesque (the hell of the mice), the lyrical (a nocturne), and the polemical (statements against nature), Leopardi alludes to many Italian and European political realities of the first third of his century, without leaving too much room to doubt the identities of some of his characters, such as Camminatorto (Prince Clemens von Metternich),

Senzacapo (Francis I of Austria), Mangiaprosciutti (the Bourbon Ferdinand I), Rubatocchi (Joachim Murat, the "Dandy King" of Naples and Napoléon's ally), and so on. To regard the poem strictly as a political allegory of contemporary events, however, does not do it justice, for beyond the satirical and grotesque presentation in all its varied fantasy is a panoramic view of human society conceived in broad, historical terms.

Canti

The poetry of the *Canti* is elegant in its classical simplicity, its unpretentious yet effective imagery, its meditative philosophical tone, and its profoundly human tenderness. It reveals an overabundant inner life characterized by endless searching and by intellectual sincerity, a sincerity that found no compromise with reality. In the long run, Leopardi explained nothing (the mystery of life, after all, defies explanation), but he said everything. The "beautiful and mortal thing passes and lasts not"; all is vanity to which humans fall prey, and those things they think they can turn to and rely on—such as love, beauty, and nature—deceive them cruelly, for each person is a microcosm in a macrocosm, subject to the universal destiny of sorrow existing in a world of ultimate nothingness. However, as often as Leopardi proclaims universal disillusionment, the poet continues to nourish illusions of love, goodness, beauty, and human fraternity. The paradox harbors one implied refuge: art, that shaper of benign illusions. This is why he was a poet.

The *Canti* as read today follow the arrangement of the poems, approved by the poet, in the posthumous Florentine edition of 1845, faithfully executed by Ranieri. The form is free, usually in blank verse in lines of varying length but with sparse rhyme and above all a sophisticated use of assonance. For Leopardi, the lyric represented the summit of literary expression. With a truly classical regard for the importance of the word, he aimed at Homeric clarity—eschewing complexity and the pathological somberness of many of his northern contemporaries—no matter how pessimistic the thought. Suppleness and the cleanly contoured line had to coexist to maintain the tone of serenity that made for a feeling of beauty and a sense of music. In addition, the free style of the canzones allowed a more relaxed incorporation of philosophical reflection than would have been possible in a more rigid versification. At no time, however, did the poet lapse into discursiveness or pedantry. Meditations, like emotions, were subject to the simplicity and directness of Leopardi's style.

Patriotic canzones

The first poems in the *Canti*, the patriotic canzones "To Italy" and "On the Monument to Dante," do not fit the ideological profile of a person who stood, ultimately, like his contemporary Alessandro Manzoni, above the political fray. Indeed, in later years, liberals who expected more utterances in this vein from Leopardi were disappointed. His conversations with Pietro Giordani undoubtedly underlie the nationalistic, youthful fervor reflected in these early poems, though as the years went by, his philosophical nature could not yield to political pragmatism, and he adopted more and more a metaphysical view of life's vicissitudes.

Of the two patriotic canzones, "To Italy" has enjoyed somewhat greater acclaim. It contains seven strophes of twenty lines each. The poet portrays a prostrate and reviled Italy, once so glorious yet today subject to foreign masters; its sons die fighting on alien ground, unlike the handful of noble Greeks, victors over the Persians at Thermopylae, who died for their own land. The poet Simonides could sing of that deed to posterity and thereby commingle his own fame with that of the Hellenic heroes. Tainted by occasional tones of "high-sounding oratory," in the opinion of Gian Carlo D'Adamo, the poem betrays the idealistic background of Petrarch and Ugo Foscolo, yet more personally it also rings with sincere concern and reveals that at twenty years of age, Leopardi was already an accomplished poet.

IDYLLS

Unlike the classical, Theocritan idylls that resembled verbal vignettes, Leopardi's idylls bear an autobiographical imprint. He defined them as "experiments, situations, feelings, historical adventures of my soul." Five poems in hendecasyllabic blank verse, the "small" idylls "The Infinite," "Sunday Evening," "To the Moon," "Il sogno," and "The Solitary Life," constitute the first significant phase in Leopardi's poetic development.

"The Infinite" is a mere fifteen-line idyll, yet it is a work of extraordinary depth. The poet is near Recanati, atop a hill that has always been dear to him. A hedge blocks his view of the horizon, but he imagines the silence of boundless space beyond it. The factor of time intrudes through the sound of the wind in the leaves, reminding him of eternity, of history, and of the present. "And so," he concludes, "in this immensity my thought is drowned: and in this sea is foundering sweet to me." The meditation strikes the reader because of the absence of concrete details; its indeterminateness is made vital by the evocative power of the words, the pauses, the enjambments, the oxymoronic arrangement of "foundering" and "sweet"—indeed, a whole rhythm of inner contemplation that halts on the threshold of fear before nothingness and reverts to losing itself completely in the immensity of being. A miniature drama played out in the mind, the poem has been considered Leopardi's masterpiece.

"Sunday Evening" recounts in forty-six lines how the poet cannot, like his beloved, indulge in pleasant fantasies during the calm evening after the holiday; nature allows him only tears. He compares the experience to the artisan's song that vanishes in the night's silence; on a grander scale, to the fall of the Roman Empire; and finally, to the anxiously awaited holiday that deceived him as a youth and choked his heart. The private theme of deception following in the wake of expectation is treated more objectively in "Saturday Evening in the Village." The effectiveness of this "holiday" poem derives from the moonlit setting, the sad, sentimental recollection, the dimmed semblance of a loved one, and the harshness of nature that favors others in preference to the poet.

"The Solitary Life" anticipates "The Solitary Thrush" with its theme of yearned-for solitude. A whole day is traced in its four unequal stanzas comprising 107 lines, from the morning patter of raindrops and the hen's fluttering wings, through the poet's lazy meditation by a quiet lake at noontime, where he remembers—despite the moving song he hears sung by a working girl from a nearby house—a disillusionment in love, to his greeting of the moon, which, unlike a thief or an adulterer, he wholly welcomes, as it sees him "wander through the woods and by the verdant banks, mute and solitary, or sit upon the grass, content enough, if only heart and breath be left for me to sigh." The movement of thought here surrenders to the motionlessness of silence.

Philosophical canzones

The next group of poems in the *Canti* is distinguished by a loftier language, and by a shift in subject matter from private to public concerns. These philosophical canzones number seven in all: "To Angelo Mai," "Nelle nozze della sorella Paolina," "Hymn to the Patriarchs," "A un vincitore nel pallone," "The Younger Brutus," "To Spring," and "Sappho's Last Song." This group of the early 1820's is usually expanded to include two poems composed slightly later, "To His Lady" and "To Count Carlo Pepoli," which share similar motifs.

In "To Angelo Mai," written in twelve fifteen-line strophes, Leopardi takes his Italian contemporaries to task because of their neglect of their illustrious past. To his "dead century" he opposes the philological discoveries of the erudite philologist and head librarian of the Ambrosiana and Vatican library, Angelo Mai, who had resurrected many significant texts. Philology is transfigured here to serve as a metaphor for civic regeneration. Though the poet feels decimated by sorrow and by lack of faith in the future, he evokes those "heroes" who lived and wrote before nature lifted the veil of comforting illusions from reality, before too much knowledge of the truth diminished humanity's imagination, before the sole certainty of existence—sorrow— had been fully disclosed, and before common opinion's notion of the sciences had pushed poetry into the background. Dante, Petrarch, Christopher Columbus, Ludovico Ariosto, Torquato Tasso, and Conte Vittorio Alfieri—all (except Ariosto) experienced deep sorrow, to which Leopardi relates his own experience in a manner that adumbrates the dominant pessimism of his subsequent poetry.

"The Younger Brutus," in eight fifteen-line stanzas, recalls the Roman hero after the Battle of Philippi ridiculing the concept of virtue. The gods, he opines, are not moved by the fate of humans, who accept death with resignation. The hero claims a limited victory over such a destiny through suicide, which the gods are incapable of understanding. Why the divine injunction against suicide? Animals are not ruled by it, only the sons of Prometheus. Beasts and birds are ignorant of the world's destiny, and the stars are indifferent (adumbrations of the coming song of the Asian shepherd). On the threshold of death, Brutus will not invoke the gods or the stars or posterity; his greatness will not enjoy understanding among men, so let his name and memory be lost. The poem stresses the hero's isolation; virtue, bitterly denounced at the outset, is exalted at the end. Leopardi's "agonism," as it has been called, consists of an active, if finally resigned, acceptance of fate, together with an eloquent protest against the laws of nature.

"Sappho's Last Song" portrays, in four sixteen-line stanzas, a legendary rather than historical Sappho: in Leopardi's words, "the unhappiness of a delicate, tender, sensitive, noble, and warm soul located in an ugly and young body," and, like Brutus, near suicide. The serene night and setting moon disclose a natural spectacle that once had brought comfort, but now, because of an adverse destiny, brings only misery. Why? No one can understand the lot of humankind; all is suffering, all is externality—the music and poetry of the deformed find no appreciation. Sappho will die; with illusions and youth gone, she will descend into the infernal black night. The poem mixes with great lyrical fantasy some of Leopardi's favorite themes, particularly the ironic contrast between the beauty of the world and the bleakness of human infelicity.

Great idylls of 1828-1830

As distinguished from the "small" idylls of 1819 to 1821—a term that many critics hesitate to accept (there is certainly nothing "small" about "The Infinite")—the "great" idylls of 1828 to 1830, perhaps better identified simply as further *canti*, treat Leopardi's familiar themes with more complex meditation and richer inspiration. They number seven: "The Revival," "To Sylvia," "The Solitary Thrush," "Memories," "The Calm After the Storm," "Saturday Evening in the Village," and "Night Song of a Nomadic Shepherd in Asia." Most of them are canzones in free form; they marked Leopardi's return to writing poetry after a lapse of several years.

"To Sylvia" underscores the theme of lost youth and the insensitive deception of nature. In its sixty-three lines in six uneven, free-form stanzas, the poem recalls the daughter of a coachman in Recanati, whose "happy and elusive" eyes and "constant song" he remembers. His life then was bright with hopes in a lovely landscape of gardens outlined in the distance by mountains and sea, but all those hopes died, as Sylvia died, the victim of nature's cruelty, of a "strange disease" that preempted even her first acquaintance with words of love and praise for her beauty: "And with your hand you pointed from afar at chilling death and at a naked tomb." The poet, living on, can only lament the shattered illusions of youth, yet he does so without bitterness, with exquisite melancholy and refined sorrow that find relief in the re-creating power of the word.

"The Solitary Thrush," its three stanzas comprising fifty-nine lines, is a melancholy elegy evoking a festive spring day in the village, stressing, along with the theme of lost youth, the notion of isolation. The reasoning poet compares himself to the instinct-guided thrush that sings alone all day long while the other birds frolic in the sky. As the poet walks away from the celebrants in the village, the thrush leaves behind the joys of love and youth. It is an ending, in a way, and the sunset symbolizes it; while the bird will not mourn its losses, the poet will "many times look back at them, but quite disconsolate." Leopardi always revered solitude as a balm for the spirit and the imagination, but at the same time he recognized that it precludes communion with other people, and he saw in his penchant for solitude a dangerous inability to cope with life.

Written in seven free-style stanzas comprising 173 hendecasyllables, "Memories" recalls a train of images that had left their imprint on Leopardi's mind during his earlier years in Recanati. Returning to Recanati, the poet remembers how the "bright stars of the Bear" used to kindle dreams at night, and how by daytime the mountains suggested happiness beyond them. At that time, he did not know the malevolent crassness of his townsmen, nor did he expect a life without love. The pealing of the bell on city hall used to comfort his midnight fears, even as the "old halls" and the "frescoed walls" stirred his imagination then—when life held some promise. There was, too, the fountain in whose waters he had "thought of ending . . . my dreams." He remembers all this with tenderness and regret, all these "dulcet illusions," now that he has seen life in all its squalid reality. No one can ever forget the lovely illusions of youth, like those associated with young Nerina, who was stripped of life when it seemed most promising. She has remained for him the lamented image of all that has departed. The poem is characteristic of Leopardi's more mature style in its blend of the lyrical with the reflective.

To the double tone of the lyrical and the reflective, "The Calm After the Storm" adds a third, the descriptive. It contains fifty-four lines in three free-style stanzas. After the storm, the town's rhythm resumes: the song of birds and the "refrain" of the hen, the artisan's tune, the women hustling after rainwater, and the screeching cart on the highway. Life truly seems welcome, as when one has escaped death. This is "bounteous" nature's sole gift: the avoidance of sorrow; pleasure is "relief from pain." The human race is "blest only when death relieves you from all sorrow." The original idyll becomes—not untypically for Leopardi—an ironic meditation.

"Saturday Evening in the Village," in four very uneven stanzas comprising fifty-one lines, again presents a series of images, all of villagers eager to complete their chores before the next day's holiday: the young lady with a bouquet of roses and violets, the old lady spinning at the wheel and recalling her youth, the children playing in the square, the farmer returning from the fields, the carpenter working until dawn. However, the festive expectation will yield only ennui and the sad thought of the continuing drudgery of tomorrow. Youth is like Saturday—one should not be so eager to leave it behind. Echoes of Vergil and Tasso give this poem an archaic flavor, as do the moralizing hints at the end. Leopardi's idea is clear: Happiness is a factor of the imagination that anticipates, and to which one should cling, for it inevitably surpasses realization. The charm of the poem, however, resides in the gentleness with which it treats a potentially sermonic subject matter.

Generally acclaimed as one of Leopardi's finest poems, "Night Song of a Nomadic Shepherd in Asia," consisting of six stanzas comprising 143 lines, drew its inspiration from an item in the September, 1826, issue of *Journal des savants* concerning the Kirkis, a north-central Asian nomadic tribe, some of whom "spend the night seated on a rock and looking at the moon, and improvising rather sad words on equally sad airs." The idea, however, had occupied Leopardi's mind for some time before 1826. The shepherd watches the "eternal pilgrim," the moon, as it crosses the sky and in turn watches the land. He does the same from dawn until evening, but what is the sense of the eternal movement of the stars and humanity's brief sojourn on Earth? Such is life: an old man who finally reaches his goal and disappears. Birth is difficult to begin with; then the parents must comfort the child "for being born"—so why struggle to live out the misery? Maybe the moon knows the why of things. The shepherd asks, but the question remains unanswered. Happy is the flock that knows nothing of destiny, though perhaps the lot of animals is equally unenviable, since "the day of birth is black to anything that's born." A surrogate for the poet, the shepherd in his primitive state knows as little about existence as the poet in his advanced modern age. Humans has always asked themselves the ultimate question, long before they started organizing their thoughts in writing; the shepherd always sensed that life is but an arduous journey toward death. All whys remain unanswered, and the moon, like the one Brutus saw, shines cold. Here again, because of the themes of pain, solitude, destiny, and universal mystery, the term "idyll" seems less suited than the term "elegy." In either case, however, the poem's supple rhythms give it a haunting, dirge-like quality.

THE ASPASIA CYCLE

The Aspasia cycle consists of "The Ascendant Thought," "Love and Death," "Consalvo," "To Himself," and "Aspasia," the last being a fictional name given by Leopardi to a woman he loved—unhappily: Pericles' beautiful and cultured courtesan represents the poet's Fanny Targioni-Tozzetti. All the poems in the cycle are in blank verse, and with the exception of "Consalvo" and "Aspasia," which are in hendecasyllables, the style is free.

"The Ascendant Thought," in fourteen stanzas comprising 147 lines, refers to the effects of love, to the way in which the poet's mind is dominated by the thought of love "like a tower gigantic and alone in a solitary field." To him it seems impossible that he has tolerated unhappiness without turning to love, which thwarts death and gives life meaning. Love allows one to withdraw from reality as in a dream. What more can the poet ask than to look into the eyes of his beloved? The Platonic ideal of Leopardi's earlier "To His Lady" here modulates into a moving passion, sustained from beginning to end not with dreamy tones, but with energetic emphasis. Here, Leopardi willingly throws himself into the arms of illusion.

On the other hand, "Love and Death," a slightly shorter poem of four stanzas comprising 124 lines, opposes death to the pleasures of love. The first effect of love is a languorous desire for death: While one needs love to escape the aridity of life, one knows also its "furious desire." Often, a lover in the heat of passion invokes death, and young lovers who kill themselves do so under the indifferent eyes of the crowd (for whom the poet ironically wishes emotionally barren longevity). As Benedetto Croce suggested, Leopardi addresses here the ravaging power of the senses: love as a "sweet and tremendous, elementary force of nature."

"To Himself" is Leopardi's most despairing utterance on the delusion of love, all the more powerful for its compression into a mere seventeen lines. The poet's heart will rest forever after the latest deception of love: "Bitter and dull is life, nothing more ever; and the world is mire." The only certainty is death; for himself, he has scorn, as he has also for nature, "and the infinite vanity of all things." Leopardi's style is as tense as his message; it is full of aesthetic silences that conjure up a wasteland of emotions, yet vibrant with the energy of disillusionment.

"Aspasia," consisting of 112 lines in four stanzas, concerns the mythologizing of woman. The poet sees Aspasia as a mother of incomparable beauty, elegance, and maternal femininity, a "ray divine." When he discovers that his image of her is largely fantasy, he blames her unjustly; in turn, she is unaware of the noble feelings that feed his delusion. The enchantment broken, the poet thinks of Aspasia in his tedium, "for a life bereft of sweet illusions and of love is like a starless night," but he finds comfort in lying on the grass to smile at "mortal destiny." The poem confesses Leopardi's humiliation for having been a slave in the throes of love, then rises to smile at the vanity of all things.

The sepulchral canzones

The sepulchral canzones are only two in number: "On the Ancient Sepulchral Bas-Relief" and "On the Portrait of a Beautiful Lady." Both are written in free style, in lines of uneven length.

In the 109 lines of "On the Ancient Sepulchral Bas-Relief," the poet hesitates to call the dead young lady fortunate or unfortunate; perhaps she is happy, but her destiny inspires pity, since she passed away in the flower of her beauty. How could nature bring this on an innocent person? If death, a "most beautiful young maiden," is good, why lament it? Nature engenders illusions and struggles, so why should death appear frightening? If nature were not indifferent to humans, it would not "tear a friend from friendly arms . . . and killing the one, the other keep alive." Sadly, Leopardi meditates, questioning the finality of things human; humankind's lot leaves not even death as the ultimate comforter. Against this despair, the poem adumbrates the theme of human solidarity, "brother [for] brother, child [for] parent, beloved [for] lover," that informs his last great poem, "The Broom."

"THE BROOM"

"The Broom," the poem that concludes the *Canti*, is Leopardi's most profoundly philosophical canzone. Its seven uneven stanzas comprise 317 lines. The setting is the sloping wastes of Mount Vesuvius, where solitary broom plants grow. Under the lava once flourished famous cities; now there is only the plant's consoling scent. If one believes in humanity's "magnificent progressive destinies," one might come here to take note of nature's destructive powers and of humanity's impotence before nature. The poet's "proud and mindless age" only thinks it progresses; its intellectuals praise the supposed accomplishments of the age, but the poet, who will be forgotten because of the bitter truths he utters, knows better. A humble, sick, yet generous man has nothing to hide about himself, but the one who foolishly ignores the misery of the human condition keeps making glorious promises to those who can be wiped out by natural disasters. On the other hand, those who admit humankind's frailty are noble—he who realizes that nature is the enemy and urges self-defensive brotherhood and the renunciation of wars. Under the starry sky where the poet sits, one cannot reconcile such immensity with the self-centered importance that humanity, "a mere dot," gives its members: "Laughter or pity, I know not which prevails." Nature treats humankind as the apple that falls from the tree and crushes the ant colony. After nearly two thousand years, the husbandman tending the vineyards still watches the crater closely and with constant apprehension. Tourists visit the unearthed Pompeii while the volcano keeps smoking, and nature does not heed human affairs. The broom plant, too, will succumb to the lava, but, free of "overweening pride," it is "far wiser and so much less infirm than humans," who believe in their immortality.

As a compendium of the *Canti*, "The Broom" reveals most of the best in Leopardi, although it does not achieve the melodic magic of "To Sylvia" or "Night Song of a Nomadic Shepherd in Asia." In the course of the collection, Leopardi establishes for himself a position of marked individuality in the poetic traditions of love, beauty, death, and nature, often by virtue of his melancholy cosmic view, emotionally powered by a deep sense of wonder. Narrowing his vision to a few common and familiar objects that serve as his points of departure, he opens them up, as it were, drawing himself away into the "infinite spaces" where his thought likes to roam freely. From this vantage, serenity dominates, rather than a pathological concentration on the ego. Although Leopardi is always at the base of his poetry, he stands there as an example, not as a display, of the human condition.

In the background of this seminal poem lie some of Leopardi's basic philosophical beliefs. "Against a reborn Catholic spiritualism and the idealistic currents," explains D'Adamo, "Leopardi places his unchanged faith in materialistic and sensationalistic doctrines . . . ; he regrets that this body of thought that, after originating in Renaissance philosophy and developing successively during seventeenth century rationalism, freed us from medieval superstition and error, should be abandoned by the intellectuals of his day... in favor of new spiritualistic positions"—which included Catholic liberalism. Also in the background was the accusation of misanthropy leveled at Leopardi for his antiprogressivism, as well as the cruel charge that his pessimism was merely a consequence of his unfortunate physical condition.

As a symbol of humanity's helplessness, the broom plant encourages the poet in his message of brotherhood, which, after all, dates back to the origins of human life on Earth, and which bespeaks an innate moral sense in humanity. Leopardi appeals to humankind's reason; he wanted to end the *Canti* in this vein. The lyrical and the philosophical remain intertwined in this poetic discourse, though, as the composition unfolds, the two modes develop separately from each other in a brilliant interplay of reason and emotion.

OTHER MAJOR WORKS

PLAYS: *Pompeo in Egitto*, wr. 1812; *Telesilla*, wr. 1819.

NONFICTION: *Storia dell'astronomia*, 1813 (*History of Astronomy*, 1882); *Saggio sopra gli errori popolari degli antichi*, 1815 (*Essay on the Popular Superstitions of the Ancients*, 1882); *Discorso sopra la vita e le opere de M. Cornelio Frontone*, 1816; *Il salterio Ebraico*, 1816; *Discorso di un Italiano intorno alla poesia rom antica*, 1818 (*Discourse of an Italian Concerning Romantic Poetry*, 1882); *Operette morali*, 1827, 1834, 1836 (*Essays and Dialogues*, 1882); *Crestomazia*, 1827-1828 (2 volumes); *Cento undici pensieri*, 1845 (*Pensieri*, 1981); *Epistolario*, 1849; *Zibaldone*, 1898-1900; *The Letters of Giacomo Leopardi, 1817-1837*, 1998.

BIBLIOGRAPHY

Barricelli, Jean Pierre. *Giacomo Leopardi*. Boston: Twayne, 1986. A basic biography of Leopardi, examining his life and works.

Broggi, Francesca. *The Rise of the Italian Canto: Macpherson, Cesarotti and Leopardi—From the Ossianic Poems to the "Canti."* Ravenna, Italy: Longo, 2009. Examines the works of Leopardi, James Macpherson, and Melchiorre Cesarotti and traces the development of the Italian canto.

Carsaniga, Giovanni. *Giacomo Leopardi: The Unheeded Voice*. Edinburgh, Scotland: Edinburgh University Press, 1977. A critical introduction to Leopardi's works with bibliographic references and index.

Chambers, Ross. "On Inventing Unknownness: The Poetry of Disenchanted Reenchantment (Leopardi, Baudelaire, Rimbaud, Justice)." *French Forum* 33, no. 1/2 (Winter, 2008): 15-35. Examines the poetry of Leopardi, Charles Baudelaire, Arthur Rimbaud, and Donald Justice for what he terms "invented unknownness." He argues that poems do not discover the unknown but rather create it. Leopardi's "The Infinite" is analyzed.

Nisbet, Delia Fabbroni-Giannotti. *Heinrich Heine and Giacomo Leopardi: The Rheto-*

ric of Midrash. New York: Peter Lang, 2000. Provides a critical analysis of similarities between the rhetorical strategies of Heine's *Ludwig Börne: Eine Denkschrift von H. Heine* (1840; *Ludwig Börne: Recollections of a Revolutionist*, 1881) and Leopardi's "Il Cantico del Gallo Silvestre" and the Midrashic process. Heine and Leopardi refer to biblical and historical events in their narratives and relate them to a contemporary situation to present their interpretation of an existential experience.

Press, Lynne, and Pamela Williams. *Women and Feminine Images in Giacomo Leopardi, 1798-1837*. Studies in Italian Literature 7. Lewiston, N.Y.: Edwin Mellen Press, 2000. A study of female images and man-woman relationships in Leopardi's works. Includes bibliographical references and index.

Rennie, Nicholas. *Speculating on the Moment: The Poetics of Time and Recurrence in Goethe, Leopardi, and Nietzsche*. Göttingen, Germany: Wallstein, 2005. Examines the themes of time and recurrence in the poetry of Leopardi, Johann Wolfgang von Goethe, and Friedrich Nietzsche. An entire section is devoted to Leopardi, although much of the discussion concerns *Zibaldone*.

Veronese, Cosetta. *The Reception of Giacomo Leopardi in the Nineteenth Century: Italy's Greatest Poet After Dante?* Lewiston, N.Y.: Edwin Mellen Press, 2009. Examines Leopardi's reception in Italy and other countries. Looks at early critical analysis of Leopardi.

Jean-Pierre Barricelli

GIAMBATTISTA MARINO

Born: Naples (now in Italy); October 18, 1569
Died: Naples (now in Italy); March 25, 1625
Also known as: Giambattista Marini

PRINCIPAL POETRY
Le rime, 1602 (*Steps to the Temple*, canto 1 only, 1646)
Il ritratto del serenissimo Don Carlo Emanuello Duca di Savoia, 1608
La lira, 1615
Il tempio, 1615
Epitalami, 1616
La galeria, 1619
Egloghe boscherecce, 1620
La sampogna, 1620
L'Adone, 1623
La Murtoleide, 1626
La strage degli innocenti, 1632 (*The Slaughter of the Innocents*, 1675)
Gerusalemme distrutta, 1633 (unfinished)
L'Anversa liberata, 1956 (unfinished)
Adonis, 1967 (selections from *L'Adone*)

OTHER LITERARY FORMS

The voluminous production of Giambattista Marino (mah-REE-noh) is almost entirely in poetical form. In 1617, while he was in France, Marino wrote an invective against the enemies of the Catholic Church, *La sferza, invettiva a quattro ministri della iniquitá* (the whip: invective against four ministers of iniquity), which was first published in Paris in 1625. In addition, Marino's copious correspondence, included in *Lettere* (1627) and published in a modern edition, *Epistolario* (1912), is very important, for it provides revealing glimpses of his moral and aesthetic values.

ACHIEVEMENTS

Thematically and stylistically, Giambattista Marino is considered one of the greatest Italian poets of his age and also, perhaps, the most representative man of letters of Baroque Europe. His impact was felt immediately, not only in the various literary circles of Italy but also in France, where he produced his masterpiece, *L'Adone* (Adonis), and whence his fame spread throughout the Continent. Echoes and imitators of the Marinesque style are indeed to be found everywhere, from the Slavic world (Miklós Zríny, Dż ivo Bunić-Vucić, Igniat Djordjić, Jan Andrzej Morsztyn) to seventeenth century England (Edward Herbert, Thomas Carew, Andrew Marvell, Richard Crashaw, Samuel Daniel, Edward Sherburne, Thomas Stanley, and so on).

Although Spanish literature of this period was to produce an equally influential figure in Luis de Góngora y Argote (who was to lend his name to Gongorism, an aesthetic current that paralleled Marinism), Spanish poets such as Juan de Tasis, Luis de Carrillo y Sotomayor, and Francisco Gómez de Quevedo y Villegas became admirers and imitators of Marino, and Lope de Vega Carpio expressed his admiration for the Italian poet by dedicating one of his comedies to him. It was undoubtedly in France, however, where Marino lived for some eight years as a favorite of Queen Marie de Médicis, that his influence was most powerfully felt. Poets as diverse as Antoine-Girard de Saint-Amant, Théophile de Viau, Tristan L'Hermite, Georges de Scudéry, Vincent Voiture, Jean de La Fontaine, Claude de Malleville, and Pierre Le Moyne betray a significant debt to Marino, and it was from France that Marinism radiated all over Europe.

Biography

Giambattista (Giovan Battista) Marino (or Marini, as it is often written), one of seven children, was born in Naples on October 18, 1569, the son of Giovan Francesco Marino. The elder Marino was a lawyer and hoped that his son would follow in his footsteps, but the young Marino was more interested in literary studies than in embracing a legal career. Having disappointed his father, Marino was unceremoniously asked to leave the paternal household, but his reputation as a spirited and bright young poet and man of letters was already sufficient to open to him the doors of several aristocratic houses, and in 1592, he entered the service of Matteo di Capua, prince of Conca, as a poet and a secretary.

As a young man, Marino led a dissolute life and was twice imprisoned: first in 1598, for having taken part in the rape of a young woman (probably a nun), and again in 1600, for having falsified some documents to prepare the escape from prison of his friend, Marc Antonio d'Alessandro, who had been condemned to death. Although Marino was freed from prison, he was forced to flee to Rome, where he found protection with the influential Monsignor Melchiorre Crescenzio. In 1601-1602, Marino traveled to Venice to oversee the publication of his first two volumes of *Le rime*, later incorporated in *La lira*. Upon his return to Rome, he found employment with Cardinal Pietro Aldobrandini, the nephew of Pope Clement VIII, and in 1606, after the pope's death, Marino followed Aldobrandini to his seat at Ravenna.

Enjoying a growing reputation as a poet, Marino accompanied Aldobrandini to Torino in 1608 to attend the marriage of two daughters of Duke Carlo Emanuele I of Savoy, and Marino seized the occasion to write *Il ritratto del serenissimo Don Carlo Emanuello Duca di Savoia* (the portrait of the most serene Don Carlo Emanuele, duke of Savoy), a panegyric in honor of the duke. The duke reciprocated by conferring on him the order of the knighthood of Saints Maurizio and Lazzaro—the title of "Cavaliere," of which Marino always felt especially proud and that he henceforth always prefixed to his name.

In 1609, the duke's secretary, Gaspare Murtola—himself a poet, jealous of Marino's rapidly rising status at the court of Turin—fired a pistol at Marino, hitting instead another man who was a favorite of the duke. Murtola was condemned to death, but at Marino's request, the sentence was commuted to exile. In 1611, Marino himself was sent to prison for fourteen months. The charges are not known, but presumably he had offended the duke with some satirical verses. Marino was freed in 1612, and in 1614, he published in Venice the result of years of creative labor: part 3 of *La lira*, later reprinted in a collected edition together with *Le rime* and the *Dicerie sacre* (holy discourses). In 1615, he received permission to go to the royal court in Paris, where he had been invited first by Marguerite de Navarre and then by Marie de Médicis, who had become Queen Regent after the death of her husband, Henry IV.

In Lyon, as soon as he set foot on French territory, Marino published a laudatory poem, *Il tempio* (the temple), in honor of the queen. Marino stayed in Paris, where he became a court favorite, until 1623, enjoying enormous popularity and receiving many honors. While in Paris, he published a volume of ten nuptial odes, *Epitalami* (epithalamia); a collection of six hundred poems celebrating various works of art, real and imagined, *La galeria* (the gallery); a gathering of poems on mythological and bucolic subjects, *La sampogna* (the shepherd's pipe); and finally, in April, 1623, his masterpiece, *L'Adone*, which he dedicated to Louis XIII. Immediately after the publication of the twenty cantos of *L'Adone*—a work more than twice as long as Dante's *La divina commedia* (c. 1320; *The Divine Comedy*, 1802) or Torquato Tasso's *Gerusalemme liberata* (1581; *Jerusalem Delivered*, 1600)—Marino, at the very peak of his popularity, decided to return to his native land to savor the triumphs that inevitably would be accorded to him as the greatest living Italian poet. In Rome, he found immediate protection at the household of Cardinal Ludovico Ludovisi, the nephew of Pope Gregory XV; was feted with a banquet held in his honor by the Roman Senate; and was elected prince of the Academy of the Umoristi, of which he had been a member for several years. While in Rome, he witnessed as a special guest the ceremonies for the election of the new pope, Urban VIII (previously Cardinal Maffeo Barberini).

Arriving in May, 1623, in his native Naples, Marino entered the city as a triumphant conqueror. A statue in his honor was unveiled there, and he was welcomed by the Spanish viceroy and by the various literary academies (the Academy of the Oziosi also made him a prince). In 1624, however, his stay in Naples was marred by the unwelcome news that his *L'Adone* had been placed on the Church's Index. Perhaps tired by his many public appearances and commitments and by the pressure to complete his religious epic, *The Slaughter of the Innocents*, he became ill, initially with a slow fever and then with a painful case of strangury. Before his death on March 25, 1625, he burned many of his sensual and profane writings. By order of the Neapolitan archbishop Cardinal Decio Carafa, Marino's burial took place during the night.

Analysis

True to the spirit of his time, Giambattista Marino wrote a number of panegyrical poems, among them *Il ritratto del serenissimo Don Carlo Emanuello Duca di Savoia, Il tempio*, and *Epitalami*, a collection of ten very sensual nuptial odes patterned after traditional models, largely mythological in content, and written to celebrate the weddings of various princes and kings. Marino was equally at ease with religious subjects, which he treated with a certain emotional detachment. In 1614, he published *Dicerie sacre*, an important work that included three lengthy and elaborate metaphorical sermons on painting, music, and Heaven, inspired respectively by the "Sindone" (Christ's shroud), the seven last words of Christ, and the orders of Saints Maurizio and Lazzaro. In 1617, while in France, Marino wrote *La sferza, invettiva a quattro ministri della iniquitá*, an invective against the enemies of the Catholic Church.

Among Marino's other writings worthy of mention are his pastoral *Egloghe boscherecce* (sylvan eclogues), first published in 1620, although the only extant copies are dated 1627, and the famous *La Murtoleide* (the deeds of Murtola). *La Murtoleide*, published in 1626 but dating back to Marino's Turin period, consists of eighty-one *fischiate* (boos), satirical sonnets written against his rival, the mediocre court poet Gaspare Murtola, who had attacked Marino in a libelous *Abridgement of the Life of Cavalier Marino*. Rather predictably, Murtola retorted by writing a *Marineide* (the deeds of Marino), which consisted of thirty-two *risate* (laughs); he also tried, unsuccessfully, to kill Marino, shooting at him with a pistol.

A well-known tercet that is said to epitomize the quintessence of Marino's poetics is to be found in the thirty-third *fischiata* of *La Murtoleide*: "The goal of the poet is to cause wonder/ (I am speaking about excellent poets and not clumsy ones):/ Those who do not know how to astonish should go to the stables."

Marino also tried his hand at composing serious epic poetry, and great admirer of Tasso that he was, he attempted to deal with two themes much in the Tassian tradition: *Gerusalemme distrutta* (Jerusalem destroyed) and *L'Anversa liberata* (Antwerp delivered). Both of these poems, however, were left unfinished and were published posthumously, the first in 1633 and the second only in 1956.

L'Adone

Marino's masterpiece, *L'Adone*—an extremely long poem of twenty cantos, first published in Paris in 1623—displays his seemingly unlimited verbal and rhetorical virtuosity as well as his ability to use a surprising array of sources and themes.

Although some of the episodes in *L'Adone* can be traced to Dante, Ariosto, and Tasso, the bulk of the work derives from classical sources, particularly book 10 of Ovid's *Metamorphoses* (c. 8 C.E.; English translation, 1567). In a sense, *L'Adone* can be seen as a marvelous poetic catalog of a mythological world where the myths and Arcadian adventures of the classical deities, Satyrs, and nymphs are syncretically evoked against a lavishly sensual Baroque setting.

The plot begins unfolding when Cupid, rather ill disposed toward his mother Venus, seeks vengeance by making Adonis—the handsome prince born out of an incestuous relation between Mirrah and her father—arrive in Cyprus and fall in love with the goddess. Readily reciprocating Adonis's love, Venus takes the young prince to her palace and guides him through the Garden of Pleasure, divided into five sections that symbolize the various senses as they are engaged by lovemaking. Afterward, still guided by his pagan, unspiritual "Beatrice," Adonis experiences the pleasures of the mind. Joined by Mercury—clearly reminiscent of Dante's Vergil—Adonis visits Apollo's fountain, symbolizing poetry, and ascends to the first three Ptolemaic spheres, those of the Moon, Mercury, and Venus. There, after some adulatory verses in honor of various royalties, he learns of the most advanced scientific notions and meets some of the most representative figures of the sixteenth century.

Unfortunately, Jealousy informs Mars of Venus's new passion, and Adonis is forced to flee before the enraged god, beginning a long series of adventures. Adonis falls into the hands of the lascivious and wicked fairy Falsirena, who, after unsuccessfully trying to seduce him, transforms him into a parrot and forces him to witness love scenes between Venus and Mars. Following other fantastic encounters, Adonis finally manages to return to Cyprus, where he is elected king of the island and can once more enjoy the favors of the goddess. On a hunt, however, Adonis is killed by a wild boar aroused against him by the disgruntled Falsirena and Mars. The poem ends with Adonis's funeral and with a description of the games held in his honor, as well as with a final series of classical myths dealing with love and death.

In a dazzling display of bravura, Marino's thin treatment of the theme of life, death, and rebirth is overpowered by the pageant of sensory delights that he presents to the reader. In a changing world filled with religious upheavals and sociopolitical tensions, Marino's ornate, brilliant display of rhetorical and poetic devices and his unrestrained celebration of life and sensual love offered an escape into the unreal realm of fables and myths. Marino's exuberant affirmation of the *meraviglia* (the astonishing, the marvelous) was judged by later critics as representative of the Baroque at its worst, its most excessive, yet his virtuosity has never been questioned. His masterly use of rhetorical figures remains unsurpassed. Indeed, the abundant use of metaphors by Marino and other Baroque poets went beyond the mere rhetorical exigencies of poetry or even the desire to display exceptional creative ability. Rather, it expressed a deeply felt if unconscious need to interpret their confusing and rapidly changing world.

OTHER MAJOR WORKS

NONFICTION : *Dicerie sacre*, 1614 ; *La sferza, invettiva a quattro ministri della iniquitá*, pb. 1625 (wr. 1617); *Lettere*, 1627 (modern edition, *Epistolario*, 1912).

BIBLIOGRAPHY

Brand, Peter, and Lino Pertile, eds. *The Cambridge History of Italian Literature.* Rev. ed. New York: Cambridge University Press, 1999. Contains a chapter on the Baroque period and a section on Marino and his followers.

Guardiani, Francesco, ed. *The Sense of Marino: Literature, Fine Arts, and Music of the Italian Baroque.* New York: Legas, 1994. A critical interpretation of selected poetic works and an introduction the history of Italian poetry of the seventeenth century.

Mirollo, James V. *The Poet of the Marvelous: Giambattista Marino.* New York: Columbia University Press, 1963. A biography of Marino. Includes texts in Italian and English of "La canzone dei baci," "La maddalena di Tiziano," and an extract from "La pastorello."

Segel, Harold B. *The Baroque Poem: A Comparative Survey.* New York: Dutton, 1974. A survey of 150 texts from English, American, Dutch, German, French, Italian, Spanish, Mexican, Portuguese, Polish, Modern Latin, Czech, Croatian, and Russian poetry, in the original languages and accompanying English translations.

Roberto Severino

MICHELANGELO

Born: Caprese, Tuscany, Republic of Florence (now in Italy); March 6, 1475
Died: Rome, Papal States (now in Italy); February 18, 1564

PRINCIPAL POETRY
Rime di Michelangelo Buonarroti, 1623 (*The Sonnets*, 1878)
Le Rime di Michelangelo Buonarroti, 1863 (Cesare Guasti, editor)
The Sonnets of Michel Angelo, 1878
Sonnets of Michel Angelo, 1905
Rime di Michelangelo Buonarroti, 1960
The Complete Poems of Michelangelo, 1960
Michelangelo: Self-Portrait, 1963

OTHER LITERARY FORMS

Michelangelo (mi-kuh-LAN-juh-loh), the renowned painter and sculptor, creator of the statue of David and the epic paintings of the Sistine Chapel's ceiling, also left a literary legacy. Along with his poetry, he wrote some five hundred letters that, though never intended as publishable literature, are a rich source of psychological and biographical material. Michelangelo's letters are largely concerned with money, contracts, the difficulties of dealing with popes, family quarrels and obligations, real estate deals and speculations, politics (very obliquely referred to), premonitions, and setting his worthless brothers up in business. Rarely, if ever, does he discuss the art that was his sole reason for existence. When he completed the paintings in the Sistine Chapel after four years of hard labor, all he wrote to his father was:

> I have finished the chapel I have been painting; the Pope is very well satisfied. But other things have not turned out for me as I'd hoped. For this I blame the times, which are very unfavorable to our art....

ACHIEVEMENTS

By all accounts, Michelangelo reigned as the most important and most gifted sculptor of the Renaissance. When his *Pietà*, commissioned for Saint Peter's Basilica and carved when Michelangelo was barely twenty, was unveiled, it caused a great flurry of excitement, and when his *David* was presented less than a decade later, there was little doubt that his work would define the standards for the highest period of the Italian Renaissance. Throughout his life, he was sought after by both the Papacy and the patriarchs of Florence, not only for his talents as a sculptor but also for his gifts as an architect and a military engineer.

Michelangelo
(Library of Congress)

Michelangelo's allegiance was always to his art, and he was able to produce commissioned works as great as the Sistine Chapel or the Medici tombs without falling prey to the political rivalries between Rome and Florence—a feat in itself, attesting the esteem in which he was held by the ruling class. Four centuries after his death, Michelangelo is revered by popular opinion; his most famous works, especially the *Pietà* of Saint Peter's Basilica, the *David*, and the Sistine Chapel, draw tens of thousands of people every year and are among the most popular tourist attractions in Europe. In addition, critics have reevaluated Michelangelo's poetry, establishing its merit not simply as a sidelight to his sculpture but as an innovative and important body of work in its own right.

Biography

Michelangelo di Lodovico Buonarroti Simoni's attainments as a poet can be understood, both thematically and aesthetically, only against the background of the artist's life in the service of six popes of the Italian Renaissance and his colossal achievements in all the visual arts—sculpture, painting, and architecture.

Brought to Florence from Caprese while still an infant, Michelangelo was sent to nurse with a stonecutter's wife in Settignano, where, he later liked to say, he imbibed marble dust with his wet-nurse's milk. When he was still a child, his mother died, leaving her husband, Lodovico, with five young sons. Lodovico remarried in 1485, and about that time, Michelangelo returned to Florence to live in the Santa Croce quarter with his father, stepmother, four brothers, and an uncle. Of the brothers, only Buonarroto, two years younger than Michelangelo, married and left progeny. The eldest brother, Leonardo, became a Dominican monk; the youngest brothers, Giovansimone and Sigismondo, passed their lives in trade, soldiering, and farming. Undoubtedly the untimely death of his mother and the overwhelmingly male household in which the artist spent his early years are important clues to certain aspects of Michelangelo's personality. He never married, asserting that his art was sufficient mistress for him; his nudes are characterized by a blurring of distinctly male and female attributes, a projection of a race whose physiognomy and physiology would seem to partake of the qualities of both sexes. Similar qualities are manifest in his poetry.

Michelangelo's correspondence with his father and brothers reveals the artist's deep, almost morbid attachment to his family, despite the fact that comprehension of, or even interest in, Michelangelo's art was entirely lacking on their part. Throughout their lives, his father and brothers looked on Michelangelo only as a source of income or as a counselor in their various projects. Although in his letters Michelangelo frequently refers to his financial affairs, he never discusses art with his family and rarely indeed with anyone else.

As a boy, Michelangelo cared little for the traditional Latin and Humanist studies; his inclination to draw led his father, despite his scorn for art, to enroll him (on April 1, 1488) as a student apprentice in the workshop of Domenico Ghirlandaio, then the most popular painter in Florence. A year later, however, Michelangelo left that master to study in the Medici gardens near San Marco, where Lorenzo the Magnificent had gathered a collection of ancient statues and had assigned Bertoldo di Giovanni, a follower of Donatello, to train young men in sculpture. A faun's head (now lost) that Michelangelo had freely copied from a classic fragment attracted Lorenzo's attention, and Michelangelo, then fifteen years old, was taken to live almost as a son in the Medici Palace, first with Lorenzo de' Medici, then briefly with his son Piero. It was during these impressionable years that the youthful artist absorbed the Neoplatonic ideas of Lorenzo's famous circle of Humanists, Poliziano, Marsilio Ficino, and Giovanni Pico della Mirandola. Undoubtedly, Michelangelo's notion of reality as an essence underlying, or contained within, an enveloping substance was derived from conversations he heard in Lorenzo's "academy." The sculptural art of "taking away"—that is, revealing the figure already contained within the block—is analogous to ascending the Platonic ladder to a preexistent Form. At Poliziano's suggestion, the young sculptor carved a relief, the *Battle of the Centaurs*, that showed indications of his mastery of the nude as the ideal vehicle of expression. The Neoplatonism that Michelangelo absorbed in the Medici Palace is one of the major themes of his poetry, especially the contrast between carnal and ideal love.

After the death of Lorenzo the Magnificent on April 8, 1492, his unworthy son Piero showed little interest in Michelangelo's genius, assigning the sculptor such tasks as making a snowman. Subsequently, fearing the imminent invasion of the French under Charles VIII and the threatened fall of the Medici, Michelangelo and two companions fled to Venice and then returned to Bologna. Several times during the artist's life, unpredictable flights of this kind occurred, resulting apparently from nameless fears.

Michelangelo remained in Bologna from the fall of 1494 until the beginning of 1495 as a guest of Gianfrancesco Aldovrandi, a wealthy merchant, to whom Michelangelo read Dante, Petrarch, and other Tuscan poets. During his lifetime, Michelangelo had the reputation of being a profound scholar of Dante's *La divina commedia* (c. 1320; *The Divine Comedy*, 1802). A harsh exaltation informs the work of both Tuscans, and in Michelangelo's own poetry, the intellectual power of Dante is matched, if not his graceful style and fertile imagery.

In 1495, Michelangelo returned to Florence, where he carved in marble a *San Giovannino* and a *Sleeping Cupid* (both lost). The Cupid was such a skillful imitation of classical sculpture that it was sold to a Roman art dealer, who in turn sold the counterfeit as an authentic antique to Cardinal Raffaello Riario. Discovering the deception, the cardinal summoned Michelangelo to Rome in June, 1496, thinking to order other works from the astonishing young talent. Although the cardinal's patronage ultimately proved unrewarding, Michelangelo remained in Rome for five fruitful years. During this period, he completed a *Bacchus* in marble for the Roman banker Jacopo Galli and the *Pietà* that is now in Saint Peter's Basilica for the French cardinal Jean Villiers de la Groslaye. This first sojourn in Rome resulted in great fame for the youthful sculptor. Sharply revealed in his *Bacchus* and *Pietà* at this time are two of the main contrasting themes that served Michelangelo all his life: pagan exaltation of the nude male figure and love-pity for the Christ. Both of these works, however, in their combination of naturalistic detail, high finish, and rather cold classical beauty, still hark back to the earlier fifteenth century Florentine sculptors. A comparison of this *Pietà* with a *Pietà* from his last years shows how far the artist moved from this early, vigorous naturalism to an abstract spiritualization of form and material.

Three months before Michelangelo signed his contract for the *Pietà*, Girolamo Savonarola was burned at the stake (May 23, 1498) after his condemnation by the Borgia Pope Alexander VI. The martyrdom of the Dominican deeply affected Michelangelo, who continued to read Savonarola's sermons throughout his life. The prophetic nature of the friar was probably also a factor that led the artist to assiduous reading of the Old Testament. Nevertheless, the years of Savonarola's domination had been unfavorable to art, and it was perhaps the more propitious atmosphere that had come about in Florence, as well as the repeated urgings of his father, that drew Michelangelo back to his native city. When Michelangelo returned from Rome in 1501, he was already a famous sculptor. He was deluged with commissions, most notably for the gigantic *David*, a fourteen-foot nude extracted from a single, awkwardly shaped block of Carrara marble (1501-1504).

This colossal *David* was, both in dimension and conception, Michelangelo's first truly heroic work. The frowning hero is the first expression of the *terribilità* for which the sculptor later became so famous. In the disproportionate right hand and the strained position of the left hand holding the sling bag at the shoulder, the artist was already moving away from the more literal naturalism of his earlier work. The huge hand is an apotheosis of *la man che ubbidisce all' intelletto*—"the hand that serves the intellect." The fierce frown plays an odd counterpoint against the relaxed pose, a typical Michelangelo equilibrium between contrary forces, a coexistence of contrarieties frequently found also in his poetry.

In 1505, Pope Julius II summoned Michelangelo to Rome, assigning him the task of creating the pope's mausoleum. The project, which involved more than forty life-size figures, seemingly lacked any trace of religious spirit, and would have been a suitable secular glorification of the worldliness of the Renaissance papacy.

The intention was to place the mausoleum in the new apse then being constructed in the old basilica of Saint Peter's. The project threatened to dwarf the existing church and thus suggested to Julius the idea of reconstructing the entire basilica on a new, immense scale. It may therefore be said that the colossal dimensions of Michelangelo's plans for the tomb were an indirect cause of the construction of the new Saint Peter's. The fickleness of the pope and his failure to pay Michelangelo for the expense of carting the marble, as well as a nameless presentiment that his life was in jeopardy, caused the hypersensitive artist to depart unexpectedly for Florence on April 17, 1506, the day before the laying of the cornerstone of the new Saint Peter's. Followed in vain by messengers and threats from the pope, who sent three peremptory briefs to the Signory of Florence, Michelangelo fiercely refused to return to Rome. Several violent sonnets addressed to Pope Julius probably date from this period. Eventually Michelangelo was persuaded to attempt a reconciliation. In November, 1506, Michelangelo, "with a rope around my neck" (the traditional symbol of submission), came to Julius at Bologna, which the old pope, marching at the head of his troops, had just reconquered from the local tyrant, Giovanni Bentivoglio. In a stormy meeting, Julius pardoned Michelangelo and assigned him a new task—to cast a huge bronze statue of the pope to be set over the main portal of San Petronio in Bologna.

The bronze finished, Michelangelo returned home, planning to complete many assignments; Julius, however, summoned him again to Rome. Michelangelo sought in vain to free himself from the pope's insistence that Michelangelo fresco the vault of the Sistine Chapel instead of resuming work on the tomb. Again, the Florentine found himself engaged in a craft that he did not consider his own. Nevertheless, once Michelangelo undertook the assignment, he set to work with typical fury and confidence, resolved to surpass all other achievements in the art of fresco. Six assistants whom he had summoned from Florence were soon dismissed by the fiercely individualistic artist. Except for some manual help in preparing the plaster grounds and perhaps in painting some portions of the architectural setting, the entire stupendous task of decorating a barrel vault 128 feet long and 45 feet wide, 68 feet from the pavement, together with lunettes over twelve windows, was carried out by Michelangelo alone. From May 10, 1508, until October, 1512, with some interruptions, he worked on a special scaffolding, painting at great personal discomfort with the brush over his head "dripping a rich pavement" on his chest:

> I've already grown a goiter from this toil,
> as water swells the cats in Lombardy
> or any other country they might be,
> forcing my belly to hang under my chin.
> My beard to heaven . . .

After describing the grotesque distortions his body must assume, painting the vault 68 feet above the pavement, the poet-artist cries out:

> Therefore, fallacious, strange
> the judgment carried in the mind must fly,
> for from a twisted gun one shoots awry.
> My dead picture defend
> now, Giovanni, and also my honor,
> for I'm in no good place, nor I a painter.

Eventually the huge surface was covered with a vast panorama comprehending the story of Genesis up to the Flood and three episodes from the life of Noah. The choice of subject was Michelangelo's own, but it harmonized with the themes treated in the fifteenth century lateral-panel frescoes already in the chapel, which dealt with parallel episodes in the lives of Moses and Christ. Undoubtedly the most awesome pictorial achievement of the High Renaissance, the Sistine Chapel ceiling is the fullest expression of Michelangelo's genius in employing the human form and face in their manifold attitudes and attributes. The Sistine ceiling balances pictures from the Old Testament and nude Greek youths, pre-Christian prophets and pagan sibyls, pagan Humanism and orthodox Christianity.

Michelangelo, however, had never ceased to think of resuming work on Julius's mausoleum. Even during the creation of the most stupendous piece of painting in Western art, he had signed his letters "Michelangelo, sculptor in Rome." He had already arranged for the purchase, later concluded, of a house in Rome on the Macel de' Corvi near the area of the Trajan Forum, where he could collect and work the marble. On February 21, 1513, however, Pope Julius died, and then began the litigation with Julius's heirs, the abandonment of Michelangelo's first grand idea, the successive diminutions of the project to the present mediocrity in San Pietro in Vincoli. This much-reduced version has as its chief attraction Michelangelo's sculpture *Moses*. In the menacing *Moses*, with its hyperbolic beard and strained posture, left foot drawn back, the *terribilità* of the artist reached volcanic expression. Michelangelo was inspired more often by the heroes, prophets, and judgmental Jehovah of the Jews than by the Gospels. Only in the drawings and poems of his extreme old age does the Crucifixion appear as a theme.

In 1516, while Michelangelo was at Carrara gathering marble for the mausoleum, he had to return to Rome, where Pope Leo X (elected March, 1513) ordered him to construct and decorate with statues the facade of San Lorenzo in Florence. Thus, the artist again found himself deflected from the vast project on which he had set his heart, and once again he found himself in the service of the Medici. Leo, indeed, had known Michelangelo as a boy when they had sat together, almost as brothers, at the table of Lorenzo, Leo X's father. The pope was exactly Michelangelo's age, forty-one years old, a pleasure-loving man famous for his remark: "Let us enjoy the Papacy, since God has given it to us." Although he commissioned Michelangelo on the basis of competitive drawings and models, the contract was soon broken. Probably Leo found the sweeter and softer-natured Raphael more to his liking than the litigious and austere sculptor. At any rate, Michelangelo produced more during his tempestuous relationship with the "terrible" Julius than with the epicurean Leo.

In 1527, Rome was sacked by Emperor Charles V. At the news, the Florentines once again evicted the Medici (May 17, 1527) and restored the Republic. In July of the next year, Michelangelo's favorite brother, Buonarroto, died in his arms of the plague, and the cares of the widowed family fell on the sculptor's shoulders. When the armies of Clement VII and the reconciled Charles V moved against the city, Michelangelo was named magistrate of the Committee of Nine of the Florentine Militia, and a few months later, he was appointed governor and procurator general of the city's fortifications. Almost against his will, he participated in the defense of his city, executing missions of a military character at Pisa, Livorno, and Ferrara and fortifying the hill at San Miniato.

After the fall of Florence (August 2, 1530), the Medici returned. Pardoned by Clement VII, the artist continued working on the Medici tombs while attending to other assignments heaped on him by the pope. Then, distrusting Duke Alexander, the new Medici ruler of Florence, and desirous of concluding work on the tomb of Julius according to the last contract, Michelangelo returned to Rome to his house at Macel de' Corvi. He alternated his Rome sojourn with long stays at Florence, where he was needed for work on the library and the tombs. This was the period of his fervent friendships with the young Tommaso Cavalieri at Rome and the young Febo di Poggio at Florence. Many of Michelangelo's most beautiful poems are addressed to Cavalieri. In 1531, Michelangelo's father died at the age of ninety, prompting a touching poem of filial affection.

With the deaths of his favorite brother and father, his native city under a ruler unsympathetic to him, and feeling the urgency to free himself of what had become the incubus of the Julius mausoleum, the artist left Florence in September, 1534, never to return. Michelangelo arrived in Rome two days before the death of Clement VII. The new pope, Paul III, did not hesitate to assign work to the master, forcing him once again to reduce the part that still remained to be executed on the tomb.

Paul set Michelangelo immediately to work on the project of painting in fresco *The Last Judgment* on the wall of the Sistine Chapel (1534-1541). Thus, after having evoked on the vault the beginning of the universe, the artist depicted its end. The violence and disequilibrium of this swirl of nude bodies rising from the grave to Paradise, or descending to Hell, spiraling around a central figure of Christ the judge, a Christ with the body of a Heracles and the face of an Apollo, is in startling contrast to the luminous, floating balance of the ceiling. The abundant and violent nudity, the athletic Christ, the angels without wings, all stirred violent condemnation during the artist's lifetime and resulted in subsequent painting of loincloths over most of the nudities, in the first instance by Michelangelo's pupil Daniele da Volterra, who thereby won for himself the nickname Il Brachettone (the breeches maker).

Some critics see in *The Last Judgment* a reflection in plastic terms of the crisis of Reformation and Counter-Reformation set off by Martin Luther's theses. Certainly, the artist, who grew increasingly religious with the years, was deeply troubled by the civil war in the body of Christianity. He was an intimate member of a reform Catholic movement centering on the poet Vittoria Colonna, whom the artist had met in 1536 and with whom he maintained a passionate platonic relationship until her death in 1547. He made many drawings for the poet, with whom he also exchanged poetry and discussed theological questions, some of which are expressed in intricate and ambiguous verse.

While working on *The Last Judgment*, Michelangelo had been named in 1535 architect, sculptor, and painter of the Apostolic Palace, wherein from 1541 to 1550, he frescoed the Pauline Chapel with the *Conversion of St. Paul* and the *Crucifixion of St. Peter*, thus completing his last paintings at the age of seventy-five. In 1547, Michelangelo was named architect of Saint Peter's. From then on, he was primarily involved with architecture: The disturbances and disequilibrium that still raged within the artist's soul found plastic expression in the broken pediments, recessed columns, blind niches, and frequently grotesque, abstract architectural forms.

Michelangelo's appointment as architect of Saint Peter's was reconfirmed by Julius III (1552), Paul IV (1555), and finally Pius IV (1559). Michelangelo resisted the insistent demands of the Medici Cosimo I that he return to Florence. More than eighty years old, Michelangelo was obsessed above all with the desire to push ahead the construction of Saint Peter's.

During these last years, the artist's thoughts dwelt constantly on the theme of death. It is probable that many of his finest sonnets and the last great drawings of the Crucifixion were executed during this time. After his seventy-fifth year, Michelangelo had begun work on the tragic *Pietà* now in the Duomo of Florence, in which the artist portrays himself as Nicodemus, the Pharisee who came to Jesus by night and raised troubled questions: "How can these things be?" According to biographer Giorgio Vasari, his contemporary, the work was intended for Michelangelo's own tomb.

At the end, Michelangelo seems to have broken through his suffering, gone beyond it into that tranquil yet tragic realm of his last two *Pietà* sculptures. The Rondanini *Pietà* leaps out of the Renaissance entirely, in two directions, one might say. The slender verticality—mother and Son merged—looks back to the column statues of Gothic portals and forward to the abstraction of Constantin Brancusi's *Bird in Space*—an almost macabre reduction of tragedy to pure essence.

Analysis

Michelangelo's tomb in Santa Croce symbolizes his titanic achievements as a sculptor, painter, and architect. Curiously, the fourth crown of laurel is missing, despite the fact that he is currently recognized as the greatest Italian lyric poet of the sixteenth century. Michelangelo himself refused to take seriously the verses that (especially from his sixtieth year on) he was forever scribbling and revising on the backs of letters, on sheets of drawings, or any other odd scraps of paper at hand. After all, he was not the only artist of his day who wrote poetry. The Renaissance ideal was *l'uomo universale*, the universal man, not the specialist.

Thus, the fact that Michelangelo wrote poetry is not surprising; what is surprising is the extraordinary quality of the best of his work. His contemporaries recognized it. The poems circulated in manuscript; a number of his madrigals were set to music by celebrated Italian and foreign composers, including Jakob Arcadelt; and in 1546, the Humanist Benedetto Varchi lectured on one of Michelangelo's sonnets before the Academy of Florence. Michelangelo was even persuaded to gather a selection of his verses for publication.

The unforeseen death of his friend, the banker Luigi del Riccio, who had been the patron for such a collection, dissuaded the artist from continuing the project. As it turned out, the poems were not published until 1623 in a corrupt edition misedited by Michelangelo's great-nephew, a Florentine academician. Fearful for his ancestor's reputation, the younger Michelangelo committed mayhem on the text, bowdlerizing anything remotely questionable, turning masculine into feminine, making elegant what was rough, and rewriting images. Not until Cesare Guasti's edition of 1863 did a responsible text appear. Individual poems have been translated by such well-known English and American poets and writers as William Wordsworth, Robert Southey, Henry Wadsworth Longfellow, Ralph Waldo Emerson, George Santayana, and Robert Bridges.

Sonnets, Madrigals, Fragments

The poetic works comprise 343 pieces—everything from sonnets and madrigals to fragments. Many of them appear to be a personal journal; others, such as the fifty epitaphs written at Riccio's request to commemorate the death of his nephew, serve some social purpose. The bulk of the verses seem to be the musings of an old man, although some love poems, full of conventional mannerisms, probably are earlier. All dating of the poems is speculative, deductive, but the assumption that very little of the earliest poetry has survived is supported by the fact that in 1518 the artist, in a burst of ire, burned many of his poems and drawings.

Michelangelo was particularly fond of the sonnet. Within its small space, as from a constricted block of marble, he hammered out harsh Dantesque lines that profoundly express his agony of spirit, now and again lightened by bursts of rough humor. Recurrent themes are the war of himself against himself; repentance for a nameless guilt; art as a symbol of the relationship of God to man; exalted platonic love; and a religious exaltation of death as liberation.

Conflicts Revealed

Despite frequent obscurities and abstract knotted metaphors, Michelangelo's poetry is striking for its ultimate confessional power, a nakedness of soul akin to his nudes in the visual arts. "Be silent! Enough of pallid violets and liquid crystals and sleek beasts," the poet Francesco Berni, a contemporary of Michelangelo, cries out in exasperation against the facile Petrarchan warblers of the time. "He speaks things, and you speak words." Berni struck to the core: "Ei dice cose . . ." ("He speaks things"), and in this, Michelangelo is rare not only among Italian poets. His lines seem to struggle out of the matrix of language as his "prisoners" struggle out of the rock. Seldom mellifluous, frequently imageless (or making use of conventional conceits), Michelangelo's verse derives its power from a texture of language that seems to be reproducing the very contours of thought itself: its spurts, its exaltations, its hesitations, its withdrawals. Sometimes ungrammatical, these strained, hammered lines are undoubtedly those of a sculptor. The combination of idealism, harshness, and crude jest reminds Italian readers of Dante. English readers, however, will be reminded of John Donne; there is the same love of paradox, the same coexistence of contraries, the same conflict between sensuality and austerity, the same mannered and overextended conceits, the same war of self against self: "Vorrei voler, Signor, quel ch'io non voglio . . ." ("I would want to want, O Lord, what I do not want . . .").

Just as in Michelangelo's sculpture (and in the painted sculpture that is the vault of the Sistine Chapel) *terribilità* coexists with melancholy resignation, so in these poems all the varieties of love—of God, of man, of woman, of art, of country—are celebrated in a grappling of ardor and ashes, the power to do anything frozen at the brink of a desire to do nothing.

Michelangelo was nourished on Dante, whose poetry he knew intimately; indeed, among his contemporaries, he was extolled as a Dante scholar. In Donato Giannotti's *Dialogues* on Dante, the artist figures as a major protagonist. However, if Michelangelo's spirit vibrated to that of his fellow Florentine, Dante, the forms and imagery of his verse were derived from the fashionable neo-Petrarchianism of the first half of the sixteenth century. The result is that Dantesque vigor and Michelangelesque spiritual suffering sometimes burst the fragile and stereotyped Petrarchan container. When these elements are in balance, the poetic achievement is of the very first order.

Tension and suffering

Michelangelo's poems are those of a man deeply ill at ease with himself and with his world, and it is this tension that makes them seem so neurotically modern. Like a salamander, Michelangelo is always living in flame; like a phoenix, he is always being reborn from the ashes of his suffering: "A single torment outweighs a thousand pleasures." Indeed, there is something masochistic, passive, feminine in many of his curious images. Like gold or silver, the poet's desire must be melted by the fires of love, and then poured into him "through such narrow spaces" to fill his void. As a goldsmith or silversmith must break the form to extract the work, so he must be broken and tortured to draw forth the perfect beauty of his lady. In another poem, one whose effectiveness is destroyed by its exaggerations, love enters through the eyes like a bunch of sour grapes forced into a narrow-necked bottle, and swelling within, is unable to escape.

Elsewhere, Michelangelo compares himself to a block of stone that, being smashed, reveals its inner sparks, and then, pulverized and re-formed, is firebaked to a longer life.

> So in love with the stone, in which it lies,
> Is fire, that, soon drawn forth, with its quick blaze
> It binds it, burns it, breaks it, and in new guise
> It makes it live in some immortal place.
> And that same stone, when baked, can brave and face
> All seasons, and acquires a higher price,
> Just like a soul that soars to blessèd days
> After the flames that cleanse while they chastise.
> Thus, if it is my fate that I soon must
> Be dissolved by this fire that hides in me,
> My new life shall be vast and manifold.
> Therefore, if I am now but smoke and dust,
> Cleansed by this flame, eternal I shall be:
> No iron chisel carves me—one of gold.

The imagery of the first six lines, relating to the preparation of a ground for fresco-painting, is typically masochistic: Suffering, being smashed, pulverized, is a necessary condition for the creation and rewards of art. In swift transition, the poet goes on to compare such purgation to the ascension of souls from Purgatory to Heaven and immediately returns to his central metaphor: Suffering enriches. Suffering is the fiery furnace for the creation of the most precious values.

NEOPLATONISM

The initial quatrain of another sonnet expresses with remarkable concision Michelangelo's entire Neoplatonic aesthetic and throws light on his technique of stone carving as well:

> The greatest artist has no single concept
> Which a rough marble block does not contain
> Already in its core; *that* can attain
> Only the hand that serves the intellect

Just as Plato's transcendental forms or ideas exist before their specific manifestations on earth, so the statue, fully formed, exists within the block of marble; there, it awaits the liberating hand of the artist, who finds it by stripping away the excess (*superchio*). Such a liberating hand does not function merely by instinct: It is guided to its goal by intelligence (*la man che ubbidisce all' intelletto*). Thus, the artist is a discoverer in the strictest etymological sense of the word.

ARTISTIC CONSISTENCY

What is so fascinating is that Michelangelo is always the same artist, whether he is twisting an idea or twisting David's right wrist, whether he is trying to fit all the ancestors of Christ into a spandrel of the Sistine Chapel or trying to fit too much concept into too little language. Just as the last great *Pietàs* and drawings have almost been dematerialized in the effort to render pure Idea, so in many of Michelangelo's poems language is being smashed, distorted, pulverized, almost as if the artist were trying to dispense with it.

The same poet addressed punning lines to a courtesan named Mancina, "Left-Handed"; lashed out at the bellicose Pope Julius, who was more devoted to the cult of Mars than to the Prince of Peace; and wrote stupendous sonnets to Night, whose dominions may be warred against by a single firefly; at the last, he held out his hands to Christ, longing for death to liberate him as he himself had liberated the perfect forms sleeping within the stone:

> Painting nor sculpturing no more will allay
> The soul turned toward the divine love
> Which opened to us its arms upon the cross.

OTHER MAJOR WORKS
NONFICTION: *I, Michelangelo, Sculptor: An Autobiography Through Letters*, 1962; *The Letters of Michelangelo*, 1963.
MISCELLANEOUS: *Complete Poems and Selected Letters of Michelangelo*, 1963.

BIBLIOGRAPHY
Barolsky, Paul. *The Faun in the Garden*. University Park: Pennsylvania State University Press, 1994. Barolsky's "analysis of poetic imagination" deeply relates Michelangelo's poetry to his artistic works and his contemporary biographies. He used all three to weave a fabrication of his "self" as creator and man.
Cambon, Glauco. *Michelangelo's Poetry: Fury of Form*. Princeton, N.J.: Princeton University Press, 1985. A specialized study of the diverse talents of Michelangelo.
Forcellino, Antonio. *Michelangelo: A Tormented Life*. Malden, Mass.: Polity, 2009. This biography, translated from the Italian, begins by describing Michelangelo's struggle with the powerful figures in his life, and how after his death they began to build a myth around him.
Gilbert, Creighton. *Michelangelo: On and Off the Sistine Ceiling*. New York: George Braziller, 1994. A specialized study of the diverse talents of Michelangelo.
Hallock, Ann Hayes. *Michelangelo the Poet*. Palo Alto, Calif.: Page-Ficklin, 1978. Hallock presents a reading and contextualizing of the *Rime*, emphasizing his "drive toward the essential." She uncovers elements of this in his use of language and "nuclei" (themes) of *patria*, family, friends, soul, and life and death. Often complicated language and no English translations.
Ryan, Christopher. *The Poetry of Michelangelo: An Introduction*. Madison, N.J.: Fairleigh Dickinson University Press, 1998. This introduction to the poet and poems emphasizes the individual works and the corpus itself, as it attempts to clarify the intricacies of both. Ryan lays the works out chronologically, in stages, providing relevant historical and biographical background. Translations are the author's.
Wallace, William E. *Michelangelo: The Artist, the Man, and His Times*. New York: Cambridge University Press, 2010. Wallace used Michelangelo's letters and poems for insight into the man in writing his biography, so there is more discussion of the poetry than in most biographies.

Sidney Alexander

EUGENIO MONTALE

Born: Genoa, Italy; October 12, 1896
Died: Milan, Italy; September 12, 1981

PRINCIPAL POETRY

Ossi di seppia, 1925 (partial translation, *The Bones of Cuttlefish*, 1983; full translation, *Cuttlefish Bones*, 1992)
Le occasioni, 1939 (*The Occasions*, 1987)
La bufera, e altro, 1956 (*The Storm, and Other Poems*, 1978)
Poems by Eugenio Montale, 1959
Eugenio Montale: Poesie/Poems, 1965
Selected Poems, 1965
Provisional Conclusions: A Selection of the Poetry of Eugenio Montale, 1970
Satura, 1962-1970, 1971 (English translation, 1998)
Diario del '71 e del '72, 1973 (partial translation in *New Poems*, 1976)
New Poems: A Selection from "Satura" and "Diario del '71 e del '72," 1976
Quaderno di quattro anni, 1977 (*It Depends: A Poet's Notebook*, 1980)
L'opera in versi, 1980
Diario postumo, 1991-1996 (2 volumes; *Posthumous Diary*, 2001)
Collected Poems, 1920-1954, 1998
Selected Poems, 2004

OTHER LITERARY FORMS

In addition to his several volumes of verse collected by R. Bettarini and G. Contini in a critical edition, *L'opera in versi*, Eugenio Montale (mohn-TAH-lay) wrote the obliquely autobiographical short stories of *Farfalla di Dinard* (1956; *Butterfly of Dinard*, 1971). His critical essays on literature were collected by G. Zampa in *Sulla poesia* (1976; on poetry) and those on broadly cultural or social topics in *Auto da fé* (1966). To them should be added the travelogues and interviews of *Fuori di casa* (1969; abroad), which arose from the practice of journalism, and the musical reviews posthumously reprinted in book form: *Prime alla Scala* (1981; premieres at La Scala), edited by G. Lavezzi. The revealing intellectual diary of 1917, *Quaderno genovese* (pb. 1983), also deserves mention.

ACHIEVEMENTS

Eugenio Montale won the Premio dell'Antico Fattore (1932), the Premio Manzotto (1956), Italy's Dante Medal (1959), the Feltrinelli Prize from the Accademia dei Lincei (1963, 1964), Paris's Calouite Bulbenkian Prize (1971), and honorary degrees from the

Eugenio Montale
(©The Nobel Foundation)

Universities of Milan, Rome, Cambridge, Basel, and Nice. In 1967, he was named senator of the Italian Republic. In 1975, he won the coveted Nobel Prize in Literature.

BIOGRAPHY

The youngest of five siblings, Eugenio Montale was born in Genoa on October 12, 1896, to Giuseppina Ricci and Domingo Montale, a well-to-do businessman who shared with two first cousins the ownership and management of a firm for the importation of turpentine and other chemicals. Poor health forced Montale to withdraw from school as a ninth-grader; henceforth, only his insatiable curiosity for books and the unfailing assistance of his sister Marianne—a philosophy student—were to sustain him in the pursuit of a broad cultural education, ranging from Italian, French, and English literature to modern philosophy. Entering the family firm or a bank, as his brothers did, was out of the question from the start for the dreamy adolescent, who, sharing with his family a great love for opera, soon began to train for baritone singing with Ernesto Sivori. This fine teacher's death in 1916 put an end to Montale's plans for an operatic career but not to his lifelong interest in musical theater. In 1917, Montale joined the army and soon was serving as an infantry officer on the Trentino front against the Austrians.

During the years immediately following World War I, Montale's contributions to literary journals and the limited if solid success of *Cuttlefish Bones* were not enough to earn a living, and in 1927, he moved to Florence, where he found work first with Bemporad, a publishing firm, and then as curator of the Vieusseux rare books library in the employ of the city administration. He was to lose that congenial position in 1938 for political reasons, but he remained in Florence through the war years as a freelance translator and an acknowledged leader of the literary scene until 1948, when he moved to Milan as contributing editor to the leading daily *Il corriere della sera*. Long before he received the 1975 Nobel Prize in Literature, he was made a senator for life by the president of the Italian Republic. The death in 1963 of his wife, Drusilla Tanzi, affected him deeply, as the "Xenia" sequence in *Satura* shows; from then on, the old poet was entrusted to the devoted care of their housekeeper, Gina Tiossi. Much earlier, two other women had left a durable imprint on his art: a visiting American scholar in the 1930's (who became the unnamed angelic figure of many poems in *The Occasions* and the Clizia of *The Storm, and Other Poems*) and, in the late 1940's and early 1950's, an Italian poetess (who inspired the "Volpe," or "Vixen," poems in *The Storm, and Other Poems*). Montale's funeral in mid-September, 1981, was attended by the Italian chief of state and many other prominent figures of public and artistic life.

Analysis

Emerging from the welter of experiments and iconoclasms that had marked the decade before World War I, Eugenio Montale's intense lyrics set the tone for the interwar period in Italian poetry. Giuseppe Ungaretti's verse, jotted down in the Carso trenches and first published in 1916, had already pointed the way to a new poetics of elliptical imagery, inward essentialness, modern diction, and deconstructed meter that had distilled Futurist exuberance into noiseless immediacy. Montale's first collection, *Cuttlefish Bones*, discovered the untapped possibilities of a venerable tradition, which, purged of academic sclerosis and vatic posturing or bombast, could best articulate the dilemmas, the self-criticism, and the yearning for authentic values that variously haunted so many of the war's survivors. The starkness of style of this first book sharpened into thinly veiled prophetic denunciation with Montale's next collection, *The Occasions*, which registered the gathering of a new storm. In his third collection, *The Storm, and Other Poems*, Montale responded to World War II and its aftermath in an unfashionable vein of visionary lyricism. His books of the 1970's, from *Satura* on, approach the threshold of prosiness, in keeping with the prevalently satirical and gnomic bent of his later years. The Nobel laureate of 1975 became the poetic conscience of the generation that had groped for truth in the dark times between two world wars; he showed that the best way for a writer to be modern was not to discard a tradition which went all the way back to Dante but instead (in Ezra Pound's words) to "make it new."

CUTTLEFISH BONES

Cuttlefish Bones displays simultaneously the alert richness of youth and maturity's searching control. Scrupulous attention to the formal resources of the word, far from foundering into aesthetic complacency, bespeaks an ingrained commitment to cognitive values, and since there can be no final certainty about these values, the persona wavering between sudden contemplative rapture and unappeased doubt transcends the merely autobiographical level to become as memorable a spokesperson for the modern human condition as T. S. Eliot's Prufrock or Pound's Mauberley. It was no accident that the author of *Cuttlefish Bones* should eventually become a friend of Pound (politics apart) and try his hand at translating one short section of *Hugh Selwyn Mauberley* (1920) as well as three of Eliot's "Ariel Poems," while Eliot, for his part, published "Arsenio," chronologically the last poem of *Cuttlefish Bones*, in a 1928 issue of *The Criterion*. "Arsenio," the most lucidly despondent and subtly modulated monologue in *Cuttlefish Bones* (the poem first appeared in the collection's third edition), was translated by Mario Praz, and it was Praz who, two decades later, identified certain formal and thematic affinities between Eugenio Montale's and Eliot's poetry.

The affinities are there, if one but thinks of the wasteland-like component in Montale's style and world view, but they should not overshadow the differences and, above all, Montale's independence from the Eliotic paradigm. Montale's poetics of dryness, which found an early embodiment in "Meriggiare pallido e assorto" ("The Wall"), stems from the Dantesque leanings first recognized by Glauco Cambon in 1956 and openly confirmed by the poet himself many years later.

In "The Wall," written several years before the publication of *The Waste Land* (1922), Montale's characteristic tone is already evident:

> ... e andando nel sole che abbaglia
> sentire con triste meraviglia
> comè tutta la vita e il suo travaglio
> in questo seguitare una muraglia
> che ha in cima cocci aguzzi di bottiglia.

> ... and walking on under the blinding sun
> to feel with sad amazement
> how all of life's painful endeavor is
> in this perpetual going along a wall
> that carries on its top sharp bottle shards.

The familiar sight of such walls protecting gardens and orchards in the northern Italian upland countryside has elicited an unmistakable emblem of the burdensome human condition which the stoic Montalian persona repeatedly faces. The emblem, whether in the same form or in the guise of cognate imagery, pervades Montale's poetry. In one of *Cuttlefish Bones*'s most cryptic and tensest lyrics, "Crisalide" ("Chrysalis"), it reaches its symbolic acme: "e noi andremo innanzi senza smuovere/ un sasso solo della gran muraglia" ("and we shall go right on without dislodging/ even a single stone of the huge wall"). Perhaps, the poem continues, we humans shall never meet on our way "la libertà, il miracolo,/ il fatto che non era necessario!" ("freedom, miracle,/ the fact that was not shackled by necessity!").

That cry of the heart and of the whole mind against the seeming barrier that reality opposes to humankind's need for knowledge and deliverance voices the central concern of the Montalean persona and propels his utterance beyond whatever seductions the lavish landscape of sensuous experience may offer. "The mind investigates, harmonizes, disjoins," as Montale writes in "I limoni" ("The Lemon Trees"), the first poem of *Cuttlefish Bones* after the epigraph lyric; it is a question of finding "a mistake of Nature,/ the dead point of the world, the loose chain-ring,/ the thread to be unravelled" which will finally "place us in the midst of a truth." Remarkably, and understandably, the search for truth can take place only as an attempt to disrupt the opaque compactness of existence. The revolt against closure, the distrust of intellectual systems that claim to explain everything, marks Montale's imagery and thought from beginning to end and accounts for his interest in Émile Boutroux's contingentist thought, which openly challenged the still prevalent determinist philosophies of science.

Montale is a thinking poet, a "poet on the edge" in Rebecca West's apt words; he cannot take phenomenal reality for granted but must forever question it. Denial is his concomitant gesture. With Arthur Schopenhauer (and Giacomo Leopardi), Montale at times sees and feels existence as sheer suffering. The "pain of living" can be escaped only in a kind of Buddhist "divine indifference," the privilege of the noon-haloed statue in the garden, of the floating cloud, of the high-soaring hawk—or else, acme of negations, in the Nirvanic ecstasy of the sunflower "impazzito di luce" (maddened with the light). The "glory of outspread noon" rules over Liguria's seething sea and rocky, olive-tree-studded slopes, a fierce beauty not to be forgotten by the war-tried persona who revisits the landscape of his childhood.

It was an Eden, now lost forever, as stated in "Fine dell'infanzia" (end of childhood). Here the persona, confronting the numinous turbulences and calms of the Mediterranean, rehearses what had been his initiation to poetry and self-knowledge, in self-differentiation from, and reimmersion in, the godlike native element. Alternatively, he contemplates, in the person of the lithe swimmer Esterina ("Falsetto"), the momentary bliss that immersion in the welcoming bosom of her "divine friend" can bestow, though the contemplator himself remains "on dry land," apart from that alien joy. The "Mediterraneo" ("Mediterranean") series at the center of the book has been faulted by some critics (Gianfranco Contini, Silvio Ramat, and the author himself) as a relapse into suspect exuberance from the terse spareness achieved by "Cuttlefish Bones," the eponymous series that precedes "Mediterranean" in the collection. "Mediterranean," however, with its nearly Whitmanesque expansiveness, counterpoints the systole of "Cuttlefish Bones" and thus makes the entire book pulsate with a vitality of its own.

THE OCCASIONS

When that vitality subsides into the mournfulness of "Arsenio" (a piece added to the third edition of *Cuttlefish Bones* in 1928), the stage is set for the next cycle of poems, *The Occasions*, which disappointed a friendly critic, Pietro Pancrazi; in Pancrazi's opinion, Montale with this new book had turned to abstruse "metaphysical" poetry instead of staying with the "physical" concreteness of *Cuttlefish Bones*. Actually, what occurred was no involution but a deepening of style and vision into the kind of clipped writing that can evoke an innermost reality from the barest outline of factual detail. The relative colorfulness of the sunstruck earlier book yields to a gray monochrome. The diction becomes even more conversational, the tone more low-key yet amenable to sudden soarings in elliptical concentration, and metric patterns tend to disintegrate as far as stanza form goes, even if the lines as such stay mostly within the regular cast of the hendecasyllable and alternative shorter verse types. *The Occasions*, accordingly, evinces a less literary and more penetrating voice than its predecessor, from which it nevertheless takes seminal motifs. The epistemological urge turns from the cosmic to the personal and historical, political sphere, facing the precariousness of individual existence to denounce (in guarded yet ultimately transparent allegory) the evils of Nazi and fascist totalitarianism, the threat of impending war. Liuba, in "A Liuba che parte" ("For Liuba, Leaving"), is a Jewess forced to flee persecution, carrying her household gods (a cat in a hatbox) like a diminutive Noah's ark that will tide her over the flood of "the blind times." In "Dora Markus," the title figure, an Austrian Jewess whose very "sweetness is a storm," recalling "migratory birds that crash into a lighthouse," withstands time's (and the times') ordeal by the mere strength of her womanly amulets, while it get "later, ever later"; in the teeth of Nazism's "ferocious faith," she refuses to "surrender/ voice, legend or destiny." An unnamed girl from Liguria who died young (a poem of the last years will identify her as Annetta) haunts the persona's memory in "La casa dei doganieri" ("The Shorewatcher's House"), where she will never return, while "the compass spins crazily at random" and "there is no reckoning the dice's throw." The persona's interlocutor in "Barche sulla Marna" ("Boats on the Marne") shares with him a peaceful Sunday on that French river which nevertheless conjures in his mind the fateful meandering of human history away from the dreamed possibility of a just, serene, and happy life on Earth.

In another holiday setting, the English bank holiday in "Eastbourne," the persona strolling on the beach descries dark omens; "evil is winning, the wheel will never stop," and perhaps not even the countervailing force of love, which holds the world together, will manage to stem the tide. It is a force coming from, and oriented toward, his absent beloved, who thereby acquires mythic, not to say godlike, status; the stirring hyperbole recalls Dante's myth of Beatrice in a different, if equally apocalyptic, context. No less apocalyptically, the same transfigured lady from the Atlantic's other shore battles the forces of obscurantism on a chessboard which clearly figures forth the contemporary world under the gathering storm ("Nuove stanze"), and she dawns on the persona's mind to exorcize those forces in "Elegia de Pico Farnese" (elegy for Pico Farnese) and in "Palio" (Palio at Siena), where the clamoring crowd and the wheeling horses in the folk event of worldwide renown evoke the mass hysteria and the apparent ineluctability of sinister political developments in the late 1930's.

At the heart of *The Occasions*, the Beatrice-like American woman dominates the twenty "motets" addressed to her by a modern troubadour who effortlessly renews the medieval worship of Eros in the very act of confronting a bleak modern reality. Descanting on the vicissitudes of love from afar, Montale attains a poignancy attuned to the contrapuntal polyphony of Orlando di Lasso, Giovanni Pierluigi da Palestrina, and Carlo Gesualdo:

> Un ronzìo lungo viene dall'aperto.
> Strazia com'unghia ai vetri. Cerco il segno
> smarrito, il pegno solo ch'ebbi in grazia
> da te.
> E l'infernoè certo.
>
> A long whir comes from the outside.
> It grates like a nail on windowpanes. I seek the sign
> lost, the one pledge I had as a grace
> from you.
> And hell is certain.

Even though, as Montale later saw fit to reveal, this particular motet and the two following ones were inspired by another lady (a Peruvian visitor) and not by the one whom he was to call Clizia, the Ovidian girl metamorphosed into a sunflower in *The Storm, and Other Poems*, it serves as a perfect opening to the whole series, with which it thematically and tonally coalesces.

THE STORM, AND OTHER POEMS

The "I-thou" rhetorical stance, the repudiation of the irrational times, and the persistent conversation with absent Clizia across the ocean—all these obviously link *The Occasions* to *The Storm, and Other Poems*, which at the same time shows new developments in style and theme. The first part of this book, with the title "Finisterre," had been published in Lugano, Switzerland, by Bernasconi in 1943, and one climactic poem, "Primavera hitleriana" ("The Hitler Spring"), protesting Hitler's official visit to Florence in 1938, could not appear in print before the end of the war. "Finisterre" pushes emblematic allusiveness to a truly hermetic point, covertly indicating the war unleashed by the Axis powers. The diction is melodiously stylized, there is a tendency toward legato as opposed to the earlier staccato and related percussive alliterations, and the very fact that three of the poems happen to be sonnets (albeit treated with deft sprezzatura) signals an unprecedented Petrarchan leaning—openly avowed by the author in "Intenzioni, intervista immaginaria" (intentions, an imaginary interview) of 1946, a poem later reprinted in *Sulla poesia*. These "Finisterre" lyrics are germane to the coeval translation of three sonnets by William Shakespeare, to be found in *It Depends: A Poet's Notebook*.

Family memories, a moving poem to Montale's wife (who was briefly hospitalized during the last days of the battle for Florence in August, 1944), and a series of madrigals to the poetically gifted lady addressed under the code name of the "Volpe" (Vixen), contribute to the uniqueness of *The Storm, and Other Poems*, a book also characterized by the frequent naming of God (a novelty in Montale) and by the joyous vitality that the poems to the Vixen and the breathtaking dithyramb "L'anguilla" ("The Eel"), ostensibly addressed to Clizia, hymnically convey. The two poems in the last section, "Conclusioni provvisorie" ("Provisional Conclusions"), provide a dark antiphon by casting a saturnine eye on the disappointing postwar world, where the dominant mass ideologies of Stalinism and Christian Democracy ("red" and "black clerics") seem equally unacceptable to the devotee of a humanist faith in the dignity of humankind. The impending extinction of Western civilization is allegorized in a "shadowy Lucifer," though the persona still clings to his dream of love for Clizia.

Satura

Satura (the Latin title means "satire" but also connotes a medley of offerings) picks up those somber clues in a prosaic register which would persist down to the last of Montale's books. A Lucifer-like god darkens by his very absence the allegorized historical scene of "Botta e risposta I" (thrust and riposte I), where the persona, reviewing what preceded and followed the latest catastrophe, decries the fact that Italy's liberation by the Allied armies failed to bring about a permanent cleansing of the Augean stables, public life being now repulsively shapeless. A bracing antiphon to that depressing message and tone rings out in "Xenia," and much else in *Satura*—especially "Angelo Nero" (black angel)—shows Montale's old mettle, even in the new, exceedingly deflated style. The books of the 1970's comment discursively on public issues or private events and memories, and if an aggressively flat chattiness seems at times to take over, the epigrams and some satirical pieces have a sharpness of their own. All in all, these last collections constitute the uneven aftermath of the great poetry that had reached its lyric climax in *The Storm, and Other Poems*.

OTHER MAJOR WORKS

NONFICTION: *Farfalla di Dinard*, 1956 (short articles, prose poems, memoirs; *The Butterfly of Dinard*, 1970); *Auto da fé*, 1966; *Fuori di casa*, 1969; *Nel nostro tempo*, 1972 (*Poet in Our Time*, 1976); *Sulla poesia*, 1976; *Prime alla Scala*, 1981; *The Second Life of Art*, 1982; *Quaderno genovese*, pb. 1983 (wr. 1917).

BIBLIOGRAPHY

Brook, Clodagh J. *The Expression of the Inexpressible in Eugenio Montale's Poetry: Metaphor, Negation, and Silence*. New York: Clarendon Press, 2002. Locating Montale firmly within European modernism, this book examines the struggle with language that is central to his work.

Butcher, John. *Poetry and Intertextuality: Eugenio Montale's Later Verse*. Perugia: Volumnia, 2007. This analysis of Montale's poetry concentrates on the works he produced in later years, including *Satura*.

Cambon, Glauco. *Eugenio Montale's Poetry: A Dream in Reason's Presence*. Princeton, N.J.: Princeton University Press, 1982. A critical assessment of Montale's career as a poet. Includes bibliographical references and indexes.

Cary, Joseph. *Three Modern Italian Poets*. Chicago: University of Chicago Press, 1993. Cary presents striking biographical portraits and provides an understanding of the works of Umberto Saba, Giuseppe Ungaretti, and Montale. Includes chronological tables, bibliography.

Huffman, Claire Licari. *Montale and the Occasions of Poetry*. Princeton, N.J.: Princeton University Press, 1983. A collection of the author's essays and lectures about Montale's life and works. Includes bibliographical references and index.

Montale, Eugenio. *Selected Poems*. Translated by Jonathan Galassi, Charles Wright, and David Young. Edited with an introduction by David Young. Oberlin, Ohio: Oberlin College Press, 2004. This collection of poems, translated by three well-known Montale translators, contains an introduction that provides biography and analysis of Montale's works.

Sica, Paola. *Modernist Forms of Rejuvenation: Eugenio Montale and T. S. Eliot*. Florence, Italy: L. S. Olschki, 2003. Sica examines modernism through the works of Montale and Eliot.

West, Rebecca. *Eugenio Montale: Poet on the Edge*. Cambridge, Mass.: Harvard University Press, 1981. The well-known novelist's critical interpretations of some of Montale's major works. Includes bibliographic references and an index.

Young, David. *Six Modernist Moments in Poetry*. Iowa City: University of Iowa Press, 2006. This discussion of modernism looks at Montale's "Mediterranean" as well as poems by Rainer Maria Rilke, William Butler Yeats, Wallace Stevens, William Carlos Williams, and Marianne Moore.

Glauco Cambon

CESARE PAVESE

Born: Santo Stefano Belbo, Italy; September 9, 1908
Died: Turin, Italy; August 27, 1950

PRINCIPAL POETRY

Lavorare stanca, 1936, expanded 1943 (*Hard Labor*, 1976)
La terra e la morte, 1947
Verrà la morte e avrà i tuoi occhi, 1951
Poesie edite e inedite, 1962
A Mania for Solitude: Selected Poems, 1930-1950, 1969
Disaffections: Complete Poems, 1930-1950, 2002

OTHER LITERARY FORMS

Cesare Pavese (pah-VAY-zay) was primarily a novelist. He wrote nine novels, beginning with *Paesi tuoi* in 1941 (*The Harvesters*, 1961). His nonfiction *Dialoghi con Leucò* (1947; *Dialogues with Leucò*, 1966) and the novel *La luna e i falò* (1950; *The Moon and the Bonfire*, 1952) are considered his masterpieces. Pavese is noted for dealing with classical myths and writing about characters from the countryside. R. W. Flint translated a selection of his fiction, and many of his works of fiction continue to be available in English.

Pavese was also a respected essayist. In his expanded edition of *Hard Labor*, published in 1943, he included two highly valued essays: "The Poet's Craft" and "Concerning Certain Poems Not Yet Written." His other essays were published posthumously as *La letteratura americana e altri saggi*, edited by Italo Calvino, in 1951. In 1970, they were translated in English by Edwin Fussell as *American Literature: Essays and Opinions*.

An accomplished translator of English works into Italian, Pavese began with Sinclair Lewis's *Our Mr. Wrenn* in 1931. He went on to translate such authors as Herman Melville, James Joyce, Sherwood Anderson, and William Faulkner.

ACHIEVEMENTS

Cesare Pavese was one of a group of writers to come to maturity during the mid-1930's. He is noted for his antifascist efforts and his commitment to other left-wing causes, and he was even imprisoned for his activities. His first volume of poetry, *Hard Labor*, published in 1936 and expanded in 1943, considered one of his major achievements, has been translated into English by such writers as Margaret Crosland and William Arrowsmith. Several poems were censored by the authorities, a testimony to

Pavese's subversive political thinking. Pavese concentrated on prose in the years following World War II, but he returned to verse a few years before his death, first publishing a group of poems called *La terra e la morte* in a magazine. These poems have a stark, lyrical quality to them. In 1950, Cesare Pavese received the Strega Prize, Italy's greatest literary award.

Biography

Cesare Pavese was born to parents Eugenio Pavese and Consolina Pavese in 1908, at their family vacation spot in the Piedmont region of Italy. The family, which included an older daughter, lived in Turin. His father worked as a bailiff in the court system. When Pavese was six years old, his father died. He started writing poetry while still in secondary school. In 1923, Pavese entered the Liceo Massimo d'Azeglio to complete his high school studies. Agusto Monti became his teacher and mentor. In 1926, Pavese entered the University of Turin. It was here that he began his lifelong interest in American literature. He did his thesis work on Walt Whitman, getting a degree from the university in 1930. His mother died the same year. He also started work on a cycle on poems that would become part of *Hard Labor*.

To help support himself during his postgraduate years, Pavese translated Melville's *Moby Dick: Or, The Whale* (1851), as well as works by Joyce, John Dos Passos, and Anderson. Pavese also joined antifascist groups; in 1935, he was arrested for holding letters of a jailed antifascist that he received from his girlfriend Tina Pizzardo, who was a member of the Communist Party. Pavese served seven months of a three-year sentence under house arrest and in exile.

His first book, *Hard Labor*, was published in 1936, but censors reduced the number of poems by four. Pavese would later publish this volume in a much larger edition. After his arrest, Pavese continued to write but stopped publishing for some time. His friend Guilio Einaudi restored a publishing company, and Pavese worked for and published most of his works with this publishing house. In 1941 and 1942, Pavese published two novels, as well as a translation of Faulkner's *The Hamlet* (1940). He left Turin in 1943, when the city fell under Nazi control. After the war, he returned to Turin and joined the Communist Party. After the war, Pavese published three books, *Feria d'agosto* (1946; *Summer Storm, and Other Stories*, 1966), *La terra e la morte*, and *Dialogues with Leucò*. In 1949, Pavese met and fell in love with the American actress Constance Dowling. Their affair lasted a year. Pavese was known as a troubled person. He seemed to embody the modern existentialist despair of his day. In August of 1950, despondent over a broken love affair, Pavese killed himself with an overdose of sleeping pills.

Analysis

Though influenced by American writers such as Whitman, Cesare Pavese is not particularly well known in the United States. However, he has a worldwide reputation and is a very important figure in twentieth century modern Italian literature. Pavese's work has influenced many modern poets, including Denise Levertov. Her volume *Life in the Forest* (1978) contains a section of poems inspired by Pavese's work.

Hard Labor

Pavese once said of *Hard Labor* that it "might have saved a generation." For a volume in which he wished to speak to and for a generation, it is striking to note that one of its major themes is silence—and another solitude. It is a silence at times wished for, and freeing: "Here, in the dark, alone,/ my body rests and feels it is the one master of itself" (in "Mania di solitudine," "Passion for Solitude"); at other times it seems to crush the person who cannot escape it: "every day the silence of the lonely room/ closes on the rustle of movement, of every gesture, like air" (in "La voce," "The Voice"). In his early poem "Antenati" ("Ancestors"), Pavese strongly suggests that the inability to speak is passed down through generations of rough men: "I found out I had lived, before I was born,/ in tough, sturdy, independent men, masters of themselves./ None of them knew what to say, so they just kept quiet." The women in the family also endure a hard silence: "In our family women don't matter./ What I mean is, our women stay home/ and make children like me, and keep their mouths shut." They suffer their own hard labor.

In "Gente spaesata" ("Displaced People"), the natural landscape can induce a hypnotic silence between men: "We've seen too much of the sea./ Late afternoon—the colorless water stretches dully away, disappearing into air. My friend's staring at the sea,/ and I'm staring at him, and neither says a word." The antidote to the sea is the hills, which supplant the earlier barren landscape. In Pavese's words, almost like a drinking song or boast, the hills become fleshy and fertile, ripe for dreams—dreams of women. In such a dream landscape, imagined conversation is possible: "We could stroll through the vineyards and, maybe,/ meet with a couple of girls, dark brown, ripened by the sun,/ we could strike up a conversation, we could sample their grapes." A harsh landscape swirls with levels of talk: simple talk, drunken talk, imaginary talk—all transformed by the poet's language.

Though the individual suffers in silence, a kind of collective is available that unites these lonely, working people: "All he feels is the pavement, which other men have made—/ men with calloused hands, hands like his" (in "Lavorare stanca," "Hard Labor"). The old pastoral ode of a shepherd following his flock, has fallen away to reveal a flintier modern man—worn down but bearing up—in silence: if not a part of, at least within, his or her community. In these kinds of poems, the solitary wanderer is not the only person to hold dreams or to suffer dreams being crushed. Poems such as "Pensieri di Deola" ("Deola Thinking"), "La moglie del barcaiolo" ("The Boatman's Wife"), and "Atlantic Oil" show people beaten down, exhausted, by the world of work, by the necessity of getting by, which is the hard soil to which all men must cling: "The long days work has left them dead" (in "Crepuscolo di sabbiatori," "Sand-Diggers' Twilight").

In "Atlantic Oil," a working mechanic is invited by the landscape to fall away into dreams: "And the story ends with the mechanic marrying the vineyard of his choice,/ and the girl that goes with it. He'll work outdoors in the sun." His heady dreams are contrasted with the knowledge of a drunken mechanic who sleeps in a ditch by the road. All these worlds will spiral down, "plunging in the valley below, down in the darkness."

Sometimes, memories of the past are all that are available, or fantasies of an imagined future with someone, a future that will never happen. The poems, despite their hard realities, contain romantic and lyric qualities that seem to hold out some hope of rescue. Usually it is an imagined woman who holds out the most hope for a man, as in "Paternità" ("Fatherhood"): "Every man,/ alone with a drink, will see her again. She'll always be there." Her permanent absence, her fleshly invisibility, ultimately creates longing and confusion and a return to silence in "Incontro" ("Encounter"): "I created her from the ground of everything/ I love the most, and I cannot understand her."

The poems in *Hard Labor* are often crafted with a long, proselike line. The people in the city and countryside seem fresh from a young poet's developing vision and seem to take their inspiration from another solitary wanderer: Whitman.

VERRÀ LA MORTE E AVRÀ I TUOI OCCHI

After a period of time when Pavese wrote only novels, he returned to verse. In the later poems, he uses a more spare line length. The poems are stark lyrics, often addressed directly to a "you." In 1945, he published in a magazine a group of nine poems called *La terra e la morte*. These poems were later collected in Pavese's posthumous volume *Verrà la morte e avrà i tuoi occhi* (death will come and it will have your eyes).

The later poems resonate with several of Pavese's familiar themes. The land and sea are ever-present, as is the quixotic search for a love that cannot be possessed. As always, silence pervades, and it assumes even darker forms, as in "La terre et la morte" ("Earth and Death"): "You are earth and death./ Your season is darkness/ and silence." In the series of love lyrics connected to the title poem, love becomes an open wound, a fatality, subsumed by silence:

> Death will come, and it will have your eyes.
> It will be like ending a vice, like seeing a dead face
> emerge from the mirror,
> like hearing closed lips speak.
> We'll go down in silence.

A few months after these last poems were written, Pavese took his own life. He was only forty-one.

OTHER MAJOR WORKS

LONG FICTION: *Paesi tuoi*, 1941 (*The Harvesters*, 1961); *La spiaggia*, 1942 (*The Beach*, 1963); *Il compagno*, 1947 (*The Comrade*, 1959); *La bella estate*, 1949 (includes

Il diavolo sulle colline and *Tra donne sole*; *The Beautiful Summer*, 1959); *Il carcere*, 1949 (*The Political Prisoner*, 1959); *La casa in collina*, 1949 (*The House on the Hill*, 1956); *Il diavolo sulle colline*, 1949 (*The Devil in the Hills*, 1954); *Prima che il gallo canti*, 1949 (includes *Il carcere* and *La casa in collina*); *Tra donne sole*, 1949 (*Among Women Only*, 1953); *La luna e i falò*, 1950 (*The Moon and the Bonfire*, 1952; also known as *The Moon and the Bonfires*); *Fuoco grande*, 1959 (with Bianca Garufi; *A Great Fire*, 1963); *The Selected Works of Cesare Pavese*, 1968.

SHORT FICTION: *Feria d'agosto*, 1946 (*Summer Storm, and Other Stories*, 1966); *Notte di festa*, 1953 (*Festival Night, and Other Stories*, 1964); *Racconti*, 1960 (*Told in Confidence, and Other Stories*, 1971); *The Leather Jacket: Stories*, 1980; *Stories*, 1987.

NONFICTION: *Dialoghi con Leucò*, 1947 (*Dialogues with Leucò*, 1966); *La letteratura americana e altri saggi*, 1951 (*American Literature: Essays and Opinions*, 1970); *Il mestiere di vivere: Diario, 1935-1950*, 1952 (*The Burning Brand: Diaries, 1935-1950*, 1961; also known as *The Business of Living*); *Lettere*, 1966 (partially translated as *Selected Letters, 1924-1950*, 1969).

TRANSLATIONS: *Il nostro signor Wrenn*, 1931 (of Sinclair Lewis's *Our Mr. Wrenn*); *Moby-Dick*, 1932 (of Herman Melville); *Riso nero*, 1932 (of Sherwood Anderson's *Dark Laughter*); *Il 42 parallelo*, 1935 (of John Dos Passos's *Forty-second Parallel*); *U omini e topi*, 1938 (of John Steinbeck's *Of Mice and Men*); *Tre esistenze*, 1940 (of Gertrude Stein's *Three Lives*); *Il borgo*, 1942 (of William Faulkner's *The Hamlet*).

BIBLIOGRAPHY

Hacht, Anne Marie, and David Kelly, eds. *Poetry for Students*. Vol. 20. Detroit: Thomson/Gale, 2004. Analyzes Pavese's "Two Poems for T." Contains the poem, a summary, and discussions of the poem's themes, style, historical context, critical overview, and criticism. Includes bibliography and index.

Lajolo, Davide. *An Absurd Vice: A Biography of Cesare Pavese*. New York: New Directions, 1983. Lajolo was a friend of Pavese and his first biographer. His friendship with Pavese gave him special insights, but later scholars distrusted some of his psychological and political speculations about Pavese.

O'Healy, Áine. *Cesare Pavese*. Boston: Twayne, 1988. This short, excellent biography clears away many of the myths about Pavese. It is an excellent place to begin a study of Pavese and his work.

Pavese, Cesare, and Anthony Chiuminatto. *Cesare Pavese and Anthony Chiuminatto: Their Correspondence*. Edited by Mark Pietralunga. Toronto, Ont.: University of Toronto Press, 2007. This collection of letters between Pavese and Italian American musician and educator Chiuminatto between 1929 and 1933 sheds light on the Italian poet.

Simborowski, Nicoletta. *Secrets and Puzzles: Silence and the Unsaid in Contemporary Italian Writing*. Oxford, England: Legenda, European Humanities Research Center,

2003. Traces self-censorship in postwar Italy in the writings of Pavese, Primo Levi, Natalia Ginzburg, and Francesca Sanvitale. Chapter 3 focuses on Pavese's political commitment.

Smith, Laurence G. *Cesare Pavese and America: Life, Love, and Literature.* Amherst: University of Massachusetts Press, 2008. This biography of Pavese examines his relationship with the United States, which turned from admiration into criticism. Discusses his brief affair with American actress Constance Dowling.

Robert W. Scott

PETRARCH

Born: Arezzo, Tuscany; July 20, 1304
Died: Arquà, Carrara (now in Italy); July 18, 1374

PRINCIPAL POETRY
Epistolae metricae, 1363 (*Metrical Letters*, 1958)
Bucolicum carmen, 1364 (*Eclogues*, 1974)
Africa, 1396 (English translation, 1977)
Rerum vulgarium fragmenta, 1470 (also known as *Canzoniere*; *Rhymes*, 1976)
Trionfi, 1470 (*Tryumphs*, 1565; also known as *Triumphs*, 1962)
Rime disperse, 1826 (also known as *Estravaganti*; *Excluded Rhymes*, 1976)

OTHER LITERARY FORMS

The other writings of Petrarch (PEH-trahrk), except for some prayers in Latin hexameters, are all in Latin prose and consist of epistles, biographies, a collection of exempla, autobiographical works, psalms, orations, invectives, assorted treatises, and even a guidebook to the Holy Land, which he never visited and knew only through the eyes and books of others. Ironically, although the author believed that he would achieve lasting fame because of his Latin compositions, he is remembered today largely for his vernacular poetry. Contemporary scholars do study his Latin works, but primarily to gain insight into his Italian poems. A knowledge of his classically inspired writings, however, is essential to anyone who would understand the cultural milieu that led to the birth of the Renaissance in Italy.

ACHIEVEMENTS

Two words sum up Petrarch's profound historical legacy: Petrarchianism and Humanism. The first stands for the widespread influence of the author's vernacular poetry, especially his love sonnets but also *Triumphs*, on Western European culture from the late fourteenth century to the mid-seventeenth century. It refers to the imitation in literature and the representation in art of the themes and images so carefully crafted in Petrarch's Italian verse: in literature, for example, the expression of the lover's torment through the use of antithesis, oxymoron, hyperbole, and other appropriate rhetorical figures, or the description of the beloved as an ideal yet real lady with golden hair, ivory skin, and pearl teeth; in art, the reproduction of *Triumphs* on canvas and wedding chests and in other media, such as woodcuts, enamels, tapestries, and stained glass, as well as in pageants, ballets, and theatricals. The second term, Humanism, refers to the intellectual and cultural movement that derived from the study of classical literature and civilization during the late Middle Ages and that was one of the main factors contributing to the rise of the Renaissance. Petrarch is commonly called the founder of Humanism be-

Petrarch
(Library of Congress)

cause his intense interest in antiquity led him to be the first in modern times to collect ancient manuscripts, compose letters to great Roman and Greek figures of the past, imitate Cicero in his prose and Vergil in his epic poetry, and examine classical writings in their own context, with waning regard for accrued medieval traditions and superstitions. Early fifteenth century Italian Humanists, such as Coluccio Salutati and Leonardo Bruni, were followers of Petrarch and saw him as the enlightened initiator of a new age, the epoch now known as the Renaissance. In reality, although Petrarch does embody many of the qualities of a Renaissance man because of his well-rounded nature and varied accomplishments, he is neither wholly in the Renaissance nor entirely in the Middle Ages. Rather, he is a transitional or pivotal figure. His vernacular amorous poetry, with its emphasis on the unreciprocated love for an idealized woman, is in many ways only a culmination of the Provençal troubadour tradition; his *Triumphs*, written in Dante's terza rima, could hardly be more medieval; and his psalms and autobiographical dialogues mirror the Middle Ages' confessional literature. Yet the genres and classical style of most of his Latin compositions, his anti-Scholastic attitudes, and his love of secular learning for its moral and civic teachings clearly place him in what would become the mainstream of the Renaissance cultural tradition.

Biography

Petrarch was born Francesco Petrarca in Arezzo, Tuscany (now in Italy), on July 20, 1304, the oldest child of Pietro di Parenzo, an exiled Florentine notary. Di Parenzo, more commonly called Ser Petracco ("Ser" indicates a notary), was a White Guelph and, like Dante, had been exiled from Florence and its territory in 1302. (Petrarch later formed his own surname by ingeniously reworking Petracco into an elegant Latinate form.) Early in 1305, Petrarch's mother, Eletta Canigiani, took her son to her father-in-law's home in Incisa, north of Arezzo and in Florentine territory. There, she and Petrarch lived until 1311, when her husband moved them to the independent state of Pisa. In 1312, the family moved to Carpentras, in Provence, to be near the papal seat, which Clement V had moved to Avignon in 1309. In Carpentras, Petrarch began his study of the *trivium* with Convenevole da Prato and continued his studies there until 1316, when, at the tender age of twelve, he was sent to the University of Montpellier to study law. In 1320, he and his younger brother Gherardo, of whom he was very fond, moved to Bologna to continue their legal studies. Petrarch, however, never completed the work for his degree because of his many varied interests. Upon the death of his father in 1326, he abandoned forever his pursuit of law and returned with his brother to Avignon. There, the two of them began ecclesiastical careers to improve their financial situations. Petrarch received the tonsure, but he never went further than the minor orders. Gherardo, on the other hand, later became a Carthusian monk.

On Good Friday, 1327, Petrarch saw a woman in the Church of Santa Chiara in Avignon and fell in love with her. The poet identifies her only as Laura, except once when he calls her "Laureta"; her exact identity has never been definitively established. While many critics believe her to be Laura de Noves, who married Hugues de Sade in 1325, others question her very existence. Whatever the case, the figure of Laura, ever reluctant to return the poet's love, is the inspiration or motivation for most of Petrarch's Italian poetry. He even records her death from the plague on April 6, 1348, in his precious copy of Vergil, an indication of the reality and depth of his devotion to her.

In 1330, Petrarch entered the service of Cardinal Giovanni Colonna and remained under that family's patronage for almost two decades. Petrarch soon became, as he characterized himself, a *peregrinus ubique* ("pilgrim everywhere"). In 1333, he traveled through northern France, Flanders, and Germany. He visited Paris, where Dionigi da Borgo San Sepolcro gave him a copy of Saint Augustine's *Confessiones* (397-401; *Confessions*, 1620); Liège, where he discovered two orations by Cicero; and Aachen, where he visited the tomb of Charlemagne. In 1336, he climbed Mount Ventoux with his brother. At the top, he read from his copy of the *Confessions* a passage on the vanity of man. He meditated at length on what he had read, and the experience marked the beginning of the serious introspection that characterized the rest of his life. From the top of the mountain, he also looked down on Italy and felt a strong desire to return to his native country. This he did in a trip to Rome, where he visited Giacomo Colonna toward the end of that year.

Petrarch returned to Avignon in 1337, desirous of solitude, which he found fifteen miles away, in Vaucluse, a valley that afforded him a quiet place to study and write. In that same year, his first illegitimate child, Giovanni, was born. The mother is unknown, and the son died from the plague in 1361. By Petrarch's mid-thirties, he was well known in Italy and France for his Latin verse, and in 1340, he received letters from the Senate in Rome and the University of Paris offering him the poet laureate's crown. He chose to receive the honor in Rome and left the next year for Naples, where King Robert examined him on various questions and proclaimed him worthy of the prize. On Easter Sunday, 1341, he accepted the laurel crown in Rome and delivered a coronation speech on the nature of poetry. It was the first time that such a ceremony had been held since classical times, and it dramatized the significance that the literary models of antiquity were assuming. From Rome, he traveled to Pisa, then to Parma, where he spent about a year working on his epic *Africa*.

In 1342, Petrarch was back in Avignon, where the following year, his illegitimate daughter Francesca was born. In October, 1343, he traveled again in Italy, this time as ambassador of the new pope, Clement VI, to the new queen, Joan I. In December, he left Naples, disgusted with the corruption of the court, and went to Parma, where his stay was cut short by the outbreak of war. He escaped through enemy lines and visited Modena, Bologna, and Verona before returning to Avignon by the end of 1345. Soon after arriving in Avignon, he retired to Vaucluse, where he spent all of 1346. In the summer of 1347, he learned that Cola di Rienzo had been elected tribune of Rome. Delighted with the election, Petrarch wrote him a congratulatory Latin eclogue in which he rebuffed all the Roman nobles, including members of the Colonna family, who were hostile to the tribune. At this time, he became entirely independent of Colonna patronage. In November, he headed toward Rome, but in Genoa, he learned of the despotic actions of the tribune and decided to interrupt his trip. He selected Parma as his main residence but traveled around Italy at will for three years. In the autumn of 1350, on his way to Rome for the Jubilee, he stopped in Florence, where he visited Giovanni Boccaccio. They met again in Padua in April of the following year. In June, 1351, Petrarch was back in Vaucluse, whence he traveled back and forth to Avignon in hope of papal assistance. The death of Clement VI and the election of Innocent VI to the papacy in December, 1352, caused Petrarch to lose all hope of support from the papacy, as Pope Innocent suspected him of necromancy. Petrarch bid his brother farewell for the last time in April of the next year and left in May for Italy.

Back in his native land, Petrarch accepted an offer from the Visconti family to live in Milan, where he remained for eight years (1353-1361). In June, 1361, he left Milan because of the spread of the plague and traveled to Padua, where he was a guest of Francesco da Carrara. In early 1362, he returned to Milan, but because of renewed danger from the plague, he was back in Padua in the spring. In September, he went to Venice, where he remained until 1368, alternating his sojourn there with repeated trips to

Padua, Milan, and Pavia. In 1363, Boccaccio paid him a visit in Venice that lasted for a few months. In 1368, Petrarch moved to Padua and from there, in 1370, to nearby Arquà with his daughter Francesca and her family. He spent his final years in Padua and in Arquà, where he died during the night on July 18, 1374.

ANALYSIS

Petrarch was both an Italian and a Latin poet, and any analysis of his poetry must take into consideration both aspects of his career. He continually and extensively revised most of his compositions; the exact chronology of his works, therefore, whether poetry or prose, is difficult to establish. His first book in Italian is *Rhymes*, poems written and revised between 1336 and 1374 but not printed until 1470, almost a full century after his death. Any "publication" prior to that date refers, more precisely, to the circulation of a manuscript. The earliest edition of Petrarch's collected Latin works dates from 1496; his complete works, including Italian verse, titled *Opera quae extant omnia*, were first published in Basel in 1554 and later reprinted there in 1581. No modern edition of the complete works exists, although a national edition has been in progress since 1926.

Although he longed to be remembered, as has been indicated, for his prodigious production in Latin, the smaller body of his Italian verse has been much more widely appreciated since the end of the fifteenth century. In both cases, however, his compositions have been widely influential because of the basic principle of imitation that he endorsed and that the Renaissance accepted as canon. Petrarch believed in the necessity of imitating the great Latin authors to produce works of lasting significance. His adherence to this doctrine in the bulk of his poetry and prose established the precedent for *imitatio* that later Humanists refined. Curiously, the subsequent refinement of the principle led to compositions that were much more Ciceronian, in terms of correct grammar and pure style, than Petrarch ever achieved in his own prose. This fact may account for the declining interest in his Latin prose after the fifteenth century. In his Italian poetry, Petrarch himself was not concerned with the imitation per se of preceding traditions as much as with the application of the best of those traditions, such as certain images found in the troubadour lyrics, to a real model: Laura. In the early sixteenth century, however, Pietro Bembo cited Petrarch's Italian lyrics as the best model for those who would write vernacular poetry. With the flourishing of the printing press at the same time as the cardinal's endorsement, Petrarch's Italian poems, already outstanding for their lyric quality and psychological insights, became destined to serve as models and to achieve prominence in the literature of the Western world.

RHYMES

Drawing on a literary-historical examination of the past, Petrarch's Latin writings, as critic Aldo Bernardo has emphasized, "contain a virile and noble view of mankind [and] exalt the achievements of ancient heroes and thinkers as indications of the heights that man can attain." Petrarch discovered in the classical era examples of moral and civic virtue capable of instructing modern humans, who, with the additional light of Christianity, could then surpass the accomplishments of pagan antiquity. Petrarch also shows the boundaries or limitations of paganism, with its bent for the things of this world, such as earthly fame and glory. The tension caused by attempting to balance the appeal of this world's attractions with the Christian's hope of a better life hereafter finds its ultimate expression in the poet's Italian lyrics.

In the collected *Rhymes*, Laura is both a *figura Christi* and a *figura Daphnae*, a symbol of Christ's purity and Daphne's sensuality. More than a study of Laura, however, the poems constitute a keen analysis of the poet's struggle to keep the attractions of this world in proper perspective. For the Christian, the eternal happiness of the next life should outshine the fleeting pleasure of this world; for Petrarch, this knowledge simply compounded his internal conflicts, as he struggled to bring his passions and desire for worldly renown under control and to submit to God. As in Saint Augustine's *Confessions*, the final word of the *Rhymes* is "peace," something that Petrarch's revered saint achieved but of which the poet claims only to have caught glimpses.

The Latin inscription at the head of the Vatican holograph of Petrarch's collected Italian poems is *Rerum vulgarium fragmenta* ("fragments of vernacular rhymes"). This title emphasizes the nonunitary nature of the collection of 366 lyrics. First, the poems, although mostly sonnets, include a variety of types and may be divided into the following categories: sonnets, canzones, sestinas, ballads, and madrigals. The total number corresponds to the maximum number of days in a year and makes the collection a sort of breviary. Second, the poems treat many topics in addition to the poet's love for Laura, including the themes of friendship, papal corruption, and patriotism. Petrarch continually reordered the poems from 1336 until his death, but the criteria for their final ordering are unclear. Except for the universally accepted grouping of a few sonnets either according to shared themes (such as poems 41 through 43, dealing with Laura's departure for an unknown place, and poems 136 through 138, treating the corruption of the Church in Avignon) or to juxtapose one idea to another (such as poems 61 and 62, expressing respectively the exaltation of love and reason), no single organizational principle, such as a meaningful chronology, has been established. Because of the blank pages that separate poems 263 and 264 in Vatican manuscript 3195, a two-part division of the overall framework traditionally has been made. The first 263 poems, which depict Laura as a real woman who moves, talks, laughs, cries, and travels, are usually designated "In vita di madonna Laura" (in the lifetime of Laura). The last 103 poems, which present Laura as a more ethereal being whose carnal presence is not felt, then receive the label "In morte di madonna Laura" (after the death of Laura). Although the headings are not original to Petrarch, they seem generally appropriate.

The true subject of the poems in which Laura appears, either in person or more often in the form of a conceit, such as the laurel tree or the dawn (*l'aurora*, in Italian), is not really Laura. Rather, it is the love of Petrarch for Laura. The *Rhymes* is the intimate story of the poet's emotions, perceptions, feelings, and changing moods produced by the sight or memory of his beloved. The actual descriptions of Laura, whose hair is always blond like gold and whose skin is white like snow or ivory, are not nearly as significant as the depictions of the poet's melancholic or exalted states as he contemplates her beauty or ruminates over his unreciprocated love. Closely connected with the repeated motif of one-sided love are the themes of the transitoriness of time, the brevity of life, and the vanity of earthly objects and honors.

Two famous canzones, "Spirito gentil" ("Noble Spirit") and "Italia mia" ("My Italy"), best exemplify the category of patriotic or political poems in the *Rhymes*. The first poem was probably written either to Cola di Rienzo in 1347, when he attempted to reinstate the Roman Republic, or to Bosone de' Raffaelli da Gubbio, a Roman senator. It pleads with the "noble spirit" to call Rome's erring citizens back to its ancient path of virtue and glory. Rivalries should be put away and a sense of national pride engendered to wake Italy from its lethargy. "My Italy" constitutes an eloquent plea for peace and is addressed to Italy's warring lords; the most famous section, "Ancient Valor Is Not Yet Dead in Italic Hearts," was chosen by Niccolò Machiavelli to conclude *Il principe* (1532; *The Prince*, 1640). The sonnet sequence previously referred to, poems 136 through 138, represents possibly the most colorful and violent depiction of the corruption of the Church, but references to the papal court at Avignon as "Babylon" occur throughout the *Rhymes*. The best-known poems of friendship treat members of the Colonna family: "Gloriosa columna" ("Glorious Column") and "Rottalè l'alta colonna" ("Broken Is the High Column"). Whatever the theme, all Petrarch's vernacular rhymes are characterized by a sensitivity to beautiful images and sounds that is almost without parallel in the history of Italian versification. In addition, the poet perfected the sonnet form.

TRIUMPHS

Begun in 1351 or 1352 and revised between 1356 and 1374, *Triumphs* was never completed by Petrarch. Like Dante's *La divina commedia* (c. 1320, 3 volumes; *The Divine Comedy*, 1802), Petrarch's *Triumphs* is an allegorical poem written in interlocking rhymed tercets. Its main divisions are six in number and relate the following story: "Triumphus amoris" ("Triumph of Love"), in four chapters, has Love—in a chariot and surrounded by classical figures—appear to the poet in a dream; as the poet observes the spectacle, Laura appears and he falls in love with her; thus enslaved, he follows the chariot to Cyprus, where Love's triumph is celebrated. "Triumphus pudicitiae" ("Triumph of Chastity"), in one chapter, shows Love vainly attempting to imprison Laura, who—armed with her virtues—succeeds in taking Love prisoner; then, surrounded by a court of ladies famous for their virtue, Laura ultimately celebrates her triumph in the temple of Chastity in Rome, where Love is left a prisoner. "Triumphus mortis" ("Triumph of

Death"), in two chapters, has Laura die without suffering and then visit Petrarch in a dream, at which time she reveals that she always loved him. "Triumphus famae" ("Triumph of Fame"), in three chapters, has Fame arrive as Death leads Laura away; surrounded by famous literati, Fame explains that she has the power to take a man from the grave and give him life again. "Triumphus temporis" ("Triumph of Time"), in one chapter, shows the Sun, envious of Fame, accelerating time so that the poet will realize that Fame is like snow on the mountain and that Time triumphs over her. Finally, "Triumphus aeternitatis" ("Triumph of Eternity"), in one chapter, depicts the poet's realization that everything in the world passes away; as the poet turns his thoughts to God, he sees a new world, more beautiful and outside time and space; there the righteous triumph, and there the poet hopes to see Laura.

The individual triumphs are successive until the sixth and final one, which provides a vision of the future. The allegorical meaning of the poem points to the need for humans to look to God for the ultimate fulfillment of their aspirations. The tone of the work, therefore, is undoubtedly medieval and reminiscent of Dante. Although Petrarch claimed in a letter to Boccaccio that he had never read *The Divine Comedy*, his allegorical poem, with its many Dantean echoes and allusions, including borrowed phrasing, stands as proof that he knew Dante's work very well. Unfortunately, the lyric quality of the unfinished poem fails to match that of the *Rhymes*. This is true for at least two reasons: First, the catalogs of characters are almost interminable and serve to break up the poetic rhythm almost before it is established; second, the allegorical frame, too obvious even from the brief summary provided, is so heavy as to be oppressive. Nevertheless, this composition, although vastly inferior to the collected lyrics, exerted a dramatic influence on Renaissance art because of the esteem in which its author was held. The representation of its processionals in all the major and most of the minor artistic media was an essential part of the phenomenon of Petrarchianism.

AFRICA

Petrarch believed that *Africa*, his epic poem composed in Latin hexameters and divided into nine books, was his most promising work. He began writing the poem in 1338 or 1339, reworking and revising it during the next thirty-five years but never finishing it. Because it was never completed, it was never more than promising. Part of it was presented to King Robert in Naples before Petrarch received the crown of poet laureate, but the poem never circulated during the author's lifetime. After his death, friends circulated it, and it was poorly received. In truth, the poem has never enjoyed critical acclaim or approval, except for rare passages such as the tragic love story of Masinissa and Sophonisba. The epic hero is Scipio Africanus; the sources on which the poem is based include Cicero's "Somnium Scipionis" ("Dream of Scipio") at the end of *De republica* (51 B.C.E.; *On the State*, 1817) and Livy's history.

The story begins with an account of Scipio's dream of his deceased father, who died gloriously in the Roman defeat of the Carthaginians in Spain. The father carries Scipio to Heaven, where the son sees a vision of the rise and fall of their beloved Rome and learns that to follow virtue is the duty of man on Earth. His father assures him of victory over Hannibal in the upcoming African campaign and promises him lasting fame because of a poet to be born in the distant future—a not-too-subtle reference to Petrarch himself. The poem, regrettably, is almost completely lacking in both subtlety and dramatic tension. Scipio, brimming with virtue, foils his ally Masinissa's illicit love affair and proves himself an unbelievable character. The outcome of the battle is known before it begins: Hannibal will be defeated, and Scipio will return to Rome victorious. On the voyage home, the conquering general and his friend Ennius discuss the nature of poetry. The latter relates a dream he had of Homer, in which a young poet of great genius figures prominently; the future poet of renown sits in an enclosed valley (read Petrarch seated in Vaucluse). The epic, with its initial and final dream sequences in which Petrarch enjoys a conspicuous place, strikes most critics as too self-congratulatory and ill conceived from beginning to end. As Thomas Bergin has stated, the poem lacks a reading public, "for a reader of Latin epics will want to read true Latin epics and not late medieval imitations."

ECLOGUES

Petrarch's Latin eclogues number twelve, one for each month of the year. As was common in the tradition of Roman and medieval pastoral poems, the bucolic setting disguises quite contemporary events. The pastors or shepherds in a faraway idyllic landscape parallel people close at hand; rustic dialogues find their analogue in contemporary issues. In brief, Petrarch's compositions are a series of allegories placed in rural settings. The themes have all been encountered before: the Roman revolution of Cola di Rienzo, the poet's love for Laura, his coronation in Rome, the corruption of the Church, the conflict in Petrarch between worldliness and spirituality, the death of King Robert, the usefulness of sacred and secular poetry, the destructiveness of the Black Death, and the poet's decision to leave the service of the Colonna family. The eclogues, although neither notably influential nor necessarily inferior, testify to Petrarch's ability to compose countless variations on any number of themes, many of which are notably personal. His life provided almost as much source material for his work as his scholarly studies did. Most of the eclogues were composed between 1346 and 1348, with the definitive version completed in 1364.

METRICAL LETTERS

The *Metrical Letters* make up a collection of sixty-six epistles in Latin hexameters, subdivided into three books. Petrarch dedicated the collection to his friend Marco Barbato di Sulmona, who was chancellor to King Robert. Beginning in 1350, the poet reorganized the letters during a period of more than a decade, completing his task in

1363. The subjects treated range from personal confessions and descriptions of autobiographical happenings to political exhortations and stirring praises for Italy. In purpose, these varied and unequal epistles are not unlike the prose letters found in four other Petrarchan collections. Their intent is to present the poet as he wished to be remembered by posterity. Consequently, they are not filled with spontaneous comments and casual observations, no matter how they may appear at first glance. Every comment and every observation is calculated; this is especially true in those letters that have been carefully rewritten in hexameters. Petrarch's desire, from the first letter to the last, is to interpret for future readers the events of his life, to analyze the results of his studies, and to speculate on the significance of his work. What may have started as another exercise in introspection quickly evolved into a new form of autobiography: an epistolary account revised through time with the reader constantly in mind.

OTHER MAJOR WORKS

NONFICTION: *Rerum familiarium libri*, wr. 1325-1366 (English translation, 1975-1985, also known as *Books on Personal Matters*); *Collatio laureationes*, 1341 (*Coronation Oath*, 1955); *Psalmi penitentiales*, 1342-1347; *Rerum memorandum libri*, 1343-1345; *De vita solitaria*, 1346 (*The Life of Solitude*, 1924); *De viris illustribus*, 1351-1353 (later reorganized as *Quorundam virorum illustrium epithoma*, with a preface by Petrarch, completed by Lombardo della Seta); *Secretum meum*, 1353-1358 (also known as *De secreto conflictu curarum mearum*; *My Secret*, 1911); *Invectiva contra quendam magni status hominem sed nullius scientiae aut virtutis*, 1355; *Itinerarium Syriacum*, 1358 (also known as *Itinerarium breve de Ianua*); *Sine nomine*, 1359-1360 (*Book Without a Name*, 1973); *Senilium rerum libri*, wr. 1361-1374 (*Letters of Old Age*, 1966); *Rerum familiarium libri xxiv*, 1364-1366 (*Books on Personal Matters*, 1975); *De remediis utriusque fortunae*, 1366 (*Physicke Against Fortune*, 1597; also as *On Remedies for Good and Bad Fortunes*, 1966); *De sui ipsius et multorum ignorantia*, 1367 (*On His Own Ignorance and That of Many*, 1948); *Posteritati*, 1370-1372 (*Epistle to Posterity*, 1966); *Invectiva contra eum qui maledixit Italiae*, 1373; *De otio religioso*, 1376; *Miscellaneous Letters*, 1966.

MISCELLANEOUS: *Opera quae extant omnia*, 1554, 1581.

BIBLIOGRAPHY

Bloom, Harold, ed. *Petrarch*. New York: Chelsea House, 1989. Well-chosen collection of eight previously published essays by major Petrarch scholars.

Braden, Gordon. *Petrarchan Love and the Continental Renaissance*. New Haven, Conn.: Yale University Press, 1999. Sticking close to the works themselves, Braden studies Petrarch's poems and their effects on the likes of Giovanni Boccaccio, Pietro Bembo, Pierre de Ronsard, and Garcilaso de la Vega. He emphasizes the continuity of subject matter and the poets' "creative narcissism."

Fubini, Riccardo. *Humanism and Secularization: From Petrarch to Valla.* Durham, N.C.: Duke University Press, 2003. An examination of Humanism and its relationship with Petrarch, Bracciolini, and Poggio. Bibliography and index.

Jones, Frederic J. *The Structure of Petrarch's "Canzionere": A Chronological, Psychological, and Stylistic Analysis.* Rochester, N.Y.: Boydell and Brewer, 1995. An analysis of Petrarch's poetry, particularly his *Rhymes.* Bibliography and indexes.

Kennedy, William J. *The Site of Petrarchism: Early Modern National Sentiment in Italy, France, and England.* Baltimore: The Johns Hopkins University Press, 2003. An examination of Petrarch's nationalism as it manifested itself in literature and its effect. Bibliography and index.

Kirkham, Victoria, and Armando Maggi, eds. *Petrarch: A Critical Guide to the Complete Works.* Chicago: University of Chicago Press, 2009. A collection of essays that cover Petrarch's works, including poetic works such as *Triumph* and *Rhymes.*

McLaughlin, Martin, and Letizia Panizza with Peter Hainsworth, eds. *Petrarch in Britain: Interpreters, Imitators, and Translators over Seven Hundred Years.* New York: Oxford University Press, 2007. This collection of twenty essays by prominent Petrarch scholars in Italy and Britain discusses the legacy of Petrarch in Britain, including his effect on love poetry, his decline during Romanticism, and his subsequent revival.

Mazzotta, Giuseppe. *The Worlds of Petrarch.* Durham, N.C.: Duke University Press, 1993. A critical look at the poetry and other works of Petrarch, including the *Rhymes.* Also examines his Humanism. Bibliography and index.

Quillen, Carol E. *Rereading the Renaissance: Petrarch, Augustine, and the Language of Humanism.* Ann Arbor: University of Michigan Press, 1998. Examines Petrarch as a reader and writer as well as his correspondence in relation to Humanism. Also looks at Saint Augustine. Bibliography and index.

Sturm-Maddox, Sara. *Petrarch's Laurels.* University Park: Pennsylvania State University Press, 1999. The relationship between Petrarch's concerns for love and for glory is encased in that of "Laura" and "the laurel." This study of their relationship in his poetry examines the conflicts, metamorphoses, and parallels that entwine the two.

Madison U. Sowell

SALVATORE QUASIMODO

Born: Modica, Sicily, Italy; August 20, 1901
Died: Naples, Italy; June 14, 1968

PRINCIPAL POETRY
Acque e terre, 1930
Oboe sommerso, 1932
Odore di eucalyptus, ed altri versi, 1933
Erato e Apollion, 1936
Poesie, 1938
Ed è subito sera, 1942
Con il piede straniero sopra il cuore, 1946
Giorno dopo giorno, 1947
La vita non è sogno, 1949
Il falso e vero verde, 1954
La terra impareggiabile, 1958, 1962
Tutte le poesie, 1960
Noeve poesie, 1963
Dare e avere, 1959-1965, 1966 (*To Give and to Have, and Other Poems*, 1969; also known as *Debit and Credit*, 1972)
Complete Poems, 1983
Day After Day: Selected Poems, 2002
The Night Fountain = La fontana notturna: Selected Early Poems, 2008 (bilingual text)

OTHER LITERARY FORMS

Outside his native country, the reputation of Salvatore Quasimodo (kwoz-ee-MUH-doh) rests primarily on his poetry, but in Italy, he achieved prominence for his many other literary activities as well. He wrote a number of important critical studies, and his librettos have been performed in opera theaters as well known as those of Venice and Palermo. More important, however, is his work as a translator. One of the finest literary translators of his time, Quasimodo ranged from Homer to the twentieth century: His translations include classical Greek and Latin poetry, the Gospel of John, and writers as varied as William Shakespeare, Molière, Pablo Neruda, E. E. Cummings, Conrad Aiken, Tudor Arghezi, Yves Lecomte, and Paul Éluard.

ACHIEVEMENTS

Together with Giuseppe Ungaretti and Eugenio Montale, Salvatore Quasimodo unquestionably belongs to the select circle of world-renowned modern Italian poets. Of

Salvatore Quasimodo
(©The Nobel Foundation)

the three, however, Quasimodo was the first to win wide acclaim, perhaps because he was able to express most lucidly the anguish and the doubts of a poet in a time when the irrational seemed to gain steadily at the expense of the rational, when poetry had gradually turned inward, divorcing itself from its tormented historical and social context. In 1959, Quasimodo received the Nobel Prize in Literature. His other awards include the San Babila Prize (1950), the Etna-Taormina International Poetry Prize (1953, shared with Dylan Thomas), and the Viareggio Prize (1958).

Biography

Born in Modica, Sicily, the second of four children born to Gaetano Quasimodo and Clotilde Ragusa, Salvatore Quasimodo spent the first years of his life following his father, a humble stationmaster, as the family moved from one small Sicilian railroad station to another. In 1908, his father settled in Gela, where Quasimodo was able to attend grade school. In 1909, he again followed his father, this time to Messina, the Sicilian town that, along with Reggio Calabria, had just been hit by the terribly destructive earthquake of 1908. In 1916, after a few years spent near Palermo, Quasimodo returned with his family to Messina, where he and his older brother were enrolled in the local trade school.

At this time, Quasimodo's poetic vocation, nurtured by careful reading of the classics as well as the major contemporary Russian and French writers, began to surface. He published his first two lyrics, one in the journal *Humanitas* and the other, a Futurist poem, in *Italia futurista*. In 1917, together with his lifelong friends Giorgio La Pira and Salvatore Pugliatti, Quasimodo founded the *Nuovo giornale letterario*, which was in print from March to November of that year.

In 1919, Quasimodo left Messina for Rome to attend the engineering school of that city's university. He soon dropped out, however, and spent the next few years working at odd jobs and leading a rather bohemian life. In 1926, he succeeded in obtaining a position as a land surveyor with the government's Civil Engineering Department at Reggio Calabria and thus was able once again to meet regularly with his friends among the Sicilian literati. At this point, he began to write seriously; some of the poems included in *Acque e terre* (waters and lands) date from this period.

The year 1929 was a decisive one in Quasimodo's life. He was invited by his brother-in-law Elio Vittorini (later to become one of the leading literary figures of contemporary Italy) to go to Florence. There, he was introduced to an influential group of writers and poets, among them Montale, and in 1930, he published his first collection of poems, *Acque e terre*, which met with favorable critical reviews. For work-related reasons, he was sent to Liguria in 1931, where he published the widely acclaimed *Oboe sommerso* (the sunken oboe) in 1932. That same year, he was awarded the Florentine Prize of the Antico Fattore, which had been given the year before to Montale. Sent in 1934 to Valtellina (Lombardy) after a short stay in Sardinia, Quasimodo entered the Milanese intellectual milieu, and in 1935, his daughter, Orietta, was born out of wedlock.

In Milan in 1936, Quasimodo published another book, *Erato e Apollion* (Aerato and Apollyon), and in 1938, he finally quit his job as a land surveyor to begin working as an editor and assistant to Cesare Zavattini, then the editor of several Mondadori periodicals. In 1939, Quasimodo was made literary editor of the weekly magazine *Il tempo*. The same year, his son, Alessandro, was born. In 1940, Quasimodo published his controversial translation *Lirici greci* (Greek lyric poets), notable for its aggressively modern idiom, and the following year, he was appointed professor of Italian literature at the Giuseppe Verdi Conservatory in Milan. In 1942, he published the most successful of his works: *Ed è subito sera* (and suddenly it is evening), the volume that marked his shift from the Hermetic style of his early verse.

During the war years, without being overtly involved in the antifascist resistance movement, Quasimodo nevertheless took a firm stand against fascism, and in 1945, soon after the war, he joined the Italian Communist Party. That same year, he published his masterful translations of Sophocles and the Gospel of John. Belonging also to this period are a number of critical essays and two collections of socially and ideologically oriented poems: *Con il piede straniero sopra il cuore* (with an invader's foot on your heart), published in 1946, and *Giorno dopo giorno* (day after day), published the following year. In 1948, following the death of his first wife, Bice Donetti, he married Maria Cumani, the mother of his son, Alessandro; he then began his career as a theater editor for the journal *Omnibus* and in the same capacity, shortly after, for the weekly *Il tempo*, while continuing to publish translations and another collection of poems titled *La vita non è un sogno* (life is not a dream), which appeared in 1949.

In 1950, Quasimodo received the San Babila Prize and, in 1953, with Dylan Thomas, the Etna-Taormina International Poetry Prize. In 1954, *Il falso e vero verde* (the true and the false green) was published; it was republished two years later with added translations and the famous speech, "Discorso sulla poesia" (speech on poetry), in which Quasimodo maintained the necessity for the true poet to express in his verses his ideological and social commitment. In 1958, after the publication of several other translations, he published yet another collection of poems, *La terra impareggiabile* (the incomparable land), but during a trip to Russia in that same year, he had a heart attack, which forced him to remain there until the spring of 1959. His hospital expenses were covered by a subscription organized by Russian writers on his behalf. In 1959, Quasimodo attained world recognition on receiving the Nobel Prize in Literature "for his lyric poetry, which expresses with classic fire the tragic experience of life in our time." In Italy, however, this award prompted a negative reaction from critics who thought that Ungaretti and Montale were both more deserving of the honor.

Shortly after receiving the Nobel Prize, Quasimodo began to travel throughout Europe and the United States. In 1960, he separated from his second wife and published a collection of essays titled *Il poeta e il politico e altri saggi* (*The Poet and the Politician, and Other Essays*, 1964), which includes the acceptance speech he had read in Stockholm. He was thereafter the recipient of several other honors and awards. In 1966, he published his last collection of poems, *To Give and to Have, and Other Poems*, which is virtually a balance sheet of his life, strongly overshadowed by the presentiment of death. In 1967, Oxford University bestowed an honorary degree on him. He died in Naples the following year as a result of a cerebral hemorrhage suffered in Amalfi, where he had been invited to preside over a poetry competition.

Analysis

Salvatore Quasimodo lived and worked in a period that harbored innumerable contrasting poetic voices. His courageous attempt to extricate himself from the arid, desolate sphere of an excessively introspective style pointed the way to a new poetry—a poetry that, without losing its lyric essence, aspires to a modern aesthetic in which civil ethics and poetic vision can coexist.

Unlike the poetry of his two great contemporaries, Quasimodo's poetic works can be divided into two sharply distinct periods. In his first phase, before World War II, Quasimodo wrote Hermetic poetry characterized by highly compressed images, allusive language, and a pervasive existential anguish. In his second phase, Quasimodo became convinced that Hermetic poetry had exhausted itself in excessively self-absorbed, contorted, and abstract imagery. He came to believe that the poet's moral duty was to be socially committed and to express the collective despair, sorrow, and frustration of his time, a position first made clear in the collection *Ed è subito sera*.

This second phase of Quasimodo's poetry—characterized by a more discursive style, the use of a plainer language, and, above all, a strong ideological and social content—need not be interpreted, however, as an unequivocal rejection of his Hermetic past, but may rather be seen as an evolution (dictated, perhaps, by the historical situation) toward new themes and a more decisive social, political, and moral commitment. In his evolution from modernist Hermeticism to a poetry of engagement, Quasimodo was able to capture and express with rare insight and sensitivity not only his own feelings and aspirations but also those of his era.

ACQUE E TERRE

Echoes of many poetic traditions, particularly of such poets as Pascoli, D'Annunzio, Filippo Tommaso Marinetti, and Sergio Corazzini, are clearly detectable in Quasimodo's first book of verses, *Acque e terre*. The gravitational presence of Ungaretti and Montale is even more noticeable in this volume. The recurrent theme of the poet's youth, evoked through the rediscovery of the ancient myths of Sicily, is a constant in Quasimodo's work. Quasimodo further intertwines an incisive imagery, boldly carved, and a personal use of antithesis employed on a conceptual as well as on a semantic level. It is through the analysis of opposites such as life/death and joy/sorrow that the reader gradually penetrates the existential inner world of the poet and the quasi-metaphysical anguish of the moral and historical wasteland of his age.

IDEOLOGY AND SOCIAL ENGAGEMENT

World War II brought about the externalization of the poet's feelings, a sort of psychological denouement along with a measure of objectivity induced by the mercilessly all-encompassing war years. Beginning with the poems of *Giorno dopo giorno*, Quasimodo made a conscious and coherent effort to overcome early unresolved dissonances and to present the reader with his own historical experience defined within the framework of a choral poetic. As Quasimodo moved toward a poetry of ideological and social engagement, he gradually rejected the poetics of memory, seen as a negation of life as exemplified in "Quasi un madrigale" ("Almost a Madrigal") from *La vita non è un sogno*: "I have no more memories, I do not want to remember;/ memory stems from death,/ life is endless." The final assimilation of opposites was dialectically assured by

Quasimodo's realization of the necessity for a new ethical dimension; he was forced to abandon once and for all his poetic monologue in favor of a socially committed dialogue with his fellow humans. In "Epitaffio per Bice Donetti" ("Epitaph for Bice Donetti"), from *La vita non è un sogno*, life and death are no longer antithetical and their synthesis is suggested by his discovery of a shared destiny: He is "one of many others" and thus finds his roots in the sorrowful plight common to all humankind.

ED È SUBITO SERA

The collected verses of *Ed è subito sera* were the result of painstaking revision and selection of poems from Quasimodo's previous collections, from *Acque e terre* and *Oboe sommerso* to *Erato e Apollion*. With the addition of a number of new poems, *Ed è subito sera* constituted both the definitive statement of his past work and the assertion of a new aesthetic vision. With the new poems that concluded the collection, Quasimodo turned to longer, more discursive verse forms (especially the hendecasyllable) and to a less cryptic use of language. While these changes reflected to a certain extent the vogue for neorealism, Quasimodo's stylistic evolution was also influenced significantly by two other factors: first, the stylistic models that he encountered in translating the classics, and second, the urgency of speaking out against the ills of fascism and war, which necessitated the establishment of a new relationship with his readers.

FROM "I" TO "WE"

The twenty poems of *Con il piede straniero sopra il cuore*, eighteen of which were to be included the following year in *Giorno dopo giorno*, dramatically reaffirm the new poetic phase initiated in *Ed è subito sera*. Quasimodo's Hermetic phase, with its inward focus on the self and on memory, is typified by the careful choice of a few nouns and adjectives in the poem "L'eucalyptus" ("The Eucalyptus") from *Oboe sommerso*: "In me un albero oscilla/ da assonnata riva,/ alata aria/ amare fronde esala" ("Within me sways a tree/ from sleeping shores/ winged air exhales/ my bitter fronds"). By contrast, in "Alle fronde dei salici"—published in 1947 in *Giorno dopo giorno* but written three years earlier, in the winter of 1944, during the harshest period of the German Occupation—Quasimodo is painfully aware that the time has come to break away from his Hermetic past in order to speak with a new voice and of new themes: "E come potevamo noi contare/ con il piede straniero sopra il cuore,/ fra i morti abbandonati nelle piazze/ . . . Alle fronde dei salici, per voto/ anche le nostre cetre erano appese" ("And how could we sing/ with an invader's foot on your heart/ among the dead abandoned in the squares/ . . . To the branches of the willow, as a vow/ also our lyres were hung up"). The language is no longer rarefied and impenetrable; it is almost epic in tone, and the poet has switched from "I" to the choral "we." As Quasimodo himself said in a speech in 1953, something happened in the field of poetry about 1945, a dramatic destruction of the content inherited from an indifferent idealism and the poetic language flourishing up to that time. . . . All of a sudden the poet found himself thrust out of his own internal history; in war his individual intelligence was worth no more than the collective intelligence of the people. . . . The private (lyric) discourse . . . became choral.

Quasimodo continued to develop in this direction; in *La vita non è un sogno*, certain poems are unusually long, and throughout the volume, the poet actively seeks dialogue with his readers. *Il falso e vero verde* comprises fourteen poems and translations covering a wide variety of themes and levels of experience, moving from the medieval Lauds (honoring a fallen Resistance fighter) to a quasi-surrealistic search for roots. A progression of moods and subjects, from the Athenian Acropolis to Sputnik, also prevails in the twenty-five poems of *La terra impareggiabile*. A dominant theme, however, is clearly identifiable in the first poem of the collection, "Visibile, Invisibile" ("Visible, Invisible"): The search for the great divide of time, for a dividing line between the present (visible) and the past or future (invisible), bears witness to Quasimodo's unrelenting quest for a poetic and ideological fusion of form and content.

To Give and to Have

The final stage, the "synthesis" of Quasimodo's dialectical probing into the self while reaching for universal truths, is contained in the twenty-three poems of *To Give and to Have* (also published under the title *Debit and Credit*). In this last book of poems—to which are appended the text of the libretto *Billy Budd* (1949), as well as translations from Homer's *Iliad* (c. 750 B.C.E.; English translation, 1611), from Giovanni Boccaccio's *Buccolicum carmen* (c. 1351-1366; *Boccaccio's Olympia*, 1913) and from the Romanian poet Tudor Arghezi—Quasimodo makes his final statement on life and death, an absorbed and reflective pulling together of the threads of his total poetic experience. As the title implies, *To Give and to Have* is a sort of balance sheet of the poet's life, a summation, of his dialectic search.

Somberly reviewing his life and world, the poet softens the tones of his social and ideological commitment, looking again within the self, pondering his human adventure and his passage through time. The presentiment of death is everywhere, but in conjunction with calm acceptance: "I am not fearful before death/ just as I was not timid before life," he writes while lying in his hospital bed in Russia ("Varvàra Alexandrovna"). Acceptance, if not detachment, is again pervasive in "Il silenzio non m'inganna" ("The Silence Does Not Deceive Me"): "I write down words, analogies, and try/ to trace a possible link/ between my life and death. The present is outside."

Quasimodo's language, too, seems to have gained a new equilibrium in which meditative expression predominates. More accessible than his obscure and often strident early style, it is, at the same time, less discursive and more controlled than the language of the war years. The poet has taken stock of himself and appears reconciled to the idea of impending death, which he acknowledges in a kind of spiritual testament to his fellow humans, devoid of anguish and metaphysical anxieties.

OTHER MAJOR WORKS

NONFICTION: *Petrarca e il sentimento della solitudine*, 1945; *Il poeta e il politico e altri saggi*, 1960 (*The Poet and the Politician, and Other Essays*, 1964); *Scritti sul teatro*, 1961; *Leonida di Taranto*, 1968.

EDITED TEXTS: *Lirica d'amore italiana, dalle origini ai nostri giorni*, 1957; *Poesia italiana del dopoguerra*, 1958.

TRANSLATIONS: *Lirici greci*, 1940 (of Greek lyric poets); *Il fiore della Georgiche*, 1944 (of Vergil's *Georgics*); *Dall'Odissea*, 1945 (of Homer's *Odyssey*); *Veronensis Carmina*, 1945 (of Catullus); *Edipo re*, 1946 (of Sophocles' play); *La Bibbia di Amiens*, 1946 (of John Ruskin); *Romeo e Giulietta*, 1948 (of William Shakespeare's play); *Le Coefore*, 1949 (of Aeschylus's play *Choēphoroi*); *Il Vangelo secondo Giovanni*, 1950 (of the Book of John); *Macbeth*, 1952 (of Shakespeare's play); *Poesie*, 1952 (of Pablo Neruda); *Riccardo III*, 1952 (of Shakespeare's play); *Elettra*, 1954 (of Sophocles' play); *Canti*, 1955 (of Catullus); *La tempesta*, 1956 (of Shakespeare's play); *Il Tartufo*, 1957 (of Molière's play); *Poesie scelte*, 1958 (of E. E. Cummings); *Dalle Metamorfosi*, 1959 (of Ovid); *Otello*, 1959 (of Shakespeare's play); *Ecuba*, 1962 (of Euripedes' play); *Mutevoli pensieri*, 1963 (of Conrad Aiken); *Antonio e Cleopatra*, 1966 (of Shakespeare's play); *Eracle*, 1966 (of Euripides' play); *Poesie*, 1966 (of Tudor Arghezi); *Chemin de Croix*, 1967 (of Pericle Patocchi); *Dall'Iliade*, 1968 (translation from Homer's *Iliad*); *Leonida di Taranto*, 1969 (of Leonidas); *Donner à voir*, 1970 (translation of Paul Éluard's book of the same title).

MISCELLANEOUS: *The Selected Writings of Salvatore Quasimodo*, 1960.

BIBLIOGRAPHY

Condini, Ned, ed. *An Anthology of Modern Italian Poetry in English Translation, with Italian Text*. New York: Modern Language Association of America, 2009. Contains a section featuring the Hermeticists, including Quasimodo. Introduction to the bilingual text provides information on Quasimodo and places him in context.

Cro, Stelio. "Salvatore Quasimodo." In *Twentieth Century Italian Poets, First Series*, edited by Giovanna De Satasio. Vol. 114 in *Dictionary of Literary Biography*. Detroit: Gale, 1992. A full biographical treatment in English. Traces the development of Quasimodo's poetry and translation from his early explorations of Hermeticism to his more political (and less successful) poetry after World War II.

Hays, Gregory. "Le morte stagioni: Intertextuality in Quasimodo's *Lirici greci*." *Forum Italicum* 29, no. 1 (Spring, 1995): 26-43. A critical study of Quasimodo's translations of ancient Greek poetry.

Jones, F. J. "The Poetry of Salvatore Quasimodo." *Italian Studies* 16 (1961): 60-77. An overview of the poet's major themes and genres.

Loriggio, Francesco. "Modernity and the Ambiguities of Exile: On the Poetry of Salvatore Quasimodo." *Rivista di studi italiani* 12, no. 1 (June, 1994): 101-120. Loriggio examines Quasimodo's poetry on the theme of exile and shows how it was this theme that caused Quasimodo's popularity to decline in the middle of the twentieth century and to be rekindled at century's end. Loriggio's analysis is clear and readable but unfortunately the passages of poetry he examines closely are rendered in the original Italian.

McKendrick, Jamie, ed. *The Faber Book of Twentieth-Century Italian Poems*. London: Faber and Faber, 2004. Presents translations of the major Italian poets of the twentieth century, including Quasimodo. Introduction places the poet among his contemporaries.

Roberto Severino

GASPARA STAMPA

Born: Padua(?) (now in Italy); c. 1523
Died: Venice (now in Italy); April 23, 1554

PRINCIPAL POETRY
Rime, 1554
Selected Poems, 1994

OTHER LITERARY FORMS

Gaspara Stampa (STAHM-pah) is remembered only for her poetry.

ACHIEVEMENTS

Gaspara Stampa produced only one lyric collection during her short life: the *Rime*. Modeled after Petrarch's prototypical *canzoniere*, Stampa's work offers modern readers exceptional insight into the artistic aspirations and literary ideals of the Italian Renaissance, a period that cherished creative imitation. Like many of her contemporaries, Stampa emulated the language, form, and thought of the traditional master. In a period that did not favor radical innovation, the *Rime* kept to the forms favored by Petrarch— the sonnet, madrigal, and sestina—as well as to his basic motifs, rhetorical devices, and conventional images.

In addition, Stampa employed the standardized lyric vocabulary formulated by Petrarch and adopted by his followers. Stampa's borrowings from Petrarch are numerous and acknowledged. The very structure of her opus follows an established format for collections of love poetry in the sixteenth century. Like Petrarch, she presents a love story as it unfolds in a series of inner conflicts in an atmosphere of painful self-awareness; like him, she orders the loose threads of her plot line in a chronological fashion. Nevertheless, both master and disciple transcend the barriers of biographical or realistic experience and enter the realm of universality. Nor was Stampa a mere copier. Her reworking of the Petrarchan model enriches her verse by constantly functioning as a sounding board against which her own words echo forcefully. Like the most successful *Petrarchisti*, she manipulates her borrowings so that the atmosphere of the original is transferred to the new composition. This "translation" is all the more significant because Stampa was forced to operate within the masculine lexicon of the dominant Petrarchan/Neoplatonic code. One of the privileged women who received a solid education in the sixteenth century, she was one of the first poets to express the woman's view of the love experience.

Stampa's feminine sensibility is clearly expressed in her poetry. Even within the confines of her creative imitation, the writer possesses a singular lyric personality, easily recognizable for its sincerity of expression, lack of rhetorical affectation, and emotive power, in contrast to the repetitive monotony of numerous other Petrarchan adherents. These very qualities, justly appreciated by modern readers, were the probable cause for her lack of popularity in her own day. Insufficiently erudite and controlled, Stampa's compositions lacked the formal dress and decorum so admired during the late Renaissance. A minor player on the stage of Venetian culture, Stampa had little influence and no resonance. After centuries of critical neglect, however, she has come to be recognized as one of the great love poets of her tradition. The rich psychological nuances of her sonnets and the extraordinary musicality of her madrigals, joined with the spontaneity of her discourse, separate her from the scores of Petrarchan imitators and make her one of Italy's foremost women writers and one of the best lyric poets of the Renaissance.

Biography

Very little is actually known about the historical Gaspara Stampa. Documentation of her life is scarce, and most data are limited to contemporary letters and occasional poems dedicated to her. Even the exact year and location of her birth are uncertain, as is the social status of her family, although some evidence suggests that her father had been a successful Paduan jeweler whose trade permitted a comfortable bourgeois existence. Some information can be drawn from the *Rime*, although it is not always wise to use the poetry as a biographical source. It appears that sometime after 1530, the three Stampa children were taken to Venice by their widowed mother and were given a good Humanistic education. The daughters, Gaspara and Cassandra, demonstrated exceptional musical aptitude and soon achieved excellent reputations as musicians, while their brother, Baldassare, was becoming greatly admired as a promising young poet before his untimely death in 1544. The siblings, particularly Baldassare, participated actively in the social world of the Venetian *ridotti*, or salons, meeting some of the most prominent artists, musicians, patrons, and intellectuals of the time. It was a sophisticated environment where the nobility freely mingled with dandies, foreigners, students, and courtesans. It was an ambiance generally inaccessible to the maidens and matrons of the city, who lived a sheltered existence. Gaspara and Cassandra had a *ridotto* of their own, where they entertained guests with song and poetry.

Sometime in 1548, at such a gathering, Stampa met Count Collatino di Collato, a feudal gentleman-warrior known for his patronage of artists and musicians. The romantic involvement of Stampa and the count became literary history. For the first time, the young woman seriously devoted herself to poetry, producing hundreds of compositions dedicated to the man and the love that would dominate her life for three years. Collatino was an indifferent lover, however, and after a series of separations and conflicts, the two ended their affair.

Stampa found consolation in her art and in another man, the patrician Bartolomeo

Zen, who appears in a limited number of sonnets in the *Rime*. Stampa died in 1554, barely thirty, having published only three of her numerous sonnets in an anthology. Her complete opus was edited posthumously by Cassandra and appeared a few months after the poet's death. Then, for two hundred years, the writer and her work were forgotten.

The fictional Gaspara Stampa first appeared in 1738, in a biographical sketch accompanying the second edition of the *Rime*. A direct descendent of Collatino, Count Antonio Rambaldo, wrote this short profile of Stampa, and thus began the first of her legends. Describing Stampa as a sweet young noblewoman of great talent, the count accused his ancestor of cruelty and betrayal leading to the unnatural and untimely death (by poison?) of the distraught lady. This version of Stampa's life appealed to the Romantic soul, and a number of fictional renderings followed, including one novel and two plays. Stampa had become a female Werther, an unwary virgin doomed to unhappiness and death.

This mythical Stampa was ravished in 1913 when a literary scholar, Abdelkader Salza, concluded that the poet had not been a young innocent but a high-class prostitute, a courtesan. Given the independence of Stampa's life, her known participation in the Venetian demimonde, and her sexual liberty, such a conclusion remains plausible but unproved; Gaspara may also have been a *virtuosa*, or professional musician, for example. The critical debate concerning the poet's social and moral standing raged for decades, involving some of Italy's major literati. As a result, another legend was born: The eternal *appassionata* emerged to replace the virginal victim. In such a biographical furor, Stampa's *Rime* was interpreted variously as a document, a diary, even an epistolary novel in verse. The historical figure and the fictional protagonist merged, and, in the process, the poet was ignored. It is only during the past fifty years that some literary critics have begun to evaluate the artist and separate her from the woman, discovering that Stampa was a serious writer, cognizant of the difficulties of her craft and of the need to develop a personal style that would adequately express what she wished to convey.

Analysis

Most modern editions of the *Rime* are based on the one prepared in 1913 by Salza, who divided Gaspara Stampa's poetry into two major groupings: the "Rime d'amore" (love poems) and the "Rime varie" (miscellaneous poems). The former includes more than two hundred compositions, preponderantly sonnets, which chronicle the poet's love for Collatino and, later, Zen. The latter contains Stampa's occasional poetry, addressed to friends, acquaintances, and celebrities. Salza's edition concludes with eight religious sonnets, extracted from their original positioning among the love poems, so that the text ends on a morally contrite and uplifting note probably not intended by the author.

The miscellaneous poems are Stampa's most conventional works, often mere exercises in the art of writing. Adhering to shared literary expectations and the collective

Petrarchan taste, they are expressions of social courtesy, gallantry, polite exchange, and encomium. Their function was public, in a century that utilized poetry as a tool of communication and flattery. Nevertheless, the "Rima varie" offer clear indications of Stampa's personal attitudes toward poetry, poetics, and her own accomplishments. Most of her addressees were avowed, if occasionally innovative, members of Venice's Petrarchan literary elite. Their relationship to Stampa was primarily artistic, poetry functioning as the common social denominator. In her laudatory verse, Stampa is often concerned with the intellectual and stylistic attainments of those to whom her poems were addressed. By praising them, she is making an express value judgment on conventional Petrarchianism, accepting it as the ideal poetic model and stating that fame can be obtained through successful emulation.

From reading the "Rima varie," it appears that the poet had a well-formulated critical criterion, by which she judged her own work and that of others—a criterion based on the theory of creative imitation. Whereas she praises her fellow poets, Stampa projects an air of artistic insecurity in regard to her own abilities, declaring time and again that her "style" is inadequate, that she lacks sufficient eloquence, that her technique is crude. Often the poet suggests that her artistic failure is a result of her gender. The frailty of women is presented as implying intellectual inferiority as well, in a series of negative qualifiers Stampa uses to describe herself, ranging from "vile" to "humble." Within her cultural environment, these disclaimers and confessions of inadequacy were Stampa's way of defining herself as an unsatisfactory *Petrarchista*, a writer who aspires to great art but fails.

PETRARCHANISM

The Petrarchan origin of Stampa's poetry is undeniable and indeed is clearly acknowledged by the poet herself in the *Rime*'s opening sonnet, which both paraphrases and pays homage to Petrarch's prefatory poem to *Rerum vulgarium fragmenta* (1470, also known as *Canzoniere*; *Rhymes*, 1976). Similar paraphrases open many Renaissance collections of love poetry, immediately acknowledging their artistic origins in the medieval master. In Stampa's case, this declared derivation serves two purposes. On one hand, the poet directly associates her compositions with those of their literary source; on the other, she also contrasts the two works by altering the premises of the sonnets. Thus, Stampa's prefatory sonnet informs the reader that she is about to construct an exemplary love story in the pattern established for *canzonieri*, but it also declares that Petrarch's moral environment is not operative in this Renaissance work. Petrarch had from the outset of his collection emphasized the victory of the soul over earthly *vanitas*; Stampa, the disciple, retains none of her master's religious conflicts.

The first sonnet of Petrarch's *Rhymes* had emphasized spiritual repentance; the first sonnet of the *Rime* proposes the unending exaltation of human love, not its moral rejection. From the beginning, Stampa distinguishes her poetic universe from Petrarch's and initiates her subversive interpretation of the model. Here, and throughout her collection, Stampa divests her borrowings of their original moral and religious implications. She uses Petrarchan themes, images, metaphors, poetic devices, forms, vocabulary, and even whole lines but rejects the Christian consciousness that shapes the psychological ambiance of the medieval source. One example is the poem "La vita fugge," which replicates the first line of a famous Petrarchan sonnet. Both poems are concerned with the passage of time and the ensuing emotions of loss and dread, but Stampa purposely distorts the original's premises. Whereas Petrarch had been preoccupied with time wasted in transient pleasures, Stampa regrets the loss of pleasure in the transience of time. What had been a poem of spiritual suffering is transformed into a complaint against the fleeting nature of earthly love. In similar fashion, Stampa's anniversary poems—also derived from Petrarch's *Rhymes*—engage in an argument with their model. In contrast to Petrarch's Good Friday, a feast of death, Stampa proposes Christmas, a celebration of birth, as the anniversary of her love.

Stampa's rejection of Petrarch's spiritual battles places her directly in the more naturalistic world of the Renaissance but does not negate her greatest contact with his poetic universe. It is in the act of loving and in psychological self-awareness that Stampa comes closest to her literary mentor. Both are exceptional landscapers of their interior worlds, delving into the deepest recesses of emotion and thought. For both, the principal issue is love. More intense than Petrarch's collection, Stampa's "Rime d'amore" is compactly powerful in its analysis of the states and stages of loving. Nothing deflects the poet from her theme. Love is omnipresent in the *Rime*, an overwhelming force that controls the poetic persona, ranging from feelings of extreme joy to painful masochism.

Equally present is the beloved, principally Collatino, who is never named directly but who is consistently idealized. The beloved is the poet's *signore*, or lord, concurrently feudal master, gentleman, superior, and god. To create such an exceptional figure, Stampa borrowed from both Petrarchianism and Platonism, easily associating him with abstractions such as the true, the beautiful, and the good as well as linking him poetically to the representation of Christ in the anniversary poems. Like an idol, the beloved receives amorous tributes but does not reciprocate, being enamored of his own beautiful self. Stampa deifies her man, rendering him as a Platonic emanation, a translucent reflection, or an immaterial beauty. She compares him to the planets, the elements, and the seasons, attributing mystical qualities to him. He is a celestial Mars, an Apollo, and an Adonis—a figure of myth, not a mere man. In keeping with Stampa's Petrarchan inspiration, however, this idol is also a cruel beloved, a pagan icon who demands immolation as a sacrifice for love. Even the Platonic desire to acquire beauty through union with the loved one becomes a means of torment, for union—understood physically as well as spiritually—is denied through separation, abandonment, and rejection. The glorification of the beloved in Stampa is concurrent with the self-denigration of the lover. The Stampean persona loses self to love, as exemplified by the figure of Echo, the nymph who had wasted away for love of Narcissus (the Count?), retaining only her voice (poetry?). Gaspara also associates love with death, in Platonic terms, for the lover is lost to the beloved. To these standard themes, the poet adds the novel one of jealousy, whose pain survives even as the persona's identity withers.

Language

It is Stampa's language that most clearly separates her from the other imitators of Petrarch and lyric poets of the sixteenth century. Common, everyday speech often intrudes into the courtly diction of emulation. The poet tends toward spoken language, creating an atmosphere of directness and sincerity often lacking in the work of her more polished contemporaries. To achieve such spontaneity, Stampa employs direct and indirect discourse, dialogue, apostrophe, invocation, and direct address. Her verse is also unique for its musicality. Given her instrumental and vocal training, it is not surprising that her poems are often melodious, rhythmic, and aurally suggestive, linking her to the later contributions of the Arcadian school and the melodrama of Pietro Metastasio. Stampa's lyric idiom has a distinct identity, a private language that unites conventional style, colloquialisms, musical cadence, and directness.

Sensuality

Also unique to Stampa is her sensual honesty. Her poetry is not explicitly erotic, but it is sensuous, its sexuality being contained by the generalities of Petrarchan diction. The carpe diem theme, the call to the beloved to enjoy pleasure and beauty before they disappear in time, links some of her poetry to that of Christopher Marlowe, Robert Herrick, and Andrew Marvell. The pain and negativity of love found in Stampa is also given rhetorical dress in her unusual use of the hyperbole. Just as the Petrarchan antithesis had served Stampa well in describing the dichotomy of loving, so the conceit serves to express love's pain and imperiousness, as well as the beloved's cruelty. Contradictory feelings, the tensions and extremes of emotion, frustration, passion, anger, and hopelessness are dramatized through language. It is this emotive tension that separates Stampa from other lyric poets in her century, justifying her famous line: "Love has made me such that I live in fire."

Bibliography

Bassanese, Fiora A. *Gaspara Stampa*. Boston: Twayne, 1982. Comprehensive and authoritative, this rare full-length critical study of Stampa in English synthesizes the full range of continental scholarship, with sound original conclusions. Annotated bibliography of Italian sources is also useful.

Benfell, V. Stanley. "Translating Petrarchan Desire in Vittoria Colonna and Gaspara Stampa." In *Translating Desire in Medieval and Early Modern Literature*, edited by Craig Barry and Heather Hayton. Tempe: Arizona Center for Medieval and Renaissance Studies, 2005. Traces the Petrarchian influence in the poetry of Stampa and the poet Vittoria Colonna, particularly in the area of desire.

De Rycke, Dawn. "On Hearing the Courtesan in a Gift of Song: The Venetian Case of Gaspara Stampa." In *The Courtesan's Arts: Cross-Cultural Perspectives*, edited by Martha Feldman and Bonnie Gordon. New York: Oxford University Press, 2006. This essay concentrates on the madrigals and works that Stampa set to music. An accomplished lute player and singer, she performed her works in public. Another chapter in this work, "The Courtesan's Voice: Petrarchan Lovers, Pop Philosophy, and Oral Traditions," by Feldman also discusses Stampa and places her in context, briefly touching on the debate over whether she was a courtesan.

Moore, Mary B. *Desiring Voices: Women Sonneteers and Petrarchism*. Carbondale: Southern Illinois University Press, 2000. Places Stampa within a larger European poetic community, providing feminist insights. Devotes a chapter to Stampa, with new translation of several poems.

Philippy, Patricia Berrahou. *Love's Remedies: Recantation and Renaissance Lyric Poetry*. Lewisburg, Pa.: Bucknell University Press, 1995. A chapter on Stampa elucidates her position in Italian literature and her deviation from the established male Petrarchan conventions.

Stampa, Gaspara. *Gaspara Stampa: Selected Poems*. Edited by Laura Anna Stortoni and Mary Prentic Lillie. New York: Italica Press, 1994. A bilingual edition, with new translations and notes. The introduction is particularly helpful with its insights into Stampa's life and times. The translations are both lyrical and faithful. A chronology of Stampa's life prefaces the text.

Warnke, Frank J. *Three Women Poets: Renaissance and Baroque*. Lewisburg, Pa.: Bucknell University Press, 1987. Presents a convincing argument that Stampa is the prime female poet of Italy. Ranks her in skill with Louise Labé and Sor Juana Inés de la Cruz. Good translations of the poetry of each poet are provided, and the comparisons of the three are particularly enlightening.

Fiora A. Bassanese

TORQUATO TASSO

Born: Sorrento, Kingdom of Naples (now in Italy); March 11, 1544
Died: Rome, Papal States (now in Italy); April 25, 1595

PRINCIPAL POETRY
Rinaldo, 1562 (English translation, 1792)
Gerusalemme liberata, 1581 (*Jerusalem Delivered*, 1600)
Rime, 1581, 1591, 1593 (*From the Italian of Tasso's Sonnets*, 1867)
Gerusalemme conquistata, 1593 (*Jerusalem Conquered*, 1907)
Le sette giornate del mondo creato, 1607

OTHER LITERARY FORMS

The literary work of Torquato Tasso (TAS-oh) begins and ends with his discussions of poetic theory. As early as 1561 but certainly before 1570, he had composed *Discorsi dell'arte poetica* (1587; discourses on the poetic art), and he published a much revised and expanded version of the same work, *Discorsi del poema eroico* (1594; *Discourses on the Heroic Poem*, 1973) the year before his death. The latter is both a defense of Tasso's own epics and an influential statement of Renaissance critical theory. Tasso's *Dialoghi* (1581) embraces a variety of subjects and often includes Tasso himself as one of the speakers; these dialogues are modeled after those of Plato. Tasso's *Lettere* (1587, 1588, 1616-1617), numbering as many as seventeen hundred, constitute a rich source of information about his life in elegantly crafted prose. Tasso's pastoral drama *Aminta* (pr. 1573; English translation, 1591), celebrates love and has been far more influential than his tragedy of mistaken identities and incest, *Il re Torrismondo* (pb. 1587; the King Torrismondo).

ACHIEVEMENTS

Torquato Tasso's importance in the history of letters is twofold: His own prodigious work has great merit, and he exerted enormous influence on artists who followed him. Tasso, the representative genius of the late Italian Renaissance, was the creator of Christian epic. In him, the erudition of classical literature and Aristotelian poetic theory combined with the force of the Counter-Reformation and court life to produce *Jerusalem Delivered*. His reputation as a writer rests on this epic, his superb pastoral drama *Aminta*, some of his lyric poetry, and his synthesis of epic poetic theory.

Tasso enjoyed almost immediate renown both in and out of Italy. The romance *Rinaldo* showed promise, but *Aminta*, on the theme of innocent and natural love triumphing over various adversities of law and circumstance, established his reputation as a poet. *Jerusalem Delivered*, completed three years later, touched off a spirited controversy over poetic theory, with comparisons to Homer, Vergil, and Ludovico Ariosto

Torquato Tasso
(Library of Congress)

that always recognized Tasso's stature, whether the commentary was hostile or admiring. Tasso's epic also excited interest in England. As early as 1584, a Latin translation of *Jerusalem Delivered* by Scipio Gentili was published in London. Edmund Spenser in his 1587 "Letter to Raleigh" mentioned Tasso as one of his models for *The Faerie Queene* (1590, 1596). In 1594, the second part of the British play *Godfrey of Bulloigne* was performed by the Admiral's Men. Also in 1594, Richard Carew published the Italian text and English translation of the first five cantos of *Jerusalem Delivered*. In the early seventeenth century, Tasso influenced Samuel Daniel, Michael Drayton, Abraham Cowley, and John Milton. Later Tasso's reputation suffered an eclipse, although John Hoole's 1763 translation of *Jerusalem Delivered* into heroic couplets was very popular. The nineteenth century saw as many as eight new translations of the epic, the most influential being Jeremiah Holmes Wiffen's 1824 version in Spenserian stanzas. Whether Tasso's epic was read for its own sake or used as a source, it was admired for its love stories. Leigh Hunt, for example, chose the romantic trials of Olindo and Sofronia, Tancred and Clorinda, and Rinaldo and Armida for his *Stories from the Italian Poets* (1846). Early in the twentieth century, however, many critics evinced little sympathy for Tasso's works or his reputation.

That reputation, the picture of a man driven to or feigning madness because of persecutions endured for love, was fostered by the biography *Vita di Torquato Tasso* (1621), published by the poet's friend G. B. Manso. As early as 1594, a now lost play, *Tasso's Melancholy*, was performed in London. The Romantic age saw in Tasso's writings his supposed love for Leonora d'Este and made Tasso a symbol of the suffering artist. The legend that grew up around his life inspired the drama *Torquato Tasso* (pb. 1790; English translation, 1827) by Johann Wolfgang von Goethe and the monologue *The Lament of Tasso* (1817) by Lord Byron, in addition to numerous musical and pictorial works. Psychological interest in Tasso has not completely disappeared, but interest in his legend no longer overshadows the worth of his writing.

Biography

Torquato Tasso was born on March 11, 1544, in Sorrento, the son of the poet and courtier Bernardo Tasso and Porzia de' Rossi. He began his education in Naples with Jesuit teachers. His family life was disrupted first when young Tasso followed his father, exiled from the Kingdom of Naples, to Rome in 1554, and again in 1556 when his mother died unexpectedly. Perhaps influenced in choice of genre by his father's recently completed epic *Amadigi* (1560) and in choice of a subject by his sister's escape from an Ottoman attack on Sorrento, Tasso wrote 116 stanzas of what was to become later his epic *Jerusalem Delivered* but laid aside the story of Godfrey and the First Crusade when his father sent him to Padua to study law in 1560. In Padua, law was far less interesting than Sperone Speroni and the discussion of philosophy, rhetoric, and poetic theory. Tasso wrote and published the chivalric romance *Rinaldo* and began writing Petrarchan love lyrics. After a period of study interspersed with escapades at the University of Bologna, he returned to Padua, probably where he wrote *Discorsi dell'arte poetica*. In 1565, Tasso left school (without a degree) for Ferrara and the service of Cardinal Luigi d'Este.

In Ferrara, Tasso resumed work on his epic on the liberation of Jerusalem. He also wrote lyrics for the two sisters of Duke Alfonso II, Lucrezia and Leonora d'Este. Tasso suffered the death of his father in 1569; in 1570, he traveled to Paris, his only trip outside Italy.

Entering the service of Duke Alfonso in January, 1572, Tasso began a very productive period of his life. His pastoral masterpiece *Aminta* was performed in 1573; he began a tragedy based on classical models in 1574; and he completed *Jerusalem Delivered* in 1575 at the age of thirty-one. Although he was eager to publish his epic, Tasso submitted it to the criticism of Scipione Gonzaga and others. Tasso wished nothing in his work to offend either poetic theory or Roman Catholic Church doctrine, but he could not bear the criticism that resulted. He left Ferrara only to return; he felt spied on and attacked a servant with a knife; he was placed under guard, but escaped to stay with his sister in Sorrento. Tasso returned to Ferrara, then soon left to wander through Mantua, Padua,

Venice, Urbino, Pesaro, and Turin before returning again to Ferrara in 1579. This time, his accusations and irrational behavior led Duke Alfonso to imprison him in Sant'Anna, where Tasso remained for seven years.

Biographers have variously attributed Alfonso's imprisonment of Tasso to the duke's anger at Tasso's love for Alfonso's sister, pique at the suggestions that his poet wished to find a new patron, fear over what Tasso might reveal to the Inquisition, or the sincere concern of an exasperated ruler to save all concerned, including Tasso himself, from the effects of real madness. Regardless of the causes of Tasso's madness or melancholy, the conditions of his long imprisonment did not prevent him from writing, although it did prevent him from having any control over the many unauthorized editions of his works published in those years. During the years of his imprisonment, Tasso composed more than four hundred letters, many of his dialogues, considerable occasional poetry, and an *Apologia* (1586) for *Jerusalem Delivered*.

Released from prison in 1586, Tasso first went to Mantua, where he completed his tragedy, renaming it *Il re Torrismondo*. He traveled restlessly and published his earlier epic, *Jerusalem Conquered*. He also composed a number of religious poems, one of which was the religious epic *Le sette giornate del mondo creato* (the seven days of the creation of the world). The last of Tasso's many journeys was to Rome, where he was to be crowned poet laureate by the pope. Tasso became ill, however, and died at the monastery of Sant'Onofrio on April 25, 1595.

Analysis

It is apparent that, from the first, Torquato Tasso set out to reconcile a number of seeming opposites in his work: lyric and heroic, myth and history, fantasy and religion, romance and epic, popular variety and Aristotelian principle. The tension of this attempt at synthesis caused Tasso to abandon his early draft of an epic poem for a series of less ambitious compositions. Many critics believe that the tension remains unresolved.

Tasso's lyric voice is amply represented in the almost two thousand short poems produced throughout his life. Many of them are imitative of Petrarch. In 1589, Tasso planned to publish his poems in separate volumes according to subject—amorous, encomiastic, and sacred. The love poems are among the earliest lyrics, sometimes linked to historical women such as Lucrezia Bendidio or Laura Peperara, but often general and diffuse in praise of beauty, love, and emotion. Rich in poetic devices, the lyrics luxuriate in the suffering of the poet.

If the middle style characterizes Tasso's amorous verse, the grand style characterizes his encomiastic verse. Many of these poems in praise of influential men risk being sterile or self-serving, but they can also be poignant. Many of the lyrics written in Sant'Anna are pleas for help or pardon, addressed to Duke Alfonzo, the Ferrara princesses, or the duke of Urbino. The Sant'Anna lyrics exhibit a remarkable variety in tone and mood and include a famous and atypical sonnet addressed to the cats of the prison.

Religious Lyrics

Tasso's religious lyrics reflect both personal experience and the general tenor of the Counter-Reformation. There are sonnets, canzones, madrigals, and ballads. They are concerned with both his personal fears and common religious themes such as "Le lagrime di Gesu Cristo" ("The Tears of Jesus Christ"), "Le lagrime di Maria Vergine" ("The Tears of the Virgin Mary"), and "Monte Oliveto" ("Mount Olivet"), a poem on the founding of the religious order that sheltered Tasso in Naples in 1588. The poems reflect the restlessness, melancholy, and personal suffering that are also present in so many of Tasso's other works. Just as Erminia in *Jerusalem Delivered* finds a temporary respite from her troubles in a pastoral sanctuary, so various people in the sonnets retire from the world to an idealized, cloistered life that Tasso envies but cannot join. Tasso's sacred verse is similar in language, style, and tone to his secular verse.

Le sette giornate del mondo creato

Le sette giornate del mondo creato illustrates some of Tasso's characteristic strengths and weaknesses. Tasso wrote the poem about the Creation between 1592 and 1594 after he had finished *Jerusalem Conquered*, a version of his great epic that he felt to be immune from any possible religious or stylistic criticism, and this new theme would allow him to expand his unimpeachable views. *Le sette giornate del mondo creato* is eight thousand lines of blank verse. It is derivative of pagan authors, the Bible, the Church fathers, and Renaissance writers including Guillaume du Bartas. It is neither original nor coherent, although it does attempt to reconcile Aristotle and the Neoplatonists. It is digressive; it succumbs to superfluous praise of noble contemporaries, such as the pope; it subordinates art to moral lesson. For all this, the poem also sees in nature a reflection of the poet's own circumstance. Even at the end of his life, Tasso reflects his person in his art: doubt, suffering, a love of the marvelous, and the lyric mood in epic expression.

Rinaldo

Tasso seems always to have aspired to the writing of epic and, like Vergil, trained for his magnum opus by writing less noble works. *Rinaldo* is just such an exercise. It is a romance in the tradition of Ariosto's *Orlando Furioso* (1516, 1521, 1532; English translation, 1591) or Bernardo Tasso's *Amadigi*. *Rinaldo* is composed of twelve cantos of ottava rima, preceded by an address, "A i lettori" ("To the Readers") which discusses his artistic choices. Tasso was influenced by the study of Aristotle, which blossomed following new translations of and commentaries on Aristotle's *De poetica* (c. 334-323 B.C.E.; *Poetics*, 1705). Tasso claims to follow Aristotelian precedent and to improve on Ariosto by limiting the action to the unity of a single hero and eliminating personalized prologues to each canto. Tasso, however, places the enjoyment of his readers above even Aristotle, and so the unity of action in Tasso's plays will admit considerable variety, along with love interest and marvels.

Both Tasso's method and his material are derivative. Commentators have found in *Rinaldo* echoes of Bernardo Tasso, Petrarch, Matteo Maria Boiardo, and Ariosto, as well as Homer, Theocritus, Vergil, Ovid, and others. The story tells of the trials endured by the protagonist in his search for glory and love. Rinaldo, Orlando's cousin, falls in love with Clorice, the sister of the king of Gascony, but must undergo many adventures on land and sea before at last rescuing Clorice from the infidels and marrying her. There are battles, magic, the glitter of the court, and the suffering of love. Just as Rinaldo in *Jerusalem Delivered* is seduced by Armida but ultimately renounces passion in favor of duty, so is this Rinaldo temporarily wooed away from his true love by the alluring Floriana. When Rinaldo ultimately rejects Floriana, she, like Armida, attempts suicide but is saved. In another incident, Clizia is accidentally shot by her husband just as Clorinda is slain by the unsuspecting Tancred in *Jerusalem Delivered*. *Rinaldo* is the story of the education of a young knight who must prove himself both moral and brave in order to win his love. In theme, incident, style, and tone, this early romance prepares for the epic that follows. *Rinaldo* was written in ten months and published in 1562 when Tasso was only eighteen years old. It was immediately popular, going through six editions during Tasso's lifetime.

JERUSALEM DELIVERED

Tasso then returned to the 116 stanzas of the *Jerusalem Delivered*, which he had begun in 1559. Manuscripts of that text, an intermediate version of about 1570, and the final version of 1575 all survive, and comparisons of the three show some of the poem's development. The original *Jerusalem Delivered* was militaristic and moralistic. It described the arrival of the Christian army, an unsuccessful negotiation, and the anticipation of strife. Almost half of these stanzas survive in the final version of *Jerusalem Delivered*, but there are no love adventures and no supernatural marvels. Tasso expanded his epic to six cantos by 1566, and by 1570, the whole poem had been written. In the 1570 version, Armida and the accompanying love interest were present, but the poem's protagonist was still Ubaldo, a forebear of the duke of Urbino. Significant changes and deletions occurred before the poem, first called *Il Goffredo*, was completed in 1575.

The twenty cantos of ottava rima, which now followed the exploits of an imaginary Rinaldo d'Este rather than Ubaldo, were submitted by Tasso to his friend Gonzaga and others for suggestions for further revision. The period of revision lasted for two years. Tasso did alter some things, but the most sweeping criticisms were followed only when Tasso rewrote the epic as *Jerusalem Conquered* in 1593. Tasso was imprisoned in Sant'Anna when the first unauthorized and incomplete version of his epic was published in 1580 under the title *Godfrey*. This was followed in 1581 by a complete but still unauthorized edition printed by Angelo Ingegneri, who was responsible for naming the epic *Jerusalem Delivered*. Tasso himself apparently collaborated with Febo Bonnà in preparing two corrected editions that followed in the same year.

Jerusalem Delivered is a conscious effort to exceed the accomplishments of Homer, Vergil, and Ariosto. Tasso wished to surpass his predecessors by reconciling the antithetical genres represented by those authors—classical epic and chivalric romance—all within the context of Christian history. He refused to admit that romance is a genre distinct from epic. Judith Kates, in her 1974 essay "Revaluation of the Classical Heroic in Tasso and Milton" persuasively argues that Tasso is the creator of Christian epic.

Jerusalem Delivered is the story of the First Crusade, in which Godfrey of Boulogne recaptures the Holy City from the Turks. As a subject, it is neither too ancient nor too modern. In canto 1, the Archangel Gabriel tells Godfrey, who is discovered praying, that he has been elected commander of the army about to set out for Jerusalem. Pagan defenders reinforce the city and the fortunes of war sway back and forth, with each side aided by supernatural agents of good or evil. After a last terrible battle, the victorious and bloodstained Godfrey leads his men in prayer at the Sepulcher of Christ. C. M. Bowra, in *From Virgil to Milton* (1963), sees the three main heroes as representative of three different ideal virtues. The historical Godfrey is here the consummate Christian leader, renowned for wisdom and piety. He is a Christian Aeneas, subordinating even personal glory to divine plan. The nonhistorical Rinaldo, in comparison, comes close to exemplifying a Homeric ideal. He is an Achilles, with "a brave heart impatient of repose" and "a burning boundless thirst for fame." Tancred exemplifies the courtly virtues and suffers from the courtly malady, laid low by a doomed love "which feeds on grief and grows forevermore."

These Christian warriors are opposed by an array of pagan heroes, the mightiest of whom are Argante and Solyman, differentiated and noble as much as any mortal outside a state of grace can be. The most memorable pagans, however, are women, exhibiting and eliciting very different types of love. The three women, Clorinda, Erminia, and Armida, are very different manifestations of an ideal of feminine beauty and love. Clorinda is an Amazon, like Vergil's Camilla, but also capable of tears, when she is moved by the plight of the lovers Olindo and Sophronia (canto 2), and of forgiveness, when she experiences God's grace through baptism at the moment of her death (canto 12). She is loved by Tancred, who unwittingly kills her, as Achilles did Penthesilea. Erminia, in contrast, epitomizes shy and delicate tenderness. Her love for Tancred is revealed only at the end of the epic, but Tasso leaves its resolution ambiguous. Nevertheless, it allows the poet to include two famous episodes: Erminia's venture, dressed in Clorinda's armor, to look for Tancred (canto 6), and her sojourn among shepherds (canto 7), a pastoral idyll in which the evil life of a court suffers by comparison with the humble, tranquil life of shepherds. Armida, the third pagan woman, is a temptress who, like Circe, changes men into nonhuman forms and, like Dido, seduces heroes from their heaven-appointed duty. Armida's garden (canto 16) is the pattern for Spenser's Bower of Bliss (*The Faerie Queene*, book 2, canto 12). Her enchantments based on sensual beauty are effective against all but direct heavenly intervention. Even when Tasso ends a love story happily, as here when Armida submits to Rinaldo and to Christianity with the words of the Virgin at the Annunciation, the lasting impression is one of tears and suffering.

The whole problem of justifying the love interests in the epic concerned Tasso very much. He set out to surpass Ariosto, and considered *Jerusalem Delivered* to be superior to Ariosto's *Orlando Furioso* in many respects. Tasso's epic conforms to ancient poetic theory, as he proves in his *Discorsi dell'arte poetica*, and expands upon in *Discourses on the Heroic Poem*. It also expresses the true piety of a man of the Counter-Reformation. The classical and religious elements are as much a part of the epic as are the love episodes, although the latter are what readers of all ages have tended to remember.

Tasso writes in an elevated style, decorous and humorless, describing a single action and beginning in medias res. The scope of the action encompasses Heaven, Earth, and Hell. He uses supernatural elements, Homeric similes, and a Latinate vocabulary. In addition to the correspondences between Tasso's characters and characters from previous epics (such as Godfrey/Aeneas or Rinaldo/Achilles), specific actions are reminiscent of earlier epic scenes: God the Father ratifies his decrees with a nod similar to that of Homer's Zeus; a statue of the Virgin, rather than the Palladium of Troy, is stolen; there are night sorties, single combats, troop reviews, espionage missions, the burning of enemy strongholds, and a beautiful woman who stands on the battlements and names the enemy combatants on the field below.

Tasso never forgets, however, that he is writing a Christian epic. As much as he admires the classical tradition, he sees it as deficient in several respects. Tasso speaks of his epic as an allegory in a letter in which he calls Godfrey "the head" and Rinaldo "the right hand." Later, the Bonnà editions of *Jerusalem Delivered* include Tasso's *Allegoria del poema* (1581), in which Tasso claims that the entire plot of his epic ought to be read as a continuous allegory. Spenser seems to have believed this, but some modern critics dismiss the *Allegoria del poema* as an afterthought, a ruse to placate the Inquisition and excuse the marvels and love interest.

Despite their classical and romantic antecedents, Tasso's characters are always judged from a Christian perspective. Admitting the nobility of an Argante or the seductive power of an Armida does not alter this fact. Some critics see the shape of Tasso's epic as reflecting the workings of Providence through history. All the diverse episodes are subordinated to this perspective and ranked by it. *Jerusalem Delivered* is divided into twenty cantos, not the usual twelve or twenty-four. The action divides these cantos in half, with the pagans in ascendance throughout the first half, the Christians throughout the second. The first half begins with the action of God, the second with that of Godfrey. The poem also divides into quarters, with Rinaldo present and active in the first and last sections, absent and enchanted in the middle two. Lastly, the poem exhibits mirror-symmetry, in which each pair of cantos, starting with the first and last, deals with parallel or opposite material. For example, Argante enters the action in canto 3 and is killed in canto 19; the Crusaders first see Jerusalem in canto 3 and first breach its walls in canto 18.

JERUSALEM CONQUERED

Near the end of his life, Tasso himself completed a version of his epic so substantially revised that it deserved and was given a new name, *Jerusalem Conquered*. The new poem, in twenty-four books instead of twenty cantos, is increasingly allegorical and doctrinaire. It purges many of the most fondly remembered episodes (Sophronia and Olindo, Erminia among the shepherds, the trip to the Fortunate Islands) and the most magical or sentimental ones (Armida transforming the knights into fish, the reconciliation of Rinaldo and Armida). Diction is smoothed; Homeric elements are increased; and many characters are renamed (Rinaldo becomes Riccardo, for example). Tasso considered *Jerusalem Conquered* to be far superior to his earlier epic; critics have not agreed with him, however, and have either dismissed the poem or vilified it.

This, however, does not negate Tasso's achievements. He is a consummate storyteller. He epitomizes the Renaissance in his veneration of classical learning and human worth. He redefines the meaning of "heroic" by transforming both the epic poem and its heroes to conform to religious ideals and his own emotional sensibility. No poet more effectively reflects the Renaissance spirit while anticipating the Romantic.

OTHER MAJOR WORKS

PLAYS: *Aminta*, pr. 1573 (verse play; English translation, 1591); *Il re Torrismondo*, pb. 1587 (verse play).

NONFICTION: *Allegoria del poema*, 1581; *Dialoghi*, 1581; *Apologia*, 1586; *Discorsi dell'arte poetica*, 1587; *Lettere*, 1587, 1588, 1616-1617; *Discorsi del poema eroico*, 1594 (*Discourses on the Heroic Poem*, 1973).

BIBLIOGRAPHY

Brand, C. P. *Torquato Tasso*. New York: Cambridge University Press, 1965. A classic biography and critical work on Tasso. Discusses the author's use of historical sources, gives a detailed account of his life, and analyzes his major works. Includes an interesting essay on the legend of Tasso's life and presumed madness, and ends with a lengthy chapter on the poet's contribution to English literature. Bibliographic references are included in the notes.

Cavallo, Jo Ann. *The Romance Epics of Boiardo, Ariosto, and Tasso: From Public Duty to Private Pleasure*. Buffalo, N.Y.: University of Toronto Press, 2004. Examines the epics of Tasso, Matteo Maria Boiardo, and Ludovico Ariosto within their literary contexts. Cavallo places emphasis on genre, ideology, and politics, and how these writers influenced one another.

Finucci, Valeria, ed. *Renaissance Transactions: Ariosto and Tasso*. Durham, N.C.: Duke University Press, 1999. This collection of essays represents a cross-section of critical approaches to "foster a dialogue" among schools of thought on *Jerusalem Conquered* and its relationship with Ariosto's work.

Gariolo, Joseph. *Lope de Vega's "Jerusalén conquistada" and Torquato Tasso's "Gerusalemme liberata" Face to Face*. Kassel, Germany: Edition Richenberger, 2005. Compares Lope de Vega Carpio's *Jerusalén conquistada* (1609) and Tasso's *Jerusalem Conquered*. Looks at the influence of Tasso's work on that of Lope de Vega and provides considerable analysis of both works.

Günsberg, Maggie. *Epic Rhetoric of Tasso: Theory and Practice*. Oxford, England: Legenda, 1998. An in-depth study of *Jerusalem Delivered*.

Sherberg, Michael. *Rinaldo: Character and Intertext in Ariosto and Tasso*. Saratoga, Calif.: ANMA Libri, 1993. Part 2 examines Tasso's treatment of the Carolingian "knight," which downplays Rinaldo's rebellious nature and actions while expanding his character, especially through psychological depth.

Zatti, Sergio. *The Quest for Epic: From Ariosto to Tasso*. Buffalo, N.Y.: University of Toronto Press, 2006. Examines Tasso's *Jerusalem Conquered* and Ludovico Ariosto's *Orlando Furioso*. Zatti has written books examining both authors' works as well as works explaining the development of the epic.

Elizabeth A. Holtze

GIUSEPPE UNGARETTI

Born: Alexandria, Egypt; February 8, 1888
Died: Milan, Italy; June 1, 1970

PRINCIPAL POETRY
Il porto sepolto, 1916
Allegria di naufragi, 1919
La Guerre, 1919
L'allegria, 1931, 1942 (includes revisions of *Il porto sepolto* and *Allegria di naufragi*)
Sentimento del tempo, 1933
Il dolore, 1947
La terra promessa, 1950
Gridasti, soffoco..., 1951
Un grido e paesaggi, 1952
Life of a Man, 1958
Il taccuino del vecchio, 1960
Morte delle stagioni, 1967
Dialogo, 1968
Giuseppe Ungaretti: Selected Poems, 1969
Vita d'un uomo: Tutte le poesie, 1969
Selected Poems of Giuseppe Ungaretti, 1975
The Buried Harbour: Selected Poems of Giuseppe Ungaretti, 1990 (Kevin Hart, translator and editor)
A Major Selection of the Poetry of Giuseppe Ungaretti, 1997

OTHER LITERARY FORMS

Giuseppe Ungaretti (ewng-gah-REHT-tee) published literary and critical essays as well as poetry. Perhaps as a consequence of the negative criticism his work drew at first, Ungaretti was concerned to show his connection with the greatest voices of the Italian literary tradition. In discussing the importance of Giacomo Leopardi, Petrarch, or the poets of the Baroque period, Ungaretti provided a framework that assists in the interpretation of his own work. These essays also contain autobiographical information and descriptions of travel and foreign places.

Ungaretti translated poetry by such diverse figures as William Shakespeare, William Blake, Luis de Góngora y Argote, Sergei Esenin, Jean Paulhan, Saint-John Perse, and Jean Racine. Notable for the English reader is Ungaretti's essay on Shakespeare's sonnets, "Significato dei sonetti di Shakespeare," in *Vita d'un uomo: Saggi e interventi*

(1974; life of a man: essays and interventions), and an essay accompanying his translations of Blake.

Achievements

With Eugenio Montale and Salvatore Quasimodo, Giuseppe Ungaretti stands as a leader of contemporary Italian poetry. His is the first modern poetic idiom in Italian. He renewed interest in, and criticism of, the tradition of Italian poetry and is considered the founder of the dominant school of poetry in Italy in the twentieth century, the Hermetic school. Though he never won the Nobel Prize in Literature, he had a significant international reputation and influence. He won the most prestigious prizes in Italy; the earliest was the Gonfaloniere Prize in Venice in 1932, followed by the Premio Roma in 1949, the Premio Montefeltro from Urbino in 1960, and the Etna-Taormina International Poetry Prize in 1966. Outside Italy, his poetry was honored in 1956 when he shared the Knokke-le-Zoute Poetry Prize with Juan Ramón Jiménez and W. H. Auden; in 1970, he received the Books Abroad Award (now the Neustadt International Prize for Literature) at the University of Oklahoma.

Ungaretti was perhaps the major voice in establishing Leopardi as the most important traditional influence on Italian poetry of the first half of the twentieth century, for he found in Leopardi a bridge between his own poetics and the long Italian tradition that had begun with Petrarch. He also wrote significantly of Baroque poetry, of Shakespeare and Blake, and of several poets of the French tradition.

Difficult in its austere, understated beginnings, Ungaretti's poetry grew deeper and yet more complex as he became responsive to traditional metrics; indeed, he was often accused of purposeful obscurity. There was no doubt, however, that Ungaretti spoke to other poets, for when Francesco Flora called his poetry Hermetic because of its subjective content, involuted forms, and French Symbolist influences, he was unwittingly acknowledging Ungaretti's leading position in Italian poetry. Ungaretti himself, however, did not remain within what came to be called the Hermetic school. The Hermetics, it might be claimed, developed mannerisms and an abstruse poetic idiom. Ungaretti, with a possible exception here and there, though writing a difficult poetry, always used that difficulty to intensify communication, and not merely for its own sake.

Biography

Giuseppe Ungaretti was born on February 8, 1888, to Italian parents, Antonio Ungaretti and Maria Ungaretti, in Alexandria, Egypt. Ungaretti's parents had emigrated from an area near Lucca, Italy, to Egypt, where his father, who was employed for a short time at the Suez Canal site, contracted an illness that was to lead to his death in 1890. The Ungarettis had opened a bakery in the Arab quarter of the city, however, and Maria Ungaretti, after her husband's death, continued this business quite successfully.

Ungaretti's education was French, but he was familiar with the Italian intellectual scene in Alexandria. He knew the Italian writer Enrico Pea and frequented Pea's house, called the *baracca rossa*, a gathering place for anarchists. Between 1906 and 1912, Ungaretti's interests included politics, for he wrote and published some political essays. More important, however, Ungaretti came to know several writers both from Alexandria and abroad. He corresponded with Giuseppe Prezzolini, editor of the important literary magazine *La voce*. It was through Prezzolini, in part, that Ungaretti met many of the most notable writers and artists of his day when he finally left Alexandria in 1912, at the age of twenty-four, to travel to Italy and then to Paris.

Paris was the place of Ungaretti's first self-awakening. There, he met with men such as artists Pablo Picasso, Georges Braque, Fernand Leger, Giorgio Di Chirico; writer Max Jacob; sculptor Amedeo Modigliani; and the Italian Futurists. In 1913, Ungaretti followed Henri Bergson's courses at the Collège de France; in the same year, Mohammed Sheab, Ungaretti's friend since childhood, unable to adjust to European life, committed suicide. Ungaretti remembered him in the poem "In Memoria" ("In Memoriam"): "And only I perhaps/ still know/ he lived," he wrote, foreshadowing, his conviction that immortality is gained only in the memory of others.

By 1914, Ungaretti was in Italy, where he wrote the first poems later collected in *L'allegria* (the joy). In 1915, he was inducted into the Italian army and was sent to the Austro-Italian Front. The poems of *Il porto sepolto* (the buried port) were written while Ungaretti was on active duty; these poems also became a part of *L'allegria*. Ungaretti did not want to print the poems written at the front, because he felt that such an act would break the solidarity he had with his countrymen, but a friend of his, Ettore Serra, took them and insisted on publishing them in 1916. In 1918, Ungaretti was in Paris again. (Guillaume Apollinaire, a friend of Ungaretti, died soon after he arrived.) He stayed in Paris until 1921, supporting himself by working for an Italian newspaper. While there, he met and married Jeanne Duprix. During this time, Ungaretti's reputation was growing, and he began lecturing in France and Belgium.

In 1921, Ungaretti returned to Rome, where he was to live until 1936. Here the Baroque art of the city had a great impact on him, and eventually this influence led to the writing of *Sentimento del tempo* (the feeling of time). He continued his lecturing and worked in the press division of the Foreign Ministry. In 1925, a daughter, Anna Maria, was born, and in 1930 a son, Antonietto. In 1931, *L'allegria* was given its definitive title and published; this collection included the poems from 1914 to 1919. In 1932, Ungaretti received the Venice Premio Gondoliere, and in 1933, *Sentimento del tempo* was published.

In 1936, Ungaretti accepted a teaching position in Italian literature at the University of São Paulo, Brazil. His stay in Brazil was a dark time, for in 1937, his older brother, Constantino, died, and in 1939, his son, Antonietto, died after a mistreated attack of appendicitis. The trials Italy faced during World War II compounded Ungaretti's sense of loss, and his writing from this period represents a hiatus in the unfolding of his poetic vision. *Il dolore* (the grief), which emerged from this time, was published in 1947.

When Ungaretti returned to Italy in 1942, he accepted a position at the University of Rome. After the war, his right to retain his teaching post was disputed, for many criticized his apparent acceptance of fascism. In spite of this controversy, he retained his position and was very productive during the period following the war. Most of his translations were published during this time, as were several commemorative editions of his works. In his seventieth year, his wife, Jeanne, died.

During his last years, Ungaretti traveled around the world. In 1964, he gave a series of lectures at Columbia University in New York City. On a visit to São Paulo in 1966, Ungaretti met a young Brazilian poetess named Bruna Bianco, with whom he pursued a platonic love affair. *Dialogo* is a poetic dialogue between them. In 1967, *Morte delle stagioni* (death of the seasons), which collected the poems of Ungaretti's old age, was published. Ungaretti was to have one more passionate relationship, with a young Croatian girl, Djuna. In 1970, he traveled again to the United States to receive the Books Abroad Award at the University of Oklahoma. While on this trip, he developed bronchitis. He died in Milan on the night of June 1, 1970.

Analysis

Giuseppe Ungaretti believed that great poets write "seemly biographies," for "poetry is the discovery of the human condition in its essence." Friendship, love, death, and the fate of humanity, the great lyric themes, are the subjects of Ungaretti's poetry. Though his poems show a contemporary concern for autobiographical material, they blend this material with the imagery of the poetic tradition. The form of this poetry is discontinuous, sensuous, and elusive. Metonymy, hyperbaton, ellipsis, surprising juxtapositions of images, and the cultivation of unusual language are all characteristic of Ungaretti's style.

As "seemly biography," Ungaretti's lifework developed with the movement of his experience. His first major collection, *L'allegria*, reflected his experience of World War I. *Sentimento del tempo*, written during his first extended stay in Rome, unfolded around a religious crisis. *Il dolore*, the book Ungaretti said he loved most, chronicled the poet's struggle to come to terms with the loss of his brother and son and the disaster Italy faced at the end of World War II. *La terra promessa* (the promised land) and the later works grew out of the realization that aging and its consequences, the fading of the senses and of feeling, offer a final challenge to the poet.

L'ALLEGRIA

Ungaretti's first major collection, *L'allegria*, includes revisions of two earlier collections, *Il porto sepolto* and *Allegria di naufragi*, which had been published separately, as well as a group of poems written in France just before World War I. *L'allegria* is a work of self-discovery. In his notes to *Il porto sepolto*, Ungaretti says that though his first awakenings came in Paris, it was not until the war that he fully came to know himself. The young Ungaretti was an atheist. There was for him no God, nor any Platonic ideals, somehow infiltrating time, to serve as a basis for life's meaning. The war and its desolate landscapes came to take on something of the significance of his youthful experience of the desert. The desert was a void—as such it represented the emptiness of blind existence—but the desert was also a space in which mirages could blossom. So, too, the war brought Ungaretti to the bones of existence, and there he discovered his courage. The self-discovery he spoke of was the courage to resist the sweep of objective, hence depersonalized, events that depress the human spirit and force it into a life of merely private pleasures and pains. Poetry was the courage to transform the worn images of everyday existence into the perfection of dreams, to find an eternal moment even in the face of desolation. Of all the poets of World War I, Ungaretti is arguably the most affirmative. He cries out in "Pellegrinaggio" ("The Pilgrimage"), "Ungaretti/ man of pain/ you need but an illusion/ to give you courage."

Also arising from Ungaretti's Alexandrian experience of the desert is his identification of himself as a Bedouin poet. This image emerges as central in *L'allegria* and recurs throughout his works in any number of transformations. Ungaretti implies in the use of this image that the poet cannot be submerged in the familiar. Movement and change nourish the quintessential condition of poetry, *disponibilità* ("availability to things"). The Bedouin nature of the poet is required by the solitary reality that the emptiness of blind existence imposes on him. In "Agonia" ("Agony"), Ungaretti pulls these themes together:

> To die at the mirage
> like thirsty skylarks
> Or like the quail
> past the sea
> in the first thickets
> when it has lost
> the will to fly
> But not to live on lament
> like a blinded finch.

The migration of the Bedouin, like that of birds, is a kind of eternal return. Human individuals are not lost in time if they allow the mirage (beauty, or the flash of poetic insight) to beckon them to the depths of experience. The Bedouin poet's courage is his recognition that thirst and the loss of the will to fly are circumstances, as death is a circumstance. Though he knows that these will overtake him, they do not diminish his passion for flight and song. The poet is always moving back, but with openness; the truth he finds can be held in an image, briefly, but it can never become fixed or permanent. Ungaretti's spirit persists in its capacity to evoke the dream in the midst of the wasteland.

Ungaretti's poetic vision shares a great deal with that of the French Symbolists, for whom the world is a kind of nullity until it is transformed by human subjectivity—hence Charles Baudelaire's celebrated notion that humans know the world through "forests of symbols." In Ungaretti's "Eterno" ("Eternal"), there is a whole poetics in epigrammatic form: "Between one flower gathered and the other given/ the inexpressible null. . . ." If the gathering and giving of the flower stand for poetry, then every poem results from a struggle with the inexpressible, what Ungaretti calls the void, or blind existence. As in the Platonic idea of recollection, the soul perfects itself only through repeated struggles with forgetfulness until it gains real knowledge; so too, in Ungaretti, a movement through repeated loss and gain is implied. In his work, however, this movement is one of renewing, or re-creating, in such a way that the poet, thereby humankind, is brought in touch with his deepest nature.

In *L'allegria*, Ungaretti abandoned the rhetorical devices that had become rife in nineteenth century Italian poetry. He conceived the poet's task to be an "excavation of the word" to release its latent power and music. In "Commiato" ("Leavetaking"), Ungaretti addresses his friend Serra, saying, "poetry/ is the world humanity/ one's own life/ flowering from the word," and concluding, "When I find/ in this my silence/ a word/ it is dug into my life/ like an abyss." The abyss of which he speaks here is not the nullity between the gathered and the given word; it is, rather, the depth of memory that carries back beyond the individual into a mythic past. The abyss is present not in the expressive content of the words but in their power. "To find a *parola* [word]," Ungaretti declared in a note to the poems in *L'allegria*, "means to penetrate into the dark abyss of the self without disturbing it and without succeeding in learning its secret."

The culmination of this vision in *L'allegria* is found in "I fiumi" ("The Rivers"), which opens with a scene from the battlefront. It is evening, a world of moonlight; a crippled tree evokes the desolation of war. The poet recalls that in the morning, he had "stretched out/ in an urn of water/ and like a relic/ rested." This is a ritual act, a baptism, for the poem goes on to recount something of a rebirth. Each epoch of the poet's life is represented by a river—the Isonzo, the river of war; the Serchio, the river of his forefathers; the Nile, the river of his birth and unconsciousness; and the Seine, the river of awakening self-awareness: "These are the rivers/ counted in the Isonzo." In the ancient image of the river, Ungaretti captures the subjective moment in which all the branches of his existence blossom together. Such a moment is a consolation and a confirmation of a path but is at the same time evanescent. There is the tantalizing sense that while the outward rivers are in a moment of vision, harmonious with the flow of one's life, such moments do not last: "My torment/ is when/ I do not feel I am/ in harmony." Nevertheless, Ungaretti suggests that there is a power working through his experience that is not identifiable with himself: "hands/ that knead me/ give me/ rare/ felicity." One critic suggested that "hands" refers to the power of ancestors working through the poet and establishing a bond between him and his tradition. However one interprets this image, it is a statement of conviction that the poet has tapped the depths of his being. Unlike his friend Mohammed Sheab, who ". . . could not/ set free/ the song/ of his abandon," Ungaretti found his voice. The poem concludes: "Now my life seems to me/ a corolla/ of shadows."

SENTIMENTO DEL TEMPO

The poems of Ungaretti's second major collection, *Sentimento del tempo*, grew out of a confrontation with the spirit of Rome. Initially, Ungaretti was shocked by Baroque architecture, which seemed to lack unity. After that initial shock, he came to feel that in the Baroque style, things are "blown into the air," and the resultant fragmentation opens the way for a new ordering of things.

For Ungaretti, the Baroque bespeaks the absence of God. In Baroque art, the sense of absence is covered by an elaboration of sensuous detail and by the use of trompe l'oeil. Although Ungaretti saw in this expression of God's absence another manifestation of the emptiness of blind existence, the rhetorical responses of the Baroque did not appeal to him. Poetry was an exploration of the real; he would not abandon the concentrated forms of his first poems. Nevertheless, Baroque poetry gave him access to traditional meters and harmonies, and these he did employ. As he said in a note to *Sentimento del tempo*, he initially wanted to recover "the naturalness and depth and rhythm in the significance of each individual word," but his new project was "to find an accord between our traditional metrics and the expressive needs of today."

The traditional metrics of which he speaks were the hendecasyllable (as in Geoffrey Chaucer's "Whan that Aprill with his shoures soote/ The droghte of March hath perced to the roote") and the seven-syllable line, or *settinario*. These metrics are not simply imposed on his poetry. They are filtered through his intuition, syncopated, and brought together with a poetic style which remains staccato. Moments of passion are drawn out by the music of the line, which Ungaretti understood to be the actual rhythm of humanity's deepest self. The fragmented modern vision is sustained by underlying harmonies. A surface coherence of images achieved through rhetorical devices would be simply linear in its structure; musical harmonies in their polyvalence and rich suggestiveness make possible a multidimensional and deeper union of self and work.

Philosopher Bergson, with whom Ungaretti had studied in Paris, provided the poet with one of the central distinctions of his poetics. Bergson distinguished between two forms of memory: voluntary and involuntary. Voluntary memory is analogous to the sense of space that focuses on space as an aggregate of discrete parts. Life, however, is primarily temporal, not spatial, and this analogy between memory and space conveys the essentially superficial character of voluntary memory. In voluntary memory, a person stands in an extrinsic relationship to his or her past; forgetfulness is the essence of such a relationship. Ungaretti saw in this idea the psychological symbol for the void. What Bergson called involuntary memory, however, was as a unified flow. In involuntary memory, everything is retained. One gains access to involuntary memory through free action, action in which the past flows into and enriches the present. Ungaretti saw in involuntary memory the concept that would unify his poetics: Poetry was a mode of free action. Blending autobiographical elements with the appropriate imagery and language of the tradition, Ungaretti felt that he had returned to the living reality of poetry: a momentary making conscious of the collective unconscious.

Sentimento del tempo is written in several sections. "Fine di Crono" ("The End of Chronos") is both the title of a poem and the name of an important section of the work. Ungaretti presupposes a knowledge of the underlying myth: the murder of Chronos by his son, Zeus, who in his action revolted against the dark world of the Titans and successfully established the world of justice, the Olympian world. For Ungaretti, this revolution reflects the discovery of the deeper, liberating flow of memory beneath the fragmented memory of blind existence. Ungaretti, however, radically alters the traditional association of the Olympians with light. He associates the deeper sense of memory with the inner, subjective world of humans; hence, things must be drawn out of the daylight experience of life into the world of memory and imagination that he associates with night. In *Sentimento del tempo*, Ungaretti inverts the values of life and death. He carries this inversion as far as he can, making death the realm of perfection and day the realm of imperfection—imagery recalling Plato's dialogue *Phaedōn* (fourth century B.C.E.; *Phaedo*, 1675) in which Socrates argues that philosophy is a preparation for death. True life is the life of the spirit, and what most people take as life, the life of enjoyment, is death. Such a view expresses an ultimate human desire to give even death, that unknown standing wholly outside experience, a meaning.

The central collection of *Sentimento del tempo* is "Inni" ("Hymns"), whose subject is a religious crisis. Here Ungaretti introduces the idea of *pietà* (compassion, pity, or piety), which fuses the ancient notion of respect for ancestors with the Christian notion of love for all humankind. In these poems, Ungaretti's self-declared condition is that of alienation, and through *pietà*, he seeks a sense of solidarity with other people. This search adds a moral dimension to the ambitions of a poet whose earlier works might be taken as seeking purely aesthetic resolutions.

The poem in "Hymns" titled "La pietà" ("Pity") is the most important single poem in *Sentimento del tempo*. It opens with an echo of Ungaretti's earlier self-depiction as "a man of pain." "I am a wounded man," he declares dramatically, going on to describe himself as an exile. This sense of exile is the profoundest sense of being out of harmony with the depth of experience Ungaretti has yet expressed: "I have peopled the silence with names./ Have I torn heart and mind to shreds/ to fall into the slavery of words?/ I rule over phantoms." Ungaretti conjures up his previous work and throws its value into doubt. The absence of God confronts the poet with the possibility that he has built on sand. In this, he is like Michelangelo, whom he regarded as the greatest Baroque artist (and after a group of whose works this poem is titled).

The second section of "Pity" develops the inversion of death and life met within all sections of *Sentimento del tempo*. "They [the dead] are the seed that bursts within our dreams," he says. If there is a road open to God, it must be by way of memorial reawakening and restoration of the past. This is the very path that has led Ungaretti to the possibility of despair, but just as the desert had the double significance of the void and the mirage, so also might Ungaretti's religious despair be the other face of hope.

In "Pity," Ungaretti achieved something akin to prayer, but there was no discovery of a way back to a poetry of the divine. The poem's fourth section is, therefore, a portrayal of human life without God. "Man, monotonous universe," it begins. Every human action, considered by itself, is a frustration: "Nothing issues endlessly but limits." When man tries to turn toward God, "He has but blasphemies." This final line echoes the earlier ". . . do those who implore you/ Only know you by name?" "Pity" ends, then, without resolution. Ungaretti has moved away from the atheism of his early years—in fact, he embraced Roman Catholicism—but, in his poetry, the stance of this Bedouin poet is that of an agnostic who seeks to believe. There is no room for dogma here.

Scholar Glauco Cambon suggests that the metaphysical connection among memory, consciousness of the void, and "the dream of becoming" is paralleled in Ungaretti's later work by a moral connection among innocence, sin, and conscience. What had been, in the earlier work, the condition of humanity lost in blind existence deepens in the later work, taking on the significance of the Fall. Indeed, the next section of *Sentimento del tempo*, titled "La morte meditata" ("Death Meditated"), takes place in the Garden of Eden, and Eve is its central figure. Ungaretti gives a particularly modern shading to Eve by introducing an element of sensuality; he does this in order to include the sensuous, poetry's medium, in an image of restored innocence. As the symbol of restored innocence, Eve carries the double significance of death as a realm of perfection and as the realm of the terrible loss of innocence. If death is another face of blind existence, then Eve emerges against the void of death as the mirage emerges on the desert. Ungaretti's choice of a female symbol to express the restored innocence for which poetry strives is characteristically Italian, recalling Petrarch's Laura, Dante's Beatrice, and Leopardi's Silvia.

IL DOLORE

The poems of *Il dolore* grew out of Ungaretti's experience of profound loss. In a poem about his brother Constantino's death, he writes: "I have lost all of childhood—/ Never again can I/ Forget myself in a cry." This nihilistic chord underlies the "bitter accord" of the collection.

"Tu ti spezzisti" ("You Shattered") is the greatest poem of the collection. It opens with the alien Brazilian landscape—a landscape unnerving and threatening: "That swarm of scattered, huge, gray stones/ Still quivering in secret slings/ Of stifled flames of origin. . . ." The references to nonhuman creation call to mind the poetic task of inwardly re-creating the world, but this landscape is presented with a force and a strangeness that make such a task overwhelming, if not impossible. Against this landscape, Antonietto, Ungaretti's son who died, is likened to a small bird: on one hand, the recalcitrantly primitive and foreboding; on the other, the fragile but keenly alive. Disaster is inevitable. "How could you not have shattered/ In a blindness so inflexible/ You, simple breath and crystal." The oppressive powers that brought down this small life are focused by reference to the sun: "Too human dazzling for the ruthless,/ Savage, droning, tenacious/ Roar of naked sun."

The rest of *Il dolore* grows out of a preoccupation with the possible destruction of Italy. A notable aspect of these poems is the emergence of the figure of Christ. Like Michelangelo, who desired faith but from whom God hid himself, Ungaretti might be seen as an odd sort of agnostic. The Christ of Ungaretti's poems is modified by the poet's humanism.

LA TERRA PROMESSA

La terra promessa contains poems written in the early 1930's, although the volume was not published until 1950. If, as Ungaretti says, the dominant season of *Sentimento del tempo* is summer, then the dominant season of *La terra promessa* is autumn. In this season, as Jones comments, "detached as the aging mind becomes from the flesh, it begins to see the world as a sensational Pascalian abyss . . . , which neither the fancy nor the imagination can any longer bridge over." Pascal, however, took joy in the promised liberation from the senses, something that Ungaretti cannot do. There would be no way to the restoration of "innocence with memory" without the sensuous imagination. For Ungaretti, the separation of sense and mind—the dying of sense—which threatens to undermine the poet's immediate engagement with things can be overcome through memory. The poet returns to the memories of youth to restructure them out of the knowledge of a full life, breathing new life into them.

The "promised land" of which Ungaretti speaks is promised because it is the place of renewed innocence. This symbol repeats and transforms his attempt to resolve the problem which was central to his writing from the beginning: How, without absolutes, does one live a human life in time? The answer he gave should be seen against a guiding mythology. As he says in *Vita d'un uomo: Tutto le poesie*:

> Once upon a time there was a pure universe, humanly speaking . . . an absurdity: an immaterial materiality. This purity became a material materiality as a result of some offence perpetrated against the Creator by who knows what event. But anyway, through some extraordinary happening of a cosmic order, this material became corrupt—thereby time originated, and history originated. This is my manner of feeling things, it is not the truth, but it is a way of feeling: I feel things in this way.

This note to the poems of *La terra promessa* makes clear Ungaretti's mythological cast of mind. The Golden Age cannot be restored, but its power can be evoked by a process of memory akin to the ritual. Poems are such evocations, and in this collection, the rites of poetry are reconstitutions of memories through the informing insight of maturity. If old age is characterized by the decline, even death, of the senses, this does not imply that there is no bridge between the sensuous visions of youth and the understanding of old age. A purification of memory is possible, and such a purification leads back through the "tunnel of time" to innocence.

The key figure in this collection is Aeneas, though he never takes the stage, and the *Aeneid* (c. 29-19 B.C.E.; English translation, 1553) of Vergil is a source of much of its symbolic material. One of the most important poems of the collection is titled "Cori descrittivi di stati d'animo di Didone" ("Choruses Descriptive of Dido's States of Mind"). In this group of nineteen fragments, the passing of Dido's beauty is mourned. This image has obvious resonance with the image of Eve as a figure of lost innocence, but only to contrast Dido with Eve. Dido is ultimately lost. She is here, as she was for Vergil, the contrast to Aeneas's virtue. She has no inner spiritual world. If Dido negatively echoes Eve, Aeneas positively echoes the image of the Bedouin poet.

Ungaretti's lifework was to open a way to cultural origins by means of his adventure in language. For Ungaretti, whatever measure of salvation can be found is to be found only through history. Humans are alone, but through *pietà* they can move beyond their alienation toward solidarity with their fellows. The poet's access to the cultural flow of memory is gained through language. The language of poetry, Ungaretti said, is always in crisis, but this is a condition of its renewal. Through the purification of language, the poet hands on the tradition intact and creatively reworked. In doing so, he holds open the possibility of perpetual renewal.

OTHER MAJOR WORKS

NONFICTION: *Il povero nella citta*, 1949; *Il deserto e dopo*, 1961; *Innocence et memoire*, 1969; *Lettere a un fenomenologo*, 1972; *Vita d'un uomo: Saggi e interventi*, 1974.

TRANSLATIONS: *Traduzioni*, 1936 (various poems and authors); *Venti-due sonetti de Shakespeare: Scelti e tradotti da Giuseppe Ungaretti*, 1944; *Vita d'un uomo: Quaranta sonetti di Shakespeare tradotti*, 1946; *L'Après-midi et le monologue d'un faune di Mallarmé*, 1947; *Vita d'un uomo: Da Góngora e da Mallarmé*, 1948; *Vita d'un uomo: Fedra di Jean Racine*, 1950; *Finestra del caos*, 1961 (of Murilo Mendes); *Vita d'un uomo: Visioni di William Blake*, 1965.

BIBLIOGRAPHY

Godorecci, Maurizio. "The Poetics of the Word in Ungaretti." *Romance Languages Annual* 9 (1997): 197-201. A critical analysis of selected poems by Ungaretti.

Hacht, Anne Marie, and David Kelly, eds. *Poetry for Students*. Vol. 20. Detroit: Thomson/Gale, 2004. Analyzes Ungaretti's "Variations on Nothing." Contains the poem, a summary, themes, style, historical context, a critical overview, and criticism. Includes bibliography and index.

Jason, Philip K., ed. *Masterplots II: Poetry Series*. Rev. ed. Pasadena, Calif.: Salem Press, 2002. This set contains summaries and analyses of the poem "La pietà."

Jones, Frederic J. *Giuseppe Ungaretti: Poet and Critic*. Edinburgh: Edinburgh University Press, 1977. An assessment of Ungaretti's life and career. Includes bibliographic references.

Moevs, Christian. "Ungaretti: A Reading of 'Alla noia.'" *Forum Italicum* 25, no. 2 (Fall, 1991): 211-227. A critical study of one of Ungaretti's poems.

Re, Lucia. "Alexandria Revisited: Colonialism and the Egyptian Works of Enrico Pea and Giuseppe Ungaretti." In A *Place in the Sun: Africa in Italian Colonial Culture from Post-unification to the Present*, edited by Patrizia Palumbo. Berkeley: University of California Press, 2003. Examines the writings of Ungaretti and Pea, both of whom lived in Alexandria.

Suvini-Hand, Vivienne. *Mirage and Camouflage: Hiding Behind Hermeticism in Ungaretti's "L'allegria."* Market Harborough, Leicester, England: Troubador/Hull Italian Texts, 2000. Provides in-depth analysis of *L'allegria*, including the issue of hermeticism.

Robert Colucci

CHECKLIST FOR EXPLICATING A POEM

I. The Initial Readings

A. Before reading the poem, the reader should:
   1. Notice its form and length.
   2. Consider the title, determining, if possible, whether it might function as an allusion, symbol, or poetic image.
   3. Notice the date of composition or publication, and identify the general era of the poet.

B. The poem should be read intuitively and emotionally and be allowed to "happen" as much as possible.

C. In order to establish the rhythmic flow, the poem should be reread. A note should be made as to where the irregular spots (if any) are located.

II. Explicating the Poem

A. *Dramatic situation.* Studying the poem line by line helps the reader discover the dramatic situation. All elements of the dramatic situation are interrelated and should be viewed as reflecting and affecting one another. The dramatic situation serves a particular function in the poem, adding realism, surrealism, or absurdity; drawing attention to certain parts of the poem; and changing to reinforce other aspects of the poem. All points should be considered. The following questions are particularly helpful to ask in determining dramatic situation:
   1. What, if any, is the narrative action in the poem?
   2. How many personae appear in the poem? What part do they take in the action?
   3. What is the relationship between characters?
   4. What is the setting (time and location) of the poem?

B. *Point of view.* An understanding of the poem's point of view is a major step toward comprehending the poet's intended meaning. The reader should ask:
   1. Who is the speaker? Is he or she addressing someone else or the reader?
   2. Is the narrator able to understand or see everything happening to him or her, or does the reader know things that the narrator does not?
   3. Is the narrator reliable?
   4. Do point of view and dramatic situation seem consistent? If not, the inconsistencies may provide clues to the poem's meaning.

C. *Images and metaphors*. Images and metaphors are often the most intricately crafted vehicles of the poem for relaying the poet's message. Realizing that the images and metaphors work in harmony with the dramatic situation and point of view will help the reader to see the poem as a whole, rather than as disassociated elements.
  1. The reader should identify the concrete images (that is, those that are formed from objects that can be touched, smelled, seen, felt, or tasted). Is the image projected by the poet consistent with the physical object?
  2. If the image is abstract, or so different from natural imagery that it cannot be associated with a real object, then what are the properties of the image?
  3. To what extent is the reader asked to form his or her own images?
  4. Is any image repeated in the poem? If so, how has it been changed? Is there a controlling image?
  5. Are any images compared to each other? Do they reinforce one another?
  6. Is there any difference between the way the reader perceives the image and the way the narrator sees it?
  7. What seems to be the narrator's or persona's attitude toward the image?

D. *Words*. Every substantial word in a poem may have more than one intended meaning, as used by the author. Because of this, the reader should look up many of these words in the dictionary and:
  1. Note all definitions that have the slightest connection with the poem.
  2. Note any changes in syntactical patterns in the poem.
  3. In particular, note those words that could possibly function as symbols or allusions, and refer to any appropriate sources for further information.

E. *Meter, rhyme, structure, and tone*. In scanning the poem, all elements of prosody should be noted by the reader. These elements are often used by a poet to manipulate the reader's emotions, and therefore they should be examined closely to arrive at the poet's specific intention.
  1. Does the basic meter follow a traditional pattern such as those found in nursery rhymes or folk songs?
  2. Are there any variations in the base meter? Such changes or substitutions are important thematically and should be identified.
  3. Are the rhyme schemes traditional or innovative, and what might their form mean to the poem?
  4. What devices has the poet used to create sound patterns (such as assonance and alliteration)?
  5. Is the stanza form a traditional or innovative one?
  6. If the poem is composed of verse paragraphs rather than stanzas, how do they affect the progression of the poem?

7. After examining the above elements, is the resultant tone of the poem casual or formal, pleasant, harsh, emotional, authoritative?

F. *Historical context.* The reader should attempt to place the poem into historical context, checking on events at the time of composition. Archaic language, expressions, images, or symbols should also be looked up.

G. *Themes and motifs.* By seeing the poem as a composite of emotion, intellect, craftsmanship, and tradition, the reader should be able to determine the themes and motifs (smaller recurring ideas) presented in the work. He or she should ask the following questions to help pinpoint these main ideas:
   1. Is the poet trying to advocate social, moral, or religious change?
   2. Does the poet seem sure of his or her position?
   3. Does the poem appeal primarily to the emotions, to the intellect, or to both?
   4. Is the poem relying on any particular devices for effect (such as imagery, allusion, paradox, hyperbole, or irony)?

BIBLIOGRAPHY

GENERAL REFERENCE SOURCES

BIOGRAPHICAL SOURCES

Jackson, William T. H., ed. *European Writers*. 14 vols. New York: Scribner, 1983-1991.

Kunitz, Stanley, and Vineta Colby, eds. *European Authors, 1000-1900: A Biographical Dictionary of European Literature*. New York: Wilson, 1967.

Magill, Frank N., ed. *Critical Survey of Poetry: Foreign Language Series*. 5 vols. Englewood Cliffs, N.J.: Salem Press, 1984.

_____. *Critical Survey of Poetry: Supplement*. Englewood Cliffs, N.J.: Salem Press, 1987.

Serafin, Steven, ed. *Encyclopedia of World Literature in the Twentieth Century*. 3d ed. 4 vols. Detroit: St. James Press, 1999.

CRITICISM

Coleman, Arthur. *A Checklist of Interpretation, 1940-1973, of Classical and Continental Epics and Metrical Romances*. Vol. 2 in *Epic and Romance Criticism*. 2 vols. New York: Watermill, 1974.

Jason, Philip K., ed. *Masterplots II: Poetry Series, Revised Edition*. 8 vols. Pasadena, Calif.: Salem Press, 2002.

The Year's Work in Modern Language Studies. London: Oxford University Press, 1931.

DICTIONARIES, HISTORIES, AND HANDBOOKS

Auty, Robert, et al. *Traditions of Heroic and Epic Poetry*. 2 vols. Vol. 1, *The Traditions*; Vol. 2, *Characteristics and Techniques*. Publications of the Modern Humanities Research Association 9, 13. London: Modern Humanities Research Association, 1980, 1989.

Bede, Jean-Albert, and William B. Edgerton, eds. *Columbia Dictionary of Modern European Literature*. 2d ed. New York: Columbia University Press, 1980.

France, Peter, ed. *The Oxford Guide to Literature in English Translation*. New York: Oxford University Press, 2000.

Henderson, Lesley, ed. *Reference Guide to World Literature*. 2d ed. 2 vols. New York: St. James Press, 1995.

Oinas, Felix, ed. *Heroic Epic and Saga: An Introduction to the World's Great Folk Epics*. Bloomington: Indiana University Press, 1978.

Index of Primary Works

Hoffman, Herbert H. *Hoffman's Index to Poetry: European and Latin American Poetry in Anthologies*. Metuchen, N.J.: Scarecrow Press, 1985.

Poetics

Gasparov, M. L. *A History of European Versification*. Translated by G. S. Smith and Marina Tarlinskaja. New York: Oxford University Press, 1996.

Wimsatt, William K., ed. *Versification: Major Language Types: Sixteen Essays*. New York: Modern Language Association, 1972.

Italian Poetry

Biographical Sources

De Stasio, Giovanna Wedel, Glauco Cambon, and Antonio Illiano, eds. *Twentieth-Century Italian Poets: First Series*. Dictionary of Literary Biography 114. Detroit: Gale Research, 1992.

_____. *Twentieth-Century Italian Poets: Second Series*. Dictionary of Literary Biography 128. Detroit: Gale Research, 1993.

Dictionaries, Histories, and Handbooks

Bohn, Willard, ed. and trans. *Italian Futurist Poetry*. Toronto: University of Toronto Press, 2005.

Bondanella, Peter, and Julia Conaway Bondanella, eds. *Dictionary of Italian Literature*. Rev. ed. Westport, Conn.: Greenwood Press, 1996.

Cavallo, Jo Ann. *The Romance Epics of Boiardo, Ariosto, and Tasso: From Public Duty to Private Pleasure*. Toronto: University of Toronto Press, 2004.

Condini, Ned, ed. and trans. *An Anthology of Modern Italian Poetry in English Translation, with Italian Text*. New York: Modern Language Association of America, 2009.

Dombroski, Robert S. *Italy: Fiction, Theater, Poetry, Film Since 1950*. Middle Village, N.Y.: Council on National Literatures, 2000.

Holmes, Olivia. *Assembling the Lyric Self: Authorship from Troubador Song to Italian Poetry Book*. Minneapolis: University of Minnesota Press, 2000.

Italian Poets of the Twentieth Century. Florence, Italy: Casalini Libri, 1997.

Kleinhenz, Christopher. *The Early Italian Sonnet: The First Century, 1220-1321*. Collezione di Studi e Testi n.s. 2. Lecce, Italy: Milella, 1986.

Payne, Roberta L., ed. *Selection of Modern Italian Poetry in Translation*. Montreal: McGill-Queen's University Press, 2004.

Zatti, Sergio. *The Quest for Epic: From Ariosto to Tasso*. Translated by Sally Hill with Dennis Looney, edited by Looney. Toronto: University of Toronto Press, 2006.

WOMEN WRITERS

Blum, Cinzia Sartini, and Lara Trubowitz, eds. and trans. *Contemporary Italian Women Poets: A Bilingual Anthology*. New York: Italica Press, 2001.

Frabotta, Biancamaria, ed. *Italian Women Poets*. Translated by Corrado Federici. Toronto: Guernica Editions, 2002.

Stortoni, Laura A., and Mary P. Lillie, eds. *Women Poets of the Italian Renaissance: Courtly Ladies and Courtesans*. New York: Italica, 1997.

GUIDE TO ONLINE RESOURCES

WEB SITES

The following sites were visited by the editors of Salem Press in 2010. Because URLs frequently change, the accuracy of these addresses cannot be guaranteed; however, long-standing sites, such as those of colleges and universities, national organizations, and government agencies, generally maintain links when their sites are moved.

LitWeb
http://litweb.net

LitWeb provides biographies of hundreds of world authors throughout history that can be accessed through an alphabetical listing. The pages about each writer contain a list of his or her works, suggestions for further reading, and illustrations. The site also offers information about past and present winners of major literary prizes.

The Modern Word: Authors of the Libyrinth
http://www.themodernword.com/authors.html

The Modern Word site, although somewhat haphazard in its organization, provides a great deal of critical information about writers. The "Authors of the Libyrinth" page is very useful, linking author names to essays about them and other resources. The section of the page headed "The Scriptorium" presents "an index of pages featuring writers who have pushed the edges of their medium, combining literary talent with a sense of experimentation to produce some remarkable works of modern literature."

Poetry Foundation
http://www.poetryfoundation.org

The Poetry Foundation, publisher of *Poetry* magazine, is an independent literary organization. Its Web site offers links to essays; news; events; online poetry resources, such as blogs, organizations, publications, and references and research; a glossary of literary terms; and a Learning Lab that includes poem guides and essays on poetics.

Poetry in Translation
http://poetryintranslation.com

This independent resource provides modern translations of classic texts by famous poets and also provides original poetry and critical works. Visitors can choose from several languages, including English, Spanish, Chinese, Russian, Italian, and Greek. Original text is available as well. Also includes links to further literary resources.

Poetry International Web
http://international.poetryinternationalweb.org

Poetry International Web features information on poets from countries such as Indonesia, Zimbabwe, Iceland, India, Slovenia, Morocco, Albania, Afghanistan, Russia, and Brazil. The site offers news, essays, interviews and discussion, and hundreds of poems, both in their original languages and in English translation.

Poet's Corner
http://theotherpages.org/poems

The Poet's Corner, one of the oldest text resources on the Web, provides access to about seven thousand works of poetry by several hundred different poets from around the world. Indexes are arranged and searchable by title, name of poet, or subject. The site also offers its own resources, including "Faces of the Poets"—a gallery of portraits—and "Lives of the Poets"—a growing collection of biographies.

Western European Studies
http://wess.lib.byu.edu

The Western European Studies Section of the Association of College and Research Libraries maintains this collection of resources useful to students of Western European history and culture. It also is a good place to find information about non-English-language literature. The site includes separate pages about the literatures and languages of the Netherlands, France, Germany, Iberia, Italy, and Scandinavia, in which users can find links to electronic texts, association Web sites, journals, and other materials, the majority of which are written in the languages of the respective countries.

ELECTRONIC DATABASES

Electronic databases usually do not have their own URLs. Instead, public, college, and university libraries subscribe to these databases, provide links to them on their Web sites, and make them available to library card holders or other specified patrons. Readers can visit library Web sites or ask reference librarians to check on availability.

Canadian Literary Centre
Produced by EBSCO, the Canadian Literary Centre database contains full-text content from ECW Press, a Toronto-based publisher, including the titles in the publisher's Canadian fiction studies, Canadian biography, and Canadian writers and their works series; *ECW's Biographical Guide to Canadian Novelists*; and *George Woodcock's Introduction to Canadian Fiction*. Author biographies, essays and literary criticism, and book reviews are among the database's offerings.

Literary Reference Center

EBSCO's Literary Reference Center (LRC) is a comprehensive full-text database designed primarily to help high school and undergraduate students in English and the humanities with homework and research assignments about literature. The database contains massive amounts of information from reference works, books, literary journals, and other materials, including more than 31,000 plot summaries, synopses, and overviews of literary works; almost 100,000 essays and articles of literary criticism; about 140,000 author biographies; more than 605,000 book reviews; and more than 5,200 author interviews. It contains the entire contents of Salem Press's MagillOnLiterature Plus. Users can retrieve information by browsing a list of authors' names or titles of literary works; they can also use an advanced search engine to access information by numerous categories, including author name, gender, cultural identity, national identity, and the years in which he or she lived, or by literary title, character, locale, genre, and publication date. The Literary Reference Center also features a literary-historical time line, an encyclopedia of literature, and a glossary of literary terms.

MagillOnLiterature Plus

MagillOnLiterature Plus is a comprehensive, integrated literature database produced by Salem Press and available on the EBSCOhost platform. The database contains the full text of essays in Salem's many literature-related reference works, including *Masterplots, Cyclopedia of World Authors, Cyclopedia of Literary Characters, Cyclopedia of Literary Places, Critical Survey of Poetry, Critical Survey of Long Fiction, Critical Survey of Short Fiction, World Philosophers and Their Works, Magill's Literary Annual,* and *Magill's Book Reviews.* Among its contents are articles on more than 35,000 literary works and more than 8,500 poets, writers, dramatists, essayists, and philosophers; more than 1,000 images; and a glossary of more than 1,300 literary terms. The biographical essays include lists of authors' works and secondary bibliographies, and hundreds of overview essays examine and discuss literary genres, time periods, and national literatures.

Rebecca Kuzins
Updated by Desiree Dreeuws

CATEGORY INDEX

BALLADS
    Cavalcanti, Guido, 75
    Tasso, Torquato, 221

CLASSICISM: NINETEENTH CENTURY
    Carducci, Giosuè, 67

DOLCE STIL NUOVO
    Boccaccio, Giovanni, 61
    Cavalcanti, Guido, 75
    Dante, 97
    Petrarch, 194

EKPHRASTIC POETRY
    Ariosto, Ludovico, 51
ELEGIES
    Leopardi, Giacomo, 145
EPICS
    Ariosto, Ludovico, 51
    Boccaccio, Giovanni, 61
    Dante, 97
    Tasso, Torquato, 221

FEMINIST POETS
    Christine de Pizan, 81
FUTURISM
    Montale, Eugenio, 179

HERMETICISM
    Montale, Eugenio, 179
    Quasimodo, Salvatore, 205
    Ungaretti, Giuseppe, 231
HYMNS
    Foscolo, Ugo, 125

LOVE POETRY
    Christine de Pizan, 81
    Dante, 97
    Petrarch, 194
    Stampa, Gaspara, 214
    Tasso, Torquato, 221
LYRIC POETRY
    Ariosto, Ludovico, 51
    Carducci, Giosuè, 67
    Cavalcanti, Guido, 75
    Christine de Pizan, 81
    D'Annunzio, Gabriele, 87
    Dante, 97
    Foscolo, Ugo, 125
    Leopardi, Giacomo, 145
    Michelangelo, 166
    Montale, Eugenio, 179
    Pavese, Cesare, 188
    Petrarch, 194
    Quasimodo, Salvatore, 205
    Tasso, Torquato, 221

MODERNISM
    D'Annunzio, Gabriele, 87
    Montale, Eugenio, 179
    Ungaretti, Giuseppe, 231

NARRATIVE POETRY
    Ariosto, Luovico, 51
    Boccaccio, Giovanni, 61
    Dante, 97
    Fracastoro, Girolamo, 133
NEOCLASSICAL POETS
    Foscolo, Ugo, 125

NEOPLATONISM
    Michelangelo, 166
    Stampa, Gaspara, 214
NEOREALISM
    Pavese, Cesare, 188
    Quasimodo, Salvatore, 205

OCCASIONAL VERSE
    Christine de Pizan, 81
    Stampa, Gaspara, 214
ODES
    Carducci, Giosuè, 67
    Marino, Giambattista, 160

PASTORAL POETS
    Marino, Giambattista, 160
    Petrarch, 194
    Tasso, Torquato, 221
PETRARCHAN SONNETS
    Michelangelo, 166
    Petrarch, 194
    Stampa, Gaspara, 214
POLITICAL POETS
    Pavese, Cesare, 188

RELIGIOUS POETRY
    Christine de Pizan, 81
    Marino, Giambattista, 160
    Tasso, Torquato, 221

RENAISSANCE, ITALIAN
    Ariosto, Ludovico, 51
    Boccaccio, Giovanni, 61
    Fracastoro, Girolamo, 133
    Michelangelo, 166
    Petrarch, 194
    Stampa, Gaspara, 214
    Tasso, Torquato, 221
ROMANTICISM
    Foscolo, Ugo, 125
    Leopardi, Giacomo, 145

SATIRIC POETRY
    Ariosto, Ludovico, 51
SONGS
    Leopardi, Giacomo, 145
    Stampa, Gaspara, 214
SONNETS
    Cavalcanti, Guido, 75
    Foscolo, Ugo, 125
    Marino, Giambattista, 160
    Petrarch, 194
    Stampa, Gaspara, 214
    Tasso, Torquato, 221

VERSE DRAMATISTS
    Ariosto, Ludovico, 51
    Tasso, Torquato, 221

WOMEN POETS
    Christine de Pizan, 81
    Stampa, Gaspara, 214

SUBJECT INDEX

Accademia dell'Arcadia, 16
Acque e terre (Quasimodo), 209
Adone, L' (Marino), 15, 163
Africa (Petrarch), 201
"Agony" (Ungaretti), 235
Aleramo, Sibilla, 30
Alfieri, Vittorio, 19
Allegria, L' (Ungaretti), 234
Anile, Antonino, 43
Ariosto, Ludovico, 10, 51-60
    Ariosto's Satyres, 58
    Orlando Furioso, 10, 55
Ariosto's Satyres (Ariosto), 58
Art for art's sake, 24
Avant-garde poets, 48

Barbarian Odes (Carducci), 73
Bembo, Pietro, 31
Betocchi, Carlo, 43
Boccaccio, Giovanni, 6, 61-66
    The Book of Theseus, 65
    The Filostrato, 64
Boiardo, Matteo Maria, 9
Book of Theseus, The (Boccaccio), 65
"Broom, The" (Leopardi), 157

Camerata dei Bardi, 14
Campana, Dino, 36
Canti (Leopardi), 150
Canto novo (D'Annunzio), 91
Carducci, Giosuè, 25, 67-74
    Barbarian Odes, 73
    Giambi ed epodi, 72
    "Hymn to Satan," 72
    Juvenilia, 71

Levia gravia, 72
The Lyrics and Rhythms, 74
Nuove poesie, 73
"Song of Love," 72
Cavalcanti, Guido, 75-80
    "My Lady Asks Me," 79
Cent Ballades d'amant et de dame (Christine de Pizan), 83
Chiabrera, Gabriello, 15
Christine de Pizan, 81-86
    Cent Ballades d'amant et de dame, 83
    The Tale of Joan of Arc, 84
Colonna, Vittoria, 14
Crepuscular poets, 34
Cuttlefish Bones (Montale), 182

D'Annunzio, Gabriele, 28, 87-96
    Canto novo, 91
    Intermezzo di rime, 91
    Le laudi, 92
    Poema paradisiaco, 92
    Primo vere, 91
Dante, 3, 97-124
    The Divine Comedy, 104
Della Valle, Federico, 16
De Robertis, Giuseppe, 36
Di Giacomo, Salvatore, 32
Divine Comedy, The (Dante), 104
Dolce stil nuovo, 2
Dolore, Il (Ungaretti), 239

Ed è subito sera (Quasimodo), 210
"End of Chronos, The" (Ungaretti), 238
Enlightenment, 18
Erba, Luciano, 48

Filostrato, The (Boccaccio), 64
Foscolo, Ugo, 125-132
    Le Grazie, 130
    On Sepulchers, 129
    "Perhaps Because of the Fateful Quiet," 128
    "Sonetti," 127
    "To Louise Pallavicini Fallen from a Horse," 129
    "To the Healed Friend," 129
    "You Nurturer of the Muses," 127
Fracastoro, Girolamo, 133-144
    Naugerius sive de poetica dialogus, 142
    Syphilis, 137
Futurism, 35

Giambi ed epodi (Carducci), 72
Govoni, Corrado, 34
Gozzano, Guido, 34
Grazie, Le (Foscolo), 130
Guarini, Battista, 13

Hard Labor (Pavese), 190
Hermeticism, 42
Humanism, 7
"Hymn to Satan" (Carducci), 72

Intermezzo di rime (D'Annunzio), 91
Italian poetry
    origins to nineteenth century, 1-23
    nineteenth century to present, 24-50

Jahier, Piero, 36
Jerusalem Conquered (Tasso), 229
Jerusalem Delivered (Tasso), 12, 226
Juvenilia (Carducci), 71

Laudi, Le (D'Annunzio), 92
Leopardi, Giacomo, 145-159
    "The Broom," 157

    Canti, 150
    "Night Song of a Nomadic Shepherd in Asia," 155
    "Sappho's Last Song," 153
    "To Italy," 151
    "The Younger Brutus," 152
Levia gravia (Carducci), 72
Luzi, Mario, 42
Lyric poetry, 2
Lyrics and Rhythms, The (Carducci), 74

Marinetti, Filippo Tommaso, 35
Marinismo, 14
Marino, Giambattista, 14, 160-165
    L'Adone, 15, 163
Medici, Lorenzo de', 7
Metastasio, Pietro, 16
Metrical Letters (Petrarch), 202
Michelangelo, 166-178
Montale, Eugenio, 38, 179-187
    Cuttlefish Bones, 182
    The Occasions, 184
    Satura, 186
    The Storm, and Other Poems, 185
Monti, Vincenzo, 21
"My Lady Asks Me" (Cavalcanti), 79

Naugerius sive de poetica dialogus (Fracastoro), 142
Negri, Ada, 45
Neo-Hermeticism, 48
Neoclassicism, 22
Neorealism, Italy, 47
"Night Song of a Nomadic Shepherd in Asia" (Leopardi), 155
Nuove poesie (Carducci), 73

Occasions, The (Montale), 184
On Sepulchers (Foscolo), 129
Onofri, Arturo, 36

Orlando Furioso (Ariosto), 10, 55
Orlando Innamorato (Boiardo), 9

Parini, Giuseppe, 18
Pascarella, Cesare, 32
Pascoli, Giovanni, 27
Pasolini, Pier Paolo, 33
Pavese, Cesare, 188-193
    Hard Labor, 190
    Verrà la morte e avrà i tuoi occhi, 191
"Perhaps Because of the Fateful Quiet" (Foscolo), 128
Petrarch, 4, 194-204
    Africa, 201
    Metrical Letters, 202
    Triumphs, 200
"Pity" (Ungaretti), 238
Poema paradisiaco (D'Annunzio), 92
Poliziano, 8
Primo vere (D'Annunzio), 91
Pulci, Luigi, 9

Quasimodo, Salvatore, 40, 205-213
    Acque e terre, 209
    Ed è subito sera, 210
    To Give and to Have, 211

Regional poetry, Italy, 30
Religious poetry, 1, 43
Renaissance, Italian, 7
Resistance poetry, 45
Rhymes (Petrarch), 5
Rime (Stampa), 216
Rinaldo (Tasso), 225
"Rivers, The" (Ungaretti), 236
Rondisti, 44
Rèbora, Clemente, 43

Saba, Umberto, 40
Salustri, Carlo Alberto, 32

Sannazzaro, Jacopo, 9
"Sappho's Last Song" (Leopardi), 153
Satura (Montale), 186
Scapigliatura movement, 24
Sentimento del tempo (Ungaretti), 237
Sette giornate del mondo creato, Le (Tasso), 225
Sicilian school, 2
Sinisgalli, Leonardo, 42
"Sonetti" (Foscolo), 127
"Song of Love" (Carducci), 72
Stampa, Gaspara, 14, 214-220
    Rime, 216
Storm, and Other Poems, The (Montale), 185
Syphilis (Fracastoro), 137

Tale of Joan of Arc, The (Christine de Pizan), 84
Tasso, Torquato, 12, 221-230
    Jerusalem Conquered, 229
    Jerusalem Delivered, 226
    Rinaldo, 225
    Le sette giornate del mondo creato, 225
Terra promessa, La (Ungaretti), 240
To Give and to Have (Quasimodo), 211
"To Italy" (Leopardi), 151
"To Louise Pallavicini Fallen from a Horse" (Foscolo), 129
"To the Healed Friend" (Foscolo), 129
Triumphs (Petrarch), 200
Turoldo, David Maria, 44

Ungaretti, Giuseppe, 37, 231-242
    "Agony," 235
    L'allegria, 234
    Il dolore, 239
    "The End of Chronos," 238
    "Pity," 238
    "The Rivers," 236
    Sentimento del tempo, 237

La terra promessa, 240
"You Shattered," 239

Verismo, 24
Vernacular poetry, 1
Verrà la morte e avrà i tuoi occhi (Pavese), 191
Vociani, 36

Women poets, 14

"You Nurturer of the Muses" (Foscolo), 127
"You Shattered" (Ungaretti), 239
"Younger Brutus, The" (Leopardi), 152

Zanzotto, Andrea, 48